EX LIBRIS

VINTAGE **CLASSICS**

THE ESSENTIAL WRITINGS OF JEAN-JACQUES ROUSSEAU

Jean-Jacques Rousseau was born in Geneva in 1712. He was a writer and political theorist of the Enlightenment. In 1750 he published his first important work *A Discourse on the Sciences and the Arts* (1750) where he argued that man had become corrupted by society and civilisation. In 1755, he published *Discourse on the Origin of Inequality* and in *The Social Contract* (1762) he argued, 'Man is born free, and everywhere he is in chains'. This political treatise earned him exile from his home city of Geneva and arguably inspired the French Revolution (his ashes were transferred to the Pantheon in Paris in 1794). He also wrote *Èmile*, a treatise on education and *The New Eloise* (1761). This novel scandalised the French authorities who ordered Rousseau's arrest. In his last 10 years, Rousseau wrote his *Confessions*. In *Confessions* he remembers his adventurous life, his achievements and the persecution he suffered from opponents. His revelations inspired the likes of Proust, Goethe and Tolstoy among others. Rousseau died in France on 2 July 1778.

Peter Constantine's honours include the PEN Translation Prize, the National Translation Award, the Helen and Kurt Wolff Translation Prize, and Greece's Translators of Literature Prize. He translated Machiavelli's *The Prince* for Vintage Classics.

MAJOR WORKS BY JEAN-JACQUES ROUSSEAU

Discourse on the Arts and Sciences
Narcissus, or, The Self-Admirer: A Comedy
*Discourse on the Origin and Foundations of
Inequality Among Men*
Discourse on Political Economy
Julie, or, the New Héloise
Émile, or, on Education
The Social Contract, or, Principles of Political Right
Pygmalion: a Lyric Scene
Confessions
Constitutional Project for Corsica
Considerations on the Government of Poland
Essay on the Origin of Languages
Reveries of the Solitary Walker

JEAN-JACQUES ROUSSEAU

The Essential Writings of Jean-Jacques Rousseau

TRANSLATED BY
Peter Constantine

EDITED AND WITH AN INTRODUCTION BY
Leo Damrosch

VINTAGE BOOKS
London

Published by Vintage 2013

13

Translation, compilation, and additional text copyright © 2013
by Random House, Inc.
Introduction copyright © 2013 Leo Damrosch
Biographical note copyright © 2013 by Peter Constantine

This edition published by arrangement with Modern Library,
a division of Random House, Inc.

First published by Modern Library in the United States in 2013

Vintage
Random House, 20 Vauxhall Bridge Road,
London SW1V 2SA

www.vintage-classics.info

Addresses for companies within The Random House Group Limited
can be found at: www.randomhouse.co.uk/offices.htm

The Random House Group Limited Reg. No. 954009

A CIP catalogue record for this book
is available from the British Library

ISBN 9780099582847

Penguin Random House is committed to a sustainable future for
our business, our readers and our planet. This book is made from
Forest Stewardship Council® certified paper.

Printed and bound in Great Britain by Clays Ltd, Elcograf S.p.A.

BIOGRAPHICAL NOTE

Jean-Jacques Rousseau was born in Geneva on June 28, 1712. His father, Isaac Rousseau, was a skilled watchmaker, and his mother, Suzanne, the daughter of a prominent Calvinist clergyman. Tragically, she contracted an infection and died a few days later. Jean-Jacques and his older brother, François, were cared for thereafter by their father's sister, also named Suzanne.

Rousseau never went to school, but was taught to read and write at home. When he was ten his father withdrew from his life, leaving Geneva after a confrontation with a haughty patrician, and he was sent to board with a clergyman in the nearby village of Bossey. At thirteen it was time to begin work, and he was apprenticed to a young engraver who proved abusive. Rousseau in turn became lazy and dishonest, and at sixteen, on the spur of the moment, he ran away from Geneva for good.

In the cathedral town of Annecy, in the Savoy region to the south of the city, he made the most important acquaintance of his life. An intelligent, beautiful young woman named Mme de Warens, who had left her husband in Switzerland, took an interest in him and sent him to Turin for instruction in the Catholic faith. (At that time Turin, in the Italian Piedmont, was the capital of the Kingdom of Sardinia, whose western province was the French-speaking Savoy.) For a year Rousseau held several low-level jobs, and then resolved to go back to Annecy. Mme de Warens now took him under her wing, and he lived with her for the next nine years. He always called her *Maman,* as though she were the mother he had lost when he was born, and he was greatly alarmed when she initiated a sexual relationship.

In his autobiographical *Confessions* Rousseau would recall this period as idyllic, but actually he was lonely and depressed much of the time. He did manage to acquire some skill in music, and he began to read voraciously under the guidance of Mme de Warens and her circle of congenial priests. But eventually it became clear that he would have to move on, and he proceeded to Lyon, where he took a position as tutor to two small boys. The tutoring didn't go well, but he formed important friendships with several members of the family, and they helped him to make valuable contacts when in 1742 he moved to Paris, hoping to make a career as a musician.

Unexpectedly, Rousseau was offered a post as secretary to the French ambassador in Venice, where he discovered administrative talents he didn't know he had and formed a passionate attachment to the emotional lyricism of Italian music. A year later there was a falling-out with his aristocratic employer, and he returned to Paris, where two significant relationships began. One was with the brilliant intellectual Denis Diderot, roughly the same age but well educated and already prominent, who was editing the immensely ambitious *Encyclopédie* that would be a centerpiece of the Enlightenment. The other was with a woman ten years younger called Thérèse Levasseur, who became Rousseau's lifelong companion. Five children were born and consigned in infancy to a foundling home, a story that would greatly damage his reputation when it became known in later life. He gave various explanations for what he had done, none very convincing.

Rousseau next accepted a job as secretary and research assistant to a well-to-do family, the Dupins, and wrote some articles on music for the *Encyclopédie.* And then, in 1749 when he was thirty-seven, a chance encounter suddenly turned him into a celebrated writer. Browsing in a newspaper, he happened to notice an announcement for an essay prize competition offered by the provincial Academy of Dijon. The topic was "whether the restoration of the sciences and arts has contributed to purify morals," and Rousseau decided to argue in the negative. The progress of civilization, he acknowledged, had brought many benefits, but it had also deformed human nature, conditioning people to conceal their feelings from one another and even from themselves. The leitmotif of a life's work was suddenly revealed. As Rousseau often observed in later years, all of his thinking grew out of one central insight: nature made man good, and it is society that makes him wicked.

Rousseau's brief *Discourse on the Sciences and Arts* won the Dijon prize, and when it was published the next year it brought instant fame. After producing a successful opera, he reconverted to Protestantism in order to regain his Genevan citizenship, and in 1755 published a second and far greater discourse, *On the Origin and Foundations of Inequality Among Men,* that drew on his early experiences and argued that the very existence of society makes inequality inevitable. Only in a presocial "state of nature" could men and women have been truly independent and free.

Leaving Paris and breaking with Diderot, Rousseau settled

with Thérèse in the village of Montmorency, where he completed no fewer than three major works that were all published in an eighteen-month period in 1761–62. *Émile, or, On Education* made a compelling case for encouraging the development of each child's unique gifts and for postponing formal learning. *Julie, or, The New Héloïse,* a novel told in letters, fiercely romantic but also urging that passion be overcome, was an immediate bestseller. And *On the Social Contract* was a landmark contribution to political theory.

Rousseau's liberal political and religious views got him in trouble with the French authorities, and he was obliged to flee to Switzerland in 1762 and to go to England in 1766. There he succumbed to the paranoid delusion that a vast plot had been mounted against him, yet he also wrote the first half of his astonishingly original *Confessions,* an autobiographical narrative that has deeply influenced modern thinking about the development of the self over time.

The next year Rousseau and Thérèse returned to France, living in obscurity in rural villages while he completed the *Confessions.* By now he was convinced that his career as a public intellectual had been a disastrous wrong turn, committing him to competitiveness and insincerity, and he intended to write thereafter for posterity alone. In 1770 he settled in Paris once more and devoted himself to music, botanizing, and writing essays called *Reveries of the Solitary Walker,* left unfinished when he died of a cerebral hemorrhage in 1778.

After the French Revolution, Rousseau's remains were moved from the village of Ermenonville, where he had died, and reinterred with high honors in the Panthéon in Paris. The faithful Thérèse lived on in poverty until 1801.

CONTENTS

INTRODUCTION

Leo Damrosch

Jean-Jacques Rousseau was the most original thinker in the great movement known as the Enlightenment, although he was probably not the best at any single thing, nor did he aspire to be. Unlike Voltaire or Hume or Diderot, Rousseau had never been a brilliant student; in fact he was never a student at all. Entirely self-taught, he freely acknowledged the handicaps that that entailed. But as an outsider who saw eighteenth-century culture from a uniquely independent perspective, he penetrated to depths that nobody else did. Instead of proposing gradual reforms in society, which was the normal program of the Enlightenment, he mounted a profound critique of its unexamined assumptions. In the sense in which the word *philosophe* means an imaginative intellectual rather than a formal philosopher, Rousseau has a claim to be considered the greatest of them all.

Indeed, Rousseau was so far ahead of his time that reviewers dismissed his books as merely paradoxical. "He can't really believe that" was a frequent reaction. But he said, "I would rather be a man of paradoxes than a man of prejudices,"[1] and as his challenge sank in, his influence grew. The distinguished Rousseauian Jean Starobinski says of the groundbreaking *Discourse on the Origin of Inequality*, "The immense echo of these words expanded in time and space far beyond what Rousseau could have foreseen."[2]

Rousseau was born in the militantly Protestant city of Geneva in 1712, the son of an affectionate but temperamental watchmaker named Isaac Rousseau. Shortly after giving birth to him his mother died of an infection, and it has been suggested that he bore a lifelong burden of guilt as a result. In later life he idealized the compact city-state—Geneva was then an independent republic, not yet part of Switzerland—and believed that it inspired his belief in the emotional loyalty that citizens need to feel to their community. Praising Genevan mores in a polemical work, he recalled a scene when a citizen militia had finished drilling in the square below the apartment where he and his father lived:

> Most of them gathered after the meal in the Place Saint-Gervais and began dancing all together, officers and soldiers, around the fountain, on to which drummers, fifers, and torch-carriers had climbed. . . . The women couldn't remain at their windows for long, and they came down. Wives came to see their husbands, servants brought wine, and even the children, awakened by the noise, ran around half-dressed among their fathers and mothers. The dance was suspended, and there was only embracing, laughter, toasts, caresses. . . . My father, hugging me, was overcome by trembling in a way that I can still feel and share. "Jean-Jacques," he said to me, "love your country! Do you

see these good Genevans? They are all friends, they
are all brothers, joy and concord reign in their midst."[3]
[Translations in the introduction are by Leo Damrosch.]

But between the lines in the autobiographical *Confessions* one
senses a lonely and discouraging childhood, which concluded
in an apprenticeship from which Rousseau impulsively ran
away at the age of sixteen.

Mainly as a way of getting financial support, he converted to
Catholicism. After a year in Turin, during which he was reduced to working as a humble lackey, he went to Annecy in the
Savoy (not yet part of France) and became the protégé of a
beautiful young Catholic convert named Mme de Warens.
Under her influence, and that of kindly priests and monks in
her social circle, he began to read seriously and to develop a
lifelong passion for music. He still had no plans, however, and
it began to look as if he would always be a drifter. When his
patroness seduced him he was seriously alarmed, since he regarded her as virtually his mother, while for her part she soon
tired of responsibility for an apparently shiftless young man.

In due course Rousseau moved to Lyon, where he took a job
as tutor to two small boys, and then to Paris. There he became
close to Denis Diderot, a brilliant polymath his own age, who
did much to expand his thinking. Meanwhile he acquired a
partner for life, a young servant girl named Thérèse Levasseur.
Their relationship was in effect a common-law marriage, but
never a legal one, and when Thérèse bore five children, Rousseau insisted on consigning them to a home for foundlings.
Years later his reputation would be seriously damaged when
Voltaire, who hated him, made this conduct public.

In 1749, when Rousseau was thirty-seven, he set out on foot

to visit Diderot, who had been incarcerated in the château of Vincennes near Paris because of irreligious hints he had published. (To assure ongoing publication of the great *Encyclopédie,* of which he was co-editor, Diderot promised never to transgress again and was released.) Pausing to rest, Rousseau idly opened a newspaper and found his life permanently changed. The obscure Academy of Dijon was offering a prize for the best essay on the topic "Whether the restoration of the sciences and arts has contributed to purify morals." It was a trite question, practically taking for granted an affirmative answer, but when Rousseau suddenly saw a new way of arguing the negative, "I beheld a different universe and became a different man." He was overcome by "dizziness like that of drunkenness," his heart pounded, and tears drenched his shirt. Under a tree, he scribbled a speech by an ancient Roman who returns from the past to denounce modern sophistication, crying, "Madmen, what have you done?" Rousseau won the prize, his *Discourse on the Sciences and Arts* was published, and it was an immediate sensation.

The more searching *Discourse on the Origin of Inequality* followed in 1755, and in 1761–62, in the space of eighteen months, Rousseau produced no fewer than three great books. *Julie, or, The New Héloïse,* a novel about romantic passion transformed into friendship, became an international bestseller. *Émile, or, On Education,* urging that children should be allowed to develop their individual talents, has influenced educational reforms ever since. And the *Social Contract,* insisting that a government gains legitimacy only from the shared commitment of its citizens, would have explosive effect a generation later.

Rousseau was now a celebrated writer in a remarkable range of fields, and in fact his work was far from miscellaneous, since—as he said himself—it all flowed from a single foundational idea. Man, he held, is naturally good, and it is society that has made him wicked. In those days, whatever was wrong in the world was conventionally ascribed by preachers to the sin of pride, and by political theorists to insubordination against superiors. Rousseau held that in the state of nature, "natural man" would have been self-sufficient and uncompetitive, and although civilization has brought benefits that we can no longer bear to give up, we should strive to recover as much of our natural selves as we can. In romantic relationships, we should break free from possessive passion; in education, we should encourage individuality to blossom; and in politics, we should respect the freedom of the individual.

The heart of Rousseau's thinking, his fundamental paradox, was to honor individualism but at the same time to submit it to a devastating critique. Progressive writers in the Enlightenment thought that the good of society was served by competition among individuals, who find it in their own interest to cooperate as well as compete; Adam Smith extolled the virtues of sociability even as he called for a free market. Rousseau took a more pessimistic view of self-interest, like that of seventeenth-century moralists such as Pascal, who said grimly in his *Pensées*, "Each *me* is the enemy of all the others, and would like to be their tyrant."[4] But whereas Pascal ascribed selfishness to original sin, Rousseau ascribed it to society, and he imagined a new kind of society in which "every individual, in uniting with everyone else, will still only be answerable to himself and remain as free as before."[5]

From social criticism, Rousseau's thinking naturally moved to individual psychology. In his own life he had experienced the ways in which a trusting, affectionate child could become selfish and dishonest, and he now preached an ideal of "sincerity" in which inside and outside would be in harmony, as he believed they once were for natural man. Eventually he had to acknowledge that it was harder to be sincere than he first thought, but this, too, produced a striking insight: we are conditioned so effectively to play artificial roles that we mistake them for our true nature. Rousseau saw that when he had been acting as a righteous counterculture critic, truth telling had actually been a kind of playacting:

> I was no longer that timid person, more shamefaced than modest, who didn't dare to introduce himself or speak, whom a playful word would disconcert and a woman's glance would cause to blush. . . . The contempt that my profound meditations inspired for the mores, maxims, and prejudices of the age made me impervious to the mockery of those who entertained them, and I crushed their little bon mots with my pronouncements as I would have crushed an insect between my fingers.[6]

Most of the philosophes took it for granted that we are by nature role-players and in fact are defined by our roles. Rousseau, inner-directed rather than other-directed, sought what would later be known as authenticity: commitment to a true self that lies deeper than any role. In a riposte to Diderot's treatise *The Paradox of the Actor*, he described the skill of accomplished performers as simply a specialized version of what everyone is conditioned to do. In an eloquent critique that has much in common with the Calvinist values of his native Geneva, and also with Plato's rejection of the arts in *The Republic*, he rose to moral outrage:

> What is the talent of the actor? The art of counterfeiting himself, clothing himself with another character

> than his own, appearing different than he is, becoming
> passionate in cold blood, saying something other than
> what he thinks as naturally as if he really thought it,
> and at last forgetting his own place by taking someone
> else's. What is the profession of the actor? A trade by
> which he gives himself in performance for money,
> submits himself to the ignominy and affronts that
> people buy the right to give him, and puts his person
> publicly on sale.[7]

This was not conventional moralizing but serious reflection on the insight that civilization encourages and rewards inauthentic behavior.

During these years, Rousseau was still living in France, but his religious and political ideas provoked official outrage there. The Catholic Church, which controlled education and censored every legally published book, was scandalized by the liberal treatment of religion in *Émile*. The *Social Contract* was similarly unacceptable to the authoritarian monarchy, and both books were publicly burned. Other philosophes often held subversive views, but they published them anonymously. Rousseau defiantly signed his own name to his books, and he was singled out as a scapegoat for the entire Enlightenment movement. A warrant was issued for his arrest, and he was given warning just in time to flee the country.

Return to Geneva was impossible, even though he had reconverted to Protestantism, since *Émile* and the *Social Contract* were proscribed there, too. Instead, he made his way to the territory of Neuchâtel, ruled at that time by Frederick the Great of Prussia, who liked to think of himself as a philosopher king. Thérèse soon followed, replying when Rousseau said he would understand if she didn't share in his persecution, "My heart has always been yours and will never change, so long as God gives you life and me as well. . . . I would go to join you even if I had to cross oceans and precipices."[8]

Three years later, after local Calvinist ministers stirred up mob hostility on account of Rousseau's religious views, he and Thérèse were driven from Switzerland, too. At the invitation of David Hume they moved to England, in what proved a highly unfortunate choice. Rather than stay in London, where French was widely understood, they retreated to a remote village in the Midlands, and by the end of a bitterly cold winter Rousseau had become alarmingly paranoid. Convinced that Hume, of all people, was masterminding a vast plot against him, he fled back to France and went into hiding there. Eventually he resolved to return to Paris and confront his accusers. They failed to appear. By that time he had ceased publishing, and the authorities were reluctant to make a martyr of him.

So Rousseau lived out his final decade in Paris, enjoying music and pursuing an avocation of collecting plants in the countryside. Speaking of himself in his late, unpublished *Dialogues*, he explained: "It is through idleness, nonchalance, and aversion to dependency and bother that Jean-Jacques copies music. He does his task as and when it pleases him; he doesn't have to account for his day, his time, his labor, or his leisure to anyone. . . . He is himself, and for himself, all day and every day."[9] In effect he was trying to re-create the condition of natural man.

The paranoia remained, but it was successfully compartmentalized, a firewall that enabled Rousseau to avoid uncomfortable contact with strangers and to enjoy the simple pleasures of life. The younger writer Bernardin de Saint-Pierre, who often accompanied him on his walks, recalled an eloquent comment of his on the singing of the nightingale: "Our musicians have all imitated its high and low notes, its runs and capriccios, but what characterizes it—its prolonged piping, its sobs, the sighing sounds that go to the soul and pervade its song—that is what no one has been able to capture."[10]

A collision in the street with a galloping Great Dane resulted in concussion and lasting brain damage, and Rousseau died of a cerebral hemorrhage in 1778, at the age of sixty-six.

After his death several posthumous works were published, most notably the great *Confessions,* which stands with its namesake by Saint Augustine as the most original and influential autobiographies ever written. Rousseau seems to have been literally the first writer to do what now seems inevitable, to seek the roots of personality in early relationships and experiences. The title of Marcel Proust's great cycle of novels, *À la Recherche du Temps Perdu,* could easily be Rousseau's: "In Search of Lost Time." His richest recoveries of the past are concentrated in the first three books of the twelve-book *Confessions,* which are included in their entirety in this volume.

One of the most memorable passages in the later books recreates a sensation of unalloyed contentment that Rousseau liked to call *le sentiment de l'existence,* the consciousness of simply being alive. He and Mme de Warens had just moved to a country house known as Les Charmettes:

> Here begins the brief happiness of my life; here come the peaceful but rapid moments that have given me the right to say I have lived. Precious moments that I miss so much, ah! begin again for me your pleasant course; flow more slowly in my memory, if that is possible, than you actually did in your fleeting succession. If all of that consisted in doings, in actions, in words, I would be able to describe and render it to some extent; but how can I say what was never said, or

done, or even thought, but tasted and felt, so that I can name no object for my happiness except the feeling itself? I got up with the sun and was happy, I took a walk and was happy, I saw Maman [Mme de Warens] and was happy, I left her and was happy, I roamed the woods and hills, I wandered in the valleys, I read, I was idle, I worked in the garden, I gathered fruit, I helped around the house, and happiness followed me everywhere. It wasn't in any single thing one could identify, it was entirely in myself, and it couldn't leave me for a single moment.[11]

In truth, this was a flight of imagination more than an accurate reminiscence; we know from Rousseau's letters that most of the time at Les Charmettes he lived alone, unhappy and neglected.

Rousseau's influence as an analyst of culture developed gradually; his influence as a political thinker bore fruit more immediately. When Thomas Jefferson wrote in the Declaration of Independence, two years before Rousseau's death, that all men are created equal and possess unalienable rights, he was using Rousseauian language. And in 1789 the political time bomb of the *Social Contract* burst. The leaders of the French Revolution, with their ideals of liberty, equality, and fraternity, hailed Rousseau as a prophet. His remains were reinterred with immense pomp in the Panthéon in Paris, and according to the official account of the occasion, "The moon that shed its pale and colorless light gave this procession the aspect of those ancient mysteries whose initiates were pure or washed clean of their faults." Especially notable was a delegation from his native city, marching with a banner that read "Aristocratic Geneva proscribed him, a regenerated Geneva has avenged his memory."[12]

In the ensuing years Rousseau's influence continued to

spread. Romanticism, with its emphasis on originality, imagination, and oneness with nature, was profoundly in his debt. The growing recognition that governments should reflect their people's will, together with the conviction that social inequality is intrinsically unjust, have profound roots in his thought. The concept of childhood as a crucially formative stage of development is Rousseauian at its heart. And psychoanalysis, searching for hidden foundations of the self, carries forward the quest that he launched in the *Confessions*.

Rousseau never wanted to found a system, and he didn't. His mission was to expose the unreconciled conflicts that make human life so difficult and that conventional systems of politics and education and psychology try to iron out. At a friend's house, he once took a peach from the bottom of a pyramid of fruit, upon which the whole thing fell down. "That's what you always do with all our systems," she commented; "you pull down with a single touch, but who will build up what you pull down?"[13] By pulling down, he challenged later generations to build up again in new ways, and his style of questioning has become inseparable from our culture. "The friends of Rousseau," one friend of his remarked, "are as though related to each other through his soul, which has joined them across countries, ranks, fortune, and even centuries."[14] Many people who have barely heard of him are, at a deep level, friends of Rousseau.

LEO DAMROSCH, is Ernest Bernbaum Research Professor of Literature at Harvard University. He is the author of numerous books, including *Tocqueville's Discovery of America* and *Jean-Jacques Rousseau: Restless Genius,* a finalist for the 2005 National Book Award in nonfiction.

FURTHER READING

The standard edition in French of Rousseau's complete works is *Oeuvres Complètes,* edited by Marcel Raymond et al., 5 vols. (Paris: Gallimard, Bibliothèque de la Pléiade, 1959–1995). Rousseau's correspondence, together with valuable supporting material, is collected in *Correspondance Complète de Jean-Jacques Rousseau,* edited by R. A. Leigh, 52 vols. (Geneva: Institut et Musée Voltaire, 1965–1971; Oxford: Voltaire Foundation, 1971–1998).

English translations, with excellent notes, are available in *The Collected Writings of Rousseau,* edited by Christopher Kelly, Roger D. Masters, et al., 15 vols. (Hanover, N.H.: University Press of New England, 1992–2009). In addition, there are translations of several individual works: *Confessions,* translated by Angela Scholar (Oxford: Oxford University Press, 2000); *Émile,* translated by Allan Bloom (New York: Basic Books, 1979); and *Reveries of the Solitary Walker,* translated by Peter France (London: Penguin, 1979).

The most comprehensive biography, left unfinished, however, at the author's death, is in three volumes by Maurice Cranston: *Jean-Jacques: The Early Life and Work* (New York: Norton, 1982), *The Noble Savage* (Chicago: University of Chicago Press, 1991), and *The Solitary Self* (Chicago: University of Chicago Press, 1997). A recent award-winning biography is Leo Damrosch, *Jean-Jacques Rousseau: Restless Genius* (Boston: Houghton Mifflin, 2005).

Good introductions to Rousseau's thought are Robert Wokler, *Rousseau: A Very Short Introduction* (Oxford: Oxford University Press, 2001), and *The Cambridge Companion to Rousseau*, edited by Patrick Riley (Cambridge: Cambridge University Press, 2001). The most stimulating (and influential) interpretation is still that of Jean Starobinski, *Jean-Jacques Rousseau: Transparency and Obstruction,* translated by Arthur Goldhammer (Chicago: University of Chicago Press, 1988, originally published in French in 1957). Valuable overviews are provided by Roger D. Masters, *The Political Philosophy of Rousseau* (Princeton, N.J.: Princeton University Press, 1968); Arthur M. Melzer, *The Natural Goodness of Man: On the System of Rousseau's Thought* (Chicago: University of Chicago Press, 1990); and Christopher Kelly, *Rousseau's Exemplary Life: The Confessions as Political Philosophy* (Ithaca, N.Y.: Cornell University Press, 1987).

THE
ESSENTIAL WRITINGS
OF
JEAN-JACQUES ROUSSEAU

Discourse on the Origin and Foundations of Inequality Among Men

In 1755, five years after Rousseau's Discourse on the Sciences and Arts *made him unexpectedly famous, he once again responded to an essay competition announced by the Academy of Dijon. The topic this time was "What is the origin of inequality among men, and is it authorized by natural law?" The Academy rejected his submission because it greatly exceeded the length limit, which didn't matter to Rousseau, because it was immediately published and proved to be a work of extraordinary originality.*

Instead of tracing the phenomenon of inequality historically, as would have been usual at the time, this second Discourse *is a thought experiment that attempts to discover what would be truly natural to human beings if society had never shaped them at all. "Natural man" is imagined as essentially an animal, solitary and unsocial, open to feeling but with no need of reason, and with no wish or occasion to exploit other people. The development of society brought with it much that was good, particularly the mutual love* and support of family life, and we could never return to the state of nature. But the negative consequences have been immense: the very fact of needing other human beings has led everywhere to joyless labor, inequality, and oppression. Rousseau's central message—immensely influential in later generations—is that social inequality is universal but it is also wrong. Still, to the extent that "natural man" survives at a deep level inside us, we can try to live according to Nature and to open ourselves to spontaneity of feeling.

PREFACE

The most useful of the natural sciences, yet the least advanced, strikes me as being the science of man, and I will venture to say that at the Temple of Delphi the only inscription contained a precept more important and difficult than all the copious volumes of the moralists.[15] I also regard the subject of the following discourse as consisting of the most interesting questions that philosophy can propose and, unfortunately for us, one of the most contentious that the philosophers seek to resolve. For how can we understand the source of the inequality among men if we do not begin by understanding them? And how can man ultimately succeed in seeing himself as nature formed him through all the changes that the succession of time and circumstances must have produced in his original constitution, and disentangle what is innate in him from what circumstances and his progress have added or changed in his original state? Like the statue of Glaucus, which time, the sea, and storms had so disfigured that it resembled less a god than a wild beast, the human soul, altered in the bosom of society by a thousand perpetually recurring causes, by the acquisition of a mass of knowledge and multitude of errors, by the changes befalling the constitution of the body and by the continual impact of the passions, has changed so as to be hardly recognizable.[16] And one no longer finds beings that always act according to firm and invariable principles, beings with the celestial and majestic simplicity that their creator imprinted on them; instead one finds the misshapen contrast of a passion that believes it reasons and an understanding that is frenzied.

What is even more cruel is that all progress made by the human species ceaselessly moves it ever further from its original state: the more discoveries we make and the more new knowledge we accumulate, the more we deprive ourselves of the means of acquiring the most important knowledge of all, and it is in a sense, through studying man that we have made ourselves incapable of knowing him.

It is clear that it is in these successive changes of the human constitution that one must look for the initial origin of the differences that distinguish men who were, by common consent, naturally as equal among one another as the animals of every species until diverse physical causes introduced the varieties that we see in them. In fact, it is not conceivable that these first changes, however they may have come about, would have altered all the individuals of a species at once and in the same manner; while some would have been improved or caused to deteriorate, having acquired various good or bad qualities that were not inherent in their nature, others would have remained longer in their original state. Such was the first source of inequality among men, and it is easier to present it in general terms such as these than to assign its true causes with precision.

Let my readers therefore not imagine that I dare flatter myself at having seen what seems to me so difficult to see. I have initiated some arguments and hazarded a few conjectures, less in the hope of resolving the question than with the intention of shedding light on its true state. Others will be able to go further along the same path without it being easy for anyone to reach the end, since it is not an easy task to disentangle what is original from what is artificial in man's present nature, and to know well a state that no longer exists and that perhaps never has existed nor ever will, and yet of which it is necessary to have precise notions in order to judge our present state correctly.[17] He who would undertake to determine the precise steps necessary to make sound observations on this subject would certainly need more philosophy than one would imagine, and a good solution to the following problem strikes me as being worthy of the Aristotles and Plinys of our day: "What experiments would be necessary to achieve an understanding of natural man, and what are the methods by which such experiments should be conducted within society?" Far from undertaking to resolve this question, I believe I have meditated enough on the subject to dare reply in advance that the greatest philosophers would not be suitable for conducting these experiments, nor the most powerful sovereigns to perform them. It is hardly reasonable to expect such a collaboration to succeed, particularly as it would need perseverance, or rather a confluence of intellect and goodwill on both sides.

And yet such an investigation, which is so difficult to undertake and to which until now such little thought has been given, is the only means left to us of dispersing a multitude of difficulties that prevent our knowing the true foundations of human society. It is the ignorance of man's nature that casts so much uncertainty and obscurity on the true definition of natural right: for the idea of right, says Monsieur Burlamaqui,[18] and even more that of natural right, are incontestably ideas relating to the nature of man. It is from the very nature of man, Monsieur Burlamaqui continues, and from his constitution and condition, that the principles of this science must be deduced.

It is with some surprise or shock that one notes how little agreement prevails on this important matter among the authors who have treated these issues. Among the soundest, one will not find two who are of the same opinion on this point—not to mention the ancient philosophers, who seem to have made it their mission to contradict one another on the most fundamental principles. The Roman jurists indiscriminately placed man and all the other animals under the same natural law, since they considered natural law the law that nature imposes upon itself rather than the one it prescribes; or because of the specific meaning under which these jurists understood the word *law*, which in this instance they seem to have taken to mean the expression of the general relations established by nature among all animate beings for their preservation. As men of our era understand *law* only to mean a rule prescribed to a moral being (that is to say, a being that is intelligent, free, and considered in its relation to other beings), they consequently restrict the domain of natural law to the only animal endowed with reason, that is to say man. But while they all define this law in their own way, they base it on such metaphysical principles that there are, even among us, very few people capable of understanding them, let alone discovering them of their own accord. Accordingly, all the definitions provided by these learned men, who are otherwise in perpetual disagreement with one another, agree only on this point: that it is impossible to understand the law of nature, and consequently to obey it, without being a truly great thinker and profound metaphysician. What this means is that for the establishment of society, men have had to employ an intelligence that develops only with great difficulty, and for very few people, in the bosom of society itself.

With such limited knowledge of nature and such a lack of agreement on the meaning of the word *law*, it would be quite difficult to agree on an adequate definition of natural law. Consequently, all the definitions found in books have, besides the defect of lacking in consistency, the further defect of being derived from several fields of knowledge that men do not have innately, and from advantages of which they cannot conceive until after they have left the state of nature.[19] One begins by considering what rules would be appropriate for men to establish among themselves for the common interest, and one then gives the name *natural law* to the collection of these rules without any other proof than the good that one feels would result from their universal implementation. This is certainly a convenient way of creating definitions and explaining the nature of things through concurrences that are almost arbitrary.

But so long as we do not know man in his natural condition, it is in vain that we seek to determine the law that he has received or the one that best suits his constitution. The only thing about this law we can see clearly is that for it to be a law, the will of him whom it binds must be able to submit himself to it consciously; but in order for this law to be natural, it must also speak immediately with the voice of nature.

Casting aside all the scientific books that only teach us to see men as they have made themselves, and reflecting on the first and most simple operation of the human spirit, I believe I perceive two principles antecedent to reason, of which one interests us intensely in our well-being and self-preservation, and the other inspires in us a natural repugnance at seeing any sentient being, particularly a fellow human, perish or suffer. It is from the collaboration and combination of the two principles of which our minds are capable, without it being necessary to introduce the principle of sociability, that, it seems to me, all the rules of natural law flow; rules that reason is then forced to reestablish on other foundations when, by its successive developments, it has succeeded in stifling nature.

In this way, one is not obliged to make man into a philosopher before making him into a man. His duty toward others is not solely dictated by belated lessons of wisdom, and so long as he does not resist the inner impulse to commiserate he will never do harm to another man or another sentient being, except in the legitimate case where his self-preservation is concerned, in which he is obliged to give preference to himself. By these means one also ends the ancient disputes as to whether animals are part of natural law, as it is clear that since they lack intellect and freedom, they cannot recognize this law; and yet, sharing to some extent as they do in our nature through the sensibility with which they are endowed, it would seem that animals ought also to share in natural right, and that man is subject to some form of duty toward them. In fact, it would appear that if I am obliged not to do any harm to a fellow man, it is less because he is a rational being than because he is a sentient one, a quality which, being common to both man and beast, must at least give the one the right not to be needlessly ill-treated by the other.

This same study of original man, of his true needs and the fundamental principles of his duty, is furthermore the only good means of dispelling the myriad difficulties that arise concerning the origin of moral inequality, the true foundations of the body politic, the reciprocal rights of its members, and a thousand other such questions, which are as important as they are opaque.

Looking at society with a calm and objective eye, it at first appears to exhibit only the violence of powerful men and the oppression of the weak. Our minds are repelled by the harshness of the former, and we are driven to lament the blindness of the latter. Nothing is less stable among men than these external relationships, which are more often the product of chance than of wisdom, and which one calls weakness or power, wealth or poverty; consequently, the institutions of man seem at first glance to be built on sand. It is only upon examining them up close, when the dust and sand that surround the edifice have been swept away, that one can see the unshakable foundations upon which it is built and learns to respect these foundations. For without the serious study of man and his natural faculties and their successive development, one will never succeed in making such distinctions and in separating in the present state of things what the divine will has done from what human skill claims to have done. The political and moral investigations to which the important question I am examining give rise are consequently useful in every way, and the hypothetical history of government is in every way an instructive lesson for man. By considering what we would have become had we been abandoned to ourselves, we must learn to bless Him whose beneficent hand, by correcting our institutions and giving them an unshakable foundation, has anticipated the disorders that would have resulted, thus instigating our happiness by means that seemed destined to complete our misery.

DISCOURSE ON THE ORIGIN AND FOUNDATIONS OF INEQUALITY AMONG MEN

It is of man that I have to speak, and the question I shall examine assures that I will be speaking openly, as one does not propose such questions to one's fellow men when one is afraid of honoring the truth. I will, therefore, defend the cause of humanity with confidence before the wise men who invite me to do so, and shall be pleased if I prove worthy of my subject and my judges.

In my view there are two sorts of inequality in the human species: one I call natural or physical, because it is established by nature and consists of differences in age, health, physical strength, and qualities of the mind or soul; the other, one might call moral or political inequality, because it depends on some sort of mutual agreement, and is established, or at least authorized, by the consent of men. This inequality consists of the various privileges that some enjoy at the expense of others, such as being wealthier, more honored, and more powerful than they, or even making themselves obeyed.

One cannot ask what the source of natural inequality is, because the simple definition of the term would be provided as an answer. Even less can one inquire if there is not some essential connection between the two inequalities, for that would be to ask in different terms if those who command are necessarily better than those who obey, and if the power of the body or the mind, and wisdom or virtue, are always found in the same individuals in proportion to their power or wealth: this is a good question, perhaps, in a debate among slaves within earshot of their masters, but it is not fitting for free men of reason who are engaged in a quest for truth.

What, then, is this discourse about? Its aim is to mark within the progression of things the moment in which rights succeeded violence, and nature was subjected to law; to explain by what sequence of miracles the powerful might resolve to serve the weak and the people purchase an imaginary repose at the price of true happiness.

All the philosophers who have examined the foundations of society have felt compelled to go back to the state of nature, but not one has succeeded. Some have not hesitated to suppose that men living in a natural state had the notion of what was just and unjust, without troubling to show that they must already have had that notion, or even that it would have been useful to them to have it. Others have spoken of a natural right that each individual has to protect what belongs to him, yet without explaining what they understand by *belongs*. Others again, after first granting authority to the more powerful over the weaker, immediately created a government without giving thought to the time that had to elapse before the words *authority* and *government* could attain meaning among men. Finally, all the philosophers, speaking constantly of need, greed, oppression, desires, and pride, imbued the state of nature with ideas they had found in society. They spoke of savage man but depicted civilized man. It did not even occur to most of our philosophers to doubt that the state of nature once existed, whereas it is evident from the Holy Scriptures that the first man, having instantly received intellect and precepts from God, was himself not in a state of nature at all; and if one gives the writings of Moses the credence that every Christian philosopher owes them, one must say that even before the Deluge men never existed in a pure state of nature, unless they lapsed into it by some extraordinary occurrence; a paradox that is most difficult to defend and altogether impossible to prove.

Let us therefore begin by setting aside all the facts, for they do not touch on the problem.[20] One must not take the inquiries into which one can enter on this subject as historical truths, but merely as hypothetical and conditional reasoning. These are better suited to elucidate the nature of things than to show their true origin, and are comparable to the hypotheses that our natural scientists make every day on the formation of the world. Religion commands us to believe that God Himself drew men out of the state of nature immediately after the Creation, and that men are unequal because he willed them to be so. But religion does not forbid us to form conjectures drawn exclusively from the nature of man and the creatures surrounding him, or to conjecture what might have happened to mankind had it been left to itself. This is what I am asked, and this is what I intend to examine in this discourse. Since my subject concerns man in general, I will strive to adopt a language suited to all nations, or, rather, forgetting times and places in order to think only about the men to whom I am speaking, I shall imagine myself in the Lyceum of Athens, repeating the lessons of my masters, having as my judges Platos and Xenocrateses, and mankind as my auditors.[21]

Listen, O man, from whatever country you may be, whatever your opinions! Here is your history such as I believe to read it, not in books written by your fellow men, who are liars, but in nature, which never lies. Everything that comes from nature will be true. Nothing will be false, except what I might unintentionally have included of my own. The times of which I shall speak are very distant. How much you have changed from what you once were! It is, so to speak, the life of your species I will describe to you according to the qualities that you have received, and that your education and your habits have been able to corrupt but not destroy. There is, I believe, an age at which an individual might want to stop growing older; you will look for the age at which you wish your species to have gone no further. Discontented with your present state for reasons that herald even greater discontent for your unfortunate posterity, you might perhaps wish to be able to go back in time. And this sentiment must lead to the praise of your first ancestors, the criticism of your contemporaries, and dread for those who will have the misfortune of living after you.

PART ONE

As important as it might be to consider man from his origins in order to judge his natural state, and examine him, so to speak, in the original embryonic state of his species, I will not follow his development through its successive stages. I will not pause to search in his biology for what he might have been at the beginning in order to eventually become what he is now. I will not examine if, as Aristotle believes, man's elongated nails might originally have been hooked claws, if he was hairy like a bear, and if, walking on all fours, his eyes directed at the ground and confined to a few paces ahead, whether this did not shape the character and also the limits of his ideas. On this question I could form only vague, almost imaginary, conjectures. Comparative anatomy has still made too little progress, and the observations of natural scientists are still too uncertain, to allow for a solid foundation on such a subject. Thus, without turning to supernatural knowledge on this subject, and without regard to the changes that have taken place in man's inner and outer form as he gradually began to apply his limbs to new uses and to nourish himself on new foods, I will assume him to have always had the form I see him having today, walking on two feet, making use of his hands as we make use of ours, directing his eyes at all of nature and surveying with them the vast expanse of heaven.

In stripping this being, constituted as he is, of all the supernatural gifts he might have received, and of all the artificial faculties that he could have acquired only by a long progress; in considering this being, in short, such as he must have emerged from the hands of nature, I see an animal that is less strong than some, less agile than others, but, in sum, formed in the most advantageous way of all. I see him satisfying his hunger beneath an oak, quenching his thirst at the first stream, making his bed beneath the same tree that furnished him his meal—thus his needs are satisfied.

Abandoned to its natural fertility and covered by immense forests that the ax had never mutilated, the earth offers at every step food and shelter to animals of every species. Men, dispersed among them, observe and imitate their industry and thus raise themselves to the instinct of beasts, with the advantage that each species has merely its own instincts, while man, having perhaps none that are his own, appropriates them all, nourishing himself equally on a wide selection of foods that other animals share, consequently finding his sustenance with greater ease than any of the others.

Men have developed a robust and almost unchanging temperament, accustomed as they had been from childhood to the inclemency of the weather and the rigors of the seasons, worked to exhaustion and forced, unarmed and exposed to the elements, to guard their lives and their prey against other wild beasts or to run away from them. The children, coming into the world with the excellent constitution of their fathers, and fortifying this constitution with the same practices that created it, acquired all the vigor of which the human species is capable. Nature treated these children exactly as the law of Sparta treated the children of its citizens: it made those with a good constitution strong and robust and made all the others perish, thus differing from our societies, where the state, rendering children burdensome to their fathers, kills them indiscriminately before they are born.

As the body of the savage man is the only instrument he knows, he puts it to various uses of which our unaccustomed bodies are incapable, and it is our machines that rob us of the strength and dexterity which necessity obliges savage man to acquire. If he had had an ax, could his wrists have smashed such powerful branches? If he had had a sling, could he have thrown a stone with his hand with such might? If he had had a ladder, would he have climbed a tree with such ease? If he had had a horse, could he have run so fast? Give civilized man enough time to gather all his machines about him, and one can be certain that he will overcome savage man with ease. But if you want to see an even more unequal contest, pitch them against one another naked and unarmed, and you will soon see the true advantage of constantly having all your strength at hand, of always being ready for any eventuality, and always being, so to speak, entirely complete within oneself.

Hobbes claims that man is naturally intrepid and seeks only to attack and fight. Another illustrious philosopher, on the contrary, thinks (as both Cumberland and Pufendorf also assert) that there is nothing as timid as man in the state of nature; that he is always trembling and ready to flee at the slightest noise he hears, the slightest movement he sees.[22] That might be true of objects he does not know, and I do not doubt that he is frightened by every new thing he sees whenever he cannot distinguish the physical good or evil he is to expect, or compare his strength to the dangers he is facing—rare circumstances in the state of nature, where everything progresses in such a uniform fashion, and where the face of the earth is not subject to abrupt and continuing changes triggered by the passions and impulses of men living in society. But savage man, living dispersed among animals and finding himself compelled to measure himself against them, is quick to make the comparison, and feeling that he surpasses them, in skill more than strength, learns not to fear them anymore. Set a bear or a wolf against a savage who is strong, agile, and courageous, as all savage men are, arm him with stones and a good club, and you will see that the danger is at most mutual, and that after several encounters of the kind, ferocious beasts that avoid attacking one another will also avoid attacking man, whom they will have found just as ferocious as they are themselves. As for animals that really have more strength than he has skill, man finds himself in the same situation as other weaker species that nevertheless continue to survive. He has the advantage of being as ready to flee as they are, and finding almost certain refuge in the trees, he always has the choice of taking on or avoiding an encounter and of choosing to fight or flee. Let us add that it does not appear that any animal naturally wages war against man except in a case of self-defense or extreme hunger, or bears him any violent antipathies that seem to announce that one species is destined by nature to serve as fodder for another.

(No doubt this is why negroes and savages worry so little about ferocious beasts that they might encounter in the forests. The Caribs of Venezuela, among others, in this respect live in great security without the least trouble. Though almost naked, they boldly face danger armed only with bow and arrow, François Corréal says, but one has never heard that any of them have ever been devoured by beasts.)[23]

More formidable enemies, against which man does not have

the same means to defend himself, are the natural infirmities: infancy, old age, and illnesses of every kind—sad signs of our weakness, of which the first two are common to all animals, while illnesses mainly assail man living in society. I also note, on the subject of infancy, that a mother, carrying her child with her everywhere, can feed it with much greater ease than the females of many other species that are forced to exhaust themselves going back and forth, on one side to find food, on the other to suckle or feed their young. It is true that if the woman perishes the child is at great risk of perishing with her, but this danger is common to countless other species where the young are not capable of foraging for food on their own. And if the duration of childhood is longer among us, our lives being longer, then everything is more or less equal in this respect, although there are other rules concerning the duration of dependence and the number of young that are not relevant to my subject. With old people who are less active and perspire little, the need for food diminishes along with the ability to provide for it. And as the way of life of savages keeps gout and rheumatism at bay—and old age, among all the ills, is the one ill that human aid can least alleviate—they end up expiring without anyone discerning that they have ceased to exist, and almost without realizing it themselves.

As for illnesses, I will not repeat the futile and false declarations against medicine that most healthy people make, but will ask if there is any reliable evidence from which one can conclude that in those countries where the art of medicine is most neglected, the average life of man is shorter than in countries where it is pursued with greater zeal; and how could this be, if we unleash in ourselves more illnesses than those for which medicine can provide remedies! There is the extreme inequality in men's way of life, an excess of idleness in some and work in others; there is the ease with which our appetites and senses are aroused and satisfied; there is the food of the rich that is too sumptuous, and that inflames humors and triggers indigestion; the bad food of the poor, who often have no food at all, the lack of which leads them to voraciously overburden their stomachs when they have the chance; nights of revelry, excesses of every kind, the immodest raptures of the passions, the exhaustion of the mind, and the vexation and countless sorrows that man experiences in all stations of life and which perpetually gnaw at the soul; all this is dire proof that most of our illnesses are of our own doing, and that we could have avoided almost all of them had we conserved a way of life that is simple, constant, and retiring, as nature has prescribed. If nature destined us to be healthy, I almost dare to assume that a contemplative state is one contrary to nature, and that a man who reflects is a depraved animal.[24] When one thinks of the good condition that savages are in, at least those we have not ruined with our strong liquor, when one discerns that they barely know any illnesses other than injury and old age, one is very much led to believe that one could map the history of human illness by following the diseases of civil societies. This, at least, is the opinion of Plato, who evaluates certain remedies used or esteemed by Podalirius and Machaon at the siege of Troy that were not yet known among men. [And Celsus reports that dieting, which today is so necessary, was first invented by Hippocrates.][25]

Having such few sources of illness, men in the state of nature consequently have little need for medicine, and even less for doctors; in this respect the human species is not in worse condition than all the other species, and it is easy to inquire from hunters whether they come across many ailing animals. They encounter a number of animals that have suffered severe injuries that had healed, animals that have had bones and even limbs broken that became whole again, with time as their only surgeon, everyday life their only therapy; animals that were no less perfectly healed for not having been tormented with incisions, poisoned with drugs, or wasted by fasting. Finally, regardless of how useful well-administered medicine might be among us, it is always certain that if a sick savage, abandoned, has only nature to rely on, he has, on the other hand, nothing to fear but his illness, which frequently renders his situation preferable to ours.

Let us therefore beware of confusing savage men with the men around us. Nature treats all animals abandoned to her care with a predilection that seems to show how jealously she guards her right. The horse, the cat, the bull, even the donkey, are for the most part better formed, have a constitution that is more robust, have more vigor, strength, and courage in the forests than they do in our barns and stables. They lose half these advantages when they become domesticated, and one would say that all our efforts to feed and treat them well lead only to their being bastardized. The same is true of man: in becoming socialized and a slave he ends up weak, timid, and mean-spirited, his soft, effeminate way of life finally draining both his strength and his courage. Let us also add that between the savage state and the domestic state, the difference between one man and another must be even greater than that between one beast and another. Since nature has treated man and beast equally, all the conveniences that man gives himself beyond those he gives the animals he tames are among the many causes that lead him to degenerate more visibly.

It is consequently not such a great misfortune for these first men, nor indeed such an obstacle to their survival, to be naked and to lack shelter and all the useless things we deem so necessary. Though their skin is not covered by fur, in warm countries they have no need of it, and in cold countries they quickly learn to appropriate the skins of the beasts they have slain. If they have only two feet with which to run, they have two arms with which to provide for their defense and their needs; their children perhaps walk late and with difficulty, but the mothers carry them with ease, an advantage lacking in other species where a mother, if she is pursued, sees herself compelled to abandon her young or limit her speed to theirs. Finally, unless one considers the singular and fortuitous concurrence of the circumstances of which I will speak subsequently, a concurrence that might very well not happen, it is clear that, all things considered, the first man who made himself clothes or built himself a lodging provided himself with things that he did not particularly need, since until then he had done without them, and it is hard to see why he could not as a grown man endure the kind of life he had endured since childhood.

Alone, unconstrained by labor, and never far from danger, savage man must like to sleep as do animals that think little and so, one could say, sleep all the time that they are not thinking. Self-preservation being savage man's practically sole concern, his most developed faculties must be those that have as their object attack and defense, either to overcome his prey or to keep himself from becoming the prey of another animal. In contrast, the organs that are only perfected by a soft and sensual way of life must remain in a rough state that prevents in him any kind of delicacy; his senses end up divided, the savage man having an extremely coarse sense of touch and taste while his senses of sight, hearing, and smell are of the greatest subtlety. Such is the animal state in general, and also, according to the reports of travelers, the state of most savage peoples. It is therefore not surprising that the Hottentots of the Cape of Good Hope can with their naked eye spot ships far out at sea, for which the Dutch need a telescope, or that the savages of the Americas can scent the trail of a Spaniard as well as the best dogs might, or that all the barbarous nations can bear their nudity with ease, sharpen their taste with hot peppers, and drink European liquor like water.

So far I have considered only physical man. Let us now try to look at him from a metaphysical and moral side.

I see in every animal simply an ingenious machine that nature has endowed with senses so that it can by itself refurbish, and to a certain extent shield itself, from all that seeks to destroy or disrupt it. I see precisely the same in the human machine, with the only difference that nature alone directs everything in the life of a beast, while man in his role as free agent partakes in the process. A beast chooses or rejects by instinct, while man does so through free acts, with the result that a beast cannot distance itself from the rules prescribed for it, even when it would be to its advantage, and with the result that man often distances himself to his disadvantage. A pigeon will die of hunger beside a bowl filled with choice meat, as will a cat on a pile of fruit or grain, though each could very well have nourished itself from the food it disdains had it known to try it. It is thus that dissolute men abandon themselves to excesses that cause fever and death, because the mind depraves the senses, and the will continues to speak when nature falls silent.

Since every animal has senses it has ideas, even connecting them to a certain degree. Man differs from beasts in this respect only insofar as larger quantities differ from lesser. Some philosophers have even proposed that there is a greater difference between one man and another than between a man and a beast. Accordingly, it is not so much man's capacity to understand that specifically distinguishes him from animals, as it is his being a free agent. Nature commands every animal, and the beast obeys. Man experiences the same command but recognizes that he is free to yield to it or reject it. And it is above all in the consciousness of this freedom that the spirituality of his soul manifests itself, for physics to some extent explains the mechanism of the senses and the formation of ideas, but in the power of wanting or, rather, choosing, and in the awareness of this power, one finds purely spiritual acts in which nothing can be explained by the laws of mechanics.

But even if the difficulties surrounding all these questions would leave some room for disagreement about this difference between man and animal, there is another very specific quality that distinguishes them and about which there can be no argument, and that is the faculty of improving oneself. With the aid of circumstances, this faculty successively develops all the others, and resides within us both as a species and as individuals, while an animal, on the other hand, becomes within several months what it will be for the rest of its life, while its whole species will in a thousand years still be what it was in the very first year of that millennium. Why is man alone subject to becoming imbecilic? Is it not that in this way he is returning to his primitive state, while the beast, which has not acquired anything, has nothing to lose, always remaining with its instinct? Does not man, losing through old age or some mishap everything that his *faculty of self-improvement* has led him to acquire, fall lower even than the beast? It would be sad if we were forced to agree that this distinctive and almost boundless human faculty is the source of all man's miseries, that it is this faculty that draws him, by the action of time, from the original condition in which he would spend tranquil and innocent days; that it is this faculty, engendering over the centuries his intellect, his errors, his virtues, and his vices, which in the end makes him his own and nature's tyrant. It would be terrible to be led to praise as benefactor the man who first suggested to the people of the Orinoco the use of the boards they apply to the temples of their children's heads, which assures them of at least some of their imbecility and original happiness.

Nature leaves savage man entirely to his instincts, or, rather, compensates him for the instincts he perhaps lacks, by giving him faculties capable of initially supplementing these instincts and then raising him well above them. But savage man begins with purely animal functions: perceiving and feeling will be his initial state, a state he shares with all animals. Wanting and not wanting, desiring and fearing, will be the first and almost only function of man's soul until new circumstances bring about new developments in it.

Whatever moralists may say, human understanding owes much to the passions, which, as is commonly admitted, also owe much to human understanding. It is through the activity of the passions that our reason improves itself; we seek knowledge only because we desire pleasure, and it is impossible to conceive why he who has neither desires nor fears might go to the trouble of reasoning. Passions, on the other hand, owe their origin to our needs and their progress to our knowledge, as one cannot desire or fear things except by way of ideas that one might have of them, or by way of the simple impulse of nature. Savage man, deprived of any sort of intellect, experiences only passions of this last kind; his desires do not exceed his physical needs. The only good he recognizes in the universe is food, a female, and sleep; the only evils he fears are pain and hunger; I say pain and not death, since an animal does not ever know what it is to die, while the knowledge of death and its terrors is one of man's first acquisitions as he distances himself from the animal condition.

It would be easy, were it necessary, for me to support these impressions with facts, and to prove that in all the nations of the world the progress of the mind is exactly proportional to the needs that peoples received from nature or to which circumstances had subjected them, and consequently proportional to the passions that drove them to satisfy those needs. I would show the arts emerging in Egypt and spreading with the floodings of the Nile; I would follow their development among the Greeks, where the arts sprouted, grew, and rose to the heavens from among the sands and rocks of Attica, without being able to strike root on the fertile banks of the Eurotas. I would point out that in general the people of the north are more industrious than those of the south because they can less afford not to be, as if nature were striving in this way to balance things by giving minds the fertility it denies the soil.

Even without resorting to the uncertain testimonies of history, is it not clear that everything appears to quell savage man's impulse and means to cease being savage? His imagination depicts nothing, his heart asks nothing. His modest needs are so readily at hand, and he is so far from the degree of knowledge necessary to want to acquire more, that he can have neither foresight nor curiosity. He is indifferent to the spectacle of nature because he is so familiar with it; it is always the same order, the same pattern. He does not have the intellect to be surprised by these great wonders, and it is not to him that one turns to seek the philosophy man needs if he is to notice what he has seen every day. His soul, which nothing perturbs, gives itself solely to the feeling of his present existence without any idea of the future, regardless of how close that future might be, and his ventures, limited like his horizon, barely extend to the end of the day. Such is even today the Carib's extent of foresight: he sells his cotton mat in the morning and then comes crying in the evening to buy it back, having failed to foresee that he would need it for the coming night.

The more one reflects on the subject, the more the distance

between pure sensations and the simplest knowledge grows before our eyes, and it is impossible to conceive how man could have crossed such a great divide with nothing but his own strength, without the help of communication, and without being driven by necessity. How many centuries must have passed before man was capable of seeing another fire than that of the heavens? How many different accidents and coincidences were necessary for him to learn the simplest uses of this element? How many times must he have let the fire go out before acquiring the art of reproducing it? And how many times did these secrets perhaps die along with him who had discovered them? What can we say about agriculture, a craft that demands so much toil and foresight, is so dependent on other skills, which is obviously practicable only where a society has at least begun to exist, and which serves not so much to draw from the earth food it would readily yield, but to compel it to cater to the preferences of our taste? But let us suppose that men had multiplied to the extent that natural produce was no longer adequate to feed them, a supposition, it should be said, which would affirm the great advantage of that way of life for the human species. Let us suppose that tools for farming had fallen straight from Heaven into the hands of savages without there ever having been forges or workshops. Let us suppose that these savages had overcome mankind's abhorrence of unrelenting labor, and that they had learned to foresee their needs far enough in advance to figure out how to cultivate the soil, sow seeds, and plant trees. Let us suppose that they would have discovered the arts of grinding wheat and fermenting grapes, all of which the gods would have had to teach them, as one cannot conceive their learning these skills on their own. What man in such a condition would be senseless enough to torment himself by cultivating a field that would be plundered by the first man or beast to take a liking to its crop? And how could any man resolve to spend his life engaged in arduous labor, of which the more he needs its rewards the more certain he can be that he will not reap them? In short, how could such a situation lead men to cultivate land that has not been divided among them, that is to say, if the state of nature has not been abolished?

Even if we were to suppose savage man as adroit in the art of reasoning as our philosophers would have him be, or if we followed the example of the philosophers and made the savage an actual philosopher himself, one who independently discovers the most sublime truths and who, by a sequence of abstract reasoning, reaches principles of justice and reason derived from an innate love of order or from his knowledge of his creator's will; in short, even if we suppose that a savage man's mind has as much intelligence and intellect as it would need to have, and we then find it to be dull and stupid, what benefit would the species draw from all this metaphysics, from a philosophy that could not be communicated and that would be lost with the individual who had invented it? What progress could mankind make, scattered in the forests among the animals? And to what extent could men improve and instruct each other if they had no fixed abode or need for one another, encountering each other once or twice in their lives without knowing or speaking to the other?

Consider how many ideas we owe to the use of language, and the extent to which grammar trains and facilitates the operations of the mind; and consider the infinite effort and time that the initial invention of language must have taken. If one adds these considerations to those I have just presented, one can judge how many thousands of centuries were necessary for the progressive development in the human mind of the operations of which it was capable.

Permit me now to consider the difficulties of determining the origin of languages. I could content myself by citing or repeating the studies that the Abbé de Condillac has made in this field, which entirely confirm my views, and perhaps even gave me my initial ideas in this matter.[26] But the manner in which this philosopher resolves the difficulties he puts in his own path in the question of the origin of established signs indicates that he takes for granted what I myself call into question, namely, that among the inventors of language a kind of society had already been established. Consequently, I believe that in alluding to his ideas I must add my own in order to present the same difficulties in the light most appropriate to my subject. The first difficulty is to conceive how languages might become necessary: since men did not interact with one another or have any need for interaction, one cannot imagine the need for the invention of language or its possibility, language not being indispensable. I might claim, as many do, that languages arose from the domestic dealings among fathers, mothers, and children, but that would both fail to resolve the objections and also lead me to commit the error of those who, in reasoning about the state of nature, apply to it ideas taken from society, always seeing the family gathered in the same dwelling and its members fostering a connection among themselves as close and permanent as our connections are, united by many common familial interests. But when mankind was in a primitive state, in which there were neither houses, huts, nor belongings of any kind, everyone slept where they happened to be, often for only one night. Males and females united haphazardly, depending on chance encounters and desire, without speech being a necessary intermediary for what they had to say to one another, and they parted just as haphazardly. The mother at first nursed her children for her own needs, after which, habit having made them dear to her, she nourished them for their needs. But as soon as they were strong enough to seek their own food they did not hesitate to abandon her, and as there was scarcely any way of ever finding one another again except by remaining in one another's sight, there soon came a time when they could not even recognize one another. Observe, furthermore, that as it is the child who must express all his needs, and consequently has more things to say to the mother than she does to the child, it is the child who must have made the greatest effort in the invention of speech, and that the language the child used must, to a large extent, have been his own invention. This raises the number of languages to the number of individuals who speak them, a situation further encouraged by a life of roving and wandering that does not allow a language time to attain consistency; for to say that a mother dictates to her child the words it will use to ask her for this or that can only clarify the way that languages which have already formed are taught, but it does not explain how languages are actually formed.

Let us suppose this first difficulty overcome. Let us for a moment cross the immense gap that must have existed between the pure state of nature and the need for languages, and inquire, by assuming languages to be necessary, how they might have begun to establish themselves. This new question is even more formidable than the previous one, for if men needed language in order to learn to think, then knowing how to think was even more vital in order to discover the art of speech. And even if we understood how the sounds of the voice were first perceived to be common interpreters of ideas, it would still leave unexplained what might have been the common interpreters for ideas that were not linked to perceptible objects and could not be indicated by gesture or voice. Consequently, it is scarcely possible to form sustainable conjectures on how this skill of communicating thoughts and establishing an exchange between minds was born: a sublime skill that is already far removed from its origin, but which philosophers still consider to be at such a prodigious distance from perfection that no man is bold enough to warrant that this perfection will ever be reached, even if the inevitable revolutions of time were suspended in its favor and the prejudices of the academies vanished or fell silent so that thinkers could devote themselves to this thorny problem for centuries without interruption.

The first language of man—the most universal, the most energetic, the only language he needed before he was compelled to persuade men assembled—was the cry of nature. Since this cry was wrenched from him only by instinct during moments of great urgency, in order to seek help when in danger or relief when in intense pain, this cry was not often needed in everyday life, where more moderate emotions prevail. When men's ideas began to expand and multiply and closer communication was established, men strove for more numerous signs and a more extensive language. They multiplied the inflections of voice and linked them to gestures that are by nature more expressive and whose meaning depends less on prior agreement. Thus they expressed visible and moving objects through gesture, and objects that can be heard through imitative sounds. But gestures can almost always only indicate objects that are present or easy to describe and actions that are visible; they cannot be of comprehensive use, since darkness or the interposition of a body would render them useless—not to mention that gestures require attention rather than excite it. Mankind consequently contrived to substitute articulations of the voice for gestures, which, without having the same relationship to specific ideas, are better suited to represent all ideas as accepted signs. But such a substitution could have been made only by common consent, and was quite difficult to apply in the case of men whose rough vocal cords were not used to such articulations, not to mention harder to imagine possible, since such a unanimous agreement would have had to have been debated, with the result that speech would have been vital in establishing the use of speech.

One must conclude that the first words men used had a much wider meaning in their minds than words have in languages that have already formed, and as men were unaware of the division of speech into constitutive parts, they initially gave every word the meaning of an entire statement. When they began distinguishing the subject from the predicate and the verb from the noun—which was a not mean feat of genius— nouns were initially no more than proper nouns, the present infinitive was the only verb tense, and, as for adjectives, the very notion must have developed with great difficulty, since all adjectives are abstract words, and abstractions are difficult processes that are far from being natural.

Each object was first given an individual name without regard to genus and species, something that these first initiators of language were not in a position to distinguish: every individual object presented itself to their minds as isolated, as they are seen in nature's tableau. If one oak was called *A*, another oak was called *B*, so that the more limited man's knowledge was, the larger his vocabulary. The jumbled nomenclature could not easily be untangled, for one had to know the properties of and differences among entities in order to arrange them into common and generic denominations. Observations and definitions were necessary, in other words, more knowledge of natural history and metaphysics than men of that era could have possessed.

Furthermore, universal ideas can be introduced into the

mind only with the help of words, and the understanding can grasp these ideas only through statements. This is one of the reasons why animals cannot form such ideas, or ever acquire the capacity to improve themselves, a capacity that depends on ideas. When a monkey goes directly from one nut to another, is one to think that he has a universal concept of the type of fruit nuts are, or that he compares the two individual nuts to their archetype? Definitely not. But the sight of one of the nuts will make him recall the sensation he received from the other, and his vision, stimulated in a particular manner, will signal to his sense of taste the stimulus it is about to receive. All universal ideas are purely intellectual; the moment imagination is in any way involved, the idea immediately becomes particular. Try to picture a tree in a universal manner and you will never succeed: despite yourself you will have to picture the tree as being small or large, leafy or bare, light or dark, and if it depended on you to see in it only what is found in every tree, the image would no longer resemble a tree. Purely abstract entities are imagined in the same way, or can be conceptualized by way of speech. Only the definition of a triangle gives you a true idea of what it is: as soon as you picture a triangle in your mind it becomes a specific triangle, and you cannot avoid making its lines visible or its plane colored. It is therefore necessary to use statements: it is necessary to speak in order to have universal ideas, for as soon as the imagination stops the mind can continue only with the aid of speech. Consequently, if the first inventors of language could give names only to ideas they already had, it follows that the first nouns could only have been proper nouns.

But when, by means that I cannot conceive, our first grammarians began to expand their ideas and generalize their words, the ignorance of these inventors must have confined this method to very narrow limits, and as they initially had gone too far in multiplying the names of individual entities through their lack of knowledge of species and genera, they subsequently made too few species and genera by dint of their not having considered entities in all their differences. Expanding the divisions broadly enough would have required more experience and knowledge than they could have had, but also more research and work than they were prepared to undertake. When even today we constantly discover new species that had escaped our notice, think how many must have eluded men who always tended to judge things at first glance. As for the basic categories and most general notions, it is unnecessary to add that even these must also have escaped the notice of early man. How could they, for instance, have imagined or understood the words *matter, mind, substance, mode, figure,* or *movement,* when our philosophers, who have been using these words for such a long time, have considerable trouble understanding them themselves? The ideas attached to these words being purely metaphysical, the early inventors of language would not have found models for them in nature.

I shall stop here at these first steps, and beg my critics to interrupt their reading to consider on the basis of the invention of physical substantives alone—that is to say, the part of language that is easiest to ascertain—how far language would still have to go in order to express all the thoughts of man, to assume a constant form, and to be suitable for speaking in public and influencing society. I ask the reader to give thought to how much time and knowledge were necessary to discover numbers, abstract words, the aorist mood, and all the tenses of the verbs, particles, syntax, connecting clauses, and arguments, and to form the whole logic of discourse. As for myself, intimidated by the difficulties that multiply, and convinced of the almost demonstrated impossibility that languages could have been created and established by purely human means, I leave to whoever might wish to undertake such a task the discussion of the difficult problem of what was more necessary: a society that is already formed for languages to be established, or languages already invented for a society to be established.

Whatever the origins were, one can at least see from the little care that nature took in bringing men together through their mutual needs and to facilitate the use of speech, how negligent nature was in forming their sociability, and how limited nature's contribution was to whatever men have done to establish bonds. Indeed it is impossible to imagine why a man in this primitive state would have more need of another man than a monkey or a wolf might need another of its kind; nor, if we were to suppose such a need, what motive could induce another man to acquiesce in it, or, if he should, how the two men would agree on the conditions. I know that we are constantly being told that there was nothing as miserable as man in a state of nature; and if, as I believe I have proven, it is the case that it would have taken many centuries for man to have either the desire or the opportunity to leave that state, then this would have been a charge to be leveled against nature and not against man, whom nature has constituted that way. But if I correctly understand the term *miserable*, it is a word that has no meaning at all, or a word that merely signifies a painful hardship and the suffering of the body or the soul. Hence I would be grateful if someone could explain to me what kind of misery there can be for a free being whose heart is at peace and whose body is healthy. I ask which of the two, the natural life or the civilized life, is more prone to becoming unbearable to those who live it. Around us we see mostly people who complain about their existence, some even depriving themselves of it if they are able, the combination of divine and human law barely sufficing to stop this disorder. I ask whether anyone has ever heard of a savage living in liberty ever thinking of complaining about his life and putting an end to it? Let it be judged with less pride on which side real misery lies. Nothing, on the other hand, could be as miserable as a savage who is dazzled by enlightenment, tormented by passions, and who ventures to reason about a state that is different from his. It was through a most wise providence that the faculties he potentially had could develop only with the opportunities of exercising them so that they proved neither superfluous nor burdensome before their time, nor belated and useless when the need arose. Man had in instinct alone all he needed to live in the state of nature, while with cultivated reason he has only what is necessary to live in society.

It would at first seem that men in the state of nature, having no kind of moral relations among themselves or settled duties, were not capable of being good or bad, and had neither vices nor virtues, unless we take those terms in a physical sense and call vices the qualities that can impair the conservation of an individual, and virtues the qualities that can contribute to it; in which case one would have to call the man who least resists the simple impulses of nature the most virtuous. But without straying from the ordinary meaning of the words *vice* and *virtue*, it would behoove us to suspend any judgment we might pass on such a situation and to be wary of our prejudices, until it has been established, scales in hand, whether among civilized men there are more virtues than vices, or if their virtues are more advantageous than their vices are detrimental. One must ask if the progress of civilized men's knowledge is sufficient compensation for the harm they do one another in proportion as they learn of the good they *ought* to be doing to one another; or if they would not on the whole be in a happier state if they had neither evil to fear nor good to anticipate from anyone rather than subject themselves to a universal dependence, obliging themselves to receive everything from those who are not obliged to give them anything.

Above all, let us not conclude with Hobbes that man is naturally evil because he has no idea of goodness, that he is depraved because he does not know virtue, that he always refuses his fellow men services he does not believe he owes them, or that by the right he reasonably claims to things he needs, he foolishly imagines himself the sole proprietor of the universe. Hobbes saw very clearly the flaw of all modern definitions of natural right; but the conclusions he drew from his own definition demonstrate that his perception of natural right was no less false. By reasoning on principles he established, Hobbes should have said that the state of nature, being the state in which the care for our own preservation is least prejudicial to the preservation of others, was consequently the most suitable state for peace and the most appropriate for mankind. The reason that he says precisely the opposite is because he included in savage man's striving for his preservation the need to satisfy a multitude of passions that are the product of society and which have made laws necessary. A wicked man, he says, is a child with the strength of a man. It remains to be seen whether savage man is also such a child; even if we agreed with Hobbes, what would he conclude? That if this man when he is big and strong were as dependent on other men as when he is small and weak, he would stop at nothing: beating his mother if she were slow at breastfeeding him, strangling his younger brother if he regarded him as a nuisance, biting another man's leg if it tripped him or got in his way; but in the state of nature being strong or being dependent are two contradictory suppositions.

Man is weak when he is dependent, and emancipated before he becomes strong. Hobbes did not see that the same cause that prevents savages from using their reason, as our jurists claim to do, also keeps them from abusing their faculties, as he claims. Hence one could say that savages are not in fact wicked, because they do not know what it is to be good. For it is neither the development of their intellect nor the restraint of the law that stops them from doing evil, but the serenity of passion and ignorance of vice. *Tanto plus in illis proficit vitiorum ignoratio, quam in his cognitio virtutis.*[27] There is, furthermore, another principle that Hobbes did not discern, which, having been bestowed on man to soften in certain instances the ferocity of his amour propre or, before the onset of this amour propre, the desire for self-preservation, tempers his ardor for well-being through an innate repugnance at seeing a fellow creature suffer. I do not believe I need fear contradiction in granting to man the only natural virtue that the most extreme detractor of human virtues has been compelled to recognize. I speak of pity,[28] a disposition suited to beings as weak as we are and subject to so many ills, a virtue all the more universal and the more useful to man in that it precedes all reflection, and is so natural that even beasts at times give clear signs of it. Without speaking of the tenderness of mothers for their children and the dangers they brave in order to protect them, one commonly sees the aversion that horses have of trampling a live body. An animal never passes a dead animal of its own species without concern; some even give their kind a burial of sorts. And the sad lowing of cattle entering a slaughterhouse reveals their impression of the terrible spectacle that confronts them. One sees with pleasure how the author of *Fable of the Bees,*[29] forced to acknowledge man as a being capable of feeling and compassion, discards his cold and refined style to offer us the poignant image of an imprisoned man who sees a ferocious beast outside his prison tearing a child from the bosom of its mother, crushing its weak limbs with murderous fangs, its claws tearing out the child's throbbing entrails. The dreadful agitation that this witness to an event in which he has no personal involvement must feel! What anguish he must suffer at this sight, unable as he is to help the distraught mother or the dying child!

This is the pure movement of nature prior to all reflection, the force of natural pity that even the most depraved morals are hard put to destroy, as every day in our theaters we see men moved to tears when confronted with the miseries of some unfortunate person, men who, if they were in a tyrant's place, would not hesitate to torment an enemy. Mandeville realized that for all their morality, men would never have been anything but monsters, had nature not given them pity in support of reason. But Mandeville did not see that all the social virtues that he seeks to deny in men flow from this single quality. Indeed, what are generosity, mercy, and humaneness if not pity accorded to the weak, the guilty, or mankind in general? Even benevolence and friendship are, if correctly understood, the products of a steadfast pity centered on a particular person, for what else is wishing that someone should not suffer than wishing that he be happy? Even if it were true that commiseration is nothing but a feeling that puts us in the position of the one who suffers—a feeling obscure but powerful in a savage, and developed but weak in civilized man—what difference would this idea make to the truth of what I am saying except to give it more force? In fact, pity becomes all the more intense as the perceiving animal identifies with the suffering animal. It is clear enough that this empathy had to be infinitely closer in the state of nature than in the state of reason. It is reason that engenders amour propre, and reflection that fortifies it; it is reason that renders man introspective, and reason that separates him from all that troubles and afflicts him, while it is philosophy that isolates him. It is through philosophy that he says to himself at the sight of a man suffering, "Perish if you will—I am safe." It is only the dangers of society as a whole that disturb the tranquil sleep of the philosopher and make him start up from his bed. A fellow man could be murdered beneath his window with impunity—he need only cover his ears and reason a little with himself to prevent nature, which is rebelling within him, from his identifying with the man being assassinated. The savage man does not have this admirable talent, and one sees him, for lack of wisdom and reason, always delivering himself impetuously to the first feeling of humanity. During upheavals and street brawls the populace gathers, while the prudent man withdraws. It is the rabble and the market women who intervene, separating combatants and stopping honest men from slaughtering one another.

It is therefore certain that pity is a natural feeling that in every individual moderates the activity of love for himself, and consequently contributes to the preservation of the entire species. It is pity that moves us to aid without reflection those we see suffering; it is pity that in the state of nature takes the place of laws, morals, and virtue, with the advantage that no one is tempted to disobey its gentle voice. It is pity that deters the strong savage from robbing helpless children, or depriving feeble old men of their hard-earned sustenance, if he has the prospect of finding sustenance elsewhere. It is pity and not the sublime maxim of reasoned justice—*Do unto others as you would have them do unto you*—that inspires all men with the other maxim of natural goodness, which is less perfect, but perhaps more useful: *Do what is good for you with the least possible harm to others*. It is, in short, within this natural sentiment and not in subtle argument that one must seek the cause for the repugnance that every man would feel doing evil, even independently of the maxims of education. While Socrates and minds of his kind may be able to acquire virtue through reason, mankind would have long ceased to exist if its preservation had depended on men's reasoning.

With passions that were so little active, and with such a beneficial restraint,[30] men were more wary than evil, and more resolved to protect themselves from harm they might suffer than they were tempted to harm others, and so were not prone to particularly dangerous quarrels. Provided that there were no issues more crucial than nourishment, their disputes rarely had bloody consequences. As savage men did not interact at all with one another, they knew no vanity, consideration, esteem, or contempt; they did not have the least concept of yours and mine, or any true idea of justice, and considered any violence they might suffer as an evil that could easily be set right rather than an affront that had to be punished. They never thought of vengeance, except perhaps instinctively and impulsively, as a dog might bite the stone that is thrown at it. Yet I see a more dangerous issue, of which it remains for me to speak.

Among the passions that agitate men's hearts there is an ardent and impetuous one that renders the sexes necessary to one another, a terrible passion that braves every danger and knocks down every obstacle, and which in its frenzy seems capable of destroying the species it is destined to preserve. What must become of men who without shame or restraint fall prey to this brutal and unbridled rage, constantly fighting over their loves at the cost of their lives?

It must first of all be agreed that the more violent the passions, the more necessary the laws needed to contain them. But while the upheavals and crimes that these passions cause among us demonstrate every day the inadequacy of the laws in this regard, it would still be worth examining whether these disorders did not arise along with the laws themselves; for in that case, if the laws were capable of repressing these disorders, then surely the least one could expect of them is that they put a stop to an evil that would not exist without them.

Let us begin by distinguishing, in the feeling of love, what is moral from what is physical. The physical is the general desire that drives one sex to unite with the other; the moral is what determines this desire and fixes it exclusively on a single person, or at least that which gives the desire a greater degree of interest for the preferred person. It is easy to see that the moral aspect of love is an artificial feeling; it is born of social custom, and exalted by women with much aptitude and care with a view to establishing their power, thus rendering dominant the sex that ought to obey. In savage man this feeling must be almost nonexistent, founded as it is on certain notions of merit or beauty that he is not in a position to have, and based on comparisons that he is not capable of making. For as his mind has not managed to form abstract ideas of regularity and proportion, his heart is not susceptible to the feelings of admiration and love that arise from the application of these concepts without one even being aware of it. Savage man obeys only the temperament he has received from nature, and not the taste he might acquire; any woman is good for him.

Limited to the physicality of love, and happy enough not to know those preferences that inflame the feeling and augment the difficulties, men must feel less frequently and less intensely the ardors of temperament, and, consequently, have fewer and less cruel disputes among themselves. Imagination, which leads to so much turmoil among us, does not touch the heart of savage man at all. Everyone calmly awaits the impetus of nature, and yields to it without choice, with more pleasure than furor, and once the need is satisfied, all desire is extinguished.

It is therefore an indisputable matter that love, just like all the other passions, has acquired the impetuous ardor that renders it so often harmful to man only in society, and it is all the more ridiculous to portray savages as ceaselessly slaughtering one another in order to satisfy their brutality, since this idea directly contradicts experience; the Caribs, who of all existing peoples have until now departed least from the state of nature, are the most peaceful among all peoples in their loves and the least subject to jealousy, despite living in a scorching climate that invariably seems to give such passions a greater fervor.

As for the conclusions one could reach regarding many species of animals, the clashes between males that bloody our barnyards throughout the year, or that in springtime fill our forests with cries as they battle over females, one must begin by excluding all the species in which nature has, in the relative power of the sexes, manifestly established other relations than those among people. Thus the skirmishes of the cockerels do not offer us an explanation for the species of man. In the species where the proportion of the sexes is more uniform, such skirmishes can have as a cause only the scarcity of females in relation to the number of males, or the intervals during which the female refuses the approach of the male, which brings us back to the first cause; for if every female will suffer a male for only two months in a year, it is as if the number of females were reduced by five-sixths. Now neither of these two cases is applicable to the human species, where the number of females generally surpasses that of males, and where, even among savages, females have never been known to have periods of heat or periods in which they reject males. Furthermore, among several of the world's species, where the entire group is in heat at the same time, there is a terrible moment of common frenzy, turmoil, and fighting, a moment that does not occur in the human species, where love is never seasonal. Consequently, one cannot conclude from the fights of some animals for the possession of females that the same thing would happen to mankind in the state of nature; and even if one were to draw such a conclusion, one must assume, since these conflicts do not destroy other species, that they would at least not be more harmful to our own. It is also quite apparent that these conflicts would still cause less turmoil in the state of nature than they do in society, particularly in countries where morals still count for something and the jealousy of lovers and the vengeance of husbands lead to duels, murders, and even worse, and where the duty of eternal fidelity leads only to adultery, and the laws of continence and honor inevitably spread debauchery and multiply abortions.

Let us conclude that savage man, roaming the forests without occupation, speech, or an abode, without war and without ties, without any need of his fellow creatures, and without a desire to harm them—perhaps even without ever recognizing any of them—this savage man, self-sufficient and subject to few passions, had only the feelings and intellect suited to such a state. This savage man felt only his actual needs, looked only at what he thought it was necessary to see, his intelligence not making more progress than his vanity. If by chance he did make some discovery, he was the less capable of communicating it, as he did not recognize even his children. Anything that was invented perished with the inventor. There was neither education nor progress; the generations multiplied uselessly, and since each generation always began from the same point, the centuries unfolded in all the crudeness of the first ages; the species was already old, but man still remained a child.

If I have dwelt so extensively on the assumption of this primitive condition, it is because I have old misconceptions and ingrained prejudices to root out, and consequently have felt that I need to dig down to the root and show in the portrayal of the genuine state of nature how much inequality, even natural inequality, is far from being as real and influential a factor of this natural state as our writers claim.

Indeed, it is clear enough that there are among the differences that distinguish men a number that are considered natural, but that are in fact exclusively the result of habit and the different kinds of life that men adopt in society. Thus a hardy or delicate temperament, and the strength or weakness that depend on it, are often more a result of the hard or yielding manner in which one was raised than of the original constitution of the body. The same is true of the power of intellect; not only does education create a difference between minds that are cultivated and those that are not, but it also increases the difference between cultivated minds as they relate to the culture; for when a giant and a dwarf walk along the same road, every step that both take gives the giant an added advantage. Hence, if one compares the prodigious variety of education and ways of life that reign in the various orders of the civil state with the simplicity and uniformity of animal and savage life, where all feed on the same foods, live in the same manner, and do exactly the same things, one will understand how much less difference there is from one man to another in the state of nature than there is among men in society, and how much natural inequality must increase in the human species as a result of the inequality of institutions. But even if nature displayed as much preference as is claimed in its distribution of gifts, what advantage would those preferred draw from this at the expense of others in a kind of living that allowed for almost no form of relationship between them? What use is beauty where there is no love? What use is wit to people who do not speak, or astuteness to those who have no dealings with one another? I always hear that the stronger will oppress the weaker, but I would like an explanation as to what is meant by the term *oppression*. The stronger will dominate with violence and the weaker, subjected to all their whims, will suffer. That is precisely what I see happening among us, but I cannot comprehend how the same could be said of savage men, to whom one would have a hard enough time explaining what servitude and domination are. A man might seize the fruit another has gathered, or the prey he has killed, the den he has used for refuge—but how will he ever succeed in making the other obey him, and what would be the fetters of dependence among men who possess nothing? If I am chased away from one tree, I am free to look for another; if I am tormented in one place, who will stop me from going elsewhere? Can there be such a thing as a man whose strength is much superior to mine, and who is also depraved, lazy, and ferocious enough to force me to provide for his subsistence while he remains idle? He will have to resolve not to lose sight of me for a single moment, to keep me securely tied up when he is asleep for fear that I might escape or kill him: in other words, he would be obliged to subject himself voluntarily to far more effort than that which he is trying to avoid and is imposing on me. After all that, what if his vigilance relaxes for just an instant? What if an unexpected noise makes him turn to look? I will already have run twenty paces into the forest, my fetters broken, and he will never again set eyes on me.

Without needlessly protracting the matter, it must be clear to all that since the bonds of servitude are formed only through men's mutual dependence and the reciprocal needs that unite them, it is impossible to subjugate a man without having first put him in a situation in which he is not able to get along on his own. As such a situation does not exist in nature, it leaves everyone free of the yoke of servitude, and renders futile the law of the strongest.

Having proven that inequality and its influence are barely manifest in the state of nature, it remains for me to present the origin and progress of inequality within the sequential development of the human mind. Having demonstrated that the *faculty of self-improvement*, the social virtues, and the other faculties bestowed on original man could never have developed of themselves, that they needed the fortuitous convergence of various external causes that might never have come about, and without which man would forever have existed in his primitive condition, it now remains for me to consider and connect the different coincidences that might have improved human reason while impairing the species, rendering a being wicked while rendering him sociable, and ultimately in the distant future to lead man and the world to the point we have now reached.

I admit that as the occurrence I will describe could have come about in several ways, I can only proceed by conjecture. But beyond these conjectures turning into reasons when they are the most probable inferences that can be derived from the nature of things, and the only means of discovering the truth, the consequences that I will deduce from my conjecture will not be speculative. By the principles I have just established, one could not form any other system that does not provide the same results, and from which one could not draw the same conclusions.

This will excuse me from expanding my reflections on the manner in which the lapse of time compensates for the slight likelihood of events, or from expanding on the surprising power of slight causes when they act persistently; it will excuse me from the issue of expanding on the impossibility of destroying certain hypotheses on the one hand, if on the other hand one finds oneself unable to give them the certainty of facts; it will exempt me from reflecting on how, when two facts are presented as real and are to be linked by a sequence of intermediate facts that are unknown or thought to be unknown, it is for history (when history is available) to provide the facts that connect them, and for philosophy (when history is lacking) to determine the plausible facts that could link the facts in question; and finally this will exempt me from reflecting that in regard to outcomes, similarity reduces facts to a much smaller number of classes than one would imagine. It is enough for me to offer these issues for the consideration of my judges; it is enough to have made certain that common readers need not consider them.

PART TWO

The first man who fenced in a plot of land and dared to say, "This is mine," and found people who were sufficiently simple to believe him, was the true founder of civil society. How many crimes, wars, murders, how much misery and horror, could have been spared the human race if someone would have pulled out the stakes or filled in the ditch and called out to his fellow men: "Beware! Do not listen to this imposter! You will be lost if you forget that the fruits of the earth belong to all, and that the land belongs to no one." But it seems most likely that by this time things had already reached a point of not being able to continue as they were, for the idea of property, depending as it does on many prior ideas that could only have arisen successively, could not have suddenly taken shape in the minds of men. Much progress had to be made, much industry and intellect acquired and transmitted from one era to the next, before that final stage of the state of nature was reached. Let us thus look further back in time and try to gather under a single point of view the slow succession of events and knowledge in their most natural order.

The first feeling of man was that of his existence, his first concern his preservation. The fruits of the earth provided him with all the help he needed; instinct drove him to make use of them. Hunger, as well as other appetites, drove him to experience, one after the other, various ways of existence, one of which compelled him to perpetuate his species. And this blind impulse, devoid of all feeling, gave rise to a purely animal act. This need satisfied, the two sexes no longer recognized one another, and even the child meant nothing to the mother as soon as it could do without her.

Such was the condition of nascent man; such was the life of an animal limited at first to pure sensations and barely profiting from the fruits that nature offered him, let alone thinking of seizing these fruits. But soon difficulties arose, and man had to learn to overcome them. The height of the trees that prevented him from reaching their fruit, the competition from animals seeking to nourish themselves from them, and the ferocity of the animals that imperiled his life, all compelled him to exercise his body. He had to become agile, a fast runner, and vigorous in battle. Soon he had in hand natural weapons, such as branches and stones. He learned to surmount the obstacles of nature, to combat, if need be, other animals, and even to fight for his subsistence with other men, or recompense himself for what he had been forced to yield to those stronger than he.

The more the human species spread, the more the hardships multiplied along with the number of people. The differences of terrain, climate, and season will have forced men to differ in their ways. Barren years, long and harsh winters, scorching summers that consumed everything, demanded new enterprise. Along seacoasts and riverbanks, men invented fishing lines and hooks and became fishermen and fish eaters; in the forests, men made bows and arrows and became hunters and warriors. In cold countries they covered themselves with the skins of animals they had killed. Lightning, volcanoes, or some lucky chance introduced men to fire, a new resource against the rigors of winter. They learned to conserve this element, and then to reproduce it, and finally to cook with it the meats that in the past they had eaten raw.

Man's repeated contact with creatures that were different from him, as well as contact with other men, must have naturally prompted in his mind perceptions of certain relations. The relations we express with the words *large, small, strong, weak, fast, slow, timorous, bold,* and similar concepts, compared to one another when necessary, and almost offhand, ultimately produced in him some kind of reflection, or rather an instinctive prudence that suggested the precautions most necessary for his safety.

The new understanding that resulted from this development increased his superiority over other animals by making him aware of this superiority. He learned to set traps for them, tricking them in a thousand ways, and though a number of animals surpassed him in speed or strength of combat, he became in time the master of those that might serve him, and the scourge of those that might do him harm. This is how the first look that man directed at himself sparked the first stirring of pride; this is how, when he was still barely able to distinguish between hierarchies, he came to consider his species in the foremost rank, and so took the first step toward claiming that rank as an individual.

Though his fellow men were not to him what our fellow men are to us, and though he hardly interacted more with them than he did with other animals, he did not neglect to observe them. The resemblances that with time he learned to perceive among them, his female, and himself, led him to sense resemblances that he could not actually perceive, and, seeing that his fellow men all behaved as he would have done in similar circumstances, he concluded that their manner of thinking and feeling fully tallied with his own. This important truth, once well established in his mind, made him follow through an intuition that was as certain as, though faster than, a dialectic process, which were the best rules of conduct to observe for his advantage and safety.

Taught by experience that the love of one's own well-being is the only impetus for human action, man found himself in a position to distinguish between the rare occasions when a mutual interest ought to lead him to rely on the help of his fellow men, and the even rarer occasions when competition ought to make him mistrust them. In the first case, he united with his fellow men in a herd, or at the very most a sort of temporary association that obligated no one and lasted only as long as the passing need that led to the group's formation; in the second case, every man sought to seize his own advantage, either through force if he thought he could, or through skill and cunning if he felt himself to be the weaker.

This is how men gradually managed to acquire a rough idea of mutual endeavors and of the advantage of fulfilling them; but only to the extent that immediate and clear interest might require, since they had no concept of foresight, and, far from concerning themselves with the distant future, did not even give any thought to the next day. If a deer was to be caught, everyone knew that they had to remain faithfully at their posts, but if a hare happened to pass within the reach of one of them, it is certain he would have chased after it without scruple, and, having attained his prey, would have cared little about having caused his companions to lose theirs.

It is easy to understand that such interaction did not require a language more refined than that of crows or monkeys, who gather in more or less the same fashion. Inarticulate cries, a multitude of gestures, and a few imitative noises must for a long time have made up the universal language of man. When a few conventional articulated sounds used in particular regions were added to this, sounds whose provenance, as I have already said, it is not easy to explain, this gave rise to languages that were distinctive, but crude and flawed, such as various savage nations still have today. I am passing over many centuries in a flash, pressed by time and the abundance of what I have to say, as well as by the almost imperceptible progress of the initial stage, since the more slowly events succeed one another, the more quickly they can be described.

These initial advancements finally enabled man to progress more rapidly. The more his mind became enlightened, the more his ventures developed. Soon he stopped sleeping under the first tree he came to, or by withdrawing into a cave, and discovered that certain kinds of hard, sharp stone axes could be used to cut wood, dig the earth, and build huts out of branches, which later man thought of smearing with mud and clay. This era was a first revolution that brought about the establishment of and differentiation between families, and introduced a notion of property that perhaps also led to the first quarrels and fights. Nevertheless, as the hardiest among them will probably have been the first to build dwellings that they felt strong enough to defend, one might conjecture that the weaker found it quicker and safer to imitate them than to attempt to oust them. As for those who already had a hut, they will hardly have sought to appropriate that of their neighbor, not so much because it belonged to another, but because it was of no use to them and they could not seize it without running the risk of a confrontation with the family occupying it.

The first developments of tender sentiment were the result

of a new situation that united husbands and wives, fathers and children, in a common dwelling. The practice of living together gave rise to the sweetest feelings known to man: conjugal love and paternal love. Every family became a small society, all the more united as its only bonds were mutual affection and freedom. It was then that the first differences in the way of life of the two sexes came to be, which until then had been the same. Women became more sedentary, and grew accustomed to looking after the hut and the children, while men went out to obtain their common subsistence. As their way of life grew gentler, the two sexes also began to lose something of their ferocity and strength. But if each of them separately became less able to fight savage beasts, they could now gather together with more ease in order to resist them as a group.

In this new condition, with a simple and self-contained life, with needs that were quite limited, and the instruments they had invented to provide for these needs, men enjoyed much leisure and used it to secure conveniences unknown to their fathers. But without their realizing it, this was the first yoke they imposed on themselves and the first source of misfortune they prepared for their descendants; for not only did they continue to weaken their bodies and minds, but the conveniences they had invented soon became habitual, losing their appeal almost entirely, while at the same time deteriorating into commodities men could no longer do without. Being deprived of them became crueler than possessing them had been pleasant, and men were unhappy at losing them without ever having been happy to possess them.

One can see here somewhat more clearly how the use of speech gradually became established, or developed within each family, and one can also conjecture how various specific causes could have spread language and accelerated its progress by making it more necessary. Great floods or earthquakes surrounded inhabited areas with water or canyons, and revolutions of the globe broke off pieces of the continent as islands. One can imagine that a common language would have formed more quickly among people who were brought together in this way and forced to live together, than it would have among those who roamed the forests and continents. Hence it is quite possible that islanders, once they had learned to navigate, would have brought us the use of speech. It is quite probable that society and languages were born on islands and developed there before being introduced to the continent.

Everything now began to change. Men who had previously roamed the forests became more sedentary and gradually drew closer to one another, uniting in different groups and finally creating separate nations in every region. Here men were united by custom and character, and not by rules and laws; they were united by the same way of life and the same kind of food, and by the common influence of the climate on everyone. An enduring proximity cannot fail to ultimately create connections between separate families. Young people of different sexes lived in neighboring huts, and the transient interaction that nature demands soon led to interactions that were no less sweet and more permanent. People became accustomed to scrutinizing different individuals and making comparisons, gradually acquiring ideas of merit and beauty that created a feeling of preference. As a result of seeing one another, one cannot do without seeing more of one another. A sweet and tender feeling creeps into the soul, and through the least resistance becomes an impetuous frenzy: jealousy awakens with love, discord triumphs, and the gentlest of passions leads to sacrifices of human blood.

As ideas and feelings succeeded one another, and the heart

and mind were exercised, the human species continued to become more sociable. Relationships expanded and bonds grew stronger. People became accustomed to gathering in front of huts or around a big tree. Singing and dancing, the true offspring of love and leisure, became the amusement, or rather the occupation, of idle men and women who gathered together. Everyone began looking at other people and wishing to be looked at, and public esteem came to be prized. The person who sang or danced the best, the one who was best looking, strongest, most skillful, or most eloquent, was now the most highly regarded. This was the first step toward inequality, and also toward vice. From these first preferences arose vanity and scorn on the one hand, and shame and envy on the other;[31] and the fermentation caused by these new leavenings ended up producing compounds fatal to innocence and happiness.

As soon as men began to value one another, and the concept of esteem had formed in their minds, everyone claimed a right to it, and it was no longer possible to deprive anyone of it with impunity. This gave rise, even among savages, to the first duties of civility, and with that every intentional wrong became an insult because the offended individual saw in the harm that resulted from the insult contempt for his person, a contempt that was often harder for him to bear than the harm itself. In this fashion, with each offended individual punishing the contempt shown him in a manner proportional to the regard in which he held himself, the acts of vengeance became terrible, and men bloodthirsty and cruel. This is the stage that most savage peoples we know of had reached. Many of our writers and thinkers, for lack of having sufficiently distinguished among different ideas, and not noting how far these people had already moved from the first stage of nature, have hastened to conclude that man is naturally cruel and needs regulation to make his temperament equable, although there is no temperament more equable than that of man in his primitive state, placed as he is by nature at an equal distance between the stupidity of brutes and the fatal knowledge of civilized man. Constrained by both instinct and reason to protect himself against the harm that threatens him, he is restrained by natural pity from doing harm to others unless he is compelled to do so, even if he has been harmed; for according to Locke's wise axiom, "Where there is no property there is no injury."[32]

But it must be noted that once society had come into being and relations were established among men, these relations required them to have qualities different from those of their primitive constitution. Once morality began to enter human actions, and as before laws were established everyone had been the sole judge and avenger of offenses he had suffered, the quality of goodness that had been valid in the pure state of nature no longer suited nascent society. It must be furthermore noted that it was necessary for punishments to become more severe as the opportunities for transgression became more frequent, and in nascent society the dread of vengeance had to take the place of the restraint of the laws. Thus although men had become less hardy, and natural pity had already undergone change, this period in the development of human faculties, which maintained a golden mean between the indolence of the primitive state and the spirited activity of our amour propre, must have been the happiest and most lasting era of man. The more one reflects on it, the more one finds that this state was the least subject to revolution, the best state for man to be in, and that he can have left it only because of some dire turn of fate, which for the common good ought never to have occurred. The example of savage peoples, most of whom have been found at the nascent stage of development, seems to confirm that the human species was made to remain in that state, the true springtime of mankind. All subsequent progress has merely been a supposed progression toward the development of the individual, but in fact has been a progression toward the decline of the species.

As long as men were content with their rough and simple dwellings, limiting themselves to sewing their clothes out of animal skins with thorns or fish bones, and adorning themselves with feathers and shells, painting their bodies in different colors, improving or embellishing their bows and arrows, and using sharpened stones to make a few fishing canoes or some rudimentary musical instruments; in short, as long as men applied themselves only to the kind of labor that a single person could accomplish on his own, and to crafts that did not require the collaboration of several hands, they lived as free, healthy, good, and happy people to the extent their nature allowed, and continued to enjoy the gentleness of independent interaction among themselves. But from the moment one man needed the help of another, as soon as men realized that it was useful for an individual to have provisions for two, equality disappeared, property was introduced, work became necessary, and the vast forests turned into sunny fields that had to be watered with men's sweat, and in which one soon saw slavery and poverty sprouting and growing along with the harvest.

Metallurgy and agriculture were the two skills whose invention led to this great revolution. Poets say it was gold and silver that civilized man and ruined mankind, but philosophy will counter that it was iron and wheat. Both metallurgy and agriculture were unknown to the savages of the Americas, who for this reason have ever remained such. Other peoples seemed to have remained barbarian through practicing one of these skills without the other. The fact that Europe is the place most abundant in iron resources and the most fertile in wheat is one of the best reasons why it was, if not the earliest place to receive civil institutions, then at least the place where the institutions were more sound and constant than anywhere else in the world.

It is difficult to surmise how men might have come to know and use iron, since it is not credible that, before they knew what the outcome would be, they would on their own have come upon the idea of extracting ore from a mine and carrying out the necessary preparations for smelting it. Then again, it is even harder to attribute this discovery to some accidental conflagration, as mines are found only in arid places that are bare of plants and trees, so one might say that nature had taken precautions to keep this fateful secret from us. Consequently, there remains only the exceptional circumstance of a volcano spewing out molten metals and giving onlookers the idea of imitating this natural process. We would of course have to assume that these onlookers had to have much courage and foresight to undertake such an arduous task and to envisage from such a distance in time the advantages they might draw from it, something that is hard to imagine as possible, even if their minds had been more developed.

As for agriculture, its principle was known long before its practice was established, and it is difficult to conceive that men who were engaged in a constant struggle to gain their subsistence from trees and plants would not have fathomed fairly quickly the means that nature uses to propagate them. But they probably did not apply their skills to agriculture until quite late. This could have been because the trees that, along with hunting and fishing, provided men with nourishment did not require cultivation. It might also perhaps have been because they were not aware of the methods for cultivating wheat, or did not have the implements for doing so or the foresight to think about their future needs; or perhaps because they simply did not have the means to prevent others from appropriating the fruits of their labor. Once men began to develop skills, one can believe that they will have cultivated a few vegetables or roots around their huts using sharp stones and pointed sticks, long before they understood the process of growing wheat or had the implements necessary for more extensive cultivation. This does not take into account that in order to distance themselves from this domestic occupation, and set about sowing whole fields, they would have had to resign themselves to an initial loss in the hope of a great subsequent gain. This long view is very far from the turn of mind of savage man, who, as I have already said, has trouble foretelling in the morning the needs he might have in the evening.

Therefore, the invention of other skills was necessary in order to induce mankind to apply itself to agriculture. As soon as some men were needed to smelt and forge iron, other men were needed to feed them. As the number of workers continued to multiply, the hands devoted to providing the subsistence of the community diminished without there being fewer mouths to feed. And as some men needed food in exchange for the iron they produced, other men finally came upon the secret of using iron in order to multiply the food supply. From this arose labor and agriculture on the one hand, and the craft of working metals and multiplying the uses of these metals on the other.

With the cultivation of the land came inevitably its division, and once property was recognized, the first rules of justice followed, for in order to render to each his own, every individual must be capable of having something. Furthermore, with men beginning to extend their views into the future and envisioning that they all had possessions they could lose, there was no one who did not need to fear reprisals for wrongs he might do to another. This origin is all the more natural as it is impossible to conceive of nascent property originating from anything other than manual labor. What, besides his own labor, can man use in order to acquire things he has not created? Since it is his labor alone that gives the farmer the right to the product of the earth he has tilled, it also by extension gives him a right—at least until the harvest—to the plot of land, and this goes on from one year to the next. This makes it a continuous occupation of the land, which in this way is easily transformed into property. When the ancients, Grotius says, gave Ceres the title of *legislatrix* and the festival celebrated in her honor the name of Thesmophoria,[33] they indicated by this that the division of the land had produced a new kind of right, that is to say the right to property, which is different from the right that results from natural law.

In this state, equality could have prevailed if men's talents had been equal, and if, for example, the use of iron and the consumption of food had always been in precise balance. But this balance, not being supported by anything, was soon disrupted; the strongest did the greatest amount of work, those who were most skilled worked to best effect, and the most resourceful found ways of reducing their work. The plowman had more need of iron and the smith more need of wheat, though despite their both laboring equally, one earned much while the other could barely survive. That is how natural inequality spread imperceptibly with the inequality of function, and the differences among men resulting from the differences in circumstance became more marked, more permanent in their effects, and began to exercise a corresponding influence on the fate of individuals.

Things having reached this point, it is easy to imagine the

rest. I will not pause in order to describe with all the resulting details that anyone can easily provide the successive invention of other crafts, the development of languages, the testing and implementation of talents, the inequality of fortune, or the use or abuse of riches. I will merely limit myself to casting a quick glance at the position of the human species in this new order of things.

We are now at a stage where all man's faculties are formed, memory and imagination developed, amour propre awakened, reason activated, and man's mind has reached almost the full extent of its possible development. All the natural qualities have been put to work, and the rank and fate of every man is established, not only in relation to the number of his possessions and his capacity to help or harm, but also in relation to mind, beauty, power or skill, and merit or talent. Since these qualities were the only ones that could attract esteem, it soon became necessary either to have them or to pretend to have them. It was indispensable for one's own interest to present oneself as being different from what one in fact was. Being and appearing became two entirely different things, and from that difference arose insolent ostentation, deceitful cunning, and all the vices in their train.[34] Then again, man, who previously had been free and independent, was now, through a multitude of new needs, in fact subjugated to the whole of nature, and above all to his fellow men, whose slave one could say he became in a sense even as he became their master. If he was rich, he needed their services, and if he was poor he needed their help; even if he was of average means he could not do without them. Thus he constantly had to seek to interest others in his fate and make them perceive the real or apparent profit they would gain if they worked for his profit. This made him cunning and deceitful with some of his fellow men, imperious and hard with others, and compelled him to mislead all those whom he needed if he could not make them fear him and had no interest in being of service to them. Finally, an all-consuming ambition—man's quest to raise his relative stature, less because of an actual need than in order to place himself above others— inspired in all men a dark predilection for harming one another, a secret jealousy that is all the more dangerous in that it often assumes the mask of benevolence in order to strike its blows more effectively. In short, there was competition and rivalry on the one hand, conflict of interest on the other, and always the hidden desire to make one's profit at another's expense. All these evils were the first effect of property and the inescapable consequence of nascent inequality.

Before the invention of symbols representing wealth, wealth could consist only of land and livestock, the only real possessions that men can own. But once inheritances had increased in scope and number to the point of covering the whole land, with properties bordering on one another, one property could grow only at the expense of another, and those whom weakness or indolence had kept from acquiring property became poor without having lost anything, for they alone had not changed while everything around them had, and they were obliged to receive or seize their subsistence from the hands of the rich. From this arose, according to the different characteristics among the rich and the poor, either domination and servitude or violence and robbery. The rich, for their part, had barely known the pleasure of domination before they spurned all other pleasures, and, using their old slaves to gain new ones, their one thought was to subjugate and conquer their neighbors, much like ravenous wolves that, once they have tasted human flesh, spurn all other food and seek to devour nothing but men.

This is how the most powerful and the most wretched people claimed through their power or their need a kind of right over the property of others, equivalent, according to them, to the right of property. The end of equality was followed by terrible disorder. This is how the usurpations committed by the rich, the robbery committed by the poor, the unbridled passions of everyone that stifled natural pity, and the still weak voice of justice, rendered men greedy, ambitious, and wicked. Between the right of the strongest and the right of the first occupant of land arose a perpetual conflict that inevitably led to fights and murders. Nascent society made way for the most terrible state of war: the human species, debased and ravaged, no longer able to turn back or renounce its miserable acquisitions, and by abuse of the faculties that should do it honor working only toward its shame, brought itself to the brink of ruin.

> *Attonitus novitate mali divesque miserque*
> *effugere optat opes et, quae modo voverat, odit.*[35]

It is not possible for men not to have reflected on such a wretched situation or on the calamities that were overwhelming them. The rich, above all, must have soon felt the disadvantage of a perpetual state of civil war for which they alone had to bear the cost, and in which all parties risked their lives, while they alone risked their property. Furthermore, however they might strive to embellish their usurpations, they knew that these were established only on a precarious and abusive right, and as the usurpations had been carried out by force, force could also deprive them of what they had usurped, without their having any recourse for complaint. Even those who had become wealthy through their own industriousness could hardly base their claim to their property on better titles. In vain would they say: "I am the one who built this wall—I have earned the right to this land through my labor." To this one might reply: "Who furnished you the boundaries for that land, and on what do you base your claim to be paid at our expense for labor we did not impose upon you? Do you not know that a countless number of your brethren are suffering or perishing from lack of what you have in excess, and that you would need the unanimous consent of the entire human species for you to be allowed to appropriate from the common property anything that extends beyond your own?" The wealthy man, lacking valid reasons to justify himself and sufficient power to defend himself, might easily crush an individual, but would himself be crushed by groups of bandits. Thus, alone against all and unable because of mutual jealousies to unite with his equals against enemies united by the common hope of plunder, the rich man finally by necessity concocted the most well-thought-out scheme that ever entered man's mind: he used the power of his attackers to his advantage by turning them into his defenders, goading them on with new maxims and institutions that were as favorable to him as natural right was contrary.

To this end, he portrayed to his fellow men the horrors of a situation that was pitching them all against one another, and making their possessions as burdensome to them as their privations, and in which no one found safety—not in poverty nor in wealth—and he easily invented fallacious reasons that enticed them into furthering his designs. "Let us unite," he told them, "so that we can protect the weak from oppression, keep the ambitious in check, and secure for each man the possessions that belong to him. Let us institute rules for justice to which all will be obliged to conform, rules that will not make exceptions for anyone and that will strive to make up for the caprices of fortune by subjecting the powerful and the weak equally to mutual duties. In short, instead of turning our power against one another, let us gather it into a supreme power, which will rule us according to wise laws that will protect and defend all the members of our association, repelling common enemies, and keeping us in eternal peace and harmony."

Much less than the equivalent of such an argument was needed to fire up rough and primitive men, who were easy to seduce and had too many disputes to settle among themselves to be able to prevail without arbiters, and too much greed and ambition to endure for long without masters. They all hastened toward their chains in the belief that they were securing their freedom, for although they had enough reason to sense the advantages of a political establishment, they did not have enough experience to predict its dangers. The individuals most capable of foreseeing the abuses were those who counted on profiting from them, and even the wise saw that they had to resolve to sacrifice one part of their freedom in order to preserve the other, much in the way an injured man will have his arm cut off in order to save the rest of his body.

Such was or must have been the origin of society and of laws, the weak gaining new fetters and the wealthy new power. Natural liberty was irreversibly destroyed, and the law of property and of inequality established forevermore. Cunning usurpation now became an irrevocable right; for the profit of a few ambitious men the entire human race was subjected to labor, slavery, and poverty. One can easily see how the establishment of a simple society rendered indispensable the establishment of all other societies, and how people, in order to prevail against a united force, had no other recourse except to unite. Societies multiplied and expanded rapidly, before long covering the whole surface of the earth; soon it was no longer possible to find a single corner of the world where one might free oneself of the yoke and withdraw one's head from beneath the sword, often waved precariously, that every man saw perpetually hanging over his head. Civil right had thus become the common rule of citizens, and the law of nature no longer played a role except in the relations among different societies. There, under the name of the right of man, the law of nature was tempered by a few tacit agreements to render commerce possible and replace natural compassion, which between interacting societies had lost almost all the power it had had between interacting men; it is now to be found only in a few great enlightened souls that cross the imaginary barriers separating different peoples and embrace all mankind in their benevolence, following the example of the Sovereign Being that created them.

The bodies politic, remaining in their interactions among themselves in a state of nature, soon encountered the same disadvantages that had forced individuals to leave the state of nature, a state that became even more of a problem to these large bodies than it had previously been for the individuals who formed them. This gave rise to national wars, battles, murders, and reprisals that outrage nature and reason, and to all those terrible prejudices that rank the honor of shedding blood among the virtues. The most honest men learned to regard the slaughtering of their kind as one of their duties, and before long they were seen to massacre one another by the thousands without knowing why. More murders were committed in a single day of battle, more horrors in the sacking of a single town, than had been committed in the state of nature in all the world throughout entire centuries. Such are the first discernible effects of the division of mankind into separate societies. Let us return to the institution of these societies.

I know that some have proposed other origins for political societies, such as conquest by the most powerful or the uniting of the weak, but the choices between these causes is of no importance for what I want to establish. Nevertheless, the origin I have put forward seems to me the most natural for the following reasons:

1. That in the first case, the right of conquest is not a right, and consequently cannot serve as a foundation for other rights. The conqueror and the conquered people always remain in a state of war with one another, unless the conquered nation has its freedom fully restored and voluntarily chooses its conqueror as its ruler. Whatever capitulations may have been made up to that point were instigated by violence, and are accordingly void by that very fact. Under this hypothesis, there can be neither genuine society, nor body politic, nor any law other than that of the strongest.

2. That the words *strong* and *weak* are equivocal in the second case, and that in the interval that exists between the establishment of the right of property or first occupant and the establishment of political governments, the meaning of these terms is better rendered by the words *rich* and *poor*. This, because before the laws were established, man did not have other means of subjugating his equals than attacking their property or making them part of his own.

3. That the poor, having nothing to lose except their freedom, would have been foolish indeed to voluntarily relinquish the only thing they still possessed without gaining anything in exchange; the rich, on the contrary, were much easier to harm, as one could say that they are vulnerable in every aspect of their possessions, and consequently needed to take more precautions to protect them. Furthermore, it is reasonable to assume that something

would be invented by those to whom it would be useful rather than by those whom it would harm.

Nascent government had no constant and regular form. The lack of understanding and experience allowed men to see only present disadvantages, and they sought only to remedy disadvantages when they appeared. In spite of the efforts of the wisest legislators, the political state always remained flawed, as it was almost a product of chance, and because, having begun badly, time revealed its defects. Proposing remedies could never rectify the flaws of the constitution. It was constantly being patched up, whereas it would have been necessary to start by clearing the ground and removing all the old impediments, as Lycurgus did in Sparta,[36] in order to build a good building. Society initially consisted only of a few general conventions that all individuals undertook to observe, and of which the community made itself the guarantor toward each individual. Experience had to show how weak such a constitution was, and how easy it was for transgressors of these conventions to avoid conviction or punishment for offenses for which the public alone ought to be witness and judge.

The laws were evaded in countless ways, and problems kept mounting until it finally occurred to man to entrust individuals with the dangerous task of public authority, and bestow on magistrates the responsibility of ensuring obedience to the deliberations of the people. To say that leaders were chosen before men formed a union, and that ministers of laws existed before laws, is a supposition that does not merit serious consideration.

It is also not reasonable to believe that from the start peoples threw themselves into the arms of an absolute master unconditionally and irrevocably, and that the first means of providing for common safety that proud and wild men envisioned was to rush into slavery. Why, in fact, did they give themselves superiors if not to defend themselves against oppression and protect their possessions, their freedom, and their lives, which were, so to speak, the elements that made up their being? Since, as in the relation between one man and another, the worst thing that can happen to the one is to find himself at the mercy of the other, would it not have gone against good sense to start by relinquishing to a leader the things for which they needed his help to preserve? What equivalent could he have offered them for the concession of such a fine right? And if he had dared demand it on the pretext of defending them, would he not immediately have received the answer given in the fable: "What more can the enemy do to us?" It is therefore incontestable, and the fundamental principle of all political right, that peoples give themselves leaders in order to defend their freedom, and not in order to be enslaved. "If we have a prince," Pliny said to Trajan, "it is so that he will preserve us from having a master."[37]

Politicians pronounce the same sophisms on love of liberty that philosophers have pronounced on the state of nature. Through things they see, they judge very different things they do not see, and so attribute to men a natural inclination to slavery because of the patience with which the men they have before their eyes bear their slavery, not realizing that we can say of freedom, as we can say of innocence and virtue, that one appreciates their worth only so long as one enjoys them, and that one loses the taste for them as soon as they are lost. "I know the delights of your country," Brasidas said to a satrap who was comparing the life in Sparta to that in Persepolis, "but you cannot know the pleasures of mine."[38]

As an untamed steed will bristle its mane, stamp the ground with its hoof, and impetuously struggle against the very sight of the bit, while a trained horse patiently suffers the whip and the spur, barbarous man does not bow his head to the yoke that civilized man bears without a murmur, and will prefer the most turbulent freedom to tranquil subjection. It is therefore not through the degradation of enslaved peoples that man's natural disposition for or against slavery should be judged, but through the prodigious extremes to which all peoples have gone in order to protect themselves from oppression. I know that the enslaved do nothing but boast of the peace and tranquility they enjoy in their fetters, and that *miserrimam servitutem pacem appellant*.[39] But when I see free peoples sacrificing pleasure, tranquility, wealth, power, and even life to the preservation of the one good thing that is so disdained by those who have lost it; when I see animals that are born free bang their heads against the bars of their prison in their abhorrence of captivity; when I see countless naked savages despise European pleasures and brave hunger, fire, the sword, and death to preserve their independence, I feel that it is not for slaves to argue about freedom.

As for paternal authority, from which some thinkers have derived absolute government and all society, it is enough to remark, without falling back on the conflicting arguments of Locke and Sidney, that nothing on earth is further from the fierce spirit of despotism than the gentleness of paternal authority. This authority is more to the advantage of the one who obeys than to the benefit of the one who commands, and by the law of nature the father is the child's master only for as long as his aid is necessary. After this period they become equals, and the son, entirely independent of the father, owes him respect but not obedience; for gratitude is a duty that must be rendered, but not a right that can be exacted. Instead of maintaining that civil society is derived from paternal power, one should, on the contrary, maintain that paternal power derives its principal force from civil society: an individual was acknowledged as the father of a number of other individuals only for as long as they remained gathered around him. The possessions of the father, of which he is unquestionably the master, are the ties that keep his children dependent on him, and he can choose to leave to his children only as great a share of his inheritance as they deserve through their constant deference to his wishes. The subjects of a despot, however, can have little expectation of being favored in this way, since they and their property belong to him, at least in his view. Consequently, they are reduced to receiving as a favor whatever he might grant them of their own property. He bestows justice when he despoils them; he bestows grace when he permits them to live.

By proceeding thus to examine the facts in terms of right, we would find as little reason as we would find truth in the voluntary establishment of tyranny, and it would be difficult to prove the validity of a contract that binds only one of the parties, a contract in which all the obligations are on one side and there are none on the other, and which can be prejudicial only to the party who binds himself. This odious system is far from being, even in our times, the system of wise and good monarchs, especially the kings of France, as can be seen in various places in their edicts. We see this most clearly in the following passage of a famous writ published in 1667 in the name and by order of Louis XIV: "Let it therefore not be said that the Sovereign is not subject to the laws of his state, since the contrary proposition is a truth of the law of nations that flattery has sometimes assailed, but which good princes have always defended as a tutelary divinity of their states. How much more legitimate is it to join wise Plato in saying that the perfect happiness of a kingdom is that a prince be obeyed by his subjects, that the prince obey the laws, and that the laws be right and always directed to the public good." I will not pause to examine whether this is not debasing man's nature, liberty being his noblest faculty; whether it is not placing him on the level of beasts that are slaves to instinct; whether it is not an affront to the Creator of his being when man renounces without reserve the most precious of all His gifts, and gives in to the necessity of committing all the crimes He has forbidden in order to please a cruel or insane master; and if the sublime Creator ought to be more angered at seeing His finest creation destroyed than dishonored. (I will disregard, if one wishes, the authority of Barbeyrac, who, following Locke, plainly declares that no man can sell his liberty to the extent of submitting himself to an arbitrary power that may treat him as it likes. "For," he adds, "this would be to sell his own life, of which he is not master.")[40] I will ask only what right those, who were not afraid of debasing themselves to this extent, have to subject their posterity to the same ignominy, and to renounce for their posterity possessions that it did not inherit from their liberality, and without which life itself must be a burden to all who are worthy of life.

Pufendorf maintains that just as one man can transfer his property to another through agreements and contracts, he can also divest himself of his liberty in favor of another. But this seems to me a very bad argument. For in the first place, the property I transfer to another becomes a thing that is entirely foreign to me, nor would I care if it is abused; yet it is important to me that my freedom not be abused, and I cannot expose myself to becoming an instrument of crime without incurring the guilt of the evil I would be forced to commit. Furthermore, as the right of property is a right only by convention and human institution, any man may dispose of what he possesses as he pleases. But this is not the case with the essential gifts of nature such as life and freedom, which everyone is permitted to enjoy, and about which it is at the very least doubtful that one has the right to divest oneself of them. By giving up freedom, man debases his being; by giving up life, he attempts to destroy it to the extent that he is able; and as no temporal property can indemnify man for the loss of either freedom or life, it would be an offense against both nature and reason to give them up at any price whatever. But even if one could transfer one's liberty to another as one can transfer one's property, the difference would be very great for the offspring, who enjoy the father's property only by the transmission to them of his right; whereas freedom being a gift they receive from nature as men, their parents have no right to deprive them of it. Consequently, just as violence had to be done to nature in order to establish slavery, nature had to be altered in order to perpetuate the right of slavery, and jurists who have solemnly pronounced that the child of a slave is born a slave have decided, in other words, that a man is not born a man.

It seems to me, therefore, certain that governments did not originate in arbitrary power, which is only the corruption of government and the extremity that takes a government back to the sole law of the strongest, which governments were originally designed to remedy. It also seems certain that even if these governments had originated in this way, such power, being by nature illegitimate, could not have served as a basis for the laws of society, nor, consequently, for instituted inequality.

Without entering here into inquiries that still remain to be made into the nature of the fundamental pact of all government, I limit myself to following the common opinion, and so will consider here the establishment of the body politic as a true contract between a people and the leaders it has chosen, a contract by which both parties bind themselves to observe the laws stipulated in it and that forms the bonds of their union. The people having, in regard to social relations, united all its wills into a single will, all the articles on which this will pronounces become so many fundamental laws that bind all members of the state without exception, one of which regulates the selection and power of the magistrates who are charged with watching over the execution of the rest of the laws. This power extends to everything that can maintain the constitution, without going so far as to alter it. Honors are linked to it that render the laws and their ministers respected, and also grant the ministers personal prerogatives that recompense them for the arduous labor that good administration involves. The magistrate, for his part, binds himself to use the power with which he is entrusted solely according to the intention of his constituents, to maintain each individual in the peaceful enjoyment of what belongs to him, and to prefer on every occasion the public interest above his own.

Before experience had shown the inevitable abuses of such a system, or knowledge of the human heart had allowed men to anticipate them, such a system must have appeared all the better, since those who were charged with preserving it had themselves the greatest interest in its preservation; for since magistracy and its rights were based solely on fundamental laws, the magistrates would cease to be legitimate the instant these laws were destroyed. Then the people would no longer owe the magistrates obedience, and as it would have been the laws and not the magistrates that would have constituted the essence of a state, everyone would regain the right to his natural freedom.

If one pauses even briefly to reflect on this, it will be confirmed through further reasons, and by the very nature of the contract one would see that it could not be irrevocable, for if there were no superior power to guarantee the fidelity of the contracting parties, or to compel them to fulfill their reciprocal engagements, each party would be the sole judge in its own cause, and would always have the right to reject the contract as soon as it felt that the other party had violated its terms, or felt that the terms no longer suited it. It is upon this principle that the right of abdication might possibly be founded. Yet if we consider only the institutions set up by men, as we are doing here, and the magistrate, who holds all the power and appropriates for himself all the advantages of the contract (but nevertheless has the right to renounce his authority), there is all the more reason that the people, who must pay for all the errors of their leader, should have the right to end their subordination to him. But the terrible dissensions and the infinite disorders that this dangerous power of ending one's subordination would necessarily bring with it, would demonstrate more than anything else how much human government was in need of a foundation more solid than reason alone, and how necessary it was for the public tranquility that the divine will should intervene to give the sovereign authority a sacred and inviolable character that would deprive subjects of the fatal right of disposing of it. If religion had granted mankind this one benefit alone, it would have sufficed for men to cherish and adopt it despite its abuses, since it saves more blood than fanaticism spills. But let us follow the thread of our hypothesis.

The various forms of government derive their origins from the greater or lesser differences among individuals at the moment the governments are instituted. If a man was eminent in power, virtue, wealth, or prestige, he was elected as sole magistrate, and the state became monarchical; if several men of more or less equal standing prevailed over the rest, they were jointly elected, and the result was an aristocracy. Those whose fortunes or talents were less disparate, and who distanced themselves least from the state of nature, retained in common the supreme administration, and formed a democracy. Time proved which of these forms was most advantageous. Some men remained solely answerable to the laws; others soon obeyed masters. The citizens wanted to preserve their liberty, while the subjects of a despot thought of nothing but relieving their neighbors of theirs, unable to bear the thought that others might enjoy a good that they themselves no longer possessed. In short, riches and conquest were on one side, happiness and virtue on the other.

In these various governments all the magistracies were initially elective, and when riches did not prevail, preference was given to merit. Merit gives a natural advantage to age, which assures experience in dealings and a cool composure in deliberation: the elders of the Israelites, the Gerontes of Sparta,[41] the Senate of Rome, and even the etymology of our French word *seigneur* show the extent to which age was respected in the past. The more frequently elections chose men of advanced years, the more frequent the elections became, and the greater the problem grew. Intrigues and factions arose, parties became embittered, civil wars broke out, and the blood of citizens was sacrificed to the sham happiness of the state, which was on the brink of falling back into the anarchy of former times. In their ambition, the foremost men took advantage of these circumstances to perpetuate their offices within their families. The people were already accustomed to dependence, to ease and the comforts of life, and were no longer capable of breaking their fetters, and so they consented to their slavery being increased in order to increase their tranquility. This is how leaders, having become hereditary, grew accustomed to regarding their magistracies as a family possession and themselves as proprietors of the state, of which they had initially been mere officers. This is how they became accustomed to calling their fellow citizens their slaves and to count them like livestock along with their other possessions, viewing themselves as kings of kings, and equals of the gods.

If we follow the progress of inequality through these different revolutions, we will find that the establishment of laws and of the right of property was its first stage, the institution of magistracies the second, and its third and last stage was the changing of legitimate power into arbitrary power. Consequently, the condition of rich and poor was rendered possible by the first epoch, that of the powerful and weak by the second, and that of master and slave by the third, a condition that led to the last degree of inequality and to which all the rest ultimately lead until new revolutions either dissolve the government entirely, or draw it closer to its legitimate founding principle.

To understand the necessity of this progress, one need not consider so much the motives for the establishing of the body politic as the form that the body politic assumes in execution and the problems it brings with it; for the same vices that make social institutions necessary also make their abuse inevitable. Laws, being in general less strong than passions, control men without changing them, except in Sparta, where laws mainly concerned the education of children and where Lycurgus established mores that made it almost unnecessary for him to add laws. It would be easy to prove that any government that always kept its founding principle would have been instituted unnecessarily, and that a country where no one evaded the laws or abused magistracy would not require laws or magistrates.

Political distinctions necessarily bring with them civil distinctions. When inequality begins to grow between the people and its leaders, it also soon appears among individuals, modifying itself in a thousand ways according to their passions, talents, and circumstances. A magistrate is not able to usurp illegitimate power without creating for himself a retinue to whom he is forced to yield some of it. Moreover, citizens will not allow themselves to be oppressed unless they are in the grip of blind ambition, and, looking below rather than above themselves, perceive their being dominated as more to their advantage than independence would be. When they consent to be fettered, it is only so that they can fetter others in turn. It is exceedingly difficult to reduce to obedience a man who does not seek to command. The most adroit politician could not manage to subdue those whose only desire is to be free. But inequality easily spreads among souls that are ambitious and cowardly and always prepared to face the risks of fortune, and to command or obey, depending on which they perceive as being more favorable. This is how a time must have come when the eyes of the people were so dazzled that their leaders had only to say to the lowliest of men, "Be great, you and all your progeny," for this man immediately to appear exalted in everyone's eyes, including his own, his descendants becoming even more exalted with the passing of the generations. The more remote and uncertain the cause, the greater the effect; the more idlers a family produced, the more illustrious it became.

If this were the place to go into detail, I would readily expand on how the inequality of prestige and authority becomes unavoidable among individuals as soon as they are united into a single society and forced to compare themselves with one another and take note of the differences they find in their continual interactions. These differences are of several kinds, but since riches, nobility or rank, power, and personal merit are in general the principal distinctions by which men measure one another in society, I could demonstrate that the harmony or conflict between these different forces is the surest indication of whether a state has been well or badly constituted. I could also show how between these four kinds of inequality (personal qualities being the origin of all the others), riches is the last to which the personal qualities are finally reduced, because as wealth is the most immediately useful to well-being and the easiest to transfer, it can readily be used to purchase all the others. Through this observation one can judge with tolerable precision how far a people has distanced itself from the precepts of its original establishment, and how far it has progressed toward the ultimate stage of corruption. Could I go into detail, I would comment on how much this universal desire for reputation, honors, and preference, which consumes us all, makes us exercise and compare talents and strengths; I would comment on how much it excites and multiplies our passions, and renders all men competitors, rivals—or rather enemies— causing continual setbacks, successes, and catastrophes of every kind, forcing so many candidates to run against one another in the same race. I would show that it is to this zeal of being talked about, this frenzy to achieve distinction that forever keeps us on edge, to which we owe what is best and worst among men: our virtues and vices, our sciences and errors, our conquerors and philosophers, in other words, myriad things that are bad set against a small number that are good. I could prove, in short, that if we see a handful of rich and powerful men at the pinnacle of greatness and fortune while the masses grovel in darkness and poverty, it is merely because the former value the things they enjoy only to the extent that the latter are deprived of them, and that even if the rich remained at the pinnacle of fortune, they would cease to be happy if the people ceased to be miserable.

But these details alone would provide sufficient material for a substantial work in which one could weigh the advantages and shortcomings of every kind of government relative to the rights of the state of nature. One could expose all the guises that inequality has assumed to this day and might continue to assume throughout the centuries, according to the nature of these governments and the revolutions that time must necessarily bring about in them. One would see the multitude oppressed from within as a result of the precautions it had taken to guard itself against outside menaces. One would see oppression constantly grow without the oppressed ever knowing where it might stop, or what lawful means they might have left to halt its progress. One would see the rights of citizens and national liberty gradually dwindle, and the protests of the weak treated as seditious murmurings. One would see politics confine the honor of defending the common cause to a mercenary section of the people, making levies and tariffs necessary, the disheartened farmer abandoning his field even in times of peace, and laying down his plow to take up the sword. One would see the rise of bizarre and baneful rules concerning the code of honor. One would see defenders of their nation sooner or later become the nation's enemies, forever raising their swords against their fellow citizens, and the time would come when one would hear them say to their country's oppressor:

> *Pectore si fratris gladium juguloque parentis*
> *Condere me jubeas, gravidoeque in viscera partu*
> *Conjugis, in vita peragam tamen omnia dextra.*[42]

From the extreme inequality of conditions and fortunes, from the diversity of passions and talents, from useless crafts, pernicious skills, and frivolous sciences, countless prejudices would arise that are equally contrary to reason, happiness, and virtue. One would see leaders divide men who have joined forces, stirring up anything that might weaken them, anything that might give society an air of apparent harmony while sowing the seeds of real division; anything that can inspire the different social orders to mutual distrust and hatred by pitching their rights and interests against those of others, and consequently strengthening the power that restrains them all.

It is from the bosom of this disorder and these revolutions that despotism gradually reared its gruesome head and devoured everything it perceived as good and sound in the state, and so would finally succeed in trampling upon the laws and the people and establishing itself upon the ruins of the republic. The period immediately before this last change would be one of trouble and calamity, but in the end the monster would swallow everything up, and the people would no longer have leaders or laws, but only tyrants. Henceforth it would no longer be a question of mores and virtue, for wherever despotism reigns, *cui ex honesto nulla est spes*,[43] it tolerates no other master. The moment despotism speaks, there is no duty or probity to which anyone can resort, and blind obedience is the only virtue left to slaves.

This is the final stage of inequality, the ultimate point that draws the circle to a close, meeting the point from which we set out. It is here that all private individuals become equal once more, because they are nothing, and that as subjects of a despot they no longer have any law but the will of their master, nor does their master have any other law but his passions: the notions of good and the principles of justice disappear once more. It is here that everything returns to the single law of the strongest, and by extension to a new state of nature different from the one with which we began, the state of nature in its purity, while the later is the fruit of excessive corruption. There is otherwise so little difference between these two states, and the contract of government is so dissolved by despotism, that the despot is master only so long as he remains the strongest. Once the despot is expelled, he cannot protest against the violence done to him: the uprising that ends in the deposition or execution of a sultan is as much a juridical act as were the acts by which, the day before, he disposed of the lives and belongings of his subjects. Force alone maintained him, and force alone overthrows him. Thus all things take place according to their natural order; and whatever the consequence of these sudden and frequent revolutions may be, no one can complain of the injustice of others, but only of his own imprudence or bad fortune.

In thus discovering and following the lost and forgotten paths that must have led man from the natural state to the civil state, and in restoring, along with all the intermediate points I have laid out (as well as points that a lack of time has led me to suppress, or that my imagination failed to suggest to me), I believe that the attentive reader will be struck by the immense distance between these two states. It is in this slow succession of things that the reader will find the solution to an infinite number of problems in mores and politics that philosophers cannot solve. The reader will perceive that the human race of one age is not the human race of another, which is why Diogenes could not find a man, since he sought among his contemporaries the man of an era that no longer existed. Cato, the reader would say, perished with Rome and with liberty because he was out of place in the era in which he lived, and this greatest of men served only to amaze a world that five hundred years earlier he would have ruled. In short, the reader will discern how the soul and human passions in their imperceptible changes alter, as it were, their nature; why ultimately the objects of our needs and pleasures change; why, as original man vanishes by degrees, society no longer offers to the eyes of the wise man anything but a collection of artificial men and contrived passions that are the product of all these new relationships and that have no true foundation in nature.[44] What reflection teaches us about this subject, experience clearly confirms, namely, that savage man and civilized man differ so markedly in their basic feelings and inclinations, that what constitutes the supreme happiness of the one would reduce the other to despair. Savage man lives and breathes only repose and liberty; he wants only to live in indolence, and even the stoic's ataraxy[45] falls short of savage man's profound indifference. In contrast, civilized man is always active, in a heated rush as he ceaselessly struggles to find ever more laborious occupations. He works himself to death, and even rushes toward death in order to be in a position to live, or renounces life in order to acquire immortality. He courts grandees he hates, and rich men he despises; he spares nothing in his quest to gain the honor of serving them; he proudly boasts of his servility and of the protection that these men of wealth afford him, and, proud of his enslavement, speaks with disdain of those who do not have the honor of sharing his condition. What a spectacle the difficult and envied labors of a European minister of state must be in the eyes of a Carib! How many cruel deaths would not this indolent savage prefer to the horrors of such a life, which so often is not even sweetened by the pleasure of doing good? But for the savage man to see the purpose behind so many cares, the words *power* and *reputation* must first come to mean something in his mind; he would have to learn that there is a kind of man who considers the way the world looks upon him as vital, who is sooner happy and satisfied with himself on the testimony of others than on his own. Such is, in fact, the true cause of all these differences: the savage lives within himself, whereas civilized man always lives outside himself and knows only how to live in the opinion of others, deriving, so to speak, from their judgment alone a sense of his own existence. It is not my subject here to show how such a disposition brings about so much indifference to good and evil, with so much fine discourse on morality, nor how everything is reduced to appearances, turning into artifice and pretense honor, friendship, virtue, and often vice itself in which one ultimately learns the secret of glorifying oneself; how, in short, in that we always are asking others what we are, we never dare ask that question of ourselves. In the midst of so much philosophy, humanity, and politeness, so many sublime maxims, we are left only with a deceitful and frivolous façade, honor without virtue, reason without wisdom, and pleasure without happiness. I think it sufficient to have proven that this is not the original state of man, and that it is only society's growing sophistication and the inequality that society engenders that have changed and debased all our natural inclinations.

I have endeavored to lay out the origin and progress of inequality, the establishing and abuse of political societies, as far as such things can be deduced from the nature of man by intellect and reason, and independently of the sacred dogmas that give sovereign authority the sanction of divine right. It follows from my exposition that inequality is almost nonexistent in the state of nature, and that it derives its power and growth from the development of our faculties and the advance of the human mind, ultimately becoming permanent and legitimate through the establishment of property and laws. It also follows that moral inequality, authorized by positive law alone, is contrary to natural right whenever it is not in equal proportion with physical inequality. This distinction sufficiently determines what one should think of the kind of inequality prevailing among all civilized peoples, since it is manifestly against the law of nature, regardless of how one seeks to define it, that an infant should command an old man, an imbecile lead a sage, or a handful of men should exult in superfluities while the famished multitude lacks the bare necessities.

On the Social Contract, or, Principles of Political Right

by J. J. Rousseau,

Citizen of Geneva[46]

For many years Rousseau hoped to write a comprehensive survey of governments and institutions, and he read widely for that purpose. The only part that he completed was the relatively brief Social Contract, *but this turned out to be one of the greatest works of political theory of all time. The American founders were influenced by it, though Rousseau's reputation as a radical prompted them to be covert about it. When Jefferson wrote in the Declaration of Independence, "We hold these truths to be self-evident, that all men are created equal, that they are endowed by their creator with certain unalienable rights," he was speaking the language of Rousseau. And after 1789, the French revolutionaries venerated him virtually as a secular saint, and with great ceremony reinterred his remains in the Panthéon in Paris.*

Social contract theories had been around since ancient times, but previous versions imagined a binding agreement between rulers and ruled, whether the government was royal or elective. The philosophes' enthusiasm for enlightened despotism was grounded in that view. Theirs was a liberalizing program, working within existing institutions to improve them. But Rousseau did not want to liberalize; he wanted to rethink political life at its very heart, and he couldn't help noticing that theorists always managed to justify the status quo. "Truth does not lead to fortune," he says in the Social Contract, *"and the people does not bestow either ambassadorships, professorships, or pensions."*

The powerful opening sentence of the treatise became famous—"Man is born free, yet everywhere he is in chains"—but what follows is equally important: "How did this change come about? I do not know. What can make it legitimate? This question I believe I can answer." The entire work is devoted to finding a means by which the rights and integrity of each individual can be respected. In Rousseau's deliberately paradoxical formulation, an individual should be able to unite with all the others and yet remain "as free as before." Even more paradoxically, the entire group becomes a moi commun, *a "common self."*

Emotions are more powerful than reason, and the citizens of Rousseau's republic need to have an emotional belief in their system regardless of its faults. To create this, he imagined a lawgiver, like Lycurgus, who was supposed to have bestowed a constitution on Sparta, and a "civil religion" that would provide a shared code of values. In modern times his vision of collective unity has sometimes been accused of promoting totalitarianism, but he can hardly be blamed for massive changes that nobody in the eighteenth century could foresee. Indeed, he thought that a true "common self" could exist only in a small city-state like the Geneva of his youth, with every citizen participating in communal decision making. A big nation-state like France—or the United States—could never hope to achieve a Rousseauian social contract.

It should perhaps be added that for a modern reader, Rousseau's exposition is slowed at times by detailed discussion of ancient Greece and Rome. He seems to have felt that the intellectuals of his day, who had the classical education he lacked, would consider this necessary. However, it is not central to his chief purpose, which is to consider the nature of any social contract whatever, not to trace political systems historically.

It should be added that Rousseau enriched his analysis with numerous footnotes, all of which are included in the endnotes to this translation.

> —*foederis aequas*
> *Dicamus leges*
> *Aeneid*, BOOK XI[47]

This small treatise is an extract from a more extensive work that I undertook some time ago without giving thought to the extent of my abilities, and which I have long since abandoned. Of the various pieces I could extract from what I had already completed, this was the most substantial, and in my view the least unworthy of being presented to the public. The rest no longer exists.

BOOK I

I want to inquire into whether in the civil order there can be some sure and legitimate rule of administration, taking men as they are and laws as they can be.[48] In this inquiry I shall endeavor to always bring together that which right permits with that which interest prescribes, so that justice and usefulness do not end up divided.

I am embarking on this project without proving the importance of my subject. I will be asked whether I am a prince or a legislator that I should be writing on politics. My answer is that I am neither, and that that is the reason I am writing on politics. Were I a prince or a legislator, I would not waste my time saying what needs to be done; I would take action, or remain silent.

Born a citizen of a free state, and a member of its sovereign body,[49] I maintain that however weak my voice might be in public affairs, the right to vote suffices to impose on me the duty to instruct myself about them. Whenever I reflect upon governments, I am happy to keep finding in my studies new reasons for loving the government of my own country.

CHAPTER I:
THE SUBJECT OF THE FIRST BOOK

Man is born free, yet everywhere he is in chains. He who believes himself the master of others cannot escape being more of a slave than they. How did this change come about? I do not know. What can make it legitimate? This question I believe I can answer.

If I took into account only power and the effects derived from it, I would say: "As long as a people is compelled to obey and obeys, it does well. The instant it can shake off the yoke and does so, it does even better; for, recovering its freedom by the same right by which freedom was seized from it, the people is either justified in retaking that freedom, or those who seized it in the first place had not been justified in doing so." But the social order is a sacred right that serves as a foundation for all other rights. And yet this right does not come from nature; it is therefore founded on general agreements. It is a matter of finding out what these agreements are. But before I come to that, I must establish what I have just put forward.

CHAPTER II:
ON THE FIRST SOCIETIES

The most ancient of all societies, and the only natural one, is the family. Even so, children remain bound to their father only as long as they need him for their survival. As soon as this need ceases, the natural bond dissolves; the children are released from the obedience they owe their father, the father is released from the care he owes his children, and all return equally to independence. If they remain united, it is no longer by nature but voluntarily; the family itself is then maintained only through agreement.

This shared liberty is a consequence of man's nature, his first principle being to see to his own preservation, his first concerns being those he owes to himself. And as soon as he reaches the age of reason, he alone being the judge of the right means of preserving himself, he consequently becomes his own master.

The family, then, is, if you will, the first model of political society: the leader is the image of the father, and the people the image of the children; all, being born equal and free, give up their liberty[50] only for their advantage. The only difference is that in the family the father's love for his children repays him for his care for them, while in the state the pleasure of command takes the place of the love that the leader does not have for his people.

Grotius denies that all human power is established for the benefit of those who are governed, and cites slavery as an example.[51] His usual manner of reasoning is to always establish right by fact.[52] It would be possible to employ a more logical method, but not one more favorable to tyrants.

According to Grotius, it is doubtful, then, if the whole of mankind belongs to some hundred men or if those hundred men belong to mankind, and throughout his book he seems to lean to the former opinion, which is also that of Hobbes.[53] So here we have the human species divided into herds of cattle, each with its master who watches over them in order to devour them.

Just as a shepherd is of a nature superior to that of his flock, the pastors of men, in other words, their leaders, are also of a nature superior to that of their people. This is how, according to Philo,[54] Emperor Caligula reasoned, concluding from this analogy that kings were gods, or that the people were beasts.

Caligula's reasoning coincides with that of Hobbes and Grotius. Aristotle had been the first to say that men are not naturally equal, but that some are born for slavery and others for domination.[55]

Aristotle was right, but he mistook the effect for the cause. Nothing is more certain than that every man born in slavery is born for slavery. In their chains slaves lose everything, even the desire of escaping them. They love their servitude, as the companions of Ulysses loved being reduced to beasts.[56] If, then, there are slaves by nature, it is because there have been slaves against nature. Force created the first slaves—their cowardice perpetuated their slavery.

I have not said anything about King Adam, or Emperor Noah, father of the three great monarchs who divided up the entire world among themselves, as did the sons of Saturn, whom people have believed to recognize in those great monarchs. I hope to be commended for my moderation, for since I am a direct descendant of one of these princes—and perhaps even of the senior branch—with a verification of titles might I not, for all I know, find myself the legitimate king of mankind? Be that as it may, one cannot deny that Adam was the sovereign of the world, as Robinson Crusoe was of his island, so long as he was its only inhabitant; and the advantage that such an empire had was that its monarch, secure on his throne, had no rebellions, wars, or conspirators to fear.

CHAPTER III:
ON THE RIGHT OF THE STRONGEST

The strongest is never strong enough to be always master, unless he transforms his strength into right and obedience into duty; hence the right of the strongest, a right that is viewed ironically yet is an established principle. But will no one ever explain this word to us? Strength is a physical power, and I fail to see what morality it can produce. Yielding to force is an act of necessity, not of will. At most it is an act of prudence. In what sense can that be a duty?

Let us assume for a moment that this alleged right exists. I maintain that it can only result in utter nonsense, for as soon as it is force that creates right, the effect changes with the cause: any force superior to another will succeed to its right. As soon as one can disobey with impunity, one can do so legitimately. And if the strongest is always right, it is then only a question of seeing to it that one is the strongest. Yet what kind of right perishes when strength ceases? If one must obey by force, one need not obey by duty; and if one is no longer forced to obey, one is no longer obliged to do so. It is consequently clear that the word *right* adds nothing to strength. It has no significance here at all.

Obey the powers that be.[57] If that means yielding to strength, it is a good precept, but redundant; I counter that it will never be violated. All power comes from God, this I admit, but so does all disease; is that to say that we ought to be forbidden to call a doctor? A brigand holds me up at the edge of the woods— am I not forced to give him my purse? Even if I could refuse, am I not bound in conscience to give it to him? The pistol he is holding is, after all, also a force.

Let us agree then that strength does not create right, and that one is obliged to obey only legitimate powers. And so we are back to my original question.

CHAPTER IV:
ON SLAVERY

Since no man has natural authority over his fellow men, and since power does not generate any right, it follows that agreement must be the foundation of all legitimate authority among men.

If an individual, Grotius says, can offer up his liberty and become slave to a master, why should not a whole people be able offer up theirs and make themselves subject to a king? There are quite a few ambiguous words here that might need explaining, but let us limit ourselves to the term *offer up. To offer up* is to "give" or "sell." And yet, a man who becomes the slave of another does not give himself; at best he might sell himself for his subsistence. But why would a people sell itself? A king, far from providing his subjects with their subsistence, draws his own only from them, and, according to Rabelais, kings do not live on little. Do subjects then give their persons on condition that their property be taken, too? I fail to see what they have left to keep.

It will be said that the despot guarantees his subjects civil tranquility. Agreed. But what is their gain if the wars that his ambition brings upon them, and if his insatiable greed and the harassing by his government ministries, torment them more than their own conflicts would have done? What do they gain if the civil tranquility he guarantees them is one of their miseries? One can live a tranquil life in a dungeon, too, but is that enough to be living well there? The Greeks who were locked up in the Cyclops's cave lived there in tranquility while they awaited their turn to be devoured.[58]

To say that a man gives himself for nothing is absurd and inconceivable; such an act is unreasonable and worthless by the mere fact that he who does such a thing cannot be in his right mind. To say the same of a whole people is to suppose it to be a people composed of madmen, and madness does not beget right.

If each man could offer himself up as a slave, he could not offer up his children: they are born men and free; their liberty belongs to them, and they alone have the right to dispose of it. Before they reach the age of reason their father can stipulate conditions for their preservation and well-being in their name, but he cannot hand over his children irrevocably and without condition, for such a gift is contrary to the ends of nature and exceeds the rights of paternity. Therefore, for an arbitrary government to be legitimate, it would be necessary that in every generation the people should have the authority to accept or reject it; in which case, however, the government would no longer be arbitrary.

To renounce one's liberty is to renounce one's quality as a human being, the rights of humanity, and even its duties. There is no possible compensation for someone who renounces everything. Such a renunciation is incompatible with the nature of man; to rid one's actions of all morality is to rid one's will of all liberty. Ultimately, it is a vain and contradictory convention to stipulate absolute authority on the one hand, and unlimited obedience on the other. Is it not clear that one can be under no obligation to a person of whom one has the right to demand everything? Does not that condition alone, when there is no need for reciprocation or exchange, result in the nullification of the act? For what right can my slave have against me, since everything he has belongs to me? And if his right belongs to me, is not the idea of my having a right against myself a meaningless concept?

Grotius and the other thinkers see war as another origin for the alleged right to slavery. The victor, according to them, has the right to kill the vanquished, and consequently the vanquished can buy back their lives at the price of their liberty, an agreement all the more legitimate as both sides benefit.

But it is clear that this alleged right to kill the vanquished does not result in any way from the state of war. The mere fact that men living in their original state of independence have no connection with one another that is permanent enough to bring about either a state of peace or a state of war proves that they cannot be natural enemies. It is the connection between things, and not between men, that brings about war; and as a state of war cannot arise from personal relations but only from matters of property, a private war or a war between one man and another cannot exist in the state of nature,[59] where there is no permanent property, nor in the social state, where everything is under the authority of the laws.

Individual combats, duels, and confrontations are not acts that create a state; and private wars authorized by the ordinances of King Louis IX of France and suspended by the intervention of the Church[60] are abuses of feudal government, an absurd system if ever there was one, and contrary to the principles of natural right and all good polity.

Consequently, war is not a relation between one man and another, but a relation between one state and another in which individuals are enemies only by chance: not as men and not as citizens,[61] but as soldiers; not as members of a country, but as its defenders. A state can therefore have only other states as enemies, not men, since there can be no true relation between entities of a disparate nature.

This rule also conforms to the established principles of all times and the invariable practice of all civilized peoples. Declarations of war are not so much warnings to the powers as they are warnings to their subjects. A foreigner—whether king, individual, or a people—who robs, kills, or detains subjects without declaring war on the prince, is not an enemy but a brigand. Even in all-out war, a just prince will seize in the enemy's country everything that belongs to the public, but will respect the person and the belongings of individuals. He respects rights on which his own are founded. The aim of war being the destruction of the enemy state, one has the right to kill its defenders as long as they are bearing arms; but the instant they lay them down and surrender, they cease to be enemies or instruments of the enemy, and simply become men once again whose lives one no longer has the right to take. Sometimes it is possible to kill a state without killing a single one of its members, for war does not grant any right that is not necessary to gaining its object. These principles are not those of Grotius: they are not founded on the authority of poets, but are derived from the nature of things and are founded on reason.

As for the right of conquest, it has no foundation other than the law of the strongest. If war does not give the victor the right to massacre a vanquished people, then this right that he does not have cannot serve as the basis of the right to enslave them. One has the right to kill an enemy only when the enemy cannot be made a slave; the right to make him a slave can therefore not come from the right to kill him. It is consequently an iniquitous exchange to make him buy his life at the price of his liberty, a life over which nobody holds the right. Is it not clear that one is entering a vicious circle in basing the right of life and death on the right of slavery, and the right of slavery on the right of life and death?

Even assuming this terrible right to kill everyone, I assert that both a slave made in war, or a conquered people, is not in any way obligated to a master, except to obey him to the extent that they are forced to. The victor, by taking an equivalent for the life of the vanquished, has not done him a favor; instead of killing him pointlessly, he has killed him usefully. Therefore, far from acquiring any authority over him in connection with force, the state of war between victor and vanquished continues as before: their relation itself is the result of it, and the custom of the right of war does not suppose any treaty of peace. The victor and the vanquished have come to an agreement; so be it; but this agreement, far from ending the state of war, presupposes its continuation.

Thus in whatever sense we consider matters, the right of slavery does not exist, not only because it is illegitimate, but also because it is absurd and meaningless. The words *slave* and *right* contradict one another; they are mutually exclusive. It will always be equally absurd for a man to say to a man or a people: "I am reaching an agreement with you that is entirely at your expense and entirely to my advantage, which I shall observe for as long as I please, and you, too, will observe for as long as I please."

CHAPTER V:
ON THE NECESSITY OF ALWAYS
RETURNING TO A FIRST AGREEMENT

Even if I were to grant everything that I have refuted up to here, the supporters of despotism would not have gained ground. There will always be a great difference between subjugating a multitude and governing a society. Even if widely scattered men, however great their number, are successively enslaved by a single man, I see in that a master and slaves, not a people and their ruler. It is, if you will, an aggregation, but not an association. We have here neither public good nor body politic. That master, even if he were to enslave half the world, is never more than an individual. His interest is separate from that of other individuals, yet is never anything but a private interest. If that same man perishes, his empire will end up scattered and disorganized, just as an oak consumed by fire will collapse into a heap of ashes.

A people, Grotius says, can give itself to a king. Thus, according to Grotius, a people is a people before it gives itself to a king. The gift is in itself a civil act. It assumes a public deliberation. Thus, before examining the act by which a people elects a king, it would be good to examine the act by which a people becomes a people; for this act, being of necessity prior to the act of their electing a king, is the true foundation of society.

Indeed, if there were no prior agreement, then, unless the election was unanimous, where would be the obligation for the minority to submit to the choice of the majority? Why should a hundred men who want a master have the right to vote on behalf of ten who do not? The law of majority voting is in itself the establishment of an agreement, and assumes that there has been, on at least one occasion, unanimity.

CHAPTER VI:
ON THE SOCIAL PACT

I propose that mankind reached a point at which the obstacles that hinder self-preservation in the state of nature became greater than the strength that each individual could employ to maintain himself in that state. At that point the primitive state could no longer prevail, and the human race would have perished had it not changed its way of life.

Yet as men cannot generate new strength but only unite and direct the strength they already have, their only means of preserving themselves is to form by aggregation a sum of forces that are enough to overcome the obstacles, and activate these forces by means of a single impetus, causing them to act in unison.

This sum of forces can arise only through a number of individuals coming together. But since strength and every man's liberty are the primary instruments of his self-preservation, how can he engage these without harming himself and neglecting the obligations he owes to himself? In relation to my subject, this difficulty can be summed up in the following terms: "How does one find a form of association that will defend and protect, through the entirety of its common force, the person and belongings of every associated member, while every individual, in uniting with everyone else, will still be answerable only to himself and remain as free as before?" Such is the fundamental problem to which the social contract provides the solution.[62]

The clauses of this contract are so determined by the nature of the act that the slightest modification would render them futile and entirely ineffective; so that although these clauses have perhaps never been formally stated, they are everywhere the same, everywhere tacitly recognized and accepted, until, should the social pact be violated, everyone returns to his initial rights and resumes his natural liberty, losing the collective liberty for which he had relinquished it.

These clauses, if properly understood, can all be reduced to a single one: that each associate give himself absolutely, together with all his rights, to the entire community; for in the first place, when everyone gives himself entirely, the conditions are equal for all, and, the conditions being equal for all, it is in no one's interest to make them difficult for others.

Furthermore, each associate's giving himself being accomplished without reservation, the union is as perfect as it can be, and no associate has anything more to demand: for if individuals retain some rights, there being no common superior who can adjudicate between them and the public, everyone would be his own judge on a specific issue and would soon claim to be his own judge in all matters. The state of nature would continue, and the association would necessarily become either tyrannical or futile.

Finally, if each individual gives himself to all, he is giving himself to nobody; and as there is no associate over whom one does not acquire the same rights that one cedes to him, there is an equivalent gain for everything lost, and more power to preserve what one has.

Therefore, if one discards from the social pact everything that is not essential to it, one finds that it can be reduced to the following terms: "Each of us places his person and all his power in common under the supreme direction of the general will, and we receive into our association each member as an indivisible part of the whole."

This act of association immediately produces a moral and collective body that replaces the separate contracting individuals, a body composed of as many members as the assembly has votes, and which receives through this same act its unity, its common *self*, its life, and its will. This *public entity*, thus formed by the union of all the individual persons, formerly bore the name of *city* and has now assumed the name *republic* or *body politic*, which its members call *state* when it is passive, *sovereign* when it is active, and *power* when it is compared to others like itself.[63] As for the associate members, they collectively assume the name *people* and call themselves individually *citizens*, as participants of the sovereign authority, and *subjects*, being subjected to the laws of the state. But these terms are often confused and mistaken for one another. It is enough to know how to distinguish them when they are used most precisely.

CHAPTER VII:
ON THE SOVEREIGN AUTHORITY

It is clear from the formula I have proposed that the act of association encompasses a reciprocal engagement between the public and the individual, and that each individual, in making a contract with himself, so to speak, is engaged in a double relationship: as a member of the sovereign authority toward individuals, and as a member of the state toward the sovereign authority. But here we cannot apply the principle of civil right that no one is bound by obligations he enters with himself, since there is quite a difference between obliging oneself toward oneself and obliging oneself toward a whole of which one is a part.

It should also be noted that the public deliberation that can obligate all the subjects to the sovereign authority, owing to the two different kinds of relationship in which they are involved, cannot, for the opposite reason, obligate the sovereign authority toward itself, and that it is therefore against the nature of the body politic for the sovereign authority to impose on itself a law it cannot infringe. As the sovereign authority cannot regard itself as having the same relation with itself, it consequently finds itself in the same situation as an individual who enters a contract with himself; which demonstrates that there neither is nor can there be any kind of fundamental law that is obligatory for the body of the people, not even the social contract. This does not mean that the body politic cannot perfectly well enter into dealings with others in whatever does not infringe the contract; for with regard to outsiders, the body politic becomes a simple being, an individual.

But the body politic or the sovereign authority, drawing its existence exclusively from the sanctity of the contract, can never obligate itself, even to others, in any way that detracts from the original act, such as to transfer any part of itself or submit itself to another sovereign authority. Violation of the act by which it exists would be for it to annihilate itself; and that which is nothing produces nothing.

As soon as the multitude is thus united in one body, it is impossible to harm one of its members without attacking the body, and even less to harm the body without the members feeling the effect. Thus duty and interest both equally obligate the two contracting parties to offer each other mutual assistance, and the same individuals must seek to combine in this double relationship all the advantages that depend on it.

The sovereign authority, then, being formed entirely of the individuals who compose it, neither has nor can have any interest contrary to theirs. Consequently, the sovereign power need make no guarantee toward its subjects, because it is impossible for the body to want to harm all its members, and we will also see later that it cannot harm any one of them in particular. The sovereign authority, by the mere fact that it exists, is always that which it ought to be.[64]

But this is not the case when it comes to the relation of the subjects to the sovereign authority, which, despite a common interest, has no guarantee that the subjects will fulfill their obligations to it if it does not find means to ensure their fidelity.

Indeed, each individual, as a man, can have an individual will that is contrary to or different from the general will he has as a citizen. His individual interest can strike him as quite different from the common interest: his existence, being absolute and naturally independent, can lead him to look upon what he owes to the common cause as an unnecessary contribution, the absence of which would be less harmful to others than the payment would be onerous to him; and as for the moral person[65] that the state constitutes as a reasoning being: because it is not a man, it would enjoy the rights of a citizen without being prepared to fulfill the duties of a subject, an injustice whose progress would lead to the ruin of the body politic.

So that this social pact will not be an empty formula, it tacitly includes this obligation, which alone can give power to the others, that whoever refuses to obey the general will shall be compelled to do so by the whole body. This means nothing other than that he will be forced to be free.[66] For that is the condition which, by giving every citizen to his state, protects him from all personal dependency. This condition makes up the artifice and skill of the political machine, and alone renders legitimate the civil obligations that without it would be absurd, tyrannical, and subject to the greatest abuse.

CHAPTER VIII:
ON THE CIVIL STATE

The transition from the state of nature to the civil state produces a most remarkable change in men, substituting justice for instinct in their conduct and giving their actions the morality they previously lacked. It is only then, when the voice of duty prevails over physical impulse and right prevails over appetite, that men, who until then had considered only themselves, are forced to act on other principles and consult their reason before following their inclinations. Though in this state they deprive themselves of a number of advantages that nature gave them, they gain others that are truly great: their faculties are exercised and develop, their ideas expand, their sentiments are ennobled, and their souls are so uplifted that if the abuses of this new condition did not frequently reduce them to a state below the one they emerged from, they ought to eternally bless the happy moment that forever raised them from it, turning them from stupid and limited animals into intelligent beings and men.

Let us reduce this balancing of gain and loss to terms that are easy to understand. What a man loses through the social contract is his natural liberty and an unlimited right to anything that tempts him and that he can attain; what he gains is civil liberty and the ownership of all he possesses. In order not to misunderstand this balance, one has to make a clear distinction between natural liberty, whose only limits are the strength of the individual, and civil liberty, which is limited by the general will. One also has to make a distinction between possession, which is merely the result of force or the right of the first occupier, and property that can be founded only on a positive title.

To what is acquired in the civil state we could also add moral liberty, since it alone makes man truly a master of himself, for the impulse of mere appetite is slavery, while obedience to laws we prescribe ourselves is liberty. But I have already said too much on this matter, and the philosophical meaning of the term *liberty* is not my subject here.

CHAPTER IX:
ON PROPERTY

Each member of the community gives himself to the community at the moment of its formation just as he is at that moment, along with all his power, of which his possessions are a part. Possessions, through this act, do not change their nature by changing hands, becoming property in the hands of the sovereign authority; but just as the powers of the state are incomparably greater than those of an individual, public possession is also, by this fact, stronger and more irrevocable without being any more legitimate, at least for foreigners. This is because the state, in regard to its members, is master of all their property through the social contract, which serves as the basis of all rights within the state, while in relation to other powers the state is master only by the right of being the first occupant, which it derives from individuals.

The right of the first occupant, though it is more tangible than the right of the strongest, becomes a true right only after the right of property has been established. Every man has by nature a right to everything he needs, but the positive act that makes him the proprietor of a particular property excludes him from all the property of others. His property specified, he must limit himself to it, and can have no further claim against that of the community. This is why the right of the first occupant, which is so weak in the state of nature, is in the civil state respected by every person. Here a person respects not so much what belongs to another as what does not belong to him.

In general, to authorize the right of the first occupant over any tract of land, the following conditions are necessary: first, that the land in question not yet be inhabited by anybody; second, that one occupy only the amount of land one needs in order to subsist; and third, that one take possession not by a meaningless ceremony but by labor and cultivation, the only sign of ownership which, in the absence of a legal title, should be respected by others.

By basing the right of the first occupant on necessity and labor, are we not in fact stretching that right as far as it can go? Can one have such a right without limits? Will it suffice to set foot on a plot of common land to claim oneself its master right away? If one has the power to drive out other men even for a moment, is that enough to deprive them of the right of ever returning? How can a man or a people seize an immense territory and keep all the rest of mankind from it, except by a punishable usurpation, since it denies other men from staying on that land and harvesting the food that nature provides them in common? When Núñez de Balboa stood on those shores and took possession of the South Seas and all of South America in the name of the Crown of Castile, was his action enough to dispossess all inhabitants and exclude all the other princes of the world from ownership? Were that so, there would have been no reason for him to add to those ceremonies, and the Catholic King could, from his chamber, have taken possession all at once of the whole world, and then only subtract from his empire any territories already in the possession of other princes.

One can understand how the lands of individuals, combined and contiguous, become public territory, and how the right of sovereignty, extending from the subjects to the lands they occupy, includes both property and people. This makes proprietors more dependent and their powers a guarantee of their fidelity, an advantage that ancient monarchs did not seem to have well understood, for they called themselves only kings of the Persians, of the Scythians, or of the Macedonians, and seemed to consider themselves more rulers of men than masters of a country. The monarchs of today call themselves more cleverly kings of France, of Spain, or of England and so forth, and by controlling the land are quite certain of controlling its inhabitants.

What is remarkable in this transfer of ownership is that far from robbing individuals by taking over their property, the community simply assures them legitimate possession of it, turning usurpation into a true right, and mere possession into proprietorship. Thus the proprietors, being regarded as holders of public property, their rights respected by all the members of the state and defended against foreigners with all the state's power, have, by means of a transfer that benefits the public and themselves even more, acquired, so to speak, all that they have given up. This paradox can be easily explained by the distinction between rights that the sovereign authority and the proprietor have over the same property, as we shall see later.

It can also happen that men begin to unite before they possess anything, and subsequently seizing a piece of land sufficient for all, they use it in common, or divide it among themselves either equally or according to proportions established by the sovereign authority. In whatever manner this acquisition is made, the right that each individual has over his own property is always subordinate to the right the community has over everyone. Without this there would be neither stability in the social bond nor true power in the exercise of sovereignty.

I will end this chapter and this book with a comment that can serve as a basis for the whole social system: the fundamental pact, far from destroying natural equality, substitutes a moral and legitimate equality for whatever physical inequality nature may have imposed on men. All men who may be unequal in strength or intelligence become equal by agreement and by law.[67]

BOOK II

CHAPTER I

ON SOVEREIGNTY BEING INALIENABLE[68]

The first and most important consequence arising from the principles established so far is that the general will alone can direct the power of the state according to the purpose for which the state has been instituted, which is the common good; for if the clash of private interests made the establishment of society necessary, it is the concurrence of these same interests that made it possible. What forms the social bond is what these different interests have in common, and were there not some point on which all interests agreed, no society would be able to exist. Therefore it is solely on the basis of this common interest that society ought to be governed.

I maintain, then, that sovereignty, being nothing but the exercise of the general will, can never be transferred, and that the sovereign authority, which is merely a collective entity, can be represented only by itself: the power can be delegated, but not the will.

Although it is not impossible for an individual will to agree with the general will on certain points, it is, however, impossible for such an agreement to be lasting and constant, since by its very nature the individual will tends to partiality, while the general will tends to impartiality. It would be even less possible to have a guarantee for this agreement even if the agreement were to be lasting; it would be due not to skill but to chance. The sovereign authority might well maintain: "Currently I want what this man wants, or at least what he says he wants." But it cannot say: "What that man wants tomorrow, I, too, will want," because it is absurd that a will can bind itself for the future, and because no will can consent to anything contrary to the good of the being that wills. If a people simply promises to obey, by doing so it unravels and loses the quality of being a people; the instant there is a master, sovereign authority ceases to exist and the body politic is destroyed.

This is not to say that the orders given by leaders cannot be general wills, as long as the sovereign authority, which is free to oppose them, does not do so. In such a case, one interprets universal silence as the consent of the people. This will be explained in greater detail.

CHAPTER II:
ON SOVEREIGNTY BEING INDIVISIBLE

Sovereignty is indivisible for the same reason that it is inalienable, since will is either general, or it is not.[69] It is the will of the people as a whole, or only of a part: in the first case, this will, once declared, is an act of sovereignty and constitutes law; in the second case, it is merely an individual will or act of magistracy—at most it is a decree.

But our political thinkers, unable to divide sovereignty in its principle, divide it in its object; they divide it into force and will, into legislative power and executive power, and into rights of taxation, justice, and war; they divide it into internal administration and into the power to conduct foreign affairs. Sometimes they combine all these parts and sometimes separate them, turning the sovereign authority into a fantastic being made up of all kinds of pieces. It is as if our political thinkers were assembling a man out of several bodies, in which one would have the eyes, another the arms, another the feet, and none anything more. It is said that Japanese conjurers will carve up a child before the eyes of the audience, and then, throwing its limbs into the air one after another, the child falls back down reassembled and alive. Such are more or less the conjuring tricks of our politicians: after dismembering the social body with a trick worthy of a fair, they throw the pieces together at random.

This error comes from our not having formed exact notions concerning the sovereign authority, and from mistaking for parts of this authority what are mere products of it. Thus, for example, the act of declaring war and that of making peace have been regarded as acts of sovereignty, which they are not. Neither of these acts is a law but merely the application of a law: a specific act that determines the application of the law, as will be clearly seen when I define the idea attached to the word *law*.[70]

By examining the other divisions in the same way, one would find that whenever one is under the impression that sovereignty is divided, one is mistaken, and that the rights that are assumed to be part of this sovereignty are all subordinate to it, invariably implying a supreme will which these rights merely put into effect. It would be impossible to overstate the extent to which this lack of precision has clouded the opinions of authors who have written on political law, when they wanted to judge the respective rights of kings and peoples on principles they had established. In chapters III and IV of the first book of Grotius, anyone can see how that learned man and his translator, Barbeyrac, became entangled and confused in their own sophisms for fear of saying too much or too little depending on their points of view, and thus offending the interests they needed to conciliate. Grotius, a refugee in France, dissatisfied with his own country and wishing to pay court to Louis XIII, to whom his book is dedicated, spares no pains to deprive the people of all their rights and invest them in kings through every conceivable artifice. This would also have been very much to the taste of Barbeyrac, who dedicated his translation to King George I of England, though unfortunately the expulsion of James II, which he called an "abdication," forced him to tread carefully, to obfuscate, so as not to present William as a usurper.[71] If these two authors had adopted the real principles, all difficulties would have been resolved and would always have been consistent; yet they would have been telling a sad truth, paying court only to the people. But truth does not lead to fortune, and the people does not bestow either ambassadorships, professorships, or pensions.

CHAPTER III:
ON WHETHER THE GENERAL WILL CAN ERR

It follows from the preceding that the general will is always honest and attentive to the public benefit, but it does not follow that the deliberations of the people always have the same rectitude. We always desire our own good but do not always discern it. The people can never be corrupted but is often deceived, and it is only then that it seems to want what is wrong.

There is often considerable difference between the will of all and the general will; the latter looks only to the public interest, while the former looks to private interest and is only a sum of individual wills. But take away from these same wills the pluses and minuses that cancel each other out,[72] and the general will remains as the sum of the differences.

If, when a sufficiently informed people deliberates, the citizens had no communication with one another,[73] the general will would always result from the great number of minor differences, and the process of deliberating would always be good. But when factions arise, partial associations at the expense of the large association, the will of each of these associations becomes general in relation to its members, and particular in relation to the state. It can consequently be said that there are no longer as many voters as there are men but only as many as there are associations. The differences become less numerous and yield a result that is less general. Lastly, when one of these associations is so great as to prevail over all the rest, the result is no longer a sum of small differences but a single difference; in this case there is no longer a general will, and the opinion that prevails is purely limited.

It is therefore important, if the general will is to be expressed clearly, that there be no partial association within the state and that each citizen assert his own opinion.[74] Such was the sublime and unique institution of the great Lycurgus. If there are partial associations, their number must be multiplied in order to prevent inequality, as was done by Solon, Numa, and Servius.[75] These precautions are the only ones that can assure that the general will may always be stated clearly, and that the people will not be deceived.

CHAPTER IV:

ON THE LIMITS OF THE SOVEREIGN POWER

If the state or the city were merely a moral person whose life comes from the union of its members—and its most important concern being for its own preservation—it must have a universally compelling force in order to arrange each part in a manner most advantageous to the whole. As nature gives each man absolute power over all his limbs, the social pact gives the body politic absolute power over its members, too; and it is this very power that, directed by the general will, bears, as I have said, the name of sovereignty.

But beyond the public person, we must consider the private persons who compose it, and whose life and liberty are naturally independent of it. One must therefore distinguish clearly between the respective rights of the citizens and the sovereign authority,[76] and between the duties the citizens have to fulfill as subjects and the natural right they must enjoy as men.

It is agreed that according to the social pact, each individual transfers only that part of his powers, goods, and liberty that is important for the community to use; but one must also agree that the sovereign authority alone should be the judge of which part is important.

A citizen owes the state every service he is capable of rendering, as soon as the sovereign authority requires it; but the sovereign authority, for its part, cannot bind its subjects with fetters useless to the community, nor can it even aspire to do so, for, according to the law of reason, as according to the law of nature, nothing can occur without a cause.

The undertakings that bind us to the social body are obligatory only because they are mutual, and their nature is such that in fulfilling them we cannot work for others without working for ourselves. Why is the general will always right, and why does everyone constantly strive for the happiness of each, if not because there is no person who does not appropriate the word *each* to mean himself, and thinks only of himself as he votes for all? This proves that the equality of right and the notion of justice it produces originate in the preference that each person gives to himself, and consequently originates in the nature of mankind. It proves that the general will, to be really such, must be general in its object as well as its essence; that it must come from all in order to apply to all, and that it loses its natural rectitude when it is directed to some particular and determinate object, because then we are judging by what is foreign to us and have no true principle of equity to guide us.

Indeed, the instant a particular issue or matter of law arises on a point that has not been previously regulated by general and prior agreement, the matter becomes contentious. It is a proceeding in which the individuals concerned make up one party and the public the other, but in which I can see neither the law that should be followed nor the judge who might make a ruling. It would be absurd in such a case to wish to rely on an express decision by the general will, which can be only the conclusion reached by one of the parties, and as a result can only be perceived by the other party as an alien will that is individual, in this case unjust and subject to error. Hence in the same way that an individual will cannot represent the general will, the general will, in turn, changes its nature when dealing with a particular object, and, being general, cannot pronounce on either a man or a fact. When the people of Athens, for example, appointed or dismissed its leaders, bestowed honors on one or imposed penalties on another, and, by a multitude of individual decrees, indiscriminately exercised all the acts of government, the people no longer had a general will in the strict sense; the people no longer acted as sovereign authority but as magistrate. This will appear contrary to common views, but I must be granted the time to present my own.

One must understand by this that what makes the will general is not so much the number of individuals voting, as the common interest that unites them: for under this system everyone necessarily submits to the conditions he imposes on others. This is an admirable agreement between interest and justice that gives common deliberations the impartial character that one sees vanishing when any private matter is discussed, for lack of a common interest that unites and identifies the ruling of the judge with that of the party. By whichever path one returns to the principle, one will always arrive at the same conclusion: that the social pact establishes such equality among citizens that they all must adhere to the same conditions and enjoy the same rights. Thus, by the nature of the pact, every act of sovereignty, that is to say, every authentic act of the general will, either obliges or favors all citizens equally, so that the sovereign authority knows only the body of the nation and does not distinguish any individuals who compose it. So, what is, strictly speaking, an act of sovereignty? It is not an agreement between a superior and an inferior, but an agreement between the body and each of its members. It is a legitimate agreement because it is based on the social contract, and equitable because it is common to all; it is useful because it can have no other aim than the general good, and stable because it is backed by public force and the supreme power. So long as subjects are submitted only to such agreements, they obey no one but their own will, and to ask how far the respective rights of the sovereign authority and the citizens extend is to ask to what point citizens can commit to one another, each committing to all, and all to each.

It is clear from this that the sovereign power, absolute, sacred, and inviolable as it is, does not and cannot exceed the limits of general agreements, and that every man can fully dispose of whatever goods and liberty these agreements leave him, so that the sovereign authority never has a right to burden one subject more than another, because if it does, the matter becomes individual and is beyond the bounds of the sovereign authority's jurisdiction.

Once these distinctions have been admitted, one can see that it is false to believe that the social contract compels individuals to renounce anything vital, and that in fact their position as a result of the contract is much preferable to the position in which they were before. Instead of relinquishing what is theirs, they have made an advantageous exchange of an uncertain and precarious existence for one that is better and more secure, an exchange of a natural independence for liberty, of the power to harm others for security for themselves, and of a personal strength that others might vanquish for a right that the social union makes invincible. Even the lives that individuals have devoted to the state are continually protected by the state, and when they risk their lives to defend the state, what more are they doing than giving back to the state what they have received from it? What are they doing that they would not have done more often and at greater risk if they were living in a natural condition, when, fighting inevitable battles, they would be defending at the peril of their lives what they need in order to preserve them? It is true that all must fight for their country if need be, but then no one need ever fight for himself. Does one not gain something in risking for one's safety a small part of what would have to be risked anyway if one were deprived of that safety?

CHAPTER V:

ON THE RIGHT OF LIFE AND DEATH

The question has been asked how individuals, not having the right to dispose of their own lives, can transfer to the sovereign authority this right that they do not possess. The only reason this question seems difficult is that it is badly put. Every man has the right to risk his own life in order to preserve it. Has anyone ever claimed that someone who throws himself out a window to escape a fire is guilty of suicide? Has a man ever been charged with suicide for perishing in a storm because when he embarked he was aware of the danger?

The aim of the social treaty is the preservation of the contracting parties. He who wills an end also wills the means, and these means involve some risk, and even some loss. Whoever wishes to preserve his life at the expense of others should also be ready to give it up for them when necessary. Yet the citizen is no longer the judge of the danger to which the law requires him to expose himself, and when the princely authority proclaims: "It is in the interest of the state that you die," he must die, since it is only on this condition that he has been living in safety until then, and thus his life is no longer just a bounty of nature but a conditional gift of the state.

The death penalty inflicted upon criminals can be seen from more or less the same point of view: it is in order not to become the victim of a murderer that one consents to die if one becomes a murderer oneself. By this contract, far from disposing of one's own life, one seeks only to preserve it, and it should not be assumed that either party to the contract is planning to get himself hanged.

Furthermore, every malefactor who attacks the social right becomes through his crime a rebel and a traitor to his country;

by breaking its laws, he ceases to be a member of it and is even waging war against it. Consequently, the preservation of the state is incompatible with his own preservation, and one of the two must perish; in putting the guilty man to death, he is judged not so much as a citizen as an enemy. The trial and the judgment are the proofs and declaration that he has broken the social treaty and is consequently no longer a member of the state. Yet, as he has acknowledged himself to be a member of the state, at least by living there, he must be removed through exile as a violator of the pact, or by death as a public enemy, for such an enemy is not a moral ideal but merely a man, and in this instance the right of war is to kill the vanquished.

But the condemnation of a criminal, it will be said, is an individual act. I agree. Therefore such condemnation does not belong to the sovereign authority; it is a right that the sovereign authority can bestow but that it cannot exercise itself. All my ideas are interconnected, but I cannot present them all at once.

One may add that frequent punishments are always a sign of weakness or indolence on the part of the government. There is no wicked person who could not be turned to some good. The state does not have the right to put someone to death, even for the sake of setting an example, except in the case of a person whom it cannot preserve without danger to itself.

As for the right to pardon or exempt a guilty man from the penalty imposed by law and pronounced by the judge, this belongs only to that which is above judge and law, that is to say, the sovereign authority; and the sovereign authority's right in this matter is not entirely clear-cut, and the cases in which it applies are extremely rare. There are few punishments in a well-governed state, not because there are many pardons but because there are few criminals: when a state is in decline, the multitude of crimes ensures the criminals' impunity. During the Roman Republic, neither the Senate nor the Consuls ever attempted to grant pardons; even the populace did not, though it sometimes revoked its own verdict. Frequent pardons are a sign that crime will soon no longer be checked, and everyone knows where that leads. But I feel my heart objecting to this and restraining my pen. Let us leave these questions to a righteous man who has never strayed and would never be in need of pardon.

CHAPTER VI:
ON LAW

By means of the social pact we have given the body politic existence and life: now it is a question of giving it motion and will through legislation. For the original act by which the body politic is formed and coheres does not in any way determine what it need do to preserve itself.

What is good and conforms with order is so by the nature of things, and independent of human conventions. All justice comes from God—He alone is its source. But if we knew how to receive justice from such a height, we would be in need of neither government nor laws. No doubt there is a universal justice emanating from reason alone; but in order to be accepted by us, this justice must be reciprocal. If we consider matters from a human perspective, the laws of justice are futile if they lack a sanction from nature. When the just man observes these laws toward everyone, while no one observes them toward him, they only benefit the wicked and harm the just. Agreements and laws are therefore necessary in order to unite rights and duties and bring justice back to its object. In the state of nature, where everything is held in common, I owe nothing to those to whom I have not promised anything, and I recognize as belonging to others only what is of no use to me. Things are different in a civil state, where all rights are fixed by law.

But what, then, is a law? As long as we are content to attach only metaphysical ideas to the concept, we will continue debating without understanding one another, and even once we have defined a law of nature, we will be no closer to knowing what a law of the state is.[77]

I have already said that there can be no general will concerning a particular object. Indeed, a particular object must be either inside or outside the state. If it is outside, a will that is foreign to it is not general in relation to it, and if it is within the state, it is a part of the state. Thus there is formed between the whole and its part a relation that turns them into two separate entities, of which the part is one entity while the other entity is the whole minus the part. But the whole minus a part cannot be a whole, and as long as this relation continues there can be no whole, but only two unequal parts, from which it follows that the will of one is no longer general in relation to the other.

But when the whole people legislates for the whole people, it is considering only itself, and if a connection should be formed, it is from the entire object from one point of view to the entire object from another point of view without there being any division of the whole. Thus the matter with which legislation is concerned is general, just like the will that is legislating. It is this act that I call a law.

When I say that the object of laws is always general, I mean that the law considers subjects as corporeal and actions as abstract, and never a person as an individual, nor an action as particular. Thus the law can indeed decree that there will be privileges, but it cannot confer them specifically on a specific person. The law can create several classes of citizens, and even assign the qualifications for these classes, but it cannot specify such and such a person to be admitted to them. It can establish a royal government and hereditary succession but cannot elect a king or name a royal family. In short, any function related to an individual does not belong to the legislative power.

By this principle it is immediately clear that the question is no longer to whom it falls to make laws, since laws are acts of the general will; nor whether the prince is above the law, since he is a member of the state; nor whether the law can be unjust, since no man is unjust toward himself; nor is it a valid question how one can be both free and subject to the laws, since the laws are merely registrations of our wills.

One sees, furthermore, that as a law combines the universality of will with that of the object, it stands to reason that what a man, whoever he may be, commands by his own authority cannot be a law; even what the sovereign authority commands with regard to a particular object is not a law but a decree, nor an act of sovereignty but of magistracy.

I therefore call *republic* any state governed by laws, under whatever form of administration, since only then does the public interest govern and do public matters count for something. Every legitimate government is republican.[78] I will explain later what government is.

Strictly speaking, laws are no more than conditions of civil association. The people that is subjected to the laws has to be their author: the conditions of a society should be regulated only by those who have gathered to form it. But how will they regulate these conditions? Is it by common agreement, by sudden inspiration? Does the body politic have an organ through which to express its will? Who will give the body politic the foresight necessary to formulate its acts and promulgate them in advance? Or how will it declare them in a time of need? How can a blind multitude, which often does not know what it wants because it rarely knows what is good for it, execute of its own accord so great and difficult an enterprise as a system of legislation? The people itself always wants what is good, but it does not, of itself, always discern what is good. The general will is always right, but the judgment that guides it is not always enlightened. One must make the general will discern objects as they are, and sometimes as they ought to appear to it. The general will must be shown the right path to follow and kept from being waylaid by individual wills; its attention must be drawn to times and places, and it must be made to weigh the attractions of advantages that are present and clear against the danger of distant and hidden evils. While individuals see the good they reject, the public wants the good it does not see. Both are equally in need of guidance: individuals must be compelled to conform their will to their reason, and the public must be taught to know what it wants; it is then that public enlightenment leads to the union of understanding and will in the social body, with the result that the different parts work in perfect accord, the greatest power being in the whole. And from this arises the need for a legislator.

CHAPTER VII:
ON THE LEGISLATOR

In order to determine the rules of society that are best suited to nations, a superior intelligence would be necessary that would discern all the human passions without experiencing any of them, that would have no affinity with our nature but would know it thoroughly: the happiness of this superior intelligence would have to be independent of us, and yet it would have to be willing to concern itself with our happiness; finally, it would have to cultivate within the sequence of time a distant glory, content to work in one century and reap the rewards in the next.[79] It would take gods to give laws to men.

The same reasoning that Caligula used in regard to *fact* was used by Plato in regard to *right* when he defined the civil or royal man he analyzes in *The Statesman*. But it is true that if a great prince is rare, how much rarer is a great legislator? The former has only to follow the model that the latter must propose. The legislator is the engineer who invents the machine, while the princely authority is merely the mechanic who sets it up and makes it work. "When societies are born," Montesquieu says, "it is the leaders of republics who form institutions, but afterward it is the institutions that form the leaders of republics."[80]

He who dares undertake the establishment of the institutions of a people must feel himself capable of changing, so to speak, human nature, of transforming each individual, who is by himself a perfect and solitary whole, into part of a greater whole from which this individual in a sense receives his life and being; the legislator must feel capable of assailing man's constitution in order to strengthen it, of substituting a partial and moral existence for the physical and independent existence we have all been granted by nature. He must, in short, deprive man of his own resources and give him new ones that are foreign to him, resources that he will not be capable of using without the help of others. The more these natural resources are utterly destroyed, the greater and more lasting those he acquires will be, and the more solid and perfect the institutions: so that if each citizen is nothing, and can do nothing except with the help of all the others—and the strength acquired by the whole is equal or superior to the sum of the forces of all the individuals—one can say that legislation is at the highest possible point of perfection.

The legislator is in every respect an extraordinary man within the state. If he is so through his intellect, he is no less so by his office, which is neither magistracy nor sovereignty. This office, which gives the republic its constitution, never involves itself in the constitution; it is an individual and superior function that has nothing in common with human rule. For if he who commands men ought not to command the laws, then he who commands the laws ought also not to command men. Otherwise, his laws can become ministers to his passions, perpetuating his injustices, and he would not be able to avoid having his private views tarnish the integrity of his work.

When Lycurgus gave laws to his city-state, he began by abdicating the throne. It was the custom in most Greek cities to entrust the establishment of their laws to foreigners. In many cases, the republics of modern Italy imitated this practice, as did the Republic of Geneva to good effect.[81] Rome, in its finest period, saw a revival of all the crimes of tyranny and was brought to the verge of destruction because it united in the same hands the legislative authority and the sovereign power. Yet the Decemvirs never arrogated to themselves the right to pass any law solely on their own authority.[82] "Nothing we propose to you," they told the people, "can pass into law without your consent. Romans, be yourselves the authors of the laws that will lead to your happiness!"

Consequently, he who frames the laws does not have, or should not have, any legislative right, and the people itself cannot, even if it wishes to, divest itself of this incommunicable right because, according to the fundamental pact, only the general will can bind individuals, and one can never be certain that an individual will is in conformity with the general will until it has been submitted to the free vote of the people. I have already said this, but it is worth repeating.

Thus we find two seemingly incompatible entities in the work of legislation: an undertaking beyond human power, and, to execute this undertaking, an authority that has no power.

Another difficulty merits attention. Wise men, who insist on speaking to the common people in elevated language instead of the language of the people, cannot make themselves understood. But there are also countless ideas that would be impossible to translate into the language of the people: ideas that are too general and considerations that are too removed are both out of its range. Each individual, having no taste for any other plan of government than what is related to his particular interest, finds it difficult to see the advantages he might derive from the constant privations that good laws impose. For a nascent people to be able to appreciate sound principles of politics and follow the fundamental rules of statecraft, the effect would have to become the cause; the social spirit that must be the work of that institution would have to preside over the institution itself, and men would have to be, before laws existed, what they should become by means of laws. The legislator, therefore, being unable to appeal to either force or reasoning, must have recourse to an authority of a different order that can compel without violence and persuade without coercion.

This is what has forced the fathers of nations throughout the ages to resort to divine intervention, and to honor the gods by attributing to them their own wisdom, so that the people, who are subjected both to the laws of the state and the laws of nature, perceive the same power behind the creation of man as also being behind the creation of the city, and therefore obeying freely and bearing meekly the yoke of public happiness.

It is the decisions of this sublime reason, rising beyond the reach of the common people, that the legislator puts into the mouths of the immortals in order to compel by divine authority those individuals who would not have been swayed by human prudence.[83] But it is not for every man to make the gods speak, or to be believed when he proclaims himself the interpreter of the gods. The brilliance of the legislator is the true miracle that must prove his mission. Any man may carve tablets of stone, bribe an oracle, feign secret communication with some divinity, train a bird to speak into his ear, or find other crude ways of misleading the people. Someone capable of that and nothing more might well gather around him a flock of fools, but he will never establish an empire, and his crazed endeavor will soon perish with him. Vain trickery leads to a fleeting bond—only wisdom can make a bond lasting. The Jewish law that still endures, and the law of Ishmael's son[84] that has ruled half the world for ten centuries, still to this day honor the great men who decreed them; and while proud philosophy, or the blind spirit of faction, sees in these men no more than fortunate impostors, the true politician admires in their institutions the great and powerful genius that presides over lasting foundations.

With all this we should not conclude, as did Warburton,[85] that politics and religion have a common object in our society, but that when nations are created, politics and religion each serve as the instrument of the other.

CHAPTER VIII:

ON THE PEOPLE

Just as an architect, before putting up a large building, will survey and probe the ground to ascertain whether it can bear its weight, a wise legislator does not begin by drawing up laws that are good in themselves, but will first evaluate whether the people for whom the laws are destined is capable of living under them. This was why Plato refused to give laws to the Arcadians and the Cyrenians, because he knew that both peoples were rich and could not endure equality; and this was also why in Crete there were good laws but bad men, because all that King Minos had done was to impose discipline on a people riddled with vice.

Countless nations have flourished that could have never endured good laws, and even those that could have endured them would have been able to do so for only a very brief period of their existence. A people, like an individual, is compliant only when young, and becomes set in its ways with age. Once customs have become established and prejudices rooted, it is a dangerous and useless enterprise to try to reform them; the people cannot bear that their ills be confronted even if only to cure them, like the foolish and cowardly patient who trembles at the sight of a doctor.

And yet just as there are illnesses that unhinge the minds of men and rob them of their memory of the past, there are also periods in the history of a state when times of violence or revolution do to a people what such an illness might do to an individual, and the horrors of the past are forgotten. The state, scorched by civil war, is reborn, so to speak, from its ashes and recovers the vigor of youth by escaping the clutches of death. Such was Sparta in the days of Lycurgus and Rome after the Tarquins,[86] and, in our time, Holland and Switzerland after the expulsion of their tyrants.

But such events are rare: they are exceptions because of a particular reason that is always found in the constitution of the state in question; they cannot even happen twice to the same people, for as long as it is still barbarous a people can free itself, but once civic vigor has lost its impulse it cannot. Then strife can destroy the state, and a revolution will not be able to re-establish it. And as soon as the people's chains are broken, it falls into disarray and ceases to exist as a people: from then on it needs a master, not a liberator. Remember this principle, free peoples: "Liberty can be gained but never recovered."[87]

Youth is not childhood. There is for nations, as for men, a period of maturity that one must await before subjecting them to laws. But the maturity of a people is not always easily recognized, and if one acts before the time is right, the endeavor is ruined. One people might be amenable to discipline at birth, another not after ten centuries. The Russians will never really be civilized, because civilization was imposed on them too soon. Peter the Great's genius was imitative but lacked true genius, which creates and constructs everything from nothing.[88] Some of the things he did were good, but most were misguided. He saw that his people was barbarous, but did not see that it was not ripe for a civilized political system: he wanted to civilize the people, while what it really needed was to be trained in discipline. He set out to make them Germans or Englishmen, when he ought to have begun by making them Russians. He prevented his subjects from ever becoming what they could have become by persuading them that they were something they were not. A French schoolmaster will, in the same way, educate his pupil so that he shines for an instant in his childhood, only to be nothing for the rest of his life. The Russian Empire will seek to conquer Europe but will itself be conquered. The Tatars, its subjects or neighbors, will become its masters as well as ours. In my view, such a revolution is inevitable, and all the kings of Europe are working in concert to bring it about.

CHAPTER IX:
ON THE PEOPLE (CONTINUED)

Just as nature has set limits to the stature of a well-formed man, beyond which it creates only giants or dwarfs, there are also, when it comes to the best constitution for a state, limits to the size the state can have so that it will be neither too large to be well governed nor too small to preserve itself. In every body politic there is a maximum strength that it cannot exceed and that it often relinquishes by increasing in size. The more the social tie is stretched, the looser it becomes; consequently, a small state is generally stronger than a large one.

There are countless reasons that prove this principle. First, great distances make administration more difficult, just as a weight at the end of a longer lever becomes heavier. Administration also becomes more onerous as the levels of government multiply: each town, first of all, has its own administration that is paid for by the people, as has every district, also paid for by the people; then every province, every larger administrative region, satrapy,[89] and vice regency has its own administration, to which greater amounts have to be paid the higher one goes, always at the expense of the unfortunate people. Finally, there is the supreme administration that blights all the rest. This great number of charges is a constant drain on the subjects, and far from being better governed by all these different levels of government, they are less so than if they were merely subjected to a single one. In the meantime, hardly any resources remain to meet emergencies, and when they have to be paid for, the state is invariably pushed to the brink of destruction.

This is not all. Not only are such governments less vigorous and prompt in enforcing their laws, preventing troubles, punishing abuses, and guarding against seditious endeavors that might be initiated in distant places, but the populace has less love for rulers it never sees, less love for its country that seems wide as the whole world, and also for its fellow citizens, most of whom are foreign. The same laws cannot suit so many diverse provinces, each having different customs, situated in climates that vary greatly, and incapable of existing under a uniform government. Among peoples who live under the same rulers and are in continuous communication, intermingle and intermarry, different laws give rise only to trouble and confusion. Submitted to alien customs, a people is never sure if its patrimony is indeed its own. Talent is smothered, virtue ignored, and vice goes unpunished among a multitude of such men, who are unknown to one another and who have been gathered in one place by the supreme administration. The leaders, overwhelmed with work, can see nothing of their own accord, and the state is governed by clerks. Finally, the measures that must be taken to maintain the general authority, which all these remote officials seek to escape or impose, absorb all the energy of the public; none is left for the happiness of the people, and hardly enough to defend it in times of need. This is how a body that is too large for its constitution collapses and perishes, crushed under its own weight.

On the other hand, a state must provide itself with a sound foundation in order to stand firm against the shocks it cannot avoid, as well as the efforts it will be forced to make in order to sustain itself. For all peoples have a kind of centrifugal force that makes them continually act against one another, seeking to expand at their neighbors' expense, like the vortices of Descartes.[90] Thus the weak are in danger of being quickly swallowed up, and it is impossible for a people to preserve itself except by establishing an equilibrium that will render the pressure roughly equal on all sides.

It is therefore apparent that there are reasons to expand the state and reasons to contract it, and it is no small part of the politician's skill to find the proportion that is most favorable to the preservation of the state. It may be said in general that the reasons for expansion, being merely external and relative, ought to be subordinate to the reasons for contraction, which are internal and absolute. A strong and healthy constitution is the first thing for which one must strive, and it is better to count on the vigor that comes from good government than on the resources a large territory provides.

In addition, there have been states that are instituted in such a way that the need for conquest entered into their very constitution, and to maintain themselves they were forced to expand ceaselessly. They may have congratulated themselves on this fortunate necessity, which nonetheless revealed to them, along with the limits of their greatness, the inevitable moment of their fall.

CHAPTER X:
ON THE PEOPLE (CONTINUED)

One can measure a political body in two ways: by the extent of its territory or the number of its population; and there is between these two measurements a proper relation that gives the state its true size. It is men who make the state, and it is the territory that feeds them. The proper relation is that the land should be sufficient to support the inhabitants, and that there should be as many inhabitants as the land can nourish. It is in this proportion that we find the maximum power of a given number of people. If there is too much land, protecting it becomes arduous, cultivating it inadequate, and its produce excessive—a direct cause of defensive wars. If there is not enough land, the state finds itself dependent on its neighbors to supplement its produce—a direct cause for wars of offense. Any people whose situation compels it to trade or fight wars is weak, it depends on its neighbors and on circumstances, and its existence can only be short and uncertain. Either it subjugates others and changes its situation, or it is subjugated and becomes nothing. It can maintain its liberty only by being small or large.

One cannot set a fixed relation between the extent of territory and the number of inhabitants who can adequately support one another, as much because of the difference one sees in the temperaments of the inhabitants as because of the differences in the quality of the land, its degree of fertility, the nature of its produce, and the influence of its climate. In a fertile country inhabitants might consume little, while those in a barren land might consume much. One also has to take into account the greater or lesser fertility of the women, what the country can offer that is more or less favorable to the population, and the number of people that a legislator can hope to bring together through his laws. Therefore the legislator should not base his judgment on what he sees but on what he foresees, nor should he dwell so much on the actual condition of the population as on the condition that it naturally ought to attain. Lastly, there are countless situations in a state that demand or permit the acquisition of a greater territory than appears necessary. Thus a people will expand greatly in a mountainous country, where the natural products, such as those from woodland and pastures, require less labor, where experience teaches us that women are more fertile than in the plains, and where a large amount of sloping ground provides only a small amount of level terrain, the only area that can be counted as arable. On the other hand, people can better gather on the coasts, even among rocks and sand that are all but barren, because there fishing can to a great extent supplement the produce of the terrain, because the inhabitants have to gather closely together to repel pirates, and also because it is easier to relieve the country of its surplus inhabitants by means of colonies.

To these conditions of establishing a people's institutions must be added a condition that cannot take the place of any other, but without which all the institutions are useless: that one enjoy the prosperity of peace. Because the time during which a state is being organized is like the time when a battalion is gathering, a moment when the body is least capable of resistance and easiest to destroy. One resists better at a time of complete disorder than while things are in ferment when everyone is occupied with rank and not with danger. If war, famine, or sedition should arise at such a time of crisis, the state will inevitably be overthrown.

That is not to say that many governments have not been established during such stormy times, but then those governments destroy the state. Usurpers will always choose or instigate such times of trouble in order to pass destructive laws under the cover of public terror, laws that the people would never adopt if they were in less distress. The choice of the moment to institute laws is one of the surest means of distinguishing the work of the legislator from that of the tyrant.

What kind of people, then, is fit for legislation? A people that finds itself already bound together by some link of origin, interest, or agreement, and has not yet been subjected to the true yoke of law; a people that has neither customs nor superstitions that are deeply ingrained; a people that is not in fear of being overpowered by a sudden invasion; a people that, without entering into its neighbors' quarrels, can resist each of those neighbors on its own, or secure the help of one neighbor to repel another; a people in which every member may be known to every other member, and where there is no need to inflict on any man a burden heavier than he can bear; a people that does not depend on other peoples, nor other peoples on it;[91] a people neither rich nor poor, but capable of sustaining itself; finally, a people that has both the stability of an ancient people and the malleability of a new. What makes the task of legislation difficult is not so much what must be established as what must be destroyed; what makes success so rare is the impossibility of combining the simplicity of nature with the needs of society. It is in fact hard to find all these conditions in one place, and so one sees few states that are well constituted.

In Europe there is one country still capable of being established legislatively: the island of Corsica.[92] The valor and constancy with which that brave people has been able to regain and defend its liberty merits some wise man to teach it how to preserve that liberty. I have a premonition that one day that little island will astonish Europe.

CHAPTER XI:
ON THE VARIOUS SYSTEMS OF LEGISLATION

If one considers what ought to be the greatest good that should be the aim of every system of legislation, one would find that it is limited to two main objectives: liberty and equality; liberty, because all dependence on the part of the individual implies so much strength the less for the body of the state, and equality, because liberty cannot exist without it.

I have already said what civil liberty is;[93] as for equality, the word must not be simply interpreted as meaning that the degrees of power and wealth ought to be exactly the same, but that power should take precedence over violence and be exercised only by virtue of rank and law; and as for wealth, that no citizen should be so rich that he can buy another, and that none be so poor that he should be forced to sell himself.[94] This assumes on the part of the wealthy that they be moderate in their possessions and influence, and on the part of the poor, moderation in avarice and covetousness.

Such equality, it is argued, is a figment of speculation that cannot exist in practice. But if abuse is inevitable, does it not follow that one should at least regulate it? It is precisely because the force of circumstances always tends to destroy equality that the force of legislation should always strive to maintain it.

But these general aims of every good system of legislation must be modified in each country in accordance with circumstances, which arise as much from the local situation as from the character of the inhabitants; and it is on the basis of these circumstances that one should assign to each people a particular system of institutions that may not be the best in itself, but is best for the state for which it is intended. If the soil is unproductive and barren, for example, or the land too crowded for its inhabitants, one should turn to industry and craft, trading what one manufactures for the foodstuffs one lacks. If, on the other hand, you are living in rich plains and on fertile slopes, on good land that lacks inhabitants, put all your effort into agriculture, which increases the population and drives out the crafts that result only in depopulation, since it groups a few inhabitants into a small number of locations.[95] If you occupy extensive and accessible coastlines, you should fill the sea with ships and foster commerce and navigation: your existence will be brilliant, though brief. If you are in a land where the sea only crashes against inaccessible rocks, then it is better for you to remain barbarians and fish eaters: your life will be quieter, perhaps better, and certainly happier. In short, beside the principles common to all, every people has within it some cause that arranges these principles in a particular manner and makes its legislation apt for itself alone. Thus the Jews long ago, and more recently the Arabs, had religion as their principle object, the Athenians had letters, Carthage and Tyre commerce, Rhodes shipping, Sparta war, and Rome valor. The author of *The Spirit of the Laws* has shown by countless examples the art by which the legislator directs his lawmaking in regard to each of these objects.

The constitution of a state is truly stable and lasting when what is appropriate is so well observed that natural circumstances and the laws are always in harmony on the same points, the laws serving, so to speak, only to guarantee, bolster, and rectify the circumstances. But if the legislator mistakes his object and adopts a different principle from that arising from the nature of things—one opting for servitude, the other for liberty; one opting for riches, the other for overpopulation; one opting for peace, the other for conquest—then laws will weaken imperceptibly, the constitution will change, and the state will face endless trouble until it is either changed or destroyed, and invincible nature has reestablished its power.

CHAPTER XII:
ON THE CATEGORIES OF LAW

In giving the state the best possible form, or giving order to the whole, there are various relations to be considered. First, there is the action of the entire body upon itself—in other words, the relation of the whole to the whole or of the sovereign authority to the state—and this relation consists of the relation of the intermediate terms, as we shall see hereafter.

The laws that give order to this relation bear the name of political laws and are also called fundamental laws, not without reason if these laws are wise. For if there is only one good system in any state, the people that instituted it should keep to it. But if the established order is bad, why would one view laws that prevent it from being good as being fundamental laws? Furthermore, a people is always in a position to change its laws, even its best laws, since, if it wishes to do itself harm, who has the right to stop it?

A second relation is that of the members with one another or with the body as a whole; and this relation should in the first case be as slight, and in the second as extensive as possible, so that each citizen can be completely independent of all the others, and extremely dependent on the state. This is always brought about by the same means, for it is the power of the state alone that ensures the liberty of its members. It is from this second relation that civil laws arise.

One could also consider a third kind of relation between the individual and law, that of the relation of disobedience to punishment. This gives rise to the establishment of criminal laws, which in essence are less a particular type of law than the sanctioning of all the others.

In addition to these three kinds of law there is a fourth, the most important of all, one that is not engraved in marble or bronze but in the hearts of the citizens. This kind of law forms the true constitution of the state, gathering new vigor every day, revitalizing or taking the place of other laws as they decay or die out; keeping a people close to the spirit of its constitution, and imperceptibly replacing force of habit with authority. I am speaking of mores, of customs, and above all of public opinion, a part of the laws unknown to our political thinkers, but on which the success of all the other laws depends. This is a part of the laws with which a great legislator concerns himself in secret, while in public he appears to confine himself to specific regulations. These regulations are only the arc of the arch, of which mores, slower to arise, form the unshakable keystone.

Among these various categories, the political laws that constitute the form of government are the only category relevant to my subject.

BOOK III

Before speaking of the different forms of government, let us try to fix the precise meaning of the word, which I have as yet not sufficiently explained.

CHAPTER I:
ON GOVERNMENT IN GENERAL

I warn the reader that this chapter should be read carefully, and that I lack the art of making myself clear to those who will not be attentive.

Every free action has two causes that concur to produce it: one moral, namely, the will that determines the act, and the other physical, namely, the power that executes it. When I walk toward an object, it is first necessary that I should will to go there, and, second, that my feet carry me there. If a paralytic wills to run, or a fit man wills not to, they both remain where they are. The body politic has the same impetus. Here, too, one can distinguish force and will: will under the name of legislative power, and force under that of executive power. Nothing is, or should be, done without their acting in concert.

We have seen that the legislative power belongs to the people, and only to them. It is clear, on the other hand, from the principles I have already established, that executive power cannot belong to the generality as legislature or sovereign authority, because this power consists only of particular acts that are not within the jurisdiction of the law, nor, consequently, within the jurisdiction of the sovereign authority, whose every act can only be a law.

The public force therefore needs an agent of its own that will unite it and put it to work in accordance with the directions of the general will that serves as a means of communication between the state and the sovereign authority, and that in a sense does for the holders of public office what the union of body and soul does for the person. This is why in the state there is government, which is wrongly confused with the sovereign authority, of which government is merely the minister.

What, then, is government? It is an intermediate body established between the subjects and the sovereign authority for their mutual interaction, and charged with the execution of the laws and the maintenance of liberty, both civil and political.

The members of this body are called magistrates or *kings*, that is to say *governors*, and the body as a whole bears the name *prince*.[96] Consequently, those who maintain that the act by which a people submits itself to a ruler is not a contract are quite right. It is absolutely nothing more than a commission, an employment in which mere officials of the sovereign authority exercise in their own name the power the sovereign authority has vested in them, a power it can limit, modify, or recall at will; the bestowing of such a right on these officials is incompatible with the nature of the social body, and contrary to the purpose of association.

Consequently, I call *government*, or supreme administration, the legitimate exercise of executive power, and *prince* or *magistrate* the man or body of men entrusted with that administration.

It is in government that we find the intermediate forces whose relations make up that of the whole to the whole, or of the sovereign authority to the state. This last relation can be represented as that between the extremes of a continuous proportion, of which the proportional mean is the government. The government receives orders from the sovereign authority, which it then transmits to the people; and so that the state remain well balanced, there must, on the whole, be an equality between the product or power of the government taken by itself, and the product or power of the citizens, who are on the one hand sovereign and on the other subjects.

Furthermore, one could not alter any of these three terms without instantly destroying the proportion. If the sovereign authority wants to govern, or the magistrate to make laws, or if the subjects refuse to obey, disorder replaces order, force and will no longer act with unanimity, and the dissolved state declines into despotism or anarchy. Finally, as there is only one proportional mean between each relation, there is also only one good government that is possible for a state: but, as countless events can change the relations of a people, not only may different governments be good for different peoples, but also for the same people at different times.

In an attempt to give some idea of the various relations that may prevail between these two extremes, I will take as an example the number of a people, as it is a relation that is easier to express. Let us suppose a state is composed of ten thousand citizens. The sovereign authority can only be considered collectively and as a body, but each citizen, being a subject, is regarded as an individual. Consequently, the sovereign authority is to the subject as ten thousand is to one; in other words, each member of the state has as his share only a ten-thousandth part of the sovereign authority, although he is entirely subject to it. If the people were to number a hundred thousand, the condition of the subject would still not undergo any change, every individual being equally subject to the authority of the laws, while the subject's vote, reduced to a hundred-thousandth part, would have ten times less influence in the drawing up of the laws. Thus, as the subject always remains a single unit, the sovereign authority's relation to him increases in proportion to the number of citizens; from which it follows that the more a state grows, the more liberty in it diminishes.

When I say that the relation increases, I mean that it loses in equality. Thus, the greater the relation is in the geometrical sense, the less relation there is in the general sense of the term. In the former, the relation, considered according to quantity, is expressed by the quotient; in the latter, considered in terms of identity, it is reckoned by similarity.[97]

Thus, the less relation the individual wills have in connection to the general will (in other words, the less relation there is between mores and laws), the more repressive force should be increased. The government, therefore, to be good, ought to be proportionately stronger the more numerous the population.

On the other hand, as the growth of the state offers the trustees of the public authority more temptations and opportunities to abuse their power, there should, with the increase of power that the government needs to keep the people contained, also be an increase of power available to the sovereign authority to contain the government. I am not speaking of absolute power, but of a power relative to the different sections of the state.

It follows from this double relation that the continuous proportion between the sovereign authority, the princely authority, and the people is by no means an arbitrary idea but a necessary consequence of the nature of the body politic. It also follows, since one of the extremities, in other words, the people as subjects, is fixed and represented by unity, that whenever the doubled ratio increases or diminishes, the simple ratio does likewise, and consequently the middle term is changed. This demonstrates that there is not a single and absolute form of government, but that there can be as many governments of a different nature as there are states of a different size.

If those seeking to ridicule this system were to maintain that, as I assert, if one wishes to find this proportional mean, and form the body of the government, one need only take the square root of the number of the people, then I would counter that I am merely offering this number as an example; the relations I am speaking of are not measured by the number of people alone, but by the amount of action that is the combined result of numerous causes, and I would also counter that though, for the sake of conciseness, I have made use of geometric terms, I am quite aware that geometrical precision has no place in moral quantities.

Government is a small version of what the body politic, which encloses it, is on a large scale. Government is a moral entity that is endowed with certain faculties: it is active like the sovereign authority, passive like the state, and one can further divide it into similar relations. From this a new proportion arises, within which there is another proportion corresponding to the arrangement of the tribunals, until one reaches an indivisible middle ground: that is to say, a single leader or supreme magistrate. Within that progression this magistrate can be represented as the unity between the series of fractions and that of the whole numbers.

Without involving ourselves with this multiplicity of terms, let us limit ourselves to regarding government as a new body within the state, distinct from the people and the sovereign authority, and intermediate between them.

There is an essential difference between these two bodies: namely, that the state exists by itself, while the government exists only through the sovereign authority. Thus the dominant will of the prince[98] is not, nor should be, the general will or the law; its power is merely the public power concentrated in him. As soon as he attempts some absolute and independent act on his own authority, the unity of the whole begins to weaken. If the prince happens to have an individual will that is more active than that of the sovereign authority, and in order to follow that individual will he uses the public power that is in his hands, there would be, so to speak, two sovereign authorities, one of law and the other actual, and the social union would instantly vanish and the body politic dissolve.

Yet for the body of the government to have existence, a real life distinguishing it from the body of the state, and for all its members to be able to act in concert and accomplish the aim for which the government was instituted, it must have a *self*, a sensibility common to its members, a strength and an individual will that ensures its preservation. This individual existence presupposes assemblies, councils, the power to deliberate and reach decisions, and presupposes rights, titles, and privileges belonging exclusively to the princely authority, which make the status of the magistrate more creditable in proportion as it is more onerous. The difficulties are in the manner of ordering this entire subordinate entity within the whole so that it does not weaken the general constitution in strengthening its own; so that it always distinguishes its individual power, destined for his own preservation, from the public power destined for the preservation of the state. In a word, it should always be prepared to sacrifice the government to the people, and not the people to the government.

Furthermore, although the artificial body of the government is the work of another artificial body and has, in a sense, only a borrowed and subordinate life, this does not prevent it from being able to act with more or less vigor or speed, or from enjoying, so to speak, more or less robust health. Finally, without directly departing from the aim for which it was instituted, the government may deviate from it to some extent, depending on how it is constituted.

From all these differences arise the diverse relations that the government must have with the body of the state, according to the accidental and particular relations through which that state is modified. For often the best of governments will become the most pernicious if its relations are not modified according to the defects of the body politic to which it belongs.

CHAPTER II:
ON THE PRINCIPLE UNDERLYING
THE VARIOUS FORMS OF GOVERNMENT

To explain the general cause of these differences I must distinguish between the princely authority and the government, as I have distinguished between the state and the sovereign authority.

The body of the magistracy can be composed of a greater or lesser number of members. We said that the relation of the sovereign authority to the subjects was greater in proportion to the people being more numerous, and, by clear analogy, we can say the same of the government in regard to the magistrates.

Since the total strength of the government is always that of the state, it never varies, from which it follows that the more the government expends this strength on its own members, the less it has left to act upon the people as a whole.

Consequently, the greater the number of magistrates, the weaker the government. As this principle is fundamental, let us do our best to elucidate it.

We can distinguish three essentially different wills in the person of the magistrate: first, the will of the individual, which strives only for his own particular advantage; second, the common will of the magistrates that relates solely to the advantage of the princely authority, and that one could call the corporate will, as it is general in relation to the government and particular in relation to the state of which the government forms a part; third, the will of the people or the will of the sovereign authority, which is general both in relation to the state considered as the whole and to the government considered as a part of the whole.

In a perfect system of legislation, the particular or individual will should be nil, the corporate will belonging to the government should be quite subordinate, and consequently the general or sovereign will should always be dominant and the unique rule that determines all the rest.

According to the natural order, on the other hand, these different wills become more active the more concentrated they are. Thus the general will is always the weakest, the corporate will is second, while the individual will occupies first place: so that in the government each member is first of all himself, then a magistrate, and then a citizen, a progression that is the exact opposite of what is required by the social order.

This granted, let us suppose that the entire government is in the hands of a single man, in which case the individual will and the corporate will are perfectly united, and consequently the latter is at the highest possible intensity. But since the exercising of power depends on the degree of will, and as the absolute power of the government is invariable, it follows that the most active government is that of a single man.

If, on the other hand, we unite the government with the legislative authority, and make the princely authority the sovereign authority and all the citizens into so many magistrates, then the corporate will, mingled with the general will, can have no more activity than that will, and must leave the individual will all its power. Thus the government, while always having the same absolute power, will have a minimum of relative power or activity.

These relations are indisputable, and other considerations serve only to confirm them. It is clear, for example, that every magistrate is more active in the body to which he belongs than each citizen is in the body to which he belongs. Consequently the individual will has much more influence on the acts of the government than on those of the sovereign authority, for each magistrate is almost always charged with some function of government, while each citizen, taken by himself, has no function within the sovereignty. Furthermore, the larger the state becomes, the more its real power increases, though not in proportion to its growth; but if the state remains the same size, there is no use multiplying the number of magistrates, as the government will not gain any greater power, because its power is that of the state, the amount of which always remains equal. Thus the relative power or activity of the government would decrease without its absolute or real power being able to increase.

It is furthermore certain that the execution of public business becomes slower in proportion to the increase in the number of people put in charge of it. Devoting too much to prudence, not enough is devoted to chance, and opportunities are missed; through deliberating one often loses the fruits of deliberation.

I have just proved that the government slackens in proportion to the increasing number of magistrates, and showed earlier that the more numerous the people, the greater the restraining power should be. From which it follows that the ratio of magistrates to government must be the inverse of the ratio of the subjects to the sovereign authority: that is to say, the more the state grows, the more the government should shrink, so that the number of rulers diminishes in proportion to the increase in the number of the people.

Nevertheless, I am here speaking only about the relative strength of the government and not of its rectitude, for, in the opposite case, the more numerous the magistracy, the more closely the corporate will approaches the general will. Under a single magistrate, on the other hand, the same corporate will is, as I have already stated, merely an individual will. Thus what one may gain on one side is lost on the other. The art of the legislator is to know how to fix the point at which the power and the will of the government, which are always in reciprocal proportion to each other, are combined in the relation most advantageous to the state.

CHAPTER III:
ON THE CLASSIFICATION OF GOVERNMENTS

In the previous chapter we saw how the various kinds or forms of government are distinguished according to the number of members composing them. In this chapter we shall see how the distinction is made.

First, the sovereign authority can assign control of the government to the whole people or the majority of the people, with the result that there will be more citizens who are magistrates than there are simple private individuals. The name given to this form of government is *democracy*.

Or the sovereign authority may restrict the government to a small number, so that there will be more ordinary citizens than magistrates. This form is called *aristocracy*.

Finally, the sovereign authority can concentrate the whole government in the hands of a single magistrate from whom all others draw their power. This third form is the most common and is called *monarchy*, or royal government.

It should be noted that all these forms, or at least the first two, occur in varying degrees and have a considerable range, for democracy can embrace the whole people or restrict itself to just half. Aristocracy, in turn, can restrict itself from half of the people to the smallest possible number. Even royalty is susceptible to some sharing of power. Sparta through its constitution invariably had two kings, while the Roman Empire had as many as eight emperors at once without its being possible to say that the empire was divided. Thus there is a point at which each form of government merges into the next, and it becomes clear that despite these three classifications, the government is in fact liable to have as many different forms as the state has citizens.

Furthermore, as a government can in certain respects be subdivided into different parts—one administered one way and another in another—the result of combinations of the three forms can be a multitude of mixed forms, each of which can be multiplied by all the simple forms.

There has been much debate throughout the ages concerning the best form of government, without considering that each government can in some cases be the best and in other cases the worst.

If in the different states the number of supreme magistrates should be in inverse ratio to the number of citizens, it follows that democratic government generally suits small states, aristocratic government those of medium size, and monarchy large states. This rule derives directly from the principle I have proposed, and yet circumstances can create countless exceptions.

CHAPTER IV:
ON DEMOCRACY

He who makes the law knows better than anyone else how it should be interpreted and executed. It seems, then, that one could not have a better constitution than one in which the executive power is united with the legislative: but it is just this that renders such a government inadequate in certain respects, because things that should be clearly distinguished are not, and if the prince and the sovereign authority are one and the same entity, they merely form, so to speak, a government without government.

It is not good that he who makes the laws also executes them, nor is it good that the body of the people turns its attention from general considerations to private matters. Nothing is more dangerous than the influence of private interests in public affairs, for the abuse of laws by the government is a lesser evil than the corruption of the legislator, which is the inevitable consequence of private considerations. In such a case, the state's substance being corrupted, all reform becomes impossible. A people that would never misuse governmental powers would not misuse independence, either. A people that would always govern well would not need to be governed.

If the word *democracy* is taken in the strict sense, then a real democracy has never existed, nor will it ever. It is against the natural order that the majority govern and the minority be governed. It is unimaginable that the people would remain perpetually assembled to tend to public affairs, and it is clear enough that the people would not be able to establish commissions for that purpose without a change in the form of administration.

Indeed, I believe I can lay down as a principle that when the functions of government are shared among several tribunals, the smaller number of tribunals sooner or later acquires the greatest authority, if only because of the facility in expediting affairs that naturally ensues. Besides, how many difficult elements one would have to combine in order to bring such a government about! First, one would need a very small state where the populace could be easily gathered together and where each citizen knows all the others; second, a great simplicity of values to prevent a multitude of thorny issues and discussions; next, a considerable measure of equality in rank and wealth, without which equality of rights and authority cannot prevail for long. Finally, there should be little or no luxury, for luxury is either the result of riches or renders them necessary: it corrupts both the rich and the poor, the rich through possession and the poor through covetousness; it leads the country to indolence and vanity, and robs the state of its citizens, enslaving them to one another, and one and all to public opinion.

That is why a famous author made virtue the principle of a republic, since all these conditions could not prevail without virtue.[99] But that great genius, by not making the necessary distinctions, frequently lacked precision, and sometimes clarity.

He did not see that as sovereign authority was the same everywhere, the same principle ought to be found in every well-constituted state, though in greater or lesser degree according to the form of the government.

Let us add that there is no government as prone to civil wars and internal strife as a democratic or popular one, because there is no government that has such a strong and constant tendency to change its form, nor any that requires more vigilance and courage to maintain it. It is primarily with a democratic constitution that the citizen must arm himself with strength and steadfastness, and say every day of his life with utter conviction what a virtuous Palatine once said in the Diet of Poland: *Malo periculosam libertatem quam quietum servitium*[100] [I prefer perilous freedom to peaceful slavery].

If there were a people of gods, it would govern itself democratically. But such a perfect government is not suited to mankind.

CHAPTER V:
ON ARISTOCRACY

We have here two very distinct moral entities, namely, the government and the sovereign authority, and consequently two general wills: one in relation to all the citizens, the other only in relation to the members of the administration. Thus, although the government can regulate its internal system as it pleases, it can never speak to the people except in the name of the sovereign authority, that is to say, in the name of the people itself, something that should never be forgotten.

The first societies governed themselves aristocratically. The heads of families deliberated among themselves on public affairs. The young yielded readily to the authority of experience; hence denominations such as *priests, elders, senators,* and *gerontes.* The savages of North America to this day still govern themselves in this manner and are very well governed.

But as the inequality caused by society's institutions prevailed over natural inequality, wealth or power[101] came to be preferred over age, and aristocracy became elective. Finally, power was passed on with a father's property to his children, rendering families patrician and the government hereditary, with the result that there were senators who were just twenty years old.

There are consequently three kinds of aristocracy: natural, elective, and hereditary. The first suits only simple peoples, while the third is the worst of all governments; the second, on the other hand, is the best, and is aristocracy in the true sense of the word.

Such a true aristocracy has the advantage not only of keeping the legislative and executive powers separate, but also of being able to choose its members; for in a government of the people, all the citizens are born magistrates, while in such an aristocracy, magistracy is confined to a few who become magistrates only by election,[102] a means by which probity, intellect, experience, and all the other reasons for preferment and public esteem provide additional guarantees of wise government.

Furthermore, assemblies are more easily held, public affairs are better discussed and executed with greater order and diligence, and the reputation of the state is better sustained abroad by venerable senators than by a multitude that is unknown or looked down upon.

In short, the best and most natural order is for those who are wisest to govern the multitude, as long as one is certain that they are governing it for its profit and not for their own. There is no need to multiply means for no reason, or to have twenty thousand men do what a hundred well-chosen men can do even better. But we should note that with the rule of the general will, the interest of the governing body has less influence over the public power, and that another inevitable tendency removes part of the executive power from the laws.

As for circumstances specifically suitable for such an aristocracy, it needs a state that is neither so small, nor a people so simple and upright, that the execution of the laws follows immediately from the public will, as in a good democracy; nor does it need a nation that is so large that the far-flung leaders governing it can each play the sovereign in his own province and set out to make himself independent in order to become the ruler.

But if aristocracy demands a few virtues less than a government of the people does, it also demands certain virtues that are particular to it, such as moderation among the rich and contentment among the poor, since a rigorous equality would be out of place—it was not observed even in Sparta.

Moreover, if this form of government brings with it a certain inequality of fortune, it is in order that the administration of public affairs might generally be entrusted to those most able to give it their whole time, and not, as Aristotle maintains, so that the rich may always be preferred.[103] On the other hand, it is important that at times an opposite choice should teach the people that the merit of a man is a more vital reason for preference than wealth.

CHAPTER VI:

ON MONARCHY

Up to now we have considered the princely authority as a moral and collective entity, unified by the power of the laws and holder of executive power in the state. We must now consider this power gathered in the hands of an actual person, a real man who alone has the right to exercise it in accordance with the laws. This man is what is called a *monarch* or a *king*.

In contrast to other forms of administration, where a collective being represents an individual, in this form an individual represents a collective being, so that the moral unity that constitutes the princely authority is at the same time a physical unity in which all the qualities that the law has such difficulty in uniting in the other forms of administration are found naturally united.

Thus the will of the people and the will of the prince, the public strength of the state and the private power of the government, all answer to a single impetus; all the levers of the machine are in the same hands, and everything moves toward the same end. There are no conflicting moves that cancel one another out, and one cannot imagine any kind of constitution in which a smaller amount of effort could produce a greater amount of action. Archimedes, sitting calmly on the shore, pulling with ease a great ship across the water, represents to me a skillful monarch who from his chambers governs vast states, moving everything while he himself appears immobile.

But if there is no government that has more vigor than a monarchy, there is also no government in which the individual will has more power and can more easily govern others. Everything moves toward the same end, but this end is not public happiness, and even the power of the administration invariably proves detrimental to the state.

Kings want to be absolute, and one calls out to them from afar that the best way of achieving this is to make themselves loved by their people. This principle is fine, and in some respects even true; but unfortunately it will always be ridiculed at court. The power that comes from a people's love is without doubt the greatest power. But it is precarious and conditional; princes will never be satisfied by it. The best kings want to be able to be wicked if they please without ceasing to be masters. A political sermonizer can tell a king to his heart's content that as the power of the people belongs to him, it is in his interest that the people flourish, multiply, and be strong. The king knows very well that this is untrue. His greatest personal interest is that the people be weak, wretched, and unable to defy him. I admit that if one supposes that the king's subjects were to be invariably submissive, his interest would certainly be for the people to be powerful, too, so that their power, being his, would make him formidable to his neighbors; but as this interest is only secondary and subordinate, and the two suppositions are incompatible, it is natural that princes will always prefer the principle that is to their immediate advantage. This is what Samuel argued before the Hebrews,[104] and what Machiavelli has clearly proven. In feigning to teach kings, Machiavelli taught great lessons to the people. His *Prince* is the book of republicans.[105]

We found by looking at general ratios that monarchy is suited only to great states, a principle that is reaffirmed as we analyze the monarchy itself. The more numerous the members of the public administration, the smaller the ratio of the princely authority to its subjects becomes as it approaches equality, so that in a democracy the ratio is one to one, in other words, equal. The same ratio increases in proportion as the government decreases in numbers, and is at its maximum when the government is in the hands of one man. Thus there is too great a distance between the princely authority and the people, and the state lacks cohesion. To form this cohesion one needs intermediate ranks, with princes, grandees, and nobility to fill them. But none of this is suitable for a small state, which would be ruined by all these ranks.

And yet if it is difficult for a large state to be governed well, it is even more difficult for it to be governed well by a single man, and everyone knows what happens when a king appoints substitutes to stand in for him.

An essential and inescapable defect, which will always make monarchical governments inferior to republican ones, is that in republics the public voice almost always elevates to leading positions men who are enlightened and capable, men who fill these positions with honor. But in monarchies, those who reach the top are most often petty blunderers, rogues, and intriguers, whose petty talents are of the kind that help them reach the highest positions at court and serve only to reveal their ineptitude as soon as they assume their posts. The people is far less often mistaken in its choice than the prince, so that a man with true merit in the royal ministry is almost as rare as a fool at the head of a republican government. Therefore, when by some stroke of luck a man born to rule does take the helm of government in a monarchy that has been practically destroyed by a troop of glib mountebanks, one is quite amazed at his resourcefulness, making a mark in his country's history.[106]

For a monarchical state to be well governed, its size or extent must be commensurate with the abilities of the one who governs. It is easier to conquer than to rule. With a long enough lever one can move the world with a single finger, but to carry it one needs the shoulders of a Hercules. However small a state may be, the prince is always too small. If, on the other hand, it happens that the state is too small for its ruler—which is most rare—it is still ill-governed, because the ruler, always pursuing his grand designs, neglects the interests of the people, and makes them no less unhappy by misusing his abundance of talent than a limited ruler does for want of talent. A kingdom should, so to speak, expand or contract with each reign according to the prince's capabilities; but as the talents of a senate, on the other hand, are more fixed in range, the state can have more stable limits, with the administration working just as well.

The most evident disadvantage of government by a single man is the lack of a continuous line of succession that in the other two kinds of government forms an uninterrupted continuity. When one leader dies, another is needed; elections leave dangerous intervals that are contentious, and unless the citizens are fair-minded and of an integrity that this form of government seldom encourages, intrigue and corruption come into play. It is unlikely that he to whom the state has sold itself will not in turn sell the state in order to compensate himself at the expense of the weak for the money that the powerful have extorted from him. Under an administration of this kind, everything sooner or later becomes venal, and peace enjoyed under such a king is worse than the turmoil of an interregnum.

What has been done to prevent these evils? In certain families, crowns have been made hereditary, and an order of succession established to prevent any disputes when kings die: that is to say, by substituting the disadvantages of regencies for those of elections, apparent tranquility has been preferred to wise administration. And men have preferred the risk of having as their rulers children, monsters, or imbeciles, to having debates in order to choose a good king. These men did not take into account that by exposing themselves in this way to the risks of this alternative, they are setting almost all the odds against themselves. There was good sense in what young Dionysius said to his father, who reproached him for some shameful deed, asking whether as a father he had ever set him such an example. "Ah," Dionysius replied, "but your father was not king."[107]

When a man is brought up to rule other men, everything conspires to deprive him of justice and reason. It is said that great pains are taken to teach young princes the art of ruling; it does not, however, appear that their education benefits them. One would do better to begin by teaching them the art of obeying. The greatest kings, celebrated by history, were not brought up to rule. It is a science that one is never so far from possessing as when one has studied it too much, and which one acquires better by obeying than by commanding. *"Nam utilissimus idem ac brevissimus bonarum malarumque rerum delectus cogitare quid aut nolueris sub alio principe, aut volueris"*[108] [The most useful and shortest way of distinguishing what is good from what is bad is to consider what you would have wished or not wished to happen under another prince].

One result of this shortcoming in succession is the inconstancy of royal government, which, regulated now by one plan and now by another according to the character of the reigning prince or those who reign for him, cannot have a fixed aim for long, nor a consistent policy. This inconsistency causes the state to be always shifting from principle to principle and project to project, something that does not happen in the other forms of government where the princely authority is always the same. We also generally see that if there is more cunning at court, there is more wisdom in the senate, and that republics advance toward their ends by more consistent and better-followed policies, while every upheaval in a royal ministry creates an upheaval in the state. It is the common principle for all ministries and almost all kings to do in everything the opposite of what their predecessors did.

This same incoherence also clarifies a sophism quite familiar to royalist political thinkers: that is, not only to compare civil government to a domestic one, and the prince to the head of a family, an error that has already been refuted, but also to liberally bestow on this magistrate all the virtues he would need, and to always suppose that the prince is what he should be. On the basis of this supposition, royal government clearly becomes preferable to all others because it is incontestably the strongest, and, in order also to be the best, it lacks only a corporate will that conforms more with the general will.

But if, according to Plato,[109] the ideal king is by nature such a rarity, how often will nature and fortune work toward crowning him? And if royal education necessarily corrupts those who receive it, what can one expect from a succession of men brought up to reign? It is therefore utter self-deception to confuse royal government with government by a good king. To see what such a government is in itself, one must evaluate it as it is under princes who are incompetent or wicked, for either they come to the throne incompetent or wicked, or the throne will make them so.

These difficulties have not escaped our authors, but they are not troubled by them. The remedy, they say, is to obey without a murmur: God sends bad kings in His wrath, and they must be endured as punishment from Heaven. Such discourse is doubtless edifying, but it would perhaps be more suited to a pulpit than a political book. What would we say of a doctor who promises miracles, and whose whole art is to exhort the sick man to patience? We know well enough that we have to put up with a bad government when we have one; the question is how to find a good one.

CHAPTER VII :
ON MIXED GOVERNMENTS

Strictly speaking, there is no such thing as a simple form of government. A single leader must have subordinate magistrates; a government of the people must have a leader. Therefore, in the distribution of executive power there is always a gradation from the greater to the lesser number, with the difference that sometimes the greater number is dependent on the lesser, and sometimes the lesser on the greater.

Occasionally the distribution is equal, either when the component parts are mutually dependent, as in the government of England, or when the authority of each part is independent but imperfect, as in Poland. This latter form is flawed because there is no unity in the government, and the state lacks cohesion.

Which is better: a simple or a mixed form of government? This is a question that has been much debated among political thinkers, and elicits the same answer I have previously given regarding all forms of government.[110]

Simple government is best in itself precisely because it is simple. But when the executive power is not sufficiently dependent upon the legislative power, in other words, when there is a closer relation between the princely authority and the sovereign authority than between the people and the princely authority, this disproportion must be remedied by dividing the government, for then all its parts have an equal authority over the subjects, while their division makes all of them together less powerful against the sovereign authority.

The same shortcoming can also be prevented by establishing intermediate magistrates, who, the government remaining whole, have the effect of balancing the two powers and preserving their respective rights. Then the government is not mixed but tempered.

Similar means can be used to cure the opposite shortcoming, and when the government is too weak, bodies of magistrates can be established to fortify it. This is done in all democracies. In the first case, the government is divided in order to make it weak, and in the second to give it power: for the *maximum* of power and weakness are both found in simple governments, while the mixed forms result in moderate power.

CHAPTER VIII:

ON HOW NOT EVERY FORM OF GOVERNMENT IS SUITED TO EVERY COUNTRY

Liberty is not a fruit that grows in every climate, and consequently is not within the reach of all peoples. The more one considers this principle, established by Montesquieu,[111] the more its truth is felt, while the more it is contested, the more opportunities arise for new proofs to confirm it.

In all the governments of the world the public entity consumes but does not produce anything. From where, then, does the substance come that it consumes? From the labor of its members. It is the surplus of individuals that produces the needs of the public; from which it follows that the civil state can continue to exist only so long as men's labor produces more than their needs.

And yet the surplus is not the same in every country in the world. In some countries it is considerable, in others moderate, in others again nil, and in still others negative. The proportion depends on the fertility of the climate, on the kind of labor the soil demands, on the nature of its products, on the strength of its inhabitants, on the greater or lesser amounts they need to consume, and on several other similar proportions that constitute it.

On the other hand, not all governments are of the same nature. Some are more and some less voracious than others, and the differences between them are based on the added principle that the further the contribution of the public is removed from its source, the more burdensome it becomes. It is not by the amount of taxes that this burden must be measured, but on how far this amount has to travel in order to return to the hands from which it came. When the redistribution is prompt and well established, it does not matter whether one pays little or much—the populace is always rich and the finances healthy. In contrast, regardless of how little the populace pays, if what it pays never comes back, the populace is soon worn out by the continual giving: the state will never become rich, and the people will always remain impoverished.

It follows from this that the greater the distance between the government and the people grows, the more burdensome the taxes become. Thus, in a democracy the people is least burdened, in an aristocracy more, while in a monarchy it bears the greatest burden. Consequently, monarchy is suited only to wealthy nations, aristocracy to states of average wealth and size, and democracy to states that are small and poor.

Indeed, the more one reflects on this, the greater one finds the difference to be between free and monarchical states. In the free state everything is used for a common benefit, while in a monarchy the public and private resources are reciprocal, one increasing through the weakening of the other. Ultimately, despotism does not govern subjects in order to make them happy but renders them miserable in order to govern them.

In every climate, then, we find natural causes by which we can determine the form of government toward which the force of the natural climate directs a state, and we can even determine what sort of inhabitants it should have. Unproductive and barren areas, where the product is not worth the labor, should remain uncultivated and deserted, or peopled only by savages; areas where men's labor brings in no more than what is absolutely necessary should be inhabited by barbarous peoples: in such places any polity is impossible. Lands where the surplus of product over labor is only middling are suitable for free peoples; those in which abundant and fertile soil has a great yield with little labor call for monarchical government, so that the surplus of the subjects will be consumed through the luxury of the prince, for it is better for this surplus to be absorbed by the government than to be dissipated among the subjects. There are exceptions, I know, but these exceptions themselves confirm the rule, in that they produce upheavals sooner or later that restore things to their natural order.

General laws should always be distinguished from particular causes that may modify their effect. If the entire south were filled with republics and the entire north with despotic states, it would be no less true that the effect of climate makes despotism suitable to hot countries, barbarism to cold countries, and good polity to intermediate regions. I also realize that even if the principle is granted, there may be argument over its application; it might be said that there are cold countries that are very fertile and southern countries that are very unproductive. But this issue exists only if one does not consider the question in all its aspects. We must, as I have already said, take into account labor, strength, consumption, and the like.

Let us suppose that one of two terrains of equal scope yields five quantities of product and the other ten. If the inhabitants of the first consume four quantities, and those of the second nine, the surplus of the first terrain would be a fifth of the yield, while that of the second would be a tenth. The ratio of these two surpluses being inverse to that of the yields, the terrain that produces only five quantities will give a surplus double that of the terrain that produces ten.

It is not, however, a matter of a doubled yield, for I do not think that anyone would generally venture to put the fertility of cold countries on an equal footing with the fertility of hot ones. But let us suppose this equality exists: let us, for instance, place England on a level with Sicily, and Poland with Egypt. Further south we have Africa and India, and further north nothing. But what a difference in cultivation one would need in order to achieve the same yield! In Sicily one has only to scratch the soil a little, while in England what effort men must put into tilling! Consequently, where more hands are needed to produce the same yield, the surplus must necessarily be less.

Consider furthermore that the same number of people consume much less in hot countries, where the climate requires people to be moderate in order to remain healthy. Europeans who try to live in southern lands as they do in Europe all perish from indigestion and dysentery. "Compared to the Asians," Chardin says, "we are carnivorous animals, wolves. Some attribute the temperate nature of the Persians to their country being less well cultivated; but I, on the other hand, believe that their country has fewer commodities because the inhabitants need less. If the Persians' frugality," he continues, "were the result of a scarcity of food, then only the poor would eat little, but in Persia everybody does. Furthermore, the Persians would eat more in some provinces and less in others, depending on the fertility of the land, whereas the same temperance is found throughout their kingdom. They pride themselves on their way of life, saying that one need only look at their complexion to ascertain the degree to which their way of life surpasses that of Christians. In fact, the Persians are of an even complexion—their skin beautiful, delicate, and smooth—while the complexion of their Armenian subjects, who live in a European manner, is coarse and blotchy, and their bodies are fat and heavy."[112]

The closer one approaches the equator, the less people eat: they eat scarcely any meat, while rice, maize, couscous, millet, and cassava are their everyday food. There are millions of people in India whose subsistence does not cost a sou a day. Even in Europe we see considerable differences in appetite between the peoples of the north and those of the south. A Spaniard will live for a week on what a German consumes in a single meal. In the countries where men are more voracious, luxury will also turn in the direction of consumption. In England, luxury appears in the guise of a table laden with meats, while in Italy one is regaled with sugar and flowers.

Luxury in clothes also presents similar differences. In climates where the changes of season are sudden and violent, clothes are better and simpler, while in climates where people dress just for show, they aim more for what is striking than what is useful, and the clothes themselves are a luxury. In Naples one sees men walking every day on the Posilippo in gold-embroidered jackets, but without stockings. It is the same with buildings: magnificence is all that matters when one need not fear the climate. In Paris and London people want to live in warmth and comfort, whereas in Madrid people have superb living rooms but no windows that shut, and people sleep in rat holes.

Foods are much more substantial and succulent in hot countries; this is a third difference that cannot fail to influence the second. Why do people eat so many vegetables in Italy? Because there they are good, nutritious, and tasty. In France, where vegetables are raised on little more than water, they are not nutritious and count for almost nothing at table; and yet they take up no less ground and require at least as much trouble to cultivate. It is a known fact that the wheat of Barbary, in other respects inferior to that of France, yields much more flour, and that the wheat of France in turn yields more than that of the north. From this one can infer that there is, generally speaking, a similar gradation in the direction from the equator to the pole. But is it not an obvious disadvantage for the same product to contain a smaller amount of nourishment?

To all these different considerations I can add one that both stems from them and strengthens them: that is, that hot countries have less need of inhabitants than cold countries but could feed more of them. This results in a double surplus, which again favors despotism. The greater the territory occupied by the same number of inhabitants, the more difficult rebellion is, because it is impossible to take concerted action rapidly or secretly, and it is always easy for the government to uncover schemes and disrupt communications. But the more a numerous people is united, the less the government can impinge on the sovereign authority: leaders of a rebellion can deliberate as safely in their rooms as the prince in his council, and a crowd can gather as rapidly in the squares as the troops can in their quarters. The advantage of tyrannical government is therefore that it is capable of acting over great distances. With the help of the points of support it sets up for itself, its power, like that of a lever, grows with distance.[113] The power of the people, on the other hand, acts only when it is concentrated: it dissipates and is lost as it diffuses, like gunpowder scattered over the earth that then only ignites grain by grain. Countries that are least populated are consequently the most suitable for tyranny: wild beasts reign only in the wilderness.

CHAPTER IX:
ON SIGNS THAT A GOVERNMENT IS GOOD

When, therefore, one asks which is absolutely the best government, one is asking a question both imprecise and unanswerable; or, if you will, there are as many valid answers as there are possible combinations in the absolute and relative positions of peoples.

But if one were to ask by what sign one can tell that a given people is well or badly governed, that would be another matter, since such a question of fact could be answered. And yet this question has remained unanswered, because everyone wants to answer it in his own way. The subjects of a monarchy extol public order, while the citizens of a democracy extol the freedom of the individual; the former prefer security of property, the latter security of person; the former consider the severest government best, the latter the mildest; the former want crimes punished, the latter want them prevented; the subjects of a monarchy see merit in being feared by neighboring states, while citizens of a democracy prefer to be ignored; the former are happy when money circulates, the latter demand that the people have bread. Even if an agreement were reached on these and similar points, would we be any closer to an answer? As moral qualities cannot be precisely measured, how could agreement concerning the manifest signs assume agreement about what they mean.

For my part, I am always astonished that people do not recognize so obvious a sign, or are of such bad faith as not to agree on it. What is the aim of political association? The preservation and prosperity of its members. And what is the surest sign of their preservation and prosperity? Their number and population. Hence look no further for this much disputed sign. All other things being equal, the government that is beyond question the best is the one under which citizens most readily increase and multiply without aid from outside, naturalization, or colonies. The government under which a people diminishes and declines is the worst. Mathematicians, it is now up to you to count, measure, and compare.[114]

CHAPTER X:
ON THE ABUSE OF GOVERNMENT
AND ITS TENDENCY TO DEGENERATE

Just as the individual will constantly acts against the general will, the government exerts itself constantly against the sovereign authority. The greater this exertion grows, the more the constitution deteriorates, and as there is no other corporate will to resist and balance that of the princely authority, sooner or later the princely authority ends up subjugating the sovereign authority and violating the social treaty. This is the inherent and unavoidable defect that relentlessly strives to destroy the body politic from the time it is born, just as old age and death eventually destroy the body of man.

There are two general ways in which government degenerates: when it contracts in size, or when the state dissolves.

Government contracts in size when it passes from the control of the many to the control of the few: from democracy to aristocracy, and from aristocracy to royalty. That is its natural progression.[115] If government were to retrogress from the few to the many, it could be said to slacken, but such a reverse progress is impossible.

Indeed, a government never changes its form except when it loses its elasticity, leaving it too weak to preserve its form. And if the spring were to be loosened further, the government's power would disappear altogether and it would be unable to continue. It is therefore necessary to tighten the spring as it slackens, otherwise the state that it sustains will fall into ruin.

The dissolution of the state may come about in two ways:

First, when the princely authority no longer administers the state in accordance with the laws, and usurps the sovereign power. In that case a remarkable change occurs: it is not the government that contracts, but the state. I mean that the state as a whole dissolves and another forms within it, composed solely of the members of the government, and which for the rest of the people is nothing more than its master and tyrant. So that the moment the government usurps the sovereignty, the social pact is broken and all the ordinary citizens, regaining by right their natural liberty, are forced, though not bound, to obey.

The same thing occurs when the members of the government usurp individually the power they ought to exercise only as a body, which is just as great an infraction of the laws and leads to even greater disorder. In that case there are, so to speak, as many princes as there are magistrates, and the state, no less divided than the government, perishes or changes its form.

When the state dissolves, the abuse of government, whatever form it may take, bears the common name of *anarchy*.[116] To clarify: democracy degenerates into *ochlocracy*, aristocracy into *oligarchy,* and I would add that kingship degenerates into *tyranny;* but this last word is equivocal and calls for explanation.

In common parlance, a *tyrant* is a king who governs with violence and without regard for justice and law. In the strict sense, a tyrant is an individual who arrogates to himself royal authority without having a right to it. This is how the Greeks understood the word *tyrant:* they applied it indifferently to good and bad princes whose authority was not legitimate.[117] Thus *tyrant* and *usurper* are perfectly synonymous terms.

To give different things different names, I will call the usurper of royal authority a *tyrant,* and the usurper of the sovereign power a *despot.* The tyrant is he who usurps the law in order to govern according to it; the despot is he who places himself above the laws themselves. Thus the tyrant cannot be a despot, but the despot is always a tyrant.

CHAPTER XI:
ON THE DEATH OF THE BODY POLITIC

Such is the natural and inevitable tendency of the best-constituted governments. If Sparta and Rome perished, what state can hope to last forever? If we want to form a lasting foundation, let us not seek to make it eternal. To succeed we must not attempt the impossible, nor flatter ourselves that we are giving the work of man a stability that human things cannot attain.

The body politic, like the human body, begins to die at birth and carries within it the seeds of its destruction. But both bodies can have a constitution that is more or less robust and suited to preserve them for a longer or shorter time. The constitution of man is the work of nature, while that of the state is the work of craft. It is not within men's power to prolong their lives, but it is within their power to prolong, as much as possible, the life of the state by giving it the best constitution it can have. The best-constituted state will come to an end, but later than others, unless some unforeseen misfortune brings about its premature destruction.

The principle of political life lies in the sovereign authority. While the legislative power is the heart of the state, the executive power is its brain, giving movement to all the parts. The brain can become paralyzed while the individual continues to live. A man may remain an imbecile and live, but as soon as the heart ceases to perform its function, the animal dies.

It is not by its laws that a state survives but by its legislative power. Yesterday's law is not binding today; but tacit consent is presumed from silence, and the sovereign authority is seen as constantly confirming the laws it could abrogate but does not. The state will always want whatever it has once declared it wants, unless it revokes its declaration.

Why, then, does one pay so much respect to ancient laws? Precisely because they are ancient. We must believe that there is nothing but the excellence of ancient acts of will that can have preserved them for such a long time. Had the sovereign authority not recognized them as consistently beneficial, it would have revoked them countless times. That is why in every well-constituted state the laws, far from growing weak, constantly gain new strength; a bias toward what is ancient makes them more venerable with every passing day, whereas wherever laws grow weak as they grow old, it is proof that there is no longer a legislative power and that the state is no longer viable.

CHAPTER XII:
ON HOW SOVEREIGN AUTHORITY
MAINTAINS ITSELF

The sovereign authority, having no other power than the legislative power, acts only by means of the laws; and as the laws are merely legitimate acts of the general will, the sovereign authority cannot act save when the people is assembled. "People assembling," you will say, "what a fantasy!" It might be a fantasy today, but it was not two thousand years ago. Has human nature changed?

The limits of the possible in moral matters are less narrow than we imagine: it is our weaknesses, vices, and prejudices that shrink them. Base souls do not believe in great men; contemptible slaves smile in mockery at the word *liberty*.

Let us consider what *can* be done by what *has* been done. I will not speak of the ancient republics of Greece; but the Roman Republic was, in my view, a great state, and the city of Rome a great city. The final census showed that in Rome there were four hundred thousand citizens who could bear arms, and the final population count of the Roman Empire showed more than four million citizens, not counting subject peoples, foreigners, women, children, and slaves.

What difficulty there must have been in frequently assembling the vast population of this capital and its surroundings! And yet few weeks passed without the Roman populace assembling, and assembling several times. The populace exercised not only the rights of sovereignty, but part of the rights of government as well. The populace discussed certain matters, tried certain cases, and assembled on the public square almost as often in the guise of magistrate as of citizen.

If we return to the earliest times of nations, we find that

most ancient governments, even monarchical ones such as those of the Macedonians and the Franks, had similar councils. Be that as it may, there is one indisputable fact that resolves all difficulties: surmising what is possible from what actually exists seems to me a sound proposition.

CHAPTER XIII:
ON HOW SOVEREIGN AUTHORITY
MAINTAINS ITSELF (CONTINUED)

It is not enough for the assembled populace to have once fixed the constitution of the state by giving its sanction to a body of laws; it is not enough for it to have established a perpetual government or arranged once and for all the election of magistrates. Apart from the extraordinary assemblies that unforeseen circumstances might require, there must be fixed, periodical assemblies that nothing can abolish or prolong, so that on the appointed day the people is legitimately summoned by law, without need of any further formal summoning.

But except for these assemblies that are official simply because the date has been fixed by law, every assembly of the people that has not been summoned by magistrates appointed for that purpose and in accordance with prescribed forms must be regarded as unlawful, and all its actions as void, because the order itself to assemble must emanate from the law.

As for the frequency with which the legitimate assemblies should meet, that depends on so many considerations that it is impossible to provide precise rules. One can say only in general that the more power a government has, the more frequently the sovereign authority should show itself.

I will be told that this might be fine for a single city, but what is to be done when the state includes several? Should the sovereign authority be divided among them, or should it be concentrated in a single city to which all the others are made subject?

My reply is that one should do neither the one nor the other. First, the sovereign authority is one and integral and cannot be divided without being destroyed. Second, no more can a city, than a nation, be legitimately subjected to another, because the essence of the body politic is in the accord of obedience and liberty, and because the terms *subject* and *sovereign authority* are identical correlatives, the concept of which is merged into the single word *citizen*.

I reply further that it is always bad to unite several towns into a single city, and should one want to make such a union, one should not flatter oneself that its natural disadvantages can be avoided. One should not present the malefactions of great states as a problem to one who wants only small states. But how are small states to be given enough power to resist big ones? The way the Greek cities once resisted the Great King, and the way more recently Holland and Switzerland have resisted the House of Austria.

However, if the state cannot be reduced to the proper limits, there still remains one resource: not to allow there to be any capital city, but to move the seat of government alternately from town to town, and thus also to assemble the different classes[118] of the country each in turn.

One must populate the territory evenly, extend the same rights throughout the territory, and spread abundance and life; that is how the state will become both strong and governed in the best possible way. Remember that the walls of cities are invariably built from the rubble of the houses of the countryside. For every palace I see raised in the capital, I see a whole country in ruins.

CHAPTER XIV:
ON HOW SOVEREIGN AUTHORITY
MAINTAINS ITSELF (CONTINUED)

The instant the people is legitimately gathered into a sovereign body, all governmental jurisdiction ceases, the executive power is suspended, and the person of the lowliest citizen is as sacrosanct and inviolable as that of the highest magistrate, because wherever the represented are, there is no longer a representative. Most of the turmoil in the Comitia in Rome arose either from ignorance of this rule or from its neglect. The consuls were then merely the presidents of the people, and the tribunes were simply speakers;[119] the Senate nothing at all.

These periods of suspension, during which the princely authority recognizes or should recognize an actual superior, have always alarmed it; and these assemblies of the people, which are the aegis of the body politic and a curb on the government, have at all times been dreaded by rulers, which is why rulers have always endeavored to make no end of objections, difficulties, and promises in order to keep citizens from having such assemblies. When the citizens are greedy, cowardly, and pusillanimous, favoring leisure over liberty, they cannot hold out long against the increased efforts of the government; it is in this way, with the resisting force constantly increasing, that the sovereign authority ultimately dissipates, and most cities fall and perish before their time.

But sometimes between the sovereign authority and arbitrary government an intermediary power intervenes, which must be discussed.

CHAPTER XV:
ON DEPUTIES OR REPRESENTATIVES

As soon as public service ceases to be the main concern of the citizens, and they prefer to serve through funds rather than through their person, the state is close to ruin. If there is a call to battle, they pay the troops and stay at home. If there is a summons to the council, they appoint deputies and stay at home. Because of idleness and money, they end by having soldiers enslave their country and representatives sell it.

It is the bustle of trade and craft, the avid pursuit of profit, and love of possessions and luxuriance, that change personal services into money. One yields a part of one's profit in order to have the leisure to increase it. Give money, and you will soon be in chains. The word *finance* is a word of slavery, unknown in the city.[120] In a state that is truly free, citizens do everything with their own hands and nothing by means of money: far from paying to be exempted from their duties, they pay to carry them out themselves. I am far from sharing the common view. I believe that taxes are more contrary to liberty than the *corvée*.[121]

The more soundly a state is constituted, the more public business takes precedence in the minds of the citizens over private business. There is even much less private business, because if the sum of the common happiness provides a greater portion to the happiness of each individual, there remains less for him to gain in private concerns. In a well-governed city everyone hurries to the assemblies; under a bad government no one has the slightest urge to attend them because no one is interested in what is done there, since people can foresee that the general will cannot prevail, and, finally, because private concerns dominate everything. Good laws lead to making better ones, bad laws lead to laws that are worse. As soon as anyone says about the affairs of the state "What do I care?" the state can be considered as lost.

The cooling of the love for one's country, the activity of private interest, the immense size of states, conquest, and the abuse of government have given rise to the idea of having deputies or representatives of the people in the assemblies of the nation. These are what in some countries they have dared call the Third Estate. Thus the private interest of two orders is put in first and second place, and the public interest comes third.

Sovereignty cannot be represented for the same reason that it cannot be transferred. It consists essentially in the general will, and the will cannot be represented: it is itself or it is something else, there is no middle ground. The deputies of the people are consequently not, nor can they be, its representatives, they are merely its agents. They cannot carry out any definitive acts. Any law that the people has not actually ratified is void; it is not a law. The people of England regards itself as free but is very much mistaken: it is free only during the election of the members of Parliament. As soon as they are elected, the people is enslaved and counts for nothing. The use the English people makes of its short moments of liberty shows that in fact it deserves to lose it.

The idea of representation is modern; it comes to us from feudal government, that iniquitous and absurd form of government that degrades the human race and dishonors the name of man. In the ancient republics, and even monarchies, the people never had representatives; the term itself was unknown. It is most remarkable that in Rome, where the tribunes were so sacrosanct, no one so much as imagined that they might usurp the functions of the people, and that in the midst of such a great multitude they never attempted to pass a single plebiscite on their own authority. But the trouble the masses sometimes caused can be gauged from what happened in the time of the Gracchi, when some of the citizens had to cast their votes from rooftops.

Where right and liberty are everything, restriction is nothing. The wise Romans gave everything its just value. They allowed their lictors to do what their tribunes would not have dared to do, as they did not fear that their lictors wanted to represent them.[122]

To explain, however, the way in which the tribunes sometimes represented the people, it suffices to understand how the government represents the sovereign authority. Since law is merely the declaration of the general will, it is clear that in regard to legislative power the people cannot be represented; but it can and must be represented in regard to executive power, which is merely force applied to law. This indicates that if one examines matters closely, one will find that very few nations have any laws. Be that as it may, it is certain that the tribunes, having no part of the executive power, could never represent the Roman people by the rights of their office but only by usurping the rights of the Senate.

Among the Greeks, the populace did for itself all it needed to do. It constantly assembled on the public square; it lived in a mild climate; it had no inherent greed; slaves did all the work; the people's great concern was its liberty. As we no longer have the same advantages, how can we preserve the same rights? Because of our harsher climate we have greater needs;[123] for half the year our public squares are unfit to gather in; our mumbling languages are not fit to be proclaimed in the open; we are more interested in our profit than our liberty, and less afraid of slavery than of poverty.

So is liberty to be maintained only by means of slavery? Perhaps. The two extremes meet. Everything that is not found freely in nature has its problems, civil society most of all. There are some unfortunate circumstances in which one cannot preserve one's liberty except at the expense of someone else's, and where the citizen can be completely free only if the slave is entirely a slave. Such was the case in Sparta. As for you, modern peoples, you have no slaves but are slaves yourselves; you pay for their liberty with yours. You pride yourselves in vain on this advantage—I find in it more cowardice than humanity.

I do not mean by this that one needs to have slaves, or that the right of slavery is legitimate, since I have proved the opposite. I am merely presenting the reasons why modern peoples that believe themselves to be free have representatives, and why ancient peoples did not. Be that as it may, the instant a people adopts representatives, it is no longer free; it no longer exists.

Weighing everything carefully, I do not see that it is any longer possible for the sovereign authority to preserve exercising its rights among us, unless the state is very small. But if it is very small, will it not be subjugated? It will not. I shall demonstrate elsewhere[124] how one can combine the external power of a great people with the simple administration and good order of a small state.

CHAPTER XVI:
ON THE INSTITUTION OF GOVERNMENT
NOT BEING A CONTRACT

Once the legislative power has been well established, the executive power must be established, too. Executive power, which operates only through individual acts, does not have the same essence as legislative power, and consequently is naturally separate from it. If it were possible for the sovereign authority as such to have executive power, right and fact would be so confounded that one could no longer tell what was law and what was not, and the body politic, thus denatured, would soon fall prey to the violence it was instituted to avert.

Since through the social contract all citizens are equal, they can all prescribe what all should do, whereas none has the right to demand that another should do what he does not do himself. But it is precisely this right, indispensable for giving the body politic life and movement, that the sovereign authority accords to the princely authority when it institutes the government.

Some have claimed that this act of establishing a government is a contract between the people and the leaders it has appointed, a contract in which conditions are stipulated between the two parties, under which the one binds itself to command and the other to obey. It will be agreed, I am sure, that this is quite a strange way of entering into a contract. But let us see if this opinion can be upheld.

First, the supreme authority can no more be modified than it can be transferred; to limit it is to destroy it. It is absurd and contradictory for the sovereign authority to set a superior over itself. To bind itself to obey a master is to return to complete liberty.

Furthermore, it is evident that a contract made between the people and this or that person is an individual act; from which it follows that such a contract can be neither a law nor an act of sovereignty, and would consequently be illegitimate.

It is also evident that under the law of nature alone, the contracting parties would be left to their own devices, without any guarantee of their reciprocal engagements, which in every way goes against the grain of the civil state. Since he who holds the power would always be the one to decide how the contract is to be executed, one could then call a contract any act in which one man says to another: "I give you everything I own, on condition that you give me back as much of it as you please."

There is only one contract in the state: that of association, which in itself excludes all others. One cannot conceive of any public contract that would not be a violation of this first contract.

CHAPTER XVII:
ON THE INSTITUTION OF GOVERNMENT

Under which terms, then, should one conceive of the act by which government is instituted? I will begin by saying that this act is complex, in other words, composed of two other acts: the establishing of the law and its execution.

By the first act, the sovereign authority determines that there will be a governing body established in this or that form; it is clear that this act is a law.

By the second act, the people appoints leaders who will be entrusted with the government that has been established. As this appointment is a particular act, it is not a second law but merely a consequence of the first and a function of government.

The difficulty is to understand how one can have an act of government before the government exists, and how in certain circumstances the people, which can be only sovereign or subject, can become prince or magistrate.

Here, however, we find one of those astonishing properties of the body politic by means of which it reconciles apparently contradictory operations. This is accomplished by a sudden conversion of sovereignty into democracy, so that without a perceptible change, and simply by virtue of a new relation of all to all, the citizens become magistrates and pass from general acts to particular acts, and from legislation to the execution of the law.

This change of relation is not merely speculative without example in practice: it takes place every day in the English Parliament, where on certain occasions the Lower House turns itself into a Committee of the Whole in order to better discuss affairs of state. It thus turns into a simple commission after having just a moment earlier been a sovereign court. Consequently it then reports to itself, as the House of Commons, what it has just settled as a Committee of the Whole, thus debating yet again under one title what it has already decided under another.

It is the distinctive advantage of a democratic government that it can be established by a simple act of the general will. Subsequently, if this form is adopted, the provisional government remains in power, or establishes in the name of the sovereign authority the government prescribed by law; and thus everything is in accordance with the rule. It is not possible to establish the government in any other legitimate manner and without renouncing the principles I have just presented.

CHAPTER XVIII:
ON THE MEANS OF PREVENTING USURPATIONS
BY THE GOVERNMENT

From these clarifications it follows, in confirmation of chapter XVI, that the act that establishes a government is not a contract but a law; that the trustees of the executive power are not the people's masters but its officers; that the people can appoint or dismiss these trustees whenever it pleases; that there is no question of the trustees entering into a contract, but of obeying, and that in taking on the functions that the state imposes on them they are simply fulfilling their duty as citizens without having, in any way, the right to challenge the conditions.

When, therefore, a people happens to institute a hereditary government, either monarchical and limited to one family or aristocratic and limited to a single class, the people is not making a commitment but merely giving the administration a provisional form until the people decides to reorganize it.[125]

It is true that such changes are always dangerous, and that one must never set about to change an established government except when it becomes incompatible with the public good; but this circumspection is a principle of policy and not a rule of right, and the state is no more bound to leave civil authority to its leaders than military authority to its generals.

It is also true that in such a case one must observe with the utmost care all the formalities necessary to distinguish a regular and legitimate act from a seditious uprising, and the will of a whole people from the clamor of one faction. It is here above all that one must give to any harmful case only what one cannot deny it according to the rigor of the law. And it is also from this obligation that the princely authority derives a great advantage in preserving its power despite the people, without it being possible to say it usurped it; for in appearing only to exercise its rights, it is very easy for the princely authority to extend them, and under the pretext of public peace to prevent the assemblies destined to reestablish order; accordingly the princely authority takes advantage of a silence it prevents from being broken, and of irregularities that it has instigated, to claim that it has the support of those whom fear has silenced, and to punish those who dare speak. This is how the Decemvirs, initially elected for one year and then kept in office for a second, strove to retain their power in perpetuity by not permitting the Comitia to assemble; and it is by this simple method that every government in the world, once vested with the public power, sooner or later usurps the sovereign authority.

The periodic assemblies of which I have already spoken[126] are suited to prevent or postpone this calamity, above all if they do not require a formal convocation; for then the princely authority is unable to stop them without openly declaring itself a violator of the law and an enemy of the state.

The opening of these assemblies, whose only object is the maintenance of the social treaty, should always take place with two questions that may not be suppressed and should be voted on separately.

The first: "Does it please the sovereign authority to preserve the present form of government?"

The second: "Does it please the people to leave the administration to those who are currently charged with it?"

I am presupposing here what I believe I have demonstrated: that there is not any fundamental law in the state that cannot be revoked, not even the social pact; for if all the citizens assemble in common accord in order to break this pact, there is no doubt that it would be legitimately broken. Grotius even thinks that everyone can renounce the state of which he is a member and on leaving the country recover his natural liberty and belongings.[127] But it would be absurd if all the citizens in unison could not do what each of them can do separately.

BOOK IV

CHAPTER I:
ON THE GENERAL WILL BEING INDESTRUCTIBLE

As long as several men gathered together regard themselves as a single body, they have only a single will that is directed to their common preservation and general well-being. In that case, all the vigor of the state is energetic and simple, its principles clear and transparent; there are no entangled or conflicting interests; the common good is clearly apparent everywhere, and only good sense is needed to perceive it. Peace, unity, and equality are the enemies of political intrigue. Men who are upright and simple are difficult to deceive because of their simplicity: snares and sophisticated ploys do not mislead them, for they are not subtle enough to be dupes. When one sees among the happiest people in the world bands of peasants running the affairs of state beneath an oak tree, and always proceeding wisely, can one refrain from scorning the intricacies of other nations that make themselves illustrious and wretched with so much artfulness and secrecy?

A state governed in this way needs very few laws; and as it becomes necessary to promulgate new ones, the necessity is universally understood. The first man to propose new laws merely says what all have already felt, and there is no question of eloquence or canvassing in order to make a law of what every individual has already resolved to do as soon as he is sure that the rest will do as he does.

What misleads rationalists is that as they see only states that have been badly constituted from the beginning, they are struck by the impossibility of maintaining such a political system. They laugh to think of all the foolish deeds by which a clever rogue or insinuating speaker can persuade the people of Paris or London. They do not know that Cromwell would have been condemned to hard labor by the people of Berne, or the Duc de Beaufort sent to a reformatory by the Genevans.[128]

But when the social bond begins to loosen and the state grows weak, when individual interests begin to make themselves felt and the small societies influence the larger one, the common interest deteriorates and meets with opposition: votes are no longer unanimous, and the general will is no longer the will of all. Contradictions and arguments arise, and the best opinion is not accepted without dispute.

Finally, when the state, close to ruin, subsists only in an illusory and futile form, when the social bond is severed in every heart and the meanest interest brazenly adorns itself with the sacred name of the public good, the general will falls silent: all individuals, guided by secret motives, express their position as citizens no more than if the state had never existed, and iniquitous decrees are falsely passed with private interest as their only aim.

Does it follow from this that the general will is destroyed or corrupted? It does not. The general will is always constant, unalterable, and pure; but it is subordinated to other wills that prevail over it. Each individual, detaching his interest from the common interest, sees clearly that he cannot separate them entirely; but his share in the public burden seems nothing to him compared to the exclusive advantage that he aims to seize for himself. Apart from this personal advantage, he has in his own interest as strong a desire for the public advantage as anyone else. Even if he sells his vote for money, he does not quell the general will within himself, but only avoids it. The error he commits is that of changing the nature of the question, and answering something other than what he is asked. Instead of saying with his vote, "It is advantageous to the state," he says, "It is advantageous to this man or that party that such-and-such a view should pass." Consequently, the law of public order in assemblies is not so much to maintain in these assemblies the general will as to ensure that questions will always be put to them, and that they will always respond.

I could present many reflections here on the simple right of voting in every act of sovereignty, a right that no one can take from the citizens, and also on the right of stating opinions, of making proposals, and of assembling and discussing, which the government always takes great care to allow only its members.[129] But this important subject would require a separate treatise, and I cannot say everything in this one.

CHAPTER II:
ON VOTING

We see from the previous chapter that the manner in which general affairs are conducted can provide a clear indication of the actual state of the mores and health of the body politic. The greater the degree of accord in the assemblies—that is, the closer to unanimous opinions are—the greater is also the dominance of the general will. But long debates, dissensions, and clamor indicate the ascendancy of private interests and the decline of the state.

This seems less clear when two or more orders enter into the state's constitution, as did in Rome the patricians and the plebeians, whose quarrels often disrupted the Comitia even in the best days of the Republic. But this exception is less real than apparent, for in such a case, through the defect inherent in the body politic, one could say that there are two states in one, and what is not true of the two together is true of each separately. In fact, even in the stormiest times the plebiscites of the people were always calmly passed, and by large majorities, when the Senate did not interfere. The citizens having but one interest, the people had but one will.

At the other extremity of the circle, unanimity returns. This is when citizens who have fallen into servitude have neither liberty nor will. Fear and flattery change votes into acclamations; people no longer deliberate, they only praise or curse. Such was the base manner in which the Senate acted under the emperors. Sometimes this was done with ridiculous precautions: Tacitus observes that under Otho, the senators, while heaping curses on Vitellius, contrived at the same time to make a great deal of noise so that if, by chance, he ever became their master he would not know what each of them had said.[130]

From these diverse considerations arise the principles by which the methods of counting votes and comparing opinions should be regulated, and according to which the general will is more or less easy to discover, and the state more or less in decline.

There is only one law that, by its nature, demands unanimous consent: the social pact. For civil association is the most voluntary act in the world; since every man is born free and his own master, no one can subject him without his consent under any pretext. To determine that the son of a slave is born a slave is to determine that he is not born a man.

If, then, at the time the social pact is made there are opponents, their opposition does not invalidate the contract but only prevents them from being included in it. They are outsiders among the citizens. When the state is instituted, residence constitutes consent; residing within a territory is to submit to its sovereignty.[131]

Except for this original contract, the vote of the majority always binds everyone else: it is a consequence of the contract itself. But one asks how a man can be both free and forced to conform to wills that are not his. How are the opponents both free and subject to laws to which they have not consented?

I reply that the question is wrongly put. A citizen consents to all the laws, even those that have been passed in spite of his opposition, or those that punish him should he dare to violate any of them. The basic will of all the members of the state is the general will, and it is through this will that they are citizens and free.[132] When a law is proposed in the assembly of the people, the people is not exactly being asked whether it approves or rejects the proposal, but whether the proposal does or does not conform with the general will, which is its will. Each man, in giving his vote, states his opinion on that point, and from counting the votes the declaration of the general will is derived. When, therefore, an opinion contrary to mine prevails, this simply proves that I was mistaken, and that what I had believed to be the general will was not. Had my individual opinion prevailed, I would have done something other than what was my will; then I would not have been free.

This does presuppose that all the characteristics of the gen-

eral will are still to be found in the majority: once they no longer are, then whatever side one takes, liberty is no longer
possible.

In showing earlier how individual wills were substituted for
the general will in public deliberations, I sufficiently indicated
the practicable ways of preventing this abuse, and I will have
more to say about this later. I have also provided the principles
with which one can determine the proportional number of
votes for declaring this general will. The difference of a single
vote disrupts equality; a single opponent destroys unanimity:
but between unanimity and equality there are several divisions
that are unequal, the number of each of which can be fixed according to the condition and needs of the body politic.

Two general principles can serve to regulate these relationships. The first is that the more important and weighty deliberations are, the closer the prevailing opinion should be to
unanimity. The second is that the more the matter at hand calls
for speed, the narrower the prescribed difference in the division of opinions should be. Yet in deliberations that must be
concluded immediately, a majority of one vote should suffice.
The first of these two principles seems better suited to the laws,
and the second to public affairs. Be that as it may, it is in combining the two principles that the best relationship for determining the majority can be established.

CHAPTER III:
ON ELECTIONS

With regard to the elections of the princely authority and the
magistrates, which are, as I have said,[133] complex acts, there are
two ways one can proceed: by choice or by lot. Both have been

used in various republics, and a very complicated mixture of the two can still be found in the election of the Doge of Venice.

"Election by lot," says Montesquieu, "is in the nature of democracy." I agree; but in what way? "Lot is a way of electing that does not upset anyone," he continues. "It gives every citizen a reasonable hope of serving his country."[134]

But these are not valid reasons. If one bears in mind that the election of rulers is a function of government and not of sovereignty, one will see why the path of the lot is more in the nature of democracy, where the administration is better in proportion as its acts are less numerous. However, in every true democracy, magistracy is not an advantage but an onerous burden that cannot be justly imposed on one individual rather than another. Only the law can lay the burden on him to whom the lot falls. For then, the conditions being equal for all and the choice not depending on any human will, there is no particular application that will alter the universality of the law.

In aristocracy, the prince chooses the prince, the government preserves the government, and that is where suffrage is appropriate.

The example of the election of the Doge of Venice, far from negating this distinction, confirms it: this mixed form suits a mixed government. For it is a mistake to consider the government of Venice a true aristocracy: though the people has no share in the government, the nobility is the people itself. A multitude of poor Barnabites[135] has never achieved magistracy, and the only benefit it has from its being noble is the empty title of "Excellency" and the right of presence at the Great Council. As this Great Council is as numerous as our General Council in Geneva, its illustrious members do not have more privileges than do our simple citizens. If we set aside the extreme disparity between the two republics, it is clear that the bourgeoisie of Geneva corresponds exactly to the patriciate of Venice. Our local people and inhabitants correspond to the townsmen and the people of Venice, and our peasants correspond to the subjects on Venice's mainland. But however one views the Republic of Venice, notwithstanding its size, its government is not more aristocratic than ours. The only difference is that as we do not have rulers for life, we do not, like Venice, have a need for elections by lot.

There would be few disadvantages in elections by lot in a true democracy, where, everyone being as equal in mores and talents as in principles and fortunes, it would make almost no difference who was elected. But I have already said[136] that there is no such thing as true democracy.

When elections by choice and lot are both used, positions that require specific skills, such as military positions, should be filled by elections of choice, while elections by lot are more suitable for filling positions in which good sense, justice, and integrity are sufficient, such as the judicial offices; because in a well-constituted state these qualities are common to all citizens.

Neither lots nor elections have any place in a monarchical government. The monarch being by right the sole prince and only magistrate, the choice of his lieutenants belongs to him alone. When the Abbé de Saint-Pierre proposed that the Councils of the King of France should be increased and their members elected by ballot, he did not realize that he was proposing to change the form of government.[137]

It remains for me to speak of the way of casting and collecting votes in the assembly of the people; but perhaps the history of the Roman polity in this matter will better clarify all the principles that I could establish. It is not unworthy of a judicious reader to follow in some detail the manner in which public and private affairs were conducted in a council consisting of two hundred thousand men.

CHAPTER IV:
ON THE ROMAN COMITIA[138]

We have no truly reliable records of Rome's earliest times; it even seems likely that most of the things related about it are fables.[139] Generally speaking, the most instructive part of the annals of a people, the history of its foundation, is the part that we most lack. Experience teaches us every day what gives rise to the revolutions of empires, but as no new peoples are now being established, we have little beyond conjecture to explain how a people comes to be.

The customs we find prevailing at least attest that they had an origin. Among traditions that go back to those origins, the ones supported by the greatest authorities and confirmed by the strongest reasons ought to pass for the most certain. These are the principles I have striven to follow in inquiring how the freest and most powerful people on earth exercised its supreme power.

After the foundation of Rome, the nascent republic—that is to say, the army of Romulus its founder, which was composed of Albans, Sabines, and foreigners—was divided into three classes, which through this division took the name *tribus,* "tribe." Each of these tribes was subdivided into ten Curiae, and each Curia into Decuriae, at the head of which were placed leaders called Curiones and Decuriones.

Beyond this, a body of a hundred *equites,* or horsemen, was drawn from each tribe and given the name Centuria, which shows that these divisions, hardly necessary in a town, were at first only military. But it seems that an instinct for greatness led the little town of Rome to provide itself in advance with a political organization that was suited to its becoming the capital of the world.

This first division soon led to a disadvantage, namely, that the tribe of the Albans and that of the Sabines always remained the same size, while that of the foreigners kept growing with the constant converging of more foreigners on Rome, so that before long it surpassed the others. Servius' remedy for this dangerous fault was to change the manner of division, abolishing the division by origin and substituting one based on the district of the town that was inhabited by each tribe. Instead of three tribes, Servius created four, each occupying one of the hills of Rome and bearing its name. Consequently, in remedying the existing inequality he also provided for the future; and so that the division was not only of districts but of men, he forbade the inhabitants of one district to move to another, thus preventing the merging of the different peoples.

Servius also doubled the three ancient Centuriae of horsemen and added twelve more, keeping, however, the ancient names, a simple and prudent method by which he succeeded in distinguishing between the body of horsemen and the people without sparking unrest in the latter.

To these four urban tribes Servius added fifteen more, called rural tribes because they were made up of those who lived in the country, divided into fifteen districts. Subsequently, fifteen further tribes were created, and the Roman people found itself divided into thirty-five tribes, a number that remained fixed until the end of the Republic.

This distinction between urban and rural tribes had one effect that is worth noting, because there is no other example of the kind, and because Rome owed to it both the preservation of its mores and the growth of its empire. One would have expected that the urban tribes would soon have arrogated to themselves power and honors, and would have lost no time in demeaning the rural tribes. But exactly the opposite happened. The taste of the early Romans for country life is well known, a taste they owed to their wise founder, who associated rural and military labors with liberty, and relegated to the city, so to speak, crafts, professions, intrigue, fortune, and slavery.

Thus, since all of Rome's most illustrious men lived in the country and cultivated the soil, people grew used to seeking only in the country the mainstay of the Republic. Since this condition was that of the worthiest patricians, it was honored by everyone; the simple and hardworking life of villagers was preferred to the indolent and idle life of the townspeople of Rome; and he who might have been merely a miserable proletarian in the town became a respected citizen in working the fields. It is not without reason, said Varro, that our high-minded ancestors made those villages the seedbeds of the sturdy and valiant men who defended them in time of war and fed them in time of peace. Pliny states plainly that the rural tribes were honored because of the men who composed them, whereas cowards they wanted to demean were transferred in disgrace to the town tribes. Appius Claudius the Sabine, having come to settle in Rome, was heaped there with honors and enrolled in a rural tribe that subsequently took his family name. Furthermore, freedmen always entered the urban tribes, never the rural ones, and throughout the Republic there is not a single example of a freedman attaining any magistracy, despite his having become a citizen.

This principle was excellent, but it was carried so far that ultimately it led to a change that was definitely a failing in the polity.

First, the censors, after having long before arrogated to themselves the right to transfer citizens arbitrarily from one tribe to another, permitted most of them to enroll in whatever tribe they pleased, a permission that certainly served no purpose and robbed the censor's office of one of its greatest means. Moreover, as all the great and powerful enrolled in the rural tribes, while the freedmen who had become citizens remained with the populace in the tribes of the town, the tribes in general soon ceased to have any local or territorial meaning. They all ended up so intermingled that the members of the different tribes could no longer be distinguished except through the registers, so that the idea of the word "tribe" passed from property to person, or rather ended up as little more than an illusion.

It also happened that the town tribes, being closer at hand, were often the most powerful in the Comitia and sold the state to whoever stooped so low as to buy the votes of the rabble that made up these tribes.

As for the Curiae, since Romulus had set up ten in each tribe, the whole Roman people, in those days enclosed within the city walls, was composed of thirty Curiae, each with its own temples, gods, officers, and priests, and with its own festivals, called *compitalia*, which corresponded to the *paganalia* later held by the rural tribes.

Since in the new division under Servius the number of thirty could not be divided equally among the four tribes he had instituted, and since he did not want to modify them, the Curiae became a further division of the inhabitants of Rome, independent of the tribes. But there was no question of there being Curiae among the rural tribes or the people who composed them since the military divisions of Romulus were found to be superfluous. The tribes had become a purely civil institution, and a different policy of levying troops had been introduced.

Thus, although every citizen was enrolled in a tribe, many were not members of a Curia.

Servius made yet a third division that had no connection to the two I have mentioned, which became, through its effect, the most important of all. He divided all the people of Rome into six classes, which he distinguished not by location or persons but by property, so that the first class consisted of the rich, the last of the poor, and the middle classes of people of moderate means. These six classes were subdivided into a hundred and ninety-three other bodies called Centuriae, and these bodies were distributed in such a way that the first class alone comprised more than half of them, and the last only one. Thus it happened that the class with the smallest number of men, the third, had the largest number of Centuriae, and the entire last class, the poor, counted only as a single subdivision, though it alone contained more than half the inhabitants of Rome. So that the people would be less aware of the consequences of this last subdivision, Servius endeavored to give the system a military air: he inserted two Centuriae of armorers into the second class, and two Centuriae of makers of weapons of war into the fourth. In each class, except for the last, he made a distinction between young and old, that is to say, those who were obliged to bear arms and those whose age exempted them by law, a distinction which, more than that of wealth, gave rise to a need for frequently taking a new census or count. Lastly, Servius wanted the assembly to be held in the Campus Martius, and all who were of age to serve in the army were to bring their weapons.

The reason he did not adopt the same division of young and old for this last class was that the poor populace composing it was not accorded the honor of bearing arms for its country: a man had to have a hearth in order to obtain the right to defend it, and of the countless troops of wretches who today populate the armies of kings, there is perhaps not a single man who would not have been driven out from a Roman cohort with contempt, in an era when soldiers were the defenders of liberty.

A further distinction in this poorest class was made between the *proletarians* and those called the *capite censi*. The former, not entirely reduced to penury, at least gave the state citizens, and in times of pressing need even soldiers. As for those who had nothing at all and could be counted only by heads, they were regarded as absolutely worthless, Marius being the first who condescended to enroll them.

Without deciding here whether this third count was good or bad in itself, I believe I may affirm that what made this practicable was the original Romans' simple mores, fair-mindedness, love of agriculture, and their scorn for commerce or the keen pursuit of wealth. Where is the modern people whose consuming greed, restless spirit, intrigue, and perpetual moving about and change of fortune would allow such an institution to last for twenty years without overturning the whole state? We must indeed observe that in Rome, morality and the office of censor, being stronger than this institution, corrected its defects, and that the rich man found himself relegated to the class of the poor for making too great a display of his wealth.

From all this it is easy to understand why only five classes have almost always been mentioned, though there were really six. The sixth class was rarely taken into account, as it provided neither soldiers for the army nor voters for the Campus Martius,[140] and was almost of no use to the state.

Such were the different divisions of the Roman people. Let us now see the effect they had on the assemblies. When these assemblies were legitimately convened they were called Comitia. They usually took place in the Roman Forum or the Campus Martius, and were distinguished as Comitia Curiata, Comitia Centuriata, and Comitia Tributa, according to the three forms under which they were organized. The Comitia Curiata were founded by Romulus, the Comitia Centuriata by Servius, and the Comitia Tributa by the tribunes of the people. No law was sanctioned and no magistrate elected except in the Comitia, and as every citizen was enrolled in a Curia, a Centuria, or a tribe, it follows that no citizen was excluded from the right to vote, and that the Roman people was truly sovereign in law and in fact.

Three conditions were necessary for the Comitia to be lawfully assembled and for their actions to have the force of law: first, that the body or magistrate calling them together possess the necessary authority; second, that the assembly be held on a day permitted by law; and third, that the auguries be favorable.

The reason for the first regulation needs no explanation; the second is an administrative matter; consequently, the Comitia were not allowed to be held on feast or market days when people from the country, coming to Rome on business, did not have time to spend the day in the public square. By means of the third regulation, the Senate held a proud and restive people in check, tempering the ardor of seditious tribunes, though these found more than one way of evading this constraint.

The laws and the election of leaders were not the only matters submitted to the judgment of the Comitia. Since the Roman people had appropriated the most important functions of government, one could say that the fate of Europe was decided in its assemblies. The variety of objectives gave rise to the various forms the assemblies took, according to the matters on which they had to pronounce.

In order to evaluate these various forms, it is enough to compare them. When Romulus established the Curiae, he had in view the checking of the Senate by the people, and the people by the Senate, while ruling over both. This way he gave the people all the authority of numbers in order to balance the authority of power and riches that he left to the patricians. However, in keeping with the spirit of monarchy, Romulus left a greater advantage to the patricians in the influence of their Clients on the majority of votes. This admirable institution of Patrons and Clients was a masterpiece of policy and humanity without which the patriciate, so contrary to the spirit of the Republic, could not have survived. Rome alone has had the honor of giving to the world this fine example, which never gave rise to any abuse, but which nonetheless has never been followed.

As this same form of Curiae continued to exist under the kings until the time of Servius, the reign of the last Tarquin not having been regarded as legitimate, royal laws were generally called *Leges Curiatae*.

Under the Republic, the Curiae, still limited to the four urban tribes and including only the populace of Rome, suited neither the Senate that led the patricians nor the tribunes, who, though they were plebeians, led the affluent citizens. Therefore the Curiae fell into discredit, and their degradation was such that their thirty assembled lictors did what the Comitia Curiata should have done.

The division by Centuriae was so favorable to the aristocracy that it is hard at first to see how the Senate did not always prevail in the Comitia that bore this name and that elected the consuls, censors, and other *curule* magistrates. In fact, of the hundred and ninety-three Centuriae that formed the six classes of the whole Roman people, the first class contained ninety-eight, and as the voting went only by Centuriae, this first class by itself had a majority of votes over all the rest. When the members of the Centuriae of the first class were in agreement, the rest of the votes were not even collected; the decision of the smallest number passed for the decision of the multitude, and matters in the Comitia Centuriata could be said to have been regulated rather by a majority of coins than a majority of votes.

But this extreme authority was tempered in two ways: first, as the tribunes were usually in the class of the rich, and a great number of plebeians always, they counterbalanced the influence of the patricians in this first class. Second, instead of having the Centuriae vote according to their order, which would have meant always beginning with the first, one of them was always chosen by lot, and that one[141] proceeded alone to the election; after which all the Centuriae, summoned on another day according to their rank, repeated the same election, and as a rule confirmed it. This way the authority of example was taken away from rank and given to the lot, according to the principle of democracy.

This practice resulted in a further advantage: the citizens from the country had time, between the two elections, to inform themselves of the merits of the candidate who had been provisionally nominated, and consequently they could cast their votes informed. But on the pretext of expediting the vote this custom was abolished, and both elections were held on the same day.

The Comitia Tributa were in reality the Council of the Roman people. They could be convoked only by the tribunes. It was there that the tribunes were elected and passed their *plebiscita*. Not only did the Senate have no standing in the Comitia Tributa, but it did not even have the right to be present, and the senators, forced to obey laws on which they had not been able to vote, were in this respect less free than the lowliest citizens. This injustice was quite misguided, and was in itself enough to invalidate the decrees of a body to which not all members were admitted. Even if all the patricians had been allowed to participate in these Comitia by virtue of their right as citizens, as simple individuals they would scarcely have influenced a form of voting that counted heads, where the lowliest proletarian had as much say as the leader of the Senate.

It is therefore evident that beyond the order resulting from these various arrangements for gathering the votes of so numerous a people, these distributions did not deteriorate into forms immaterial in themselves, but each form had effects relative to the views that caused them to be preferred.

Without going into greater detail about this, it follows from the clarifications I have just made that the Comitia Tributa were the most favorable to a democracy, and the Centuriata to aristocracy. As for the Comitia Curiata, in which the populace of Rome formed a majority, since all they were good for was to favor tyranny and evil designs, the Comitia inevitably fell into disrepute, and even seditious factions avoided using means that exposed their schemes too clearly. It is certain that all the majesty of the Roman people lay solely in the Comitia Centuriata, which included everyone: the Comitia Curiata lacked the rural tribes, and the Comitia Tributa lacked the Senate and the patricians.

As for the manner of collecting the votes, among the early Romans it was as simple as their mores, though still less simple than in Sparta. Each man declared his vote aloud, a scribe writing it down; a majority of votes in each tribe determined the vote of the tribe, and the majority of votes among the tribes determined that of the people; the same was true for the Curiae and the Centuriae. This practice was good as long as honesty prevailed among the citizens and each man was ashamed to cast his vote publicly in favor of an unjust proposal or an unworthy candidate; but when the people grew corrupt and votes were bought, it was thought more fitting to cast votes in secret so that those who wanted to purchase votes would not know whom to trust, thus forcing rogues not to be traitors.

I know that Cicero criticizes this change, to some extent attributing to it the ruin of the Republic. But though I respect the weight that Cicero's authority should have here, I cannot agree with him; I believe on the contrary that the loss of the state was hastened by the lack of enough such changes. Just as the regimen of the healthy is not appropriate for the sick, one must not seek to govern a corrupted people by laws suitable to a good people. There is no better proof of this principle than the Republic of Venice, the shadow of which still exists, this state owing its longevity solely to the fact that its laws are suited only to wicked men.

Writing tablets were therefore distributed to the citizens, by which means each man could vote without anyone knowing his opinion. New formalities were also established for gathering these tablets, counting votes, compiling the results, and so on, which did not prevent the trustworthiness of the officers who were assigned these functions[142] often coming under suspicion. Finally, to prevent intrigues and the trafficking of votes, edicts were issued, but their sheer number proves how useless they were.

Toward the end of the Republic, the Romans had to resort quite often to extraordinary measures in order to make up for the inadequacy of the laws. Sometimes miracles were feigned, but this ploy, which might have tricked the people, could not trick those who governed. Sometimes an assembly was suddenly called together before the candidates had time to intrigue, at other times an entire session was taken up with speeches when it was evident that the people had been deceived and were about to pass a bad resolution. But ultimately ambition overcame everything, and what is incredible is that in the midst of all these abuses such a vast people, by virtue of its ancient regulations, still managed to elect magistrates, pass laws, judge cases, and expedite private and public affairs almost as easily as the Senate itself might have done.

CHAPTER V:
ON THE TRIBUNATE

When one cannot establish an exact proportion between the constituent parts of the state, or when persistent causes continually assail the relationship of these parts with one another, one must institute a special magistracy that is not incorporated with the rest. This magistracy must restore each term to its true relation, and provide a link or middle term between either the princely authority and the people, or the princely authority and the sovereign authority, or, if necessary, both at the same time.

This body, which I shall call the *tribunate,* is the preserver of the laws and of the legislative power. It serves sometimes to protect the sovereign authority against the government, as the tribunes of the people did in Rome, and sometimes to uphold the government against the people, as the Council of Ten now does in Venice; and sometimes to maintain the balance between the two, as the Ephors did in Sparta.[143]

The tribunate is not a constituent part of the city and should not have any share in either legislative or executive power; and yet it is precisely this that makes its own power all the greater, for though it can do nothing, it can prevent everything. As the defender of the laws, it is more sacred and more revered than the princely authority that executes them or the sovereign authority that makes them. This was seen very clearly in Rome, when the proud patricians, who always had contempt for the populace as a whole, were forced to bow before a simple official of the people who had neither auspices nor jurisdiction.

A tribunate that is wisely tempered is a good constitution's strongest support; but if its power ever becomes even a little too excessive, it overturns everything. Weakness is not in its nature, and provided there is a tribunate, it is never weaker than it should be. It degenerates into tyranny when it usurps the executive power, of which it is only the moderator, and when it seeks to administer laws that it ought only to protect. The immense power of the Ephors, which was not dangerous as long as Sparta preserved its mores, hastened corruption once it had begun. The blood of Agis, slaughtered by these tyrants, was avenged by his successor: the crime and the punishment of the Ephors both hastened the fall of the republic, and after Cleomenes, Sparta ceased being of any account. Rome, too, perished in the same way, the excessive power of the tribunes, which had been usurped by decree, ultimately serving, with the help of laws made for liberty, to shield emperors who were destroying liberty. As for Venice's Council of Ten, it is a tribunal of blood, an equal horror to patricians and people alike, and which, far from loftily protecting the laws, is no longer of any use since the laws have been debased, except, under the cloak of darkness, to strike blows of which no one dares take note.

The tribunate, like the government, grows weak as the number of its members increases. When the tribunes of the Roman people, who at first numbered two and then five, wanted to double their number, the Senate let them do so, certain that it could check some of the tribunes by means of the others, which is exactly what happened.

The best means for preventing usurpations by so formidable a body—a means that no government has yet considered using—would be not to make that body permanent, but to establish periods during which it would remain suspended. These periods, which should not be long enough to allow abuses time to strike root, could be fixed by law so that they could easily be shortened as needed by extraordinary commissions.

This procedure seems to me to have no disadvantages, because, as I have said, the tribunate does not form part of the constitution and can be removed without the constitution's being harmed. It furthermore strikes me as effective, because a newly established magistrate does not start out with the power his predecessor had, but with the power the law grants him.

CHAPTER VI:
ON DICTATORSHIP

The inflexibility of laws, which prevents them from being adapted to circumstances, can in certain cases render them destructive, and in a crisis bring about the ruin of the state. The law's methods and slowness of procedure require an amount of time that circumstances sometimes do not allow. Countless situations can arise for which the legislator has made no provision, and being aware that one cannot foresee everything is a vital foresight.

One should not, therefore, seek to make political institutions so rigid as to negate the power to suspend their action. Even Sparta allowed for its laws to be suspended.

But only the greatest dangers can counterbalance the danger of compromising the public order, and one should never suppress the sacred power of the laws except when the safety of the state is at stake. In such rare and manifest cases, provision is made for public security by a special act that entrusts this security to the most worthy man. This commission can be given in two ways, according to the kind of danger that is being faced.

If, as a remedy, it is sufficient to increase the activity of the government, one must concentrate the government in the hands of one or two of its members. In this case it is not the authority of the laws one is affecting, but only the form of how the laws are to be administered. But if the peril is such that the apparatus of the law is an obstacle to the security of the state, one must nominate a supreme leader who can overrule all the laws and for a period suspend the sovereign authority. In such a case, the general will is not in doubt, as it is clear that the foremost intention of the people is that the state not perish. In this way the suspension of the legislative authority does not abolish it. The magistrate who is silencing it cannot make it speak; he overrules it without being able to represent it. He can do anything, except make laws.

The first method was used by the Roman Senate when, by means of a consecrated set of rules, it directed the consuls to provide for the safety of the Republic; the second method was used when one of the two consuls nominated a dictator,[144] a custom for which Alba had provided Rome the example.

At the beginning of the Roman Republic there was frequent recourse to dictatorship, because the state did not yet have a firm enough foundation to maintain itself through the power of its constitution alone. As mores in those days rendered superfluous many of the precautions that would have been necessary in another era, there was no fear that a dictator would abuse his authority or seek to retain it beyond its term. On the contrary, it seemed that such great power was a burden to him in whom it was vested, judging by the haste with which dictators tried to divest themselves of it, as if taking the place of the laws was too difficult and perilous a position to maintain.

Hence it is not so much the danger of the dictatorship's being abused as of its being degraded that leads me to criticize the incautious use of this supreme magistracy in the early days of the Roman Republic. Since the dictatorship was freely used at elections, at temple consecrations, and in matters of mere formality, there was danger of the dictatorship's becoming less formidable in times of need, the people having become accustomed to regarding it as a mere title used only at insignificant ceremonies.

Toward the end of the Republic, the Romans, having become more circumspect, were as unreasonably sparing in the use of dictatorship as they had previously been lavish. It is easy to see that their fears were groundless; that the weakness of the capital secured it against the magistrates who were within it, that a dictator could, in certain cases, defend public liberty without being able to violate it, and that Rome's chains would be forged not in Rome itself but in its armies. The scant resistance offered by Marius to Sulla, and Pompey to Caesar, indicated clearly what was to be expected from internal authority in the face of external force.

This error led the Romans to make great mistakes, such as, for example, not appointing a dictator in the Catiline conspiracy.[145] This conspiracy had been merely an internal matter within Rome itself, extending at most to some Italian province. Thus the unlimited authority that the laws gave the dictator would have allowed him to dispose with ease of the conspiracy, which was subsequently crushed only by a series of lucky coincidences that human prudence should never expect.

Instead, the Senate contented itself with handing its whole

power over to the consuls, with the result that, in order to take effective action, Cicero was compelled to exceed his powers on a capital point; and though in the first transports of public rejoicing, Cicero's conduct was praised, he was later justly called to account for the blood of citizens spilled in violation of the laws, a reproach that could not have been leveled at a dictator. But Cicero's eloquence swept all before it, and he himself, despite being a Roman, loved his own glory more than his country, and sought not so much the most legitimate and sure means of saving the state but the means that would garner him all the honor of the affair.[146] Cicero was therefore justly honored as liberator of Rome, and justly punished as infringer of its laws. However triumphant his recall from exile may have been, it was undoubtedly an act of pardon.

Furthermore, whatever the manner in which the important commission of dictatorship is conferred, it is vital to limit its duration to a very brief term that can never be extended. In crises that lead to the establishing of a dictatorship, the state is either quickly destroyed or quickly saved; and once the pressing need has passed, a dictatorship becomes either tyrannical or of no use. As dictators in Rome held office for only six months, most abdicated before their term ended. If their term had been longer, they might have been tempted to extend it even further, as the Decemvirs did their one-year term. The dictator had only time to provide for the emergency that had led to his being elected; he had no time to embark on further ventures.

CHAPTER VII:
ON THE CENSOR

Just as the law represents the general will, the censor represents the opinion of the public.[147] Public opinion is the type of law of which the censor is minister, and which it applies only to particular cases in the same way that the princely authority does.

Thus the censorial tribunal, far from being the arbiter of the people's opinion, merely declares it, and the instant it departs from this function its decisions are empty and ineffectual.

It is useless to differentiate between the mores of a nation and the objects of its esteem, for all these things are linked to the same principle and are necessarily mingled. Among all the peoples of the world, it is not nature that determines the choice of their pleasures, but opinion. Set men's opinions on the right path, and their mores will purify themselves of their own accord. People always love what is good, or what they consider good, but in judging what is good, people err. It is this judgment, therefore, that must be addressed. Whoever judges morality judges honor, and whoever judges honor derives his law from opinion.

The opinions of a people arise from its constitution. Although the law does not regulate mores, it is legislation that engenders them. When legislation weakens, mores degenerate, but then the judgment of the censors will not do what the power of the laws has not done.

It follows from this that the censor may be useful for the preservation of mores but never for restoring them. Establish censors while the laws are vigorous: as soon as they have lost their vigor, there is no hope; nothing legitimate has any power anymore once the laws no longer have power.

The censor maintains mores by preventing opinion from becoming corrupt, by preserving its integrity through wise application, and sometimes even by defining opinion when it is still uncertain. The use of seconds in duels, taken to extremes in the Kingdom of France, was abolished by the mere words of a royal edict: "as for those who have the cowardice to call upon seconds." This judgment, anticipating that of the public, immediately determined it. But when the same edicts sought to pronounce dueling itself an act of cowardice, which is quite true but contrary to common opinion, the public ridiculed the pronouncement, upon which its judgment had already been formed.

I have said elsewhere[148] that as public opinion is not subject to constraint, there should be no vestige of it in the tribunal established to represent it. One cannot praise highly enough the skill with which this, which has been lost among the moderns, was employed by the Romans, and even more by the Lacedaemonians.

In the Council of Sparta, when a man of bad character put forward a good suggestion, the Ephors disregarded it but had the same suggestion put forward by a virtuous citizen. What an honor for the one, and what a disgrace for the other, without either praise or blame having been bestowed on either of them! Some drunkards from Samos[149] once defiled the tribunal of the Ephors: the following day, a public edict gave Samians permission to misbehave. A true punishment would have been less severe than impunity of this kind. When Sparta pronounced on what is or is not right, Greece did not challenge its judgments.

CHAPTER VIII:
ON CIVIL RELIGION

Initially, mankind had no other kings than gods, nor any government other than theocracy. Men reasoned as Caligula did, and for that era reasoned correctly. A prolonged period of change in feelings and ideas is necessary for people to accept an equal as master, assuring themselves that it is to their benefit.

The mere fact that God was placed at the head of every political society resulted in there being as many gods as there were peoples. Two peoples alien to one another, and almost always enemies, could not long recognize the same master; two armies battling one another could not obey the same leader. Hence national divisions resulted in polytheism, which in turn gave rise to theological and civil intolerance. These are of course the same, as I shall explain hereafter.

The Greeks' notion of finding their gods among barbarians arose from their notion of considering themselves the natural sovereigns of those peoples. But in our day, erudition that revolves around the identity of the gods of different nations is quite absurd, as if Moloch, Saturn, or Chronos could be the same god! As if the Phoenicians' Baal, the Greeks' Zeus, or the Romans' Jupiter could be the same! As if imaginary beings bearing different names could have anything in common!

If one asks how it came to be that in pagan times, when every state had its religion and its gods, there were no wars of religion, my reply is that it was precisely because each state, having its own religion as well as its own government, made no distinction between its gods and its laws. Political war was also theological. The territories of the gods were, so to speak, fixed by the borders of nations. The god of one people had no rights over another people. The gods of the pagans were not jealous gods, and divided among themselves the dominion of the world. Even Moses and the Hebrew people sometimes lent themselves to this idea and spoke of the God of Israel. It is true that they looked down upon the gods of the Canaanites, a proscribed people condemned to destruction whose lands they were to occupy; but consider how they spoke of the divinities of the neighboring peoples they were forbidden to attack. "Is not what belongs to Kemosh, your god, legitimately your due?" Jephthah said to the Ammonites. "We possess, under the same title, the lands our conquering God has acquired."[150] We have here, it seems to me, a well-recognized parity between the rights of Kemosh and those of the God of Israel.

But when the Jews, subject to the Kings of Babylon and subsequently to the Kings of Syria, resolved not to recognize any god other than their own, their refusal was regarded as a rebellion against their conqueror, and drew down on them the persecutions of which one reads in their history, and of which one sees no other example before Christianity.[151]

Since every religion, then, was solely tied to the laws of the state that prescribed it, there was no way of converting a people other than by enslaving it, nor were there any other missionaries than conquerors. Since obligation to change religion was the law imposed on the vanquished, victory was necessary before any change could be stipulated. Far from men fighting for the gods, it was the gods, as in Homer, who fought for men. Each man asked his god for victory, and paid by setting up new altars. The Romans, before seizing a land, summoned its gods to leave it, and when they allowed the Tarentines to keep their shaken gods, it was because the Romans regarded these gods as subject to theirs and compelled to pay their gods homage. They left the vanquished their own gods as they left them their own laws. A wreath to the Capitoline Jupiter was often the only tribute the Romans imposed.

Eventually the Romans had, along with their empire, also spread their religion and their gods, and often adopted the gods of the vanquished by granting the vanquished and their gods the right of the city. Thus the peoples of that vast empire gradually found themselves with a multitude of gods and religions that were almost the same everywhere; this is how paganism finally became one and the same religion throughout the known world.

It was in these circumstances that Jesus established a spiritual kingdom on earth that, by separating the theological system from the political one, put an end to the unity of the state, bringing about the internal divisions that have never ceased to agitate Christian peoples. As the novel idea of a kingdom of the Other World would never have occurred to pagans, they always looked on the Christians as rebels who, while feigning to submit, were only awaiting the chance to make themselves independent and become their masters, usurping through guile the authority that they feigned to respect while they were weak. This was the cause of the persecutions.

What the pagans had feared came to pass. Everything changed: the humble Christians changed their tone, and soon this so-called kingdom of the Other World was to become, under a manifest leader, the most violent despotism in this world.

However, since there have always been princely authority and civil laws, this dual power has given rise to a perpetual conflict of jurisdiction that has made all good polity impossible in Christian states; and no one has ever succeeded in ascertaining whether one is obliged to obey the leader or the priest.

Several peoples, nevertheless, even in Europe or its vicinity, have sought in vain to preserve or restore the old system; but the spirit of Christianity has prevailed. The sacred cult has always preserved or reestablished its independence from the sovereign authority, and without any necessary link to the body of the state. Muhammad had very sound views: in his political system he linked the two powers well, and for as long as the form of his government continued under the caliphs who succeeded him, that government was entirely unified, and in that respect good. But the Arabs, having grown prosperous, lettered, civilized, soft, and cowardly, were subjugated by barbarians, after which the division between the two powers began once again. Although this division may be less apparent among the Muhammadans than among the Christians, it nevertheless exists, especially in the sect of Ali, and there are states, such as Persia, where it is still apparent.

In Europe, the Kings of England established themselves as head of the Church, as did the Czars in Russia, but by doing so they made themselves less the masters of the Church than its ministers; they have acquired not so much the right to change the Church as the power to maintain it, and are not its legislators but merely its princes. Wherever the clergy forms a body,[152] it is master and legislator in its own territories. There are therefore two powers and two sovereign authorities in England, Russia, and elsewhere as well.

Of all the Christian authors, only the philosopher Hobbes has seen the evil and its remedy and dared propose the reunion of the two heads of the eagle and the restoration of political unity, without which no state or government will ever be well constituted. But he must subsequently have recognized that the domineering spirit of Christianity is incompatible with his system, and that clerical advantage would always be stronger than that of the state. What has made his political ideas hated is not so much what is horrible and false about them, as what is just and true.[153]

I believe that by examining the historical facts from this point of view, it would be simple to refute the contrary opinions of Bayle and Warburton, the former arguing that religion can be of no use to the body politic, while the latter maintains that, on the contrary, Christianity is its strongest support. One could prove to Bayle that no state has ever been established without religion as its foundation, and to Warburton that Christian law is in essence more harmful than beneficial for strengthening the constitution of the state. To make myself fully understood, I need only give the all-too-vague ideas of religion that relate to this subject somewhat more precision.

Seen in relation to society that is either public or private, religion may also be divided into two kinds: the religion of man and the religion of the citizen. The first, without temples, altars, or rites, is limited to the purely internal religion of the supreme God and the eternal duties of morality, and is the pure and simple religion of the Gospel, true theism, and what may be called natural divine right. The second, inscribed within the limits of a single country, gives it its gods, its own tutelary patrons. This religion has its dogmas, its rites, and its external practices prescribed by law. Beyond the single nation that follows it, this religion regards the rest of the world as infidel, alien, and barbarous, and extends the duties and rights of man only as far as its own altars. Such were all the religions of the first peoples, religions to which we can give the name civil or positive divine law.

There is a third, stranger kind of religion that gives men two sets of laws, two rulers, and two fatherlands, and so subjects them to contradictory duties and prevents them from being both devout and citizens at the same time. Such is the religion of the Lamas of Tibet, such is the religion of the Japanese, and such is Roman Catholicism. This kind of religion may be called the religion of the priest. It leads to a mixed law that is detrimental to society, a law that has no name.

Considered politically, each of these three kinds of religion has its defects. The third is so obviously bad that it is an utter waste of time to set about proving it. Whatever destroys social unity is useless; all institutions that set man in contradiction with himself are useless.

The second kind of religion, the religion of the citizen, is good in that it unites the divine cult with reverence for the laws, and, by making the citizens' country the object of their worship, teaches them that to serve the state is to serve its tutelary god. It is a kind of theocracy in which there ought to be no bishop other than the prince, and no priests other than the magistrates. In this way, to die for one's country is to achieve martyrdom, whereas to break its laws is impiety, and to subject a guilty man to public execration is to deliver him to the wrath of the gods: *Sacer estod.*[154]

But this kind of religion is bad in that it is founded on lies and error and so deceives men, making them credulous and superstitious, and smothers the true cult of the divinity with empty ceremonies. It is also bad when it becomes exclusive and tyrannical and makes a people bloodthirsty and intolerant, sparking murder and massacre, its credo being that it is a holy act to kill whoever denies its gods. This places such a people in a natural state of war with all others, which is most harmful to its own security.

There remains, then, the religion of man—Christianity. Not the Christianity of today, but that of the Gospel, which is entirely different. By this holy, sublime, and true religion all men, children of one God, recognize one another as brothers, and the society that unites them does not dissolve even in death.

But this religion, having no specific relation to the body politic, leaves to the laws only the power they derive from themselves without adding any other power; and consequently, one of the great bonds of any given society remains ineffectual. Furthermore, far from binding the hearts of the citizens to the state, this religion detaches them from it as from all earthly things. I know of nothing more contrary to the social spirit.

We are told that a people composed of true Christians would form the most perfect society imaginable. I see only one great impediment to this supposition: that a society of true Christians would no longer be a society of men.

I will even venture that this supposed society, despite its perfection, would be neither the strongest nor the most lasting. By the mere fact of being perfect it would lack cohesion; its fatal flaw would lie in its very perfection. Everyone would fulfill his duty: the people would obey the laws, the rulers would be just and temperate, the magistrates honest and incorruptible; the soldiers would scorn death, and there would be neither vanity nor luxury. All this is wonderful, but let us examine it further.

Christianity is an entirely spiritual religion, solely occupied with heavenly matters; the country of the Christian is not of this world. The Christian fulfills his duty, it is true, but does so with profound indifference to the success or failure of his endeavors. Provided he has nothing to reproach himself with, it matters little to him whether things are going well or badly here on earth. If the state is flourishing, he scarcely dares enjoy the public happiness; he is afraid of taking pride in his country's glory. If the state is in decline, he blesses the hand of God that lies heavily upon His people.

In order for society to be peaceable and for harmony to be maintained, all the citizens, without exception, would have to be good Christians. But if, by some bad fortune, there should be a single ambitious man, a single hypocrite, a Catiline, for instance, or a Cromwell, this man would certainly manage to dupe his pious compatriots. Christian charity does not readily allow one to think ill of one's neighbor; as soon as the ambitious individual has, through some ruse, discovered the art of imposing on his compatriots and seizing a share in the public authority, you suddenly have a man invested with dignity, and it is the will of God that he be respected. There you now have a power, and it is God's will that it be obeyed. And if the holder of that power should abuse it? Then it is the scourge with which God punishes His children. One could not drive out the usurper in good conscience, since public peace would be disturbed, violence would have to be used, and blood would be spilled. All this is irreconcilable with Christian mildness—and what does it matter, after all, whether one is free or a serf in this vale of tears? The essential thing is to enter Paradise, and resignation is an additional means of doing so.

What if a war with a foreign state breaks out? The citizens will readily march to battle, not one of them thinking of flight—they do their duty, but without passion for victory. They are better versed in dying than in conquering. What does it matter if they win or lose? Does not Providence know better than they what should befall them? Imagine what an advantage a proud, violent, and zealous enemy could draw from their stoicism! Set a Christian people against such a valiant people consumed by ardent love of country and glory; imagine a Christian republic face to face with Sparta or Rome: the pious Christians would be beaten, crushed, and destroyed before they knew what had befallen them, and if they were saved, they would merely owe their salvation to their enemy's contempt for them. My view is that the soldiers of Fabius took a fine oath: they did not swear to conquer or die, but to return victorious; and they kept their pledge. No Christians would ever have sworn such an oath; they would have considered it as challenging God.

But I am wrong to speak of a Christian republic; the terms *Christian* and *republic* are mutually exclusive. Christianity preaches only servitude and dependence. Its spirit is too favorable to tyranny for tyranny not to invariably take advantage of it. True Christians are made to be slaves; they know it and are not troubled, for in their eyes this short life is worthless.

Christian troops are excellent, we are told. I deny it. Let them show me some. For my part, I know of no Christian troops. The Crusades, I will be told. Without contesting the valor of the Crusaders, I will reply that far from being Christians, they were soldiers of the priests and citizens of the Church. They fought for their spiritual country, which the Church had somehow managed to make temporal. Strictly speaking, this is a return to paganism, as the Gospel does not establish a national religion. A holy war among Christians is impossible.

Under the pagan emperors of Rome, the Christian soldiers were brave; every Christian writer affirms this, and I believe it: it was a matter of rivalry in honor with the pagan troops. As soon as the emperors became Christian, this rivalry ended, and once the Cross had driven out the Eagle, all Roman valor disappeared.

But let us set political considerations aside and return to the subject of rights, and define our principles on this important point. The right that the social pact grants the sovereign authority over its subjects does not, as I have already said,[155] exceed the limits of what is useful to the state.[156] The subjects therefore owe the sovereign authority an account of their opinions only to the extent that these opinions matter to the community. But it does matter very much to the state that each citizen have a religion that will make him love his duty; however, the dogmas of that religion must concern the state and its members only to the extent that these dogmas relate to the morality and to the duties that whoever professes this religion is bound to fulfill toward others. Beyond this, everyone may hold whatever opinions he pleases without its falling to the sovereign authority to know about them, for, since the sovereign authority has no jurisdiction in the Other World, whatever the fate of its subjects may be in the life to come is not its business, provided that in this life they are good citizens.

There is, therefore, a purely civil profession of faith in which it falls to the sovereign authority to determine the articles, not exactly as religious dogmas, but as predilection of sociability without which a man cannot be a good citizen or loyal subject.[157] While the sovereign authority cannot compel anyone to believe these sentiments, it can banish from the state anyone who does not believe in them. It can banish such an individual not for impiety, but as unsocial, as someone incapable of sincerely loving the laws and justice, and incapable of sacrificing, if need be, his life to his duty. If anyone, after publicly recognizing these dogmas, conducts himself as if he does not believe them, let him be punished with death. He has committed the greatest of crimes: he has lied before the law.

The dogmas of civil religion ought to be few in number, simple, precisely worded, and without explanation or commentary. The positive dogmas are: the existence of a mighty, intelligent, and beneficent Divinity who is prescient and providing, the existence of the life to come, the happiness of the just, the punishment of the wicked, and the sanctity of the social contract and the laws. As for the negative dogmas, I restrict them to just one: intolerance. This dogma belongs to the religions we have rejected.

Those who distinguish civil intolerance from theological intolerance are, in my opinion, mistaken. These two forms of intolerance are inseparable. It is impossible to live at peace with people one believes to be damned; to love them would be to hate God who punishes them. It is vital that one either convert them or persecute them. Wherever theological intolerance is allowed, it will inevitably have a civil effect;[158] and as soon as it does, the sovereign authority is no longer sovereign even in the temporal sphere. From then on, priests are the true masters, and kings no more than their officers.

Now that there no longer is and no longer can be an exclusive national religion, one should tolerate all religions that tolerate others, as long as their dogmas contain nothing contrary to the duties of the citizen. But whoever dares say "There is no salvation outside the Church" ought to be driven from the state, unless the state *is* the Church, and the prince the pontiff. Such a dogma is good only in a theocratic government; in any other, it is pernicious. The reason Henry IV is said to have embraced Roman Catholicism ought to make every honest man leave it, and above all any prince who knows how to reason.[159]

CHAPTER IX:
CONCLUSION

Having laid down the true principles of political right, and by this means having tried to give the state a solid foundation, it remains for me to elaborate on its external relations, which would include the rights of peoples, commerce, the rights of war and conquest, public law, alliances, negotiations, treaties, and so on. But all this raises a new issue that is too vast for my narrow scope.[160] As it is, I should have kept my scope narrower.

ÉMILE, OR,
ON EDUCATION

*Rousseau once spent a year as tutor to a pair of small boys,
with what he acknowledged were disappointing results, especially since he was self-taught himself and the subject of
education had long interested him. When he came to write
Émile, it was also a very personal act of expiation, because
far from educating his own children, he had placed each of
them in a foundling home as soon as they were born. This
was still a closely guarded secret, but a footnote hints at it: "I
predict that anyone who has a heart and neglects such sacred duties will weep long and bitterly for his error, and will
never be consoled."*

*Beyond personal considerations, Émile conveys the mes-
sage that Rousseau said was at the heart of all his writings:
man is naturally good but society has made him wicked. In-
terspersing argument with novelistic narrative, he imagines
an ideal tutor who undertakes full supervision of Émile
from earliest boyhood—the tutor himself is given no
name—and who leads him skillfully through experiences*

that teach him to think and act for himself. Formal instruction is postponed until the teenage years, and contact with other people is minimized so that the boy will not learn to manipulate and lie. Above all, he must be protected from the inauthenticity that social life imposes. But there is a paradox: although Émile is encouraged to believe that he is acting spontaneously, in actuality he unknowingly carries out his tutor's carefully planned scenarios.

When Émile reaches adulthood it is time for him to become a citizen rather than an outsider and loner, and at this point he meets the young woman, Sophie, who will be his wife. After some final counseling it is time for the tutor to let him go. The fifth and final book of Émile *has become the most controversial, since although Émile remained as long as possible in the independent state of "natural man," Sophie has been socialized from the very beginning, learning traditional female accomplishments and preparing to be a loyal wife and nurturing mother. When the work was first published, however, few women readers objected. They seem to have felt that Rousseau offered them a more significant role in the life of the family than the old patriarchal code allowed.*

What got Rousseau in immediate trouble was "The Savoyard Vicar's Profession of Faith," a self-contained discourse embedded in Book IV at the point when Émile's religious education is addressed. To modern eyes it may look harmless enough, and indeed Rousseau was far more religiously inclined than most of the philosophes. Nevertheless, the "Profession of Faith" is dismissive of many tenets of orthodox dogma, and it led to a warrant for Rousseau's arrest and his flight from France to Switzerland. In Paris and Geneva, copies of Émile *were publicly burned by the hangman.*

FROM BOOK II

[...]

Human institutions are folly and contradiction. We worry more about our life in proportion as it loses its value: the old regret the loss more than the young; they do not want to lose the preparations they have made for enjoying it. What a cruel fate to die at sixty, before one has begun to live. We think that man has an abiding love for his preservation, and it is true, but we do not see that this love, as we feel it, is to a large extent the work of man. Natural man worries about his preservation only to the extent that the means of ensuring it are in his power; the moment these means elude him, he resigns himself and dies without uselessly tormenting himself. Our first law of resignation comes from nature. Savages and wild beasts barely struggle against death, enduring it almost without complaint. If nature's law is destroyed, another law originating in reason arises, but few know how to take advantage of it, and this artificial resignation is never as entire or complete as nature's law.

Foresight! Foresight, that forever carries us beyond ourselves, often to places at which we will never arrive. This is the true source of all our problems. It is such folly for a transient being like man to always look far into a future that so rarely comes to be while neglecting the present of which he is sure, a folly all the more dire as it continuously increases with age. The old, who are always so wary, careful, and miserly, would rather deny themselves what they need today so they will not have to do without it a hundred years from now. Thus we become attached to everything, cling to everything. What is important to each of us are the times, places, people, things, and all that is and all that will be: our own self is now less than half of ourselves. Everyone spreads himself, so to speak, over the whole world, and becomes sentient on its vast surface. Is it surprising that our ills multiply at all the points where we can be wounded, that princes mourn the loss of lands they have never seen, that merchants will weep in Paris at a blow they have been dealt in the Indies?

Is it nature that takes men so far away from themselves? Is it her will that each shall learn his fate from others, and sometimes be the last to learn it, so that a man will die happy or in misery without realizing anything? I see a man who is vigorous, happy, and robust, a vital man whose presence inspires joy, his eyes expressing contentment and well-being, the image of happiness. A letter arrives in the mail; the happy man looks at it, it is addressed to him; he opens it and reads it. In an instant his expression changes. He turns white, faints, and when he regains consciousness begins to weep, flails around, moans, tears at his hair, his cries ring out, he is beset by terrible convulsions. Foolish man! What harm can this piece of paper have done you? What limb has it torn from you? What crime has it made you commit? What has it changed in you to put you in the state in which I see you?

Had the letter gone astray, or had a charitable hand thrown it in the fire, the fate of this mortal—at once both happy and unhappy—would, I believe, have posed a strange problem. His unhappiness, you will say, was real. That is true; but he did not feel it. So where was his unhappiness? His happiness was imaginary. I know that health, happiness, well-being, and ease of mind are merely illusions. We no longer exist where we are, we only exist where we are not. Is it worth being so afraid of death, considering that the world we live in endures?

O man, assert your existence within yourself and you will no longer be miserable. Remain in the place nature assigned you within the chain of being. Nothing can make you leave it. Do not resist the harsh law of necessity—do not exhaust yourself trying to resist it with a power to extend and prolong your existence that Heaven has not granted you. You can only live the way Heaven wants you to live, and for as long as it wants you to live. Your freedom and power extend only as far as the strength nature gave you, and not beyond. The rest is merely slavery, illusion, and fantasy. Domination is servile when it depends on opinion, since you depend on the prejudices of others when you rule them by means of those prejudices. To govern men as you please, you must conduct yourself as they please. They need only to change their manner of thinking and you will have to change your manner of action. Those who approach you need only know how to influence the opinions of the people you believe you are governing, or the favorites who govern you, or those of your family, or your own favorites, all the viziers, courtiers, priests, soldiers, servants and chatterboxes, and even children (though you might be as great a genius as Themistocles) might lead *you* like a boy amidst all your legions.[161] Try as you might, your real authority will never exceed your actual powers. As soon as you are compelled to see through the eyes of others, you must act through their wills. "My people are my subjects," you say with pride. Granted. And yet, what are you? You are the subject of your ministers. And your ministers, what are they? They are the subjects of their clerks, their mistresses, the servants of their servants. Usurp everything, take it all, and then scatter your money in all directions, prime your battery of cannons, set up gallows and torture wheels, pass laws, issue edicts, multiply your spies, soldiers, executioners, prisons, and chains. But poor little men, what use will all that be to you? You will not be better served, less robbed, less deceived, more absolved. You will always say "We want!" but will always do what others want.

The only one who can carry out his will is he who does not need to expand his reach with the hands of another to do it. Therefore, the foremost good is not authority but freedom. The man who is truly free wants only what he is capable of doing and does what he likes. That is my fundamental principle. One has only to apply it to childhood, and all the rules of education will follow.

[...]

I return to practical matters. I have already said that your child should not be given a thing just because he asks for it, but because he needs it, nor should he do anything out of obedience, but only out of necessity.[162] Thus the words *obey* and *command* must be banished from the child's vocabulary, and even more so the words *duty* and *obligation*, while *strength, necessity, weakness,* and *constraint* must be given pride of place. Before one reaches the age of reason, one cannot have a conception of moral beings or social relations; hence one must avoid using, to the extent that one can, words that express them, for fear that the child might from the beginning link these words to mistaken ideas of which you will be unaware and which you will not be able to eradicate. The first mistaken idea that enters his head becomes the seed of error and vice. It is at this initial step that it is especially important to pay attention. Make certain that as long as the child is struck only by physical things, all his ideas will be confined to sensations.[163] Make sure that he perceives only the physical world around him, otherwise you can be certain that he will not listen to you at all, or will develop fantastic notions of the moral world of which you speak to him, notions that you will never be able to eradicate.

Reasoning with children was Locke's great principle, a principle that is quite fashionable today.[164] Its success, however, does not strike me as sufficient reason to make it valid; in my view nothing is more foolish than children with whom one has done nothing but reason. Of all the faculties of man, reason, which is arguably no more than an amalgam of all the others, develops the latest and with the most difficulty: and they want to use reason to develop the first faculties! The ultimate goal of a good education is to produce a reasonable man, and they want to raise a child through reason! That is beginning with the end, attempting to make the final product the instrument. If children understood reason, there would be no need for them to be educated. But by talking to them from their earliest age in a language they do not understand at all, one is accustoming them to being satisfied with mere words, to question everything that is said to them, to believe themselves as wise as their tutors, and to become disputants and mutinous. Everything one thinks of obtaining from them by reasonable motives one can obtain only by motives of covetousness, fear, or vanity that one is then invariably compelled to add to the others.

Here is the formula to which almost all moral lessons one can and should give to children can be reduced:

TUTOR: You must not do that.

CHILD: Why mustn't I do that?

TUTOR: Because it is wrong.

CHILD: Wrong? What is the meaning of wrong?

TUTOR: It is what you are not allowed to do.

CHILD: Why is it bad to do what I am not allowed to do?

TUTOR: Because you will be punished for having disobeyed.

CHILD: Then I will do it secretly.

TUTOR: Then you will be caught.

CHILD: I will hide.

TUTOR: You will be questioned.

CHILD: I will lie.

TUTOR: One must not lie.

CHILD: Why mustn't one lie?

TUTOR: Because it is wrong, etc.

This is the inevitable circle. If you step out of it, the child will no longer understand you. Are these not quite useful instructions? I would be curious to know what might be put in place of this dialogue. Locke himself would surely have been at a loss for an answer. It is not a child's business to know what is good and what is bad, or to recognize the reason for man's obligations.

Nature wants children to be children before being adults. If we try to pervert this order, we will produce a premature fruit that will have neither ripeness nor flavor and will be quick to rot. We will have young scholars and old children. Childhood has its own ways of seeing, thinking, and feeling. Nothing is less reasonable than wanting to substitute our ways, and I should no more insist that a child of ten stand five feet tall than I would insist that he have judgment. Indeed, what use would reason be to him at that age? Reason is the bridle of strength, and a child does not need such a bridle.

When you try to persuade your pupils of the duty of obedience, you add to this supposed persuasion force and threats, or, what is worse, flattery and promises. Thus, lured by gain or constrained by force, they pretend to be convinced by reason. The minute you perceive their action, they can recognize that obedience is to their advantage and disobedience to their disadvantage. But since everything you demand from them is unpleasant and it is always disagreeable to do the will of others, they secretly do their own will, persuaded that they are doing the right thing as long as you are unaware of their disobedience, but if they are discovered they are ready to admit that they are doing wrong from fear of worse evils. As the reason for duty is not conceivable at their age, there is not a man in the world who could manage to make them comprehend it. But the fear of punishment, the hope of forgiveness, importunity, and awkwardness in answering, wring from them all the admissions you demand, and you think you have convinced them when you have only bored or intimidated them.

What is the result of all this? First, by imposing on them a duty they do not comprehend, you make them reluctant to submit to your tyranny and turn away their love for you. Second, you teach them to become deceitful, false, and liars in order to exact rewards or evade punishment; finally, by accustoming them to conceal a secret motive behind an apparent one, you yourself give them the means with which to deceive you constantly, to deflect you from knowing their true character, and to ply you and others with empty words whenever they can. Laws, you will say, though binding on the conscience, also impose constraint on grown men. I agree; but what are these men if not children spoiled by education? This is precisely what must be prevented. Use force with children, and reasoning with men. Such is the natural order. The wise man needs no laws.

Treat your pupil according to his age. Place your pupil where he should be right, and keep him there so firmly that he no longer tries to escape. So before he knows what good sense is, he will have dealt with the most important lesson. Never—absolutely never—order him to do anything, whatever it may be. Do not even let him conceive that you claim any sort of authority over him. Only let him know that he is weak and that you are strong, and that on account of his position and yours he is inevitably within your power. Let him know it, learn it, feel it: let him feel on his proud neck from an early age the heavy yoke that nature imposes on man, the yoke of necessity under which every finite being must bend. He must understand that this necessity lies in things and never in the caprice[165] of man; that the bridle restraining him is force, not authority. If there is something from which he must abstain, do not forbid him to do it, but hinder him from doing it without explanation or reasoning. What you grant him, grant at his first word without beseeching or entreaties, and above all without conditions. Grant with pleasure and refuse with repugnance, but let everything you refuse be irrevocable, and let no pleading move you. Let the *no* you pronounce be a stone wall at which the child can throw himself five or six times, exhausting his strength but failing to knock it down.

That is how you render your pupil patient, composed, resigned, and calm, even when he does not get what he wants, for it is in man's nature to patiently endure what he has to, but not the ill will of others. No child has ever rebelled against the response "There is none left," unless he believes it to be a lie. Furthermore, there is no middle course: you must either demand nothing of him, or else bend him to perfect obedience from the start. The worst education is to let him hover between his will and yours, and to carry on a constant dispute about which of the two will be master. I would prefer a hundred times that it be he.

It is very strange that ever since people have set about educating children they have never invented methods for guiding them other than emulation, jealousy, envy, vanity, greed, and cowardly fear, all of which are passions that are the most dangerous, the quickest to ferment, and the most apt to corrupt the soul even before the body is fully formed. With every precocious lesson that you seek to impress on their minds, you plant a vice in the depths of their soul. Foolish tutors think they are working miracles by making their pupils wicked in order to teach them what goodness is. And then they tell us gravely: "Such is man." Indeed, such is the man that you have created!

All the methods have been tried except one—the only method that can in fact succeed: a freedom that is well regulated. One should not set about educating a child when one does not know how to lead him where one wants by laying down the law as to what is possible and what is not. As both are equally unknown to your pupil, they can be extended or constricted as you please. While he is restrained, goaded on, or held back with nothing more than the bond of necessity, he will not utter a word. You will render him pliable and docile by the mere force of things, without giving vice a chance to sprout in him, since passions are never sparked if they can have no effect.

Do not give your pupil any kind of verbal instruction; his lessons should come from experience alone. Do not inflict any punishment on him, since he does not know what it means to be at fault. Never make him ask for forgiveness, since he does not know how to offend you. Devoid of any morality in his actions, he cannot do anything that is morally wrong that deserves either punishment or reprimand.

I already see the astonished reader comparing this child to

those he knows. He is mistaken. The incessant restriction you impose on your pupils stimulates their liveliness. The more your watchful eye holds them in check, the more rambunctious they become the moment they escape you. They must, whenever they can, compensate for the harsh constraint in which you keep them. Two schoolboys from the town will do more mischief in the countryside than all the children of a village. Lock a young gentleman and a young peasant in a room, and the former will have knocked over or smashed everything before the latter has so much as lifted a finger. Why is this, if not because the boy from the town hastens to exploit a moment of independence, while the other, always certain of his freedom, never hastens to exploit it. And yet the children of villagers, often cosseted or disciplined, are still quite far from the state in which I would want them.

Let us postulate as an incontestable principle that the first impulses of nature are always right: that there is no original sin in the human heart. It does not contain a single vice of which one could not say how or from where it entered. The only passion natural to man is love of himself, or, in a broader sense, self-respect. This self-respect is good and useful both in itself and in relation to ourselves, and since it has no necessary relation to other people, it is, in this sense, naturally neutral. It becomes good or bad only by one's application of it and the connections one establishes. Until such time as reason, the captain of self-respect, can develop, it is important that the child not do anything, because, in short, he has seen or heard nothing in relation to others, but only what nature asks of him, and thus will do only what is good. I do not mean that he will never do any mischief, never hurt himself, or never break an expensive piece of furniture within his reach. He might do much damage, but without doing wrong, because a bad action depends on an intent to destroy, and he will never have such an intention—if he did, even once, all would be lost: he would be wicked almost beyond hope.

Some things are evil when seen from the standpoint of greed that are not evil from the standpoint of reason. When you allow children to freely exercise their foolish whims, you must put away anything that might make this a costly venture, and move anything fragile or expensive out of their reach. Their quarters ought to be furnished with simple, sturdy furniture: no mirrors, porcelain, or fancy bibelots. As for my Émile, who I am raising in the country, his room will have nothing that distinguishes it from that of a peasant. What is the use of decorating it with so much care when he will be spending so little time in it? But I am wrong, since he will decorate the room himself, and we shall soon see with what.

If in spite of all your precautions the child ends up causing some disorder or breaking something useful, do not scold him or punish him for your negligence. He must not hear a word of reproach, not a hint that he has upset you: act as if the piece of furniture had broken of itself; you can consider it a great accomplishment if you manage to say nothing.

Dare I present here the greatest, the most important, and the most useful rule in all of education? It is that one should not attempt to gain time, but waste it. Simple reader, excuse my paradoxes, but they are a necessary part of reflection, and whatever you may say, I would rather be a paradoxical man than a man of prejudice. The most dangerous period in life is between birth and the age of twelve. It is the time when errors and vices germinate without the child's yet having any means to destroy them; though by the time he has the means, the roots are so deep that it is too late for them to be pulled up. If infants sprang directly from their mothers' breast to the age of reason, our current way of education might be quite suitable, but considering their natural growth, they need an education that is completely opposite. A child should do nothing with his soul until all his faculties have developed, for while the soul is blind it cannot see the torch you are offering it, or follow a path that reason traces through the vast expanse of ideas so faintly that even the keenest eyes can barely see it.

Therefore, the first education should be purely negative. It must not consist in teaching virtue or truth, but of securing the heart from vice and the mind from error. If you do nothing and allow nothing to be done, if you can lead your pupil, strong and healthy, to the age of twelve without his being able to tell his right hand from his left, then the eyes of his understanding will open to reason from your very first lessons. Free from prejudice and habits, there would be nothing in him that could defy the effect of your efforts. In your hands he will quickly become the wisest of men, and you, having started out by doing nothing, will have created a prodigy of education.

[...]

From Book III

[…]

During our early childhood, time was long; if we sought to waste time, it was only out of fear of using it badly. Now it is just the opposite: we do not have enough time to do everything we have to do. Consider that for your pupil the first passions are approaching, and when they knock at the door he will no longer pay attention to anything else. The calm age of intelligence is so short, passes by so swiftly, and has so many other necessary aspects, that it is folly to try to make a child become learned. The issue is not to teach him knowledge, but to give him a taste for cherishing it and methods for learning it once his taste is better developed. This is most certainly one of the fundamental principles of all good education.

Now is also the time to accustom your pupil little by little to pay extended attention to a given subject, though this attention should never be the result of constraint, but always of pleasure or desire. Great care must be taken that it does not overwhelm him, and that it be not pursued to the point of boredom. So be vigilant, and at all cost stop before he gets bored, for it is never as important that he learn as that he not be forced to do something against his will.

If he himself asks questions, answer to the extent that will satisfy his curiosity, but not to the extent that it will be sated. Especially when you see that instead of asking questions in order to learn, he begins overwhelming you with silly questions. This you must stop immediately, aware that he no longer cares about what is being learned, but only about subjecting you to his queries. You must pay less heed to the words he utters than to the motive that makes him speak. This warning, less necessary before this stage, becomes of the utmost importance as soon as the child begins to reason.

There is a chain of general truths by which all the sciences are linked to common principles that are developed in turn. This chain is the method of the philosophers; but that is not what we are dealing with here. There is another entirely different method by which every particular subject attracts another and always points to the subject that follows it. This method, which through continual curiosity nourishes the attention required by every subject, is the one most people follow, and is above all the method that children need. In orienting ourselves so as to create our maps, we had to draw the meridians. Two points of intersection between the equal shadows of morning and evening provide an excellent meridian for the thirteen-year-old astronomer. But the appeal of these meridians fades; it takes time to draw them, and one is always doing the one thing. So much trouble and constraint will end up boring him. But we foresaw this; we have prepared for it in advance.

Here I am again entering into minute and long-winded detail. Reader, I can hear you grumbling, but I shall brave it, as I do not want to sacrifice the most important part of this book to your impatience. Come to terms with my tedious passages, as I have come to terms with your objections.

My pupil and I had long noticed that amber, glass, wax, and certain other bodies attracted straws when rubbed, while others did not. By chance we discovered a material with an even more unusual property, that of attracting at a distance filings and other particles of iron without being rubbed. This quality amused us for a long time without our being able to see any-thing more in it! We finally discovered that this property is in-herent in the iron itself, which somehow becomes magnetized. One day we go to a fair where a conjuror is beckoning, with a piece of bread, a wax duck floating in a basin of water. Though we are greatly surprised we do not call him a magician, since we do not know what a magician is. Constantly struck by ef-fects whose causes we do not know, we are in no hurry to pass judgment, and calmly remain in our ignorance until we find an opportunity to emerge from it.

Back at home, as we keep talking about the duck at the fair, we finally resolve to imitate the trick. We take a needle that has been well magnetized, and embed it in a ball of white wax that we shape as best we can into the form of a duck, so that the needle runs through its body, the needle's eye forming the bill. We place the duck in water, bring a key ring near its beak, and, with a joy easy to comprehend, we watch our duck follow the key, just as the duck at the fair had followed the piece of bread. We leave it to another time to see in which direction the duck will point when left in the water undisturbed. For the time being this will suffice, as we are wholly occupied with the sub-ject at hand.

That same evening we return to the fair with our piece of prepared bread in our pocket, and as soon as the conjuror has performed his trick, my little scholar, who can barely contain himself, says to him that the trick is not difficult, and that he, too, can do as much. He is taken at his word. He immediately produces the bread containing the hidden piece of iron from his pocket, his heart beating as he steps up to the table. Almost shaking, he holds out the bread. The duck approaches and follows him. The child cries out, jumping with delight. The applause and the shouts from the crowd go to his head, and he is beside himself. The mountebank is confounded, but comes over and hugs the boy, congratulates him, and begs for the honor of his company the following day, adding that he will do his best to gather an even greater crowd to applaud his skill. My little scientist, bursting with pride, begins chattering away, but I immediately bid him hold his tongue, and take him home showered with praise.

With comical excitement the child counts the minutes until the following day. He invites everyone he sees, wanting all mankind to witness his glory; he can hardly await the hour. He wants to get there early, and we hurry to the appointed place. The hall is already full. As he enters, his young heart swells with excitement. Other tricks come first. The conjuror surpasses himself with the most surprising feats. The child sees nothing of all this. He is on edge, sweats, can barely breathe, and spends his time fiddling with the piece of bread in his pocket, his hand trembling with impatience. Finally his turn comes. The master announces him to the audience with great ceremony. The boy comes forward somewhat shyly, and takes out his piece of bread—O the ephemeral joy of all things human!—the duck, so tame the day before, is quite wild today. Instead of offering its beak, it turns tail and flees, avoiding the bread and the hand that holds it as persistently as it had pursued them the day before. After numerous futile attempts, the crowd jeering, the child protests that he has been tricked, that this is another duck substituted for the first one, and defies the conjuror to beckon it himself.

The conjuror, without so much as a word, takes a piece of bread and offers it to the duck, which immediately follows the bread and the retreating hand. The child takes the conjuror's piece of bread, but far from succeeding any better than before, the duck spites him, whirling around the basin. The boy, flustered, finally retreats, no longer daring to face the taunts of the crowd.

Now the conjuror takes the piece of bread the child had brought and uses it as successfully as he had his own. He pulls out the bit of iron before the crowd—more laughter at our expense—and, with the bread thus emptied, attracts the duck as before. He does the same with a piece of bread cut by a third person in the presence of the crowd. He attracts the duck with his glove, with the tip of his finger. Finally he moves to the center of the room, and with the pompousness peculiar to his kind declares that the duck will obey his voice as readily as it obeys his hand. He calls out to the duck and it complies: he tells it to swim to the right and the duck swims to the right, to swim back again and the duck swims back, to turn and it turns. The movement is as prompt as the command. The mounting applause is a mounting affront to us. We slip away unnoticed and lock ourselves in our room without proclaiming our success as we had intended.

The following morning there is a knock at our door. I open, it is the conjuror. He humbly complains about our behavior. What had he done to us that we should want to discredit his tricks and deprive him of a living? "What is so wondrous in the art of making a wax duck move toward you to seek this applause at the cost of an honest man's livelihood? I assure you, Messieurs, if I had another talent by which to earn a living, I would hardly glorify myself with this one. You ought to have realized that a man who has spent his life exercising this pitiful trade will know more about it than you, who have given it only a few moment's thought. If I did not show you my master-strokes right away, it was because one ought not hasten like a fool to show off all one knows. I am always mindful to keep my best tricks for when I need them, and beside the one you saw I have many more to foil indiscreet young fellows. That said, Messieurs, I have come in benevolence to reveal the secret that so confounded you. I beg you, however, not to use it in order to do me harm, and to be more circumspect next time."

He then shows us his contraption, and we see to our utmost astonishment that it merely consists of a very strong magnet secretly moved about by a child hidden beneath the table.

The man puts away his contraption, and we, thanking him and apologizing, try to make him a gift. But he refuses it. "No, Messieurs, I am not so pleased by what you have done that I am willing to accept your gift. I leave you in my debt despite yourselves, which is my only revenge. Learn that there is generosity in every class of men. I charge for my tricks, not for my lessons."

On leaving, he addresses a direct and lofty reprimand to me: "I am happy to forgive this child," he tells me, "he has only sinned through ignorance. But you, Monsieur, who ought to have known that he was in the wrong, why did you let him do it? As he is in your care and you are the older, you should be watching over him and giving him good counsel. Your experience is the authority that must guide him. When one day he reproaches himself for the errors of his youth, he will doubtless reproach you for the ones of which you did not warn him."

He departs, leaving us both quite perplexed. I censure myself for my thoughtlessness, and promise the child that in the future I will pay more attention to his interests and warn him of errors before he commits them, as the time is approaching when our relationship will change and when the master's severity must give way to the kindness of a friend. This change must come about by degrees. Everything must be foreseen, and foreseen well in advance.

The following day we return to the fair to see again the trick whose secret we had learned. We approach our Socratic conjuror with profound respect. We hardly dare raise our eyes to look at him, but he shows us every attention and seats us in a place of honor. He performs his routines as usual, but, clearly delighted, permits himself to linger over the trick with the duck, often looking proudly in our direction. We know exactly how it is done, but we do not breathe a word. If my pupil so much as opened his mouth, he would have deserved a whipping.

Every detail of this example is more important than it seems. So many lessons in just one! What mortifying results are brought on by the first impulse of vanity! Young tutor, eye this first impulse with care. If you make it lead to indignity and disgrace, you can be certain that a second such impulse will not reoccur for a long time. Why so many detours, you will ask. I agree, and all this just to provide a compass to serve as the meridian![166]

Having learned that a magnet acts through other bodies, we now hasten to build a contraption similar to the one we have seen. A cleared table, a shallow basin carefully placed on it and filled with a few inches of water, a duck made with a little more care, and so on. Standing watch by the basin, we come to notice that the duck, when at rest, will always point in more or less the same direction. We experiment further, examine the direction, and find that it is from south to north. What more do we need?

We have discovered our compass, or as good as discovered it! We have begun our study of physics.

There are various climates in the world, and these climates have various temperatures. The seasons vary more markedly the more one approaches the poles. All bodies contract with cold and expand with heat. This effect is more measurable in liquids and more noticeable in spirits—whence the thermometer. The wind strikes the face: consequently, air is a body, a fluid, you feel it though you cannot see it. Turn a glass upside down in the water, and the water will not fill it as long as you do not let the air escape. Air is therefore capable of resistance: push the glass deeper and the water will impinge on the space of the air without, however, being able to fill it entirely; air is therefore to a certain extent capable of compression. A ball filled with compressed air bounces better than one filled with any other substance. Consequently, air is an elastic body. When you are lying in your bath, raise your arm horizontally from the water and you will feel it weighed down by a terrible load: hence, air is a heavy body. By establishing an equilibrium between air and other fluids, one can measure its weight—whence the barometer, the siphon, the air gun, and the pneumatic pump. All the laws of statics and hydrostatics can be ascertained by experiments as simple as this. There is absolutely no need to enter a laboratory of experimental physics. I dislike all those instruments and apparatuses. The scientific atmosphere kills science. All the apparatuses will either frighten the child or their appearance will divert and steal his attention, which should be on the results.

I would have us make all our apparatuses ourselves, but I do not want to create the instrument prior to the experiment. After glimpsing the experiment as if by chance, I would have us invent step by step the instruments that will verify it. I would prefer that our instruments not be all that perfect and precise, but for us to have clearer ideas about how they ought to be and the result they ought to produce. For my first lesson in statics, instead of getting a scale, I place a stick across the back of a chair and, once the stick is balancing, measure the two lengths. I add to either end weights that are sometimes equal and sometimes not, and by pulling or pushing as needed, I eventually ascertain that equilibrium is the result of a reciprocal relationship between the number of weights and the length of the levers. Thus my little physicist is now capable of adjusting a scale before he has ever seen one.

Notions of things are without question much clearer and more definite when one learns them this way, on one's own, than are notions acquired through the teaching of others. In this way we do not accustom our reason to servile submission to authority, and we become more resourceful at finding relationships, connecting ideas, and inventing instruments than when we merely accept everything we are given and allow indifference to enfeeble our minds. The body of a man who is always dressed, shod, waited upon by his servants, and carted around by his horses will end up losing strength and the use of his limbs. Boileau prided himself on having taught Racine the art of rhyming the hard way. Among the many admirable methods to shorten the study of the sciences, we are in great need of someone to offer us a method of learning them by our own efforts.

The most perceptible advantage of these slow and laborious investigations is that while engaged in speculative studies, the pupil maintains his body active, his limbs supple, and his hands ready for the work and activities useful to man. The many instruments invented to guide us in our experiments and to substitute for the accuracy of our senses result in our neglecting to exercise them; the graphometer makes it unnecessary for us to estimate the degree of angles ourselves; the eye that once measured distances with precision relies on a chain to measure them for it; a scale exempts me from having to use my hand in order to judge what the scale can weigh. The more ingenious our tools, the cruder and more awkward our senses become. By surrounding ourselves with instruments, we no longer find the instruments within us.

But when we devote to the creating of these instruments the skill we once used in their place, when we use the intelligence to build them that we once needed to get by without them, we gain without losing anything, we add craft to nature and become more ingenious without becoming less adroit.

If I employ a child in a workshop instead of chaining him to his books, his hands working to the benefit of his intellect, he will become a philosopher while thinking himself merely a laborer. This exercise has other advantages as well, of which I shall speak later, and we will see how from the games of philosophy one can rise to the real tasks of man.

I have already mentioned that purely speculative knowledge is hardly suitable for children, even those approaching adolescence. But without having them go far into systematic physics, you should see to it that all their experiments are linked to one another by some chain of reasoning, so that with its help they can arrange these experiments into a sequence in their minds and recall them at need, for it is quite difficult for isolated facts or reasoning to remain long in one's memory when there are no links to recall them.

In an inquiry into the laws of nature, always begin with the phenomena that are most common and most evident, and accustom your pupil not to take them as reasonings, but as facts. I take a stone and pretend to place it in the air; I open my hand, the stone falls. I see Émile attentively watching my action and ask him: "Why did this stone fall?"

What child will hesitate to answer? No child will, not even Émile, had I not taken great pains to prepare him not to know how to reply. All children will say that the stone falls because it is heavy. "And what is heavy?" "What falls." "So the stone falls because it falls?" Here my little philosopher would be at a total loss. There we have his first lesson in systematic physics, but even if he does not gain from it any learning in this field, it will at least be a lesson in common sense.

As the child advances in intelligence, other important considerations oblige us to offer him a greater choice of activities. As soon as he gets to know himself sufficiently to understand what constitutes his well-being, as soon as he can grasp relations extensive enough for him to judge what suits him and what does not, then he will be in a position to feel the difference between work and amusement, and not regard amusement merely as relaxation from work. Then objects of real utility can be introduced into his studies and can lead him to a more constant application than he had devoted to simple amusements. The ever-recurring law of necessity teaches man early to do what he does not like, in order to avert an evil he would dislike even more. Such is the use of foresight, and this foresight, whether ordered or disordered, is the source of all human wisdom or misery.

Every man wants to be happy, but to succeed in this he must first know what happiness is. The happiness of the natural man is as simple as his life: it consists in not suffering. Its elements are health, freedom, and the necessities of life. The happiness of the moral man is another matter, but he does not concern us at present. I cannot repeat often enough that it is only purely physical objects that can interest children, particularly children whose vanity has not been awakened and who have not been corrupted in advance by the poison of opinion.

Once children can foresee their needs before feeling them, their intelligence is already quite advanced, and they begin to know the value of time. At that point it is important to accustom them to directing their use of time to subjects that are useful, but useful in a way fitting to their age and within the scope of their intellect. Everything connected to the moral order and the customs of society should not be presented to children so soon, as they are not in a condition to understand them. It is absurd to demand that they apply themselves to things that one tells them in vague terms are good for them, without their knowing what that good is, things one assures them will benefit them when they are grown up, though for the present they take no interest in this supposed benefit they cannot understand.

The child must not do anything on command. For him nothing is good except what he believes to be good. You think you are using foresight when you keep urging him on in his understanding, but foresight is what *you* are lacking. By arming the child with useless tools that he may perhaps never use, you are depriving him of man's most universal tool: good sense. You accustom him to being always led, nothing but an instrument in the hands of others. You want him to be docile when he is small, which is to want him to be credulous and a dupe when he is grown up. You keep saying to him: "Everything I tell you to do is for your own good, though you cannot understand that now. But what do I care whether you do what I ask or not? You are to do it for your own good." With all these fine speeches that you direct at him to make him wise, you are preparing him to fall victim to speeches he will one day hear from visionaries, alchemists, charlatans, and cheats and madmen of every kind, speeches with which they will trap him in their snares or make him adopt their madness.

A man must know many things whose usefulness a child will not understand. But can and must a child learn all that is important for a man to know? Try to teach the child everything of use to his age, and you will find that it takes up all his time. Why would you want to urge him to neglect the studies suited to his age today and apply himself to studies for an age he does not know he will reach? "But," you counter, "will it not be too late for him to learn what he must know when the time has come to put it to use?" I do not know. But what I do know is that it is impossible to learn it before that time, as our real teachers are experience and feeling, and a man never feels what suits him except in situations in which he finds himself. A child knows that he is destined to become a man. But any ideas he can have about the state of manhood can only come from what he might have been taught. He will remain in absolute ignorance about any ideas that are beyond his reach. My entire book is a constant testimony to this principle of education.

As soon as we have succeeded in giving our pupil an idea of the word *useful*, we have another great means of governing him, because this word makes a great impression on him, provided it has a meaning for him relative to his age, and that he clearly perceives its connection to his current well-being. The reason this word might make no impression on your pupils is because you have not taken care to give them an idea of it that they can grasp; others have always undertaken to provide them with what is useful to them, so they have never had to think about it for themselves and do not know what usefulness is.

"What is the use of this?" Here we now have the magic phrase, the key phrase in all our interactions. With this question I invariably counter all his questions, and it serves to check the multitude of foolish and annoying queries with which children pointlessly and tirelessly wear out everyone around them, more to gain some sort of power over them than to learn anything useful. A pupil who has been taught as the most important lesson only to want to know what is useful will ask questions like Socrates. He will not ask anything without first weighing the reason for the question, as he knows he will be required to provide this reason before he will receive an answer.

What a powerful instrument I am placing in your hands to control your pupil! As he does not know the reason for anything, you can reduce him to silence almost at will; while you, on the other hand, what an advantage your knowledge and experience gives you to show him the usefulness of everything you suggest to him! For, make no mistake: when you ask him this question you are teaching him to ask you the same question in turn, and you can be sure that whatever you propose to him thereafter, he will not fail to follow your example and ask: "What is the use of this?"

Here is perhaps the hardest trap for a tutor to avoid. If you merely try to put the child off when he asks a question, giving him a single reason that he is not at a level to understand, he, seeing you reasoning according to your own ideas and not his, will believe that what you are telling him is good for your age but not for his; he will no longer trust you, and all will be lost. But what tutor will stop to admit his faults to his pupil? Tutors tend to make it a rule never to admit to the faults they have, while I would make it a rule to admit even to faults I do not have, if I cannot otherwise make the child grasp my reasons. This way my conduct, always clear in his mind, will never strike him as suspect, and I will garner more credit in claiming supposed faults than those who conceal theirs.

First of all, you should keep in mind that it is rarely up to you to suggest what he ought to learn. It is for him to desire it, seek it out, and find it, while it is for you to bring it within his reach, skillfully awakening this desire and furnishing him with the means to satisfy it. It follows that your questions should be few but well chosen, and as he will have more questions to put to you than you to him, you will always be less exposed and more often in a position to reply: "What is the use of knowing the answer to what you are asking me?" Moreover, it is of little consequence whether he learns one thing or another, as long as he has a good understanding of what he is learning and what it is useful for, because as soon as you cannot give him an explanation about what you are telling him that satisfies him, it is better not to give him one at all. Do not hesitate to tell him: "I do not have a good answer for that. I was wrong, let us drop the subject." If your choice of subject was truly ill-advised, there is no harm in dropping it altogether, and if not, with a little care you will soon find the opportunity to make him see its usefulness.

In discoursing, I do not like explanations. The young pay little attention to them and retain hardly anything. What matters are palpable things, real things! I cannot repeat often enough that we give too much importance to the power of words: with our babbling education we can only produce babblers.

[...]

From Book IV

[...]

It is man's weakness that makes him sociable: our common sufferings draw us to other humans, and we would have no duties to humanity if we were not human. All attachment is a sign of insufficiency; if we did not need anyone else, nobody would ever think of associating with another. Consequently, our frail happiness is born from our weakness. A truly happy being is a solitary being. Only God enjoys absolute happiness, but who among us can conceive what that means? If some imperfect being could be sufficient unto himself, then what, in our eyes, would he delight in? He would be alone and miserable. I cannot conceive how he who needs nothing can love something, nor can I conceive that he who loves nothing can be happy.

It follows from this that we attach ourselves to our fellow creatures less through feeling their pleasures than through feeling their pain, for we more clearly see our nature in that, and a guarantee of their attachment to us. If our common needs unite us through interest, our common misery unites us through empathy; the sight of a happy man inspires envy rather than love. We are prepared to accuse him of seizing a right that is not his in seeking happiness for himself alone, and our self-regard suffers, too, in making us feel that that man has no need of us.[167] But who will not lament an unhappy man he sees suffering? Who would not wish to deliver him from his troubles if a simple wish sufficed? Imagination puts us in the place of the wretched man more readily than in that of the happy one; we feel that the state of the one touches us more closely than that of the other. Pity is sweet, because by putting ourselves in the place of the one who is suffering, we nevertheless feel the pleasure of not suffering as he does. Envy is bitter, because the sight of someone who is happy, far from putting the envious man in the happy man's place, sparks in him the regret that the happiness is not his. It seems that the wretched man exempts us from the misfortunes he is suffering, while the happy man robs us of the good he is enjoying.

So do you want to excite and nourish in the heart of a youth the first stirrings of an awakening sensibility, and turn his character toward beneficence and goodness? Then do not nurture in him pride, vanity, and envy with the deceptive image of the happiness of mankind. Do not show him the pomp of the courts, the ostentation of the palaces, or the attractions of the theater. Do not step out into society with him or take him to brilliant assemblies. Do not show him the face of high society until you have made him able to evaluate it for what it is. Showing him the world before he knows mankind is not educating him but corrupting him, not teaching him but misleading him.

Men are by nature neither kings, grandees, courtiers, nor persons of wealth. All are born naked and poor, and all are subject to the miseries of life, to its sorrows, evils, needs, and suffering of every kind. In the end, all are condemned to die. This is truly man's lot, from which no mortal is exempt. One must begin with the study of what is most basic to human nature, that which best embodies humanity.

At sixteen, the adolescent knows the meaning of suffering, for he himself has suffered; but he has little inkling that other beings suffer as well: to see suffering without feeling it is not to know it, and, as I have said many times, a child does not imagine what others feel but knows only his own troubles. Yet when the development of the senses first ignites in him the fire of imagination, he begins to sense himself in his fellows, to be touched by their laments, to suffer their pains. It is at this time that the sad tableau of suffering humanity ought to touch his heart with a first feeling of compassion.

If it is not easy to discover this moment in your children, then who is to blame? You teach them so early to feign feeling, you teach them its language, so that using its vocabulary they turn your lessons against you, and leave you no means of distinguishing when they stop lying and begin to feel what they are saying. But consider my Émile: at the age to which I have brought him, he has neither felt nor feigned feeling. Before knowing what love means, he has never said to anyone "I love you so much." He has never been told what expression to assume on entering the sickroom of his ailing father, mother, or tutor. He has not been shown the art of affecting a sorrow he does not feel. He has not pretended to weep at anyone's death, since he does not know what it means to die. He has the same insensibility in his heart that he has in his manners. Indifferent to everything outside himself, like all children, he shows no interest in anyone. The only thing that distinguishes him is that he does not try to feign interest and is not insincere, as others are.

Having given little thought to living, feeling creatures,

Émile consequently will learn late the meaning of suffering and dying. Laments and cries will begin to touch him deeply, the sight of blood will make him turn away, the convulsions of a dying animal will cause him I know not what anguish before he knows from where these new impulses arise. If he had remained dull and uncivilized he would not have had these impulses, and if he had been more instructed he would have recognized their source. He has already compared ideas too frequently not to feel anything, but not enough to understand what he is feeling.

Consequently, pity is born—the first relative feeling that touches the human heart according to the order of nature. To become sensitive and capable of pity, the child must know that there are beings like himself who suffer what he has suffered, who feel the pains he has felt, as well as other pains he should be able to imagine feeling. In fact, how can we let ourselves be moved to pity if we are not capable of thinking beyond ourselves and identifying with the suffering animal; by leaving, so to speak, our being in order to assume the other's being? We suffer only so far as we suppose that the other creature is suffering. It is not within ourselves that we are suffering, but within the other. Consequently, no one becomes sensitive until his imagination is awakened and begins to take him outside himself.

What can we do to stimulate and nourish this nascent sensibility, to guide it or follow it in its natural inclination? What can we do other than offer the youth objects on which the expansive force of his heart can act, making it grow and extend to other creatures? Objects that make him responsive to all that is outside himself, carefully keeping away those that restrict his heart and tighten the spring of the human self? To put this in other words, we should excite in him goodness, humanity, commiseration, and beneficence, all the gentle and attractive passions that are naturally pleasing to man, and we should prevent the birth of envy, covetousness, and hatred, all the repulsive and cruel passions that make sensibility not only nothing, but negative, and torment the person who experiences them.

[...]

Readers, do not fear that I will measure my words in a way unworthy of a lover of truth. I shall never forget my motto, but I tend too easily to distrust my own judgment.[168] So instead of telling you what I myself think, I will tell you what a man thought who was worthier than I. I avow the truth of the facts I shall recount. It is what truly happened to the author whose writings I shall transcribe, and it will be for you to decide whether useful reflections about the matter at hand can be gained from them. I am not proffering my ideas or those of another, but placing them before you for you to examine.

Thirty years ago, in an Italian town, a young exile found himself reduced to utter destitution.[169] He had been born a Calvinist, but as the result of an act of folly had ended up a fugitive in a foreign land, and, bereft of means, converted to Catholicism so that he would have bread to eat. In that town there was a hospice for proselytes. He was admitted. Instructing him in doctrine, they inspired doubts he had never had, and taught him evil he had never known. He was introduced to new dogma, and encountered even newer morals. He encountered them and almost fell victim to them. He tried to flee, but was locked up; he complained, and was punished for complaining. At the mercy of his tyrants, he found himself treated as a criminal for having refused to submit to the crime. Those who know how much the first experience of violence and injustice inflames a young inexperienced heart can imagine the state of his. Tears of anger flowed from his eyes, indignation choked him. He implored the heavens and men, he tried to confide in everyone, but no one listened. All he saw were the vile lackeys of the wretch who had attacked him, or accomplices in the same crime, who jeered at his resistance and urged him to imitate their ways. He would have been lost were it not for an honest priest who came to the hospice on some business, and to whom he contrived to speak in secret. The priest was poor, and himself in need of any help he could get, but the oppressed boy needed his help even more, and the priest did not hesitate to assist him in escaping at the risk of making dangerous enemies.

Having escaped vice only to face destitution, the youth struggled against his destiny in vain. For a moment he thought himself above it. At the first glimmer of good fortune, he forgot his woes as well as his protector. He was soon punished for this ingratitude: all his hopes vanished. Though his youth was in his favor, his romantic ideas ruined everything. He had neither talent enough nor the skill to make his path easy; not knowing how to be circumspect or evil, he aspired to so many things that he achieved nothing. Having sunk back to his former destitution, without bread, without shelter, on the point of starving to death, he remembered his benefactor.

He went back, found the priest, and was well received. The sight of the boy reminded the priest of the good deed he had done, and such a memory always lifts the soul. This priest was by nature humane and compassionate. He felt the suffering of others through his own, and his heart had not been hardened by prosperity; in a word, the lessons of wisdom and an enlightened virtue had affirmed his natural kindness. He welcomed the youth, sought lodgings and a position for him, and shared with him a meager living barely enough for two. And he did more: he tutored him, consoled him, and taught him the difficult art of enduring adversity with patience. O prejudiced people! Would you have expected all this in a priest, and in Italy?

This honest clergyman was a poor Savoyard vicar whom a

youthful romance had dishonored in his bishop's eyes, and who had crossed the Alps to find a position he could no longer attain in his own country. He lacked neither intelligence nor learning, and, as he had a pleasant countenance, he found patrons who secured him the position of tutor to the son of a government minister. But he preferred poverty to dependence, and did not know how to comport himself among the nobility. He did not long remain with the minister, but in leaving him did not lose his esteem. As he lived virtuously and won everyone's heart, he hoped to find his way back to the good graces of his bishop and be granted a small parish in the mountains where he could spend the rest of his days. Such was the ultimate goal of his ambition.

A natural liking drew the priest to the young fugitive and made him examine his qualities with care, seeing that bad fortune had already seared the boy's heart, that scorn and contempt had beaten down his courage, and that his pride had turned into bitter spite, leading him to see in the injustice and harshness of men nothing but the evil in their nature and the illusion of virtue. The boy had seen that religion served only as a mask for self-interest and the holy services as a screen for hypocrisy. He had found in the subtleties of empty disputations Heaven and Hell awarded as prizes for word play. He had seen the sublime and primitive idea of divinity disfigured by the fantastical fancies of men, and, finding that to believe in God one had to renounce the judgments received from God, he held our foolish imaginings about the deity in equal disdain with the object to which we apply them. Without any knowledge of what is, without any inkling of the origin of things, the boy immersed himself in his dull ignorance with a deep disdain for all who thought they knew more than he did.

The neglect of all religion leads to the neglect of the duties of man. That progress had already been more than half completed in the young libertine's heart. And yet he had not been born with a bad nature, though poverty and lack of faith were gradually stifling his natural disposition, and rapidly dragging him down to ruin and to the morals of a rogue and the morality of an atheist.

The evil that was almost inevitable had not, however, entirely prevailed. The youth had some knowledge, and his education had not been neglected. He was at that happy age where fermenting blood begins to heat the soul without delivering it to the raging of the senses. His soul still had its resilience. An innate modesty and timid disposition contributed to his awkwardness and prolonged the period in which one watches over one's pupil with so much care. Far from sparking his imagination, the odious examples of brutal depravity and charmless vice had deadened it. For a long time it was disgust instead of virtue that preserved his innocence, which was to succumb only later to sweeter seductions.

The priest saw both the danger and the boy's promise. He was not discouraged by the difficulties, and he delighted in the task. He was determined to complete it and lead to virtue the victim he had snatched from infamy. He trod carefully to gain his ends, the beauty of the cause firing his courage and inspiring him with means worthy of his zeal. Whatever the degree of success, he was certain not to have wasted his time: one always succeeds when one aims to do good.

The priest set out to gain his proselyte's confidence not by parading his good offices or imposing himself and sermonizing, but by always being within the boy's reach and humbling himself in order to become his equal. It was, I believe, a touching sight to see a serious man become the comrade of a rogue, to see virtue lend itself to licentiousness in order to triumph over it. When the foolish boy confided his silly secrets and poured out his heart to the priest, the priest listened and put him at ease; without approving of the evil, he took an interest in everything. No tactless reproof restrained the boy's chatter or led him to close his heart. The pleasure with which he believed that the priest was listening to him heightened the pleasure with which he revealed everything. Thus, without intending to confess, he made a complete confession.

After the priest had carefully studied the boy's character and feelings, he clearly saw that although he was not ignorant for his age, he had forgotten everything that was important for him to know, and that the disgrace to which fortune had reduced him had smothered in him all true sense of good and evil. There is a degree of debasement that robs the soul of its life, and the inner voice cannot make itself heard by one who is only thinking of how to feed himself. To protect the unlucky youth from the moral danger that was threatening him, the priest began by awakening in him esteem and regard for himself. He showed him a happier future that could be attained with the right use of his talents. He rekindled in his heart a generous warmth by relating stories of the noble deeds of others, and, by inspiring in him an admiration for those who had done these deeds, stirred the boy's desire to follow their example. In order to draw him imperceptibly away from the idle life of a vagabond, he had him copy out extracts from well-chosen books, and, pretending to need these extracts, nurtured in him the noble feeling of gratitude. He instructed him indirectly through these books, and made him regain a good opinion of himself so that he would no longer think himself a creature useless in every way, or one contemptible in his own eyes.

A trivial incident will illustrate the craft this beneficent man used to raise his pupil's heart up out of its baseness without seeming to. The priest was so renowned for his honesty and good judgment that many preferred to entrust their alms to him rather than to the rich curates of the towns. One day, when the priest had been given some money to distribute among the poor, the youth, claiming his own poverty, had the temerity to ask for some of the money for himself. "No," the priest replied, "we are brothers, and as you are part of me I cannot touch this sum for my own use." Then from his own pocket he gave the boy the amount he had asked for. Lessons of this kind are rarely lost on the heart of a young person who is not entirely corrupted.

I am tired of speaking in the third person, a superfluous precaution, as I am certain you must be aware, fellow citizen, that the unfortunate fugitive was myself. I am, I believe, far enough removed from the transgressions of my youth that I may venture to admit them, and the man who drew me away from these transgressions deserves that I should honor his kind deed at the cost of a little shame.

What had the greatest effect on me was to see in my worthy tutor's own life a virtue without hypocrisy, a humanity without weakness, a discourse that was always direct and simple, and conduct that was always in accord with his discourse. I never saw him trouble over whether those he helped went to vespers, whether they confessed often enough or fasted on the appointed days, nor did I see him impose such or similar conditions, not following which you could die of starvation sooner than expect any help from the devout.

I was encouraged by these observations, and far from affecting the zeal of the new convert, I did not make a great effort to hide from him my way of thinking, nor did he seem any the more shocked by it. There were times when I might have said to myself that he was overlooking my indifference to the religion I had embraced because he saw that I was equally indifferent to the religion I was born into, and consequently knew that my disdain was not partisan. But what was I to think when I sometimes heard him approve of dogmas contrary to those of the Roman Catholic Church, and when he seemed to show little regard for its ceremonies? I should have thought him a covert Protestant had I seen him less faithful to the same practices of which he seemed to make little. But I knew that he fulfilled his duties as a priest as punctiliously in private as he did in public, and so I did not know what to make of these contradictions. Except for the fault that had brought about his disgrace, a fault for which he had been unfairly punished, his life was exemplary, his morals beyond reproach, his discourses frank and prudent. While I lived so close to him, I learned day by day to respect him more. My heart won over entirely by so much goodness, I awaited with impatient curiosity the moment when I might learn the principle on which he founded the consistency of so singular a life.

This moment did not come quickly. Before confiding in his pupil, the priest tried his utmost to ensure that the seeds of reason and goodness he had planted in the boy's soul would sprout. What was hardest in me to eradicate was a proud misanthropy, and a certain bitterness against those who were rich and happy, as if their wealth and happiness had been gained at my expense, and as if the happiness they claimed had usurped mine. The foolish vanity of youth that resists humiliation gave me too much of an inclination to an angry humor, and the self-respect that my mentor strove to awaken in me led me to pride, which made people even more base in my eyes and succeeded only in adding contempt to my hatred of them.

Without attacking my pride directly, he prevented it from

turning into hard-heartedness, and without stripping me of my self-esteem made my pride less scornful of my fellow men. Always pushing aside vain appearance and showing me the real evils it conceals, he taught me to deplore the errors of my fellow men, to be touched by their misery, and to feel pity for them rather than envy. His deep awareness of his own weaknesses moved him to compassion for human failings as he saw people fall victim to their vices and those of others: the poor groaning under the yoke of the rich, and the rich under the yoke of prejudice. "Believe me," he said, "our illusions, far from concealing our evils from us, only increase them by giving importance to things that have no importance, and making us sensitive to a thousand false privations we would not otherwise feel. Peace of soul consists of disdain for everything that could trouble it. The man who clings most persistently to life knows least how to enjoy it, and he who aspires most eagerly to happiness is always the most miserable."

"Oh, what a sad picture!" I exclaimed bitterly. "If we must deny ourselves everything, what is the point of being born? And if we have to spurn even happiness itself, who is capable of being happy?" "I am," the priest replied one day in a tone that took me aback. "You? Happy? You, to whom fortune has been so unkind, who are poor, exiled, and persecuted, you are happy? How can that be?" "My child," he replied, "I will gladly tell you."

Thereupon he said that having heard my confessions, he would now confess to me: "I will pour out the feelings of my heart to you," he said, embracing me. "You will see me, if not as I am, then at least as I see myself. When you have heard my whole profession of faith, when you know the state of my soul, you will know why I consider myself happy; and, if you think as I do, you will know what to do in order to be happy as well.

But these avowals are not a matter of a few moments. I will need time to expose all my ideas to you about the fate of man and the true value of life. Let us choose a time and suitable place so we can continue this conversation in a calmer setting."

I expressed my eagerness to hear him. Our meeting was arranged for the very next morning. It was summer, and we woke up at the break of day. He took me to a hill outside the town above the river Po, which we could see flowing between its fertile banks. In the distance, the vast chain of the Alps crowned the landscape. The rays of the rising sun already touched the plains, casting onto the fields long shadows of trees, slopes, and houses, brightening with a thousand shimmers of light the most beautiful scene that could strike the human eye. One would have thought that nature was displaying all her splendor to give us the text for our conversation. It was there, after contemplating nature in silence, that the man of peace spoke to me as follows:

THE SAVOYARD VICAR'S PROFESSION OF FAITH

My child, do not expect from me learned speech or profound reasoning. I am not a great philosopher, nor do I desire to be one. But I have a certain amount of common sense and a profound love of truth.

[...]

If the soul is immaterial, it can survive the body, and if it survives the body, providence is justified. If my only proof of the immateriality of the soul was the triumph of everything that is wicked in this world and the oppression of all that is just, that alone would prevent me from doubt. So shocking a dissonance in the universal harmony would have led me to attempt to resolve it, and to tell myself: "Everything does not end for us with life's end—with death everything returns to order." But I would, in truth, find it difficult to ask myself what becomes of man when all his senses are destroyed. This question no longer presents any difficulty to me when I have acknowledged the two states. It is easy enough to understand that, as during my physical life I can perceive only through my senses, whatever is imperceptible to these senses will escape me. Once the union of soul and body is destroyed, I conceive that the former may be dissolved and the latter preserved. But why should destruction of the one involve destruction of the other? On the contrary, being of such different natures they exist during their union in a violent condition, but when this union comes to an end, they both return to their natural state. The active and living substance regains all the force it used in setting the passive dead substance in motion. Alas! My vices make me feel too keenly that during this life man is only half alive, and that the life of the soul begins only with the death of the body.

But what is this life, and is the soul immortal by its nature? My limited understanding can conceive of nothing without limits; everything that is called infinite escapes me. What can I deny or affirm, what judgment can I make about matters I cannot conceive? I believe that the soul survives the body long enough to maintain order, but who knows if this is enough to last forever? I can comprehend how the body uses and destroys itself by the division of its parts, but I cannot conceive a similar destruction of the thinking being, and as I cannot imagine how this being can die, I presume that it will not. Since this assumption consoles me and is not unreasonable, why should I be afraid of accepting it?

I am aware of my soul. I know it through feeling and through thought; I know that it exists, but without knowing what its essence is; I cannot reason about knowledge I do not have. What I do know is that the identity of the self is prolonged only by memory, and that to be the same in reality, I must remember that I have existed. And yet after my death I would not be able to remember what I was during my life unless I could also remember what I felt, and, consequently, what I did. And I have no doubt that this memory will one day bring happiness to those who are good and torment to those who are evil. In this world a thousand ardent passions absorb inner feeling and cheat remorse. The humiliations and disgrace that the practice of virtue attracts do not permit us to realize all its charms. But once we have been delivered from the illusions of the bodily senses, we rejoice in the contemplation of the Supreme Being and the eternal truths of which He is the source. When the beauty of order strikes and we are solely occupied in comparing what we have done with what we ought to have done, it is then that the voice of conscience will reclaim its force and power; it is then that the pure delight born of self-contentment and the bitter regret of having debased the self will distinguish by inexhaustible feeling the fate that each has prepared for himself. Do not ask me, dear friend, whether there will be other sources of happiness or torment, for I do not know; but there are enough of them to console me in this life and to lead me to hope for a life to come. I am not saying that the good will be rewarded, for what greater good can a truly excellent being attain than to live in accordance with his nature? But I do say that the good will be happy, because their creator, the creator of all justice, having made them capable of feeling, has not created them in order to suffer; and as they have not abused their freedom on earth, they have not failed to reach their destination through their own fault. They have suffered in this life and will be compensated in the life to come. This feeling relies less on the merit of man than on the notion of goodness that seems to me inseparable from the divine essence. I merely suppose that the laws of order are observed and that God is true to Himself.[170]

Do not ask me, either, whether the torments of the wicked will be eternal. I still do not know, and I do not have the curiosity to try to settle futile questions. What do I care what becomes of the wicked? I take little interest in their fate. Nevertheless, I find it hard to believe that they will be condemned to everlasting torment. If supreme justice exacts vengeance, it does so in this life. O nations! You and your errors are its ministers! Supreme justice employs the evils you do to one another to punish the crimes that attracted those evils. It is in the bosom of your false prosperity, in your own insatiable souls corroded by envy, greed, and ambition, that the avenging passions punish your crimes. What need is there to seek Hell in the next life? It is here in this life, in the heart of the wicked.

Where our fleeting needs cease, where our meaningless desires end, our passions and crimes must also end. To what perversity can pure spirits be susceptible? As they are not in need of anything, why should they be wicked? If they are cleansed of our base senses, and all their happiness consists in the contemplation of other beings, all they can know is to want good; and can whoever ceases to be wicked be miserable forever? This is what I am inclined to believe without having made much effort to come to any conclusions. O good and clement Being! I will adore Your decrees, whatever they may be! If You will punish the wicked, I shall abandon my feeble reason before Your justice, but if the remorse of these unfortunates should die out with time, if their ills should come to an end, and if the same peace one day awaits us all, I will praise You. Is not the wicked man my brother? How many times have I been tempted to resemble him? May he be as happy as I, if, delivered from his misery, he also loses the malignity that accompanies it. His happiness, far from arousing my jealousy, will only add to mine.

In this way, contemplating God in His works and studying Him through those of His attributes that are important for me to know, I have managed to reach, and by degrees augment, the initially limited and imperfect idea of this infinite Being. But if this idea has become more noble and grand, it is also less consonant with human reason. As I approach in spirit the eternal light, I am dazzled and confused by its glory, and am compelled to abandon all terrestrial notions that help me imagine it. God is no longer corporeal and accessible to the senses; the Supreme Intelligence that rules the world is no longer the world itself. I elevate and weary my mind in vain trying to conceive His essence. When I think that this essence is what gives life and activity to active and living substance that rules living bodies, when I hear it said that my soul is spiritual and that God is a spirit, I am angered by this disparagement of the divine essence, as if God and my soul were of the same nature! As if God were not the only absolute being, the only truly active, feeling, thinking, self-determining being from whom we receive thought, feeling, activity, will, freedom, and existence. We are free only because He wills our freedom, and His inexplicable substance is to our souls what our souls are to our bodies. I do not know whether He created matter, the body, the mind, or the world. The concept of creation perplexes me and is beyond my understanding. I believe it insofar as I can conceive it; but I know that He has created the universe and all that exists, that He has made all things and put them in order. God is eternal, without doubt; but can my mind grasp the idea of eternity? Why should I deceive myself with meaningless words? What I can conceive is that He existed before all things, that He will exist as long as they do, and that if all things must come to an end some day, He will still be there. A being beyond my comprehension giving existence to other beings is veiled to me and incomprehensible; but the notion that being and nothingness might be able to convert themselves one into the other is a palpable contradiction and outright absurdity.

God is intelligent, but in what way? Man is intelligent when he reasons, but the Supreme Intelligence does not need to reason; it has neither premises nor consequences: there are not even any conditions. The Supreme Intelligence is utterly intuitive, it can see equally all that is and all that might be; and all truths are for it but a single idea, all places but a single point, and all time but a single moment. Man's power acts through means, while divine power acts from within itself. God can act because He wills to—His will is His power. God is good, nothing can be clearer, but goodness in man is love for his kind, while God's goodness is love of order, because it is through order that He sustains what exists and unites each part with the whole. God is just; and I am convinced that this is a consequence of His goodness. The injustice of men is their work, not His; the moral disorder that argues against providence in the eyes of the philosophers leads only to proving it in mine. But human justice consists in rendering to each what he deserves, while God's justice is to call each of us to account for what He has given us.

If I have sequentially come upon these attributes of which I have no absolute idea, it is through consistent reasoning and the good use of my reason; but I assert them without understanding them, and ultimately that amounts to affirming nothing. It is in vain that I say, "This is how God is; I feel it, experience it," for I cannot conceive any better how God can be so.

In the end, the more I force myself to contemplate His infinite essence, the less I can conceive it; but this essence exists, and that is enough for me; the less I can conceive it, the more I adore it. I bow before it and say: "Being of beings, I am because You are; ceaselessly meditating on You raises me to my source. The most worthy use I can make of my reason is to prostrate myself before You; it is the rapture of my mind, the allure of my weakness, to feel myself overwhelmed by Your greatness."

Hence, from the impression of physical objects and the inner feeling that leads me to evaluate causes according to my natural intelligence, I have deduced the principal truths that were important for me to know. There remains for me to ascertain which principles I must draw from these truths for my conduct, and what rules I must prescribe for myself in order to fulfill my destiny in the world according to the intention of Him who placed me here. Following my method, I do not draw these rules from the principles of a high philosophy, but find them in the depths of my heart, where nature has etched them in indelible characters. With regard to what I want to do, I need only consult myself: all that I feel to be good is good; all that I feel to be bad is bad. Conscience is the best casuist, and it is only when one haggles with conscience that one has recourse to the subtleties of reasoning. The foremost care is the duty to oneself; yet how often does our inner voice tell us that in seeking our good at the expense of others we are doing wrong? We think we are following the impulse of nature, but we are resisting it. By listening to what nature says to our senses, we devalue what it says to our hearts. The active being obeys, the passive being commands. Conscience is the voice of the soul, passions are the voice of the body. Is it surprising that these two languages are often contradictory? Then to which of them should we lend our ear? Reason deceives us too often, and we have amply acquired the right to challenge it! Conscience, on the other hand, never deceives us; it is the true guide of man, and is to the soul what instinct is to the body. He who follows conscience obeys nature, and need not fear that he will stray.

[...]

When my method results in the same answer from whatever perspective I consider the problem, and avoiding one difficulty anticipates another, I consider my method good and that I am on the right path. This is what I believe I see in the method I am suggesting. If I choose to be stern and cool toward my pupil, I will lose his confidence and he will soon hide from me. If I choose not to be rigorous, or to look the other way, what good does it do him to be under my care? That would be giving my stamp of approval to his excesses, and relieving his conscience at the expense of my own. If I introduce him into society with no other object than teaching him, he might learn more than I wish. If I keep him away from society until he is of age, what will he have learned from me? Everything, perhaps, except the one skill most necessary to a man and citizen, that of knowing how to live with his fellow men. If I give him a task that will be useful too far in the future, it will be to no avail, as he is concerned only with the present. If I am merely content with supplying him with amusements, what good will that do him? He will become spoiled and learn nothing.

I will have none of this. My method alone provides for everything. "Your heart," I tell the youth, "needs a companion. Let us seek a girl who will be suitable; she will perhaps be hard to find, since true worth is always rare, but let us not be in a hurry, nor easily disheartened. No doubt there is such a girl, and we will find her in the end, or at least one as like her as possible." With a project so attractive to him, I introduce him into society. What more need I say? Have I not done everything?

You can be certain that by portraying to him the companion I have in mind for him, I will know how to prepare him properly for what he should seek or flee. I would have to be the clumsiest of men were I to fail in making him passionate for someone before he knows who she is. It does not matter that the person I portray to him is imaginary; it is enough that it will make him detest those who would have otherwise attracted him; it is enough if, wherever he looks, he finds comparisons who make him prefer the girl of his fantasy to the real women who catch his attention. For what is true love if not a chimera, lie, and illusion? One is far more in love with the image one creates than with the object to which one applies it. If we saw what we loved exactly the way it is, there would be no more love in this world. When we stop loving, the person we loved remains the same as before, but we no longer see her as such; the magic veil of illusion drops and love disappears. But by supplying the imaginary object, I am the master of comparisons, and can easily forestall the illusion of real objects.

I would not want to deceive a young man by portraying a model of perfection that cannot exist; but I will choose the kinds of faults in his mistress in such a way that they will suit him, please him, and serve to correct his own. I would not want to lie to him either, affirming falsely that the person I am depicting really exists; but if he delights in the portrait, he will soon hope for the original. The road from hope to belief is a short one; it is a matter of a few skillful descriptions, which, with some well-chosen features, will give this imaginary object a greater air of reality. I would go so far as to give her a name; I would say with a smile: "Let us call your future beloved Sophie. Sophie is a name that augurs well; if the companion you will choose does not bear this name, she will at least be worthy of it, and we can honor her with it in advance."[171] If, after all this, one

neither affirms nor denies her existence, but sidesteps with eva-
sions, his suspicions will become certainty: he will think you
are concealing his destined bride from him, and that he will see
her when the time is right. Once he has arrived at that conclusion and the beloved's traits shown to him have been well chosen, the rest is simple; there will be almost no risk in presenting
him to society. If you protect him from his senses, his heart will
be safe.

But whether or not he will perceive the model I have managed to make so attractive to him to be real, this model, if it is
well presented, will draw him to whatever resembles it and distance him from anything unlike it. This is a great means to
shield his heart from the dangers to which he will be exposed,
to repress his senses with his imagination, and above all to rescue him from those ladies who seek to educate a young man,
making him pay dearly for this education, teaching him elegant
manners by depriving him of all his honesty. Sophie is such a
modest maiden—with what eye can he view the advances of
these others? Sophie is so simple—how can he appreciate the
airs they assume? There is too great a distance between his
ideal and what he sees for the latter to be dangerous.

[...]

From Book V

[…]

Always justify the tasks you set for young girls, but keep giving them tasks. Idleness and disobedience are the two most dangerous faults for them, and the hardest to cure once contracted. Girls should be attentive and diligent. But that is not all; they ought to be kept in check from an early age. This misfortune, if they consider it one, is inherent in their sex, and they will never escape it except to suffer even more cruelly. Their whole life they will have to submit to the strictest and most enduring restraints, those of decorum. They must be trained early in this, so they can master their whims with ease, submitting themselves to the will of others. If they are eager to work, one must sometimes force them to do nothing. Extravagance, frivolity, and caprice are faults that are quick to develop from a first taste of corruption. To avert these faults, above all teach them restraint. In our senseless mores, the life of a decent woman is a constant struggle against herself. But it is only fair that womankind should bear the share of the evils they have caused mankind.

Prevent girls from becoming bored with their tasks and keen on their amusements, which always happens in vulgar methods of education where, as Fénelon says, all the boredom is on one side and all pleasure on the other.[172] Boredom with their tasks can be avoided if the rules laid down are followed, unless the girl dislikes those whose care she is under. A little girl who loves her mother or governess will work all day at her side without being bored. The chatter alone will make up for the constraint. But if she finds the person who is overseeing her unbearable, she will perceive everything she does under that person's charge as distasteful. It is unlikely that girls will turn out well if they do not enjoy their mother's company more than anyone else's; but to judge their real feelings you must observe them and not simply trust what they say, for they are flatterers and learn at an early age to dissimulate. They should not be told to love their mothers, either, as affection cannot be the result of duty; here constraint is out of place. Attachment, care, and habit alone can make a daughter love her mother, if the mother does not do anything to incur her hatred. Even the constraint under which the mother keeps her child, if it is judicious, will increase rather than diminish a daughter's affection: as dependence is a natural state for women, girls feel themselves made for obedience.

For the same reason that girls have or ought to have little freedom, they will carry to excess the freedom they are allowed. Extreme in everything, they abandon themselves to their games with even more enthusiasm than boys do. This is one of the difficulties that I have just mentioned. Such enthusiasm must be kept in check, for it is the cause of a number of faults particular to women, such as caprice and infatuation, which will lead a woman to raptures today about something she will not even look at tomorrow. A fickleness of taste is as dangerous to them as their excesses, and both come from the same source. Do not deprive them of fun, laughter, noise, and rollicking games, but do not let them have their fill of one game in order to rush to another; do not allow for a single unchecked moment in their lives. Accustom them to being interrupted in the middle of their games, and encouraged to occupy themselves with something else without complaining. Habit alone is still all that is needed, for it merely reinforces nature.

This habitual restraint results in a docility that women will need all their lives, since they never cease to be subjected to a man or to the judgments of men, and they will never be allowed to put themselves above these. The first and most important quality in a woman is gentleness; created to obey a creature as imperfect as man, who is often prone to vice and whose character is always flawed, she must learn early to suffer injustice, and bear without complaint the wrongs her husband inflicts on her. It is for her own sake, not his, that she must be gentle. Bitterness and obstinacy in women only multiply their sufferings and their husbands' bad comportment, for men feel that it is not with such weapons that they ought to be conquered. Heaven did not make women ingenious and persuasive so they might become shrews, nor weak so they might be imperious; it did not give them such soft voices to utter hard words, such delicate features so that frowns might disfigure them with anger. When women become angry, they forget themselves. They often have cause to complain, but they are always wrong to scold. One should keep the tone that befits one's sex; a husband who is too gentle can render a wife impertinent, but unless a man is a monster, the gentleness of a woman will, sooner or later, win him over, and she will ultimately triumph over him.

Girls must always be obedient, but mothers should not always be too hard on them. To make a girl docile, one must not make her unhappy; to make her modest, one must not dull her mind; on the contrary, I would not be displeased to see her permitted to show a little resourcefulness, not in order to evade punishment for disobedience, but to evade the necessity for obedience. Her dependence need not be made onerous; it is enough that she should be made to feel it. Wiliness is a talent natural to the fair sex, and as I am persuaded that all natural inclinations are good and right in themselves, I believe that this one should be cultivated just like all the others; it is only a matter of preventing its abuse.

For the truth of these remarks, I call upon every honest observer. I do not propose that you question women themselves in this matter, for our irksome mores have led them to sharpen their wits; I would rather that one examine girls—little girls, just out of the nursery, so to speak—and compare them to boys of the same age, and if you do not find the latter awkward and foolish by comparison, I will most certainly have been wrong. Permit me to give a single example with all its childish ingenuousness.

It is quite common to forbid children to ask for anything at table, since it is widely believed that the most successful upbringing is to heap them with useless rules. As if a small portion of this or that could not be easily granted or refused without leaving a poor child forever consumed by greed sharpened with hope.[173] Everyone knows the resourcefulness of a little boy subjected to this law when he has been overlooked at table and who will then ask for some salt or the like. I would not say that one could chide him for asking directly for salt and indirectly for meat; such neglect is so cruel that I cannot believe he would have been punished had he finally broken the rule and said openly that he was hungry. But here is how a little girl of six once acted in a case that was far more difficult, because not only had she been strictly forbidden to ask for anything directly or indirectly, but any such disobedience would not have been pardoned.

The little girl had eaten from every dish except one, of which they had forgotten to give her some, and which she very much wanted. So to repair this omission without anyone being able to accuse her of disobedience, she pointed to every dish in turn, saying out loud as she pointed: "I've had some of this. I've had some of that." But she made such a show of passing over in silence the dish of which she had not eaten, that someone noticed and asked: "What about that one? Haven't you had some?" "Oh, no, I haven't," the little glutton replied sweetly, lowering her eyes. I need not say more. Compare the two: this trick is the astuteness of a little girl, the other that of a little boy.

What is, is good, and no general law is bad. This special skill with which the fair sex has been endowed is a just compensation for its lesser strength, for without this ability a woman would not be man's companion but his slave. It is through this superiority of talent that she remains his equal, ruling him while obeying him. Woman has everything against her: our defects, her timidity, her weakness. She has only artfulness and beauty in her favor. Is it then not fair that she should cultivate both? Yet beauty cannot be taken for granted; it can perish in any number of accidents and disappears with time, while habit destroys its effect. Wit alone is the true resource of the fair sex; not the foolish kind of wit that society values so much and which does nothing to make life happy, but the wit of a woman's position, and her art of exploiting the positions we men hold, reaping the benefits of our particular advantages. We are not aware to what extent this ability that women have is useful to us, the charm it gives to the society of men and women, how it serves to suppress the petulance of children or restrains brutal husbands, and the extent to which it maintains a peaceful household that otherwise would be full of strife. I am aware that crafty and wicked women will misuse this quality, but is there any quality that vice will not abuse? We must not destroy the instruments of happiness because wicked people sometimes use them to do harm.

[...]

Sophie is not indulgent when it comes to the proper attentions of love; quite the opposite: in this matter she is imperious and exacting. She would rather not be loved at all than be loved in moderation. Hers is that noble pride of merit that is aware of itself and its worth and that wants to be honored as it honors itself. She would scorn a heart that did not sense the full value of hers, that did not love her for her virtues as much and more than it loved her for her charms; a heart that did not put duty to her above duty to itself, and did not prefer her to everything else. Not that she wanted a lover who knew no rules but hers: she wants to reign over a man whom she has not subdued. It was thus that Circe, having debased Ulysses' companions, disdaining them, gave herself only to the man she could not change.[174]

But apart from this sacred and inviolable right, Sophie is extremely jealous of all her own rights and observes carefully how Émile respects them, gauging the extent of his zeal to do her will, his skill in guessing her wishes, and the care with which he arrives at the appointed hour. She wants him to be neither early nor late: he must arrive exactly on time. If he arrives early, he is thinking more of himself than of her, and if late, he is neglecting her. To neglect Sophie! It will not happen twice. An undue suspicion that he had neglected her almost ruined everything, but Sophie is equitable and knows how to redress her errors.

One evening we were expected: Émile had been sent an invitation. They come out to meet us, but we do not arrive. "What has become of them? What misfortune has befallen them? Why have they not sent word?" They spend the evening waiting for us. Poor Sophie fears us dead. She is inconsolable, tormented, and spends the night weeping. Earlier in the evening a messenger had been sent to inquire after us and bring back news the following morning. The messenger returns in the company of another messenger sent by us, who delivers our excuses, saying that we are well. A moment later we appear ourselves. Suddenly the scene changes: Sophie dries her tears, or if she sheds any, they are now tears of anger. Her proud heart is not won over by the discovery that we are not dead. Émile is alive and has needlessly kept her waiting.

When we arrive, Sophie wants to lock herself in her room. Her father desires her to remain, and she must acquiesce, but she immediately affects a calm and happy air that might deceive most people. Her father comes forward to receive us and says: "You have distressed your friends; there are some here who will not readily forgive you."

"Who might they be, papa?" Sophie asks, with the most gracious smile she can affect. "Why should you care," her father says, "as long as it is not you?"

Sophie does not reply and lowers her eyes to her embroidery. Her mother receives us with a cold and formal air. Émile is so embarrassed that he does not dare address Sophie. She speaks first, inquiring how he has been keeping, inviting him to sit down, and she puts on such a good pretense that the poor youth, who as yet knows nothing of the language of violent passions, is deceived by her cool demeanor and is on the point of taking offense.

To disabuse him, I try to take Sophie's hand and raise it to my lips as I sometimes do, but she abruptly draws it back, uttering "Monsieur!" in such an unusual manner that her involuntary movement immediately opens Émile's eyes.

Sophie, seeing that she has betrayed herself, is less guarded, her apparent indifference changing into ironic contempt. She replies to everything that is said to her in monosyllables, which she utters slowly and with a wavering voice as if she were afraid that a touch of indignation might show through. Émile, half dead with fear, looks at her with anguish, trying to draw her eyes to his so he can read her true feelings. Sophie, even more irritated at his audacity, casts a glance at him that robs him of the wish for another. Fortunately, Émile, taken aback and trembling, dares neither to look at her nor speak to her, for, even if he were innocent, she would not have forgiven him his enduring her anger.

Seeing that it is now my turn, and that the time to explain has come, I return to Sophie. I again take her hand, which she does not withdraw this time, as she is close to fainting. I say to her gently: "Dear Sophie, we are in a predicament, but you are reasonable and just; you will not judge us without first hearing us out. So please listen to us."

She does not reply, and so I speak: "We set out yesterday at four o'clock; we were to be here at seven, and we always allow ourselves more time than necessary so we can rest a little before arriving. We were already three-quarters of the way here when we heard a man calling out in pain. The cries were coming from some distance away, from a hollow near the hill. We hurried toward the cries and found a poor peasant who had been riding home from town after having drunk a little too much wine, and who had fallen so heavily from his horse that he had broken his leg. We kept shouting for help, but nobody came. We tried to lift the injured man back onto his horse, but could not; at the least movement the poor man suffered terrible pain. We decided to tie the horse in the nearby woods, and joined hands to carry the man as gently as we could, following his directions for the way to his home. The way was long and we had to rest several times. At last we got there, though utterly exhausted. We realized to our bitter surprise that we knew the house, and that the poor man we had carried back with so much effort was the same man who had received us with much kindness the day we had first arrived in these parts. In all the commotion we had not recognized each other until that moment.

"There were only two little children in the house along with his wife, who was about to present him with a third. She was so distressed at the sight of him that she was beset by labor pains and gave birth a few hours later. What could we have done under these circumstances in a remote cottage where there could be no help? Émile decided to go and get the horse we had left in the woods and ride as fast as he could to find a surgeon in the town. He gave the surgeon the horse, and, unable to find a nurse, returned on foot with a servant after having dispatched a messenger to you. I, in the meantime, as you can imagine, was at a loss back at the house, caught up as I was between a man with a broken leg and a woman in labor; but I did everything I could to help them both.

"I will not burden you with all the other details, as they are not relevant. It was two o'clock in the morning before Émile or I had a moment's rest. Finally, we arrived before daybreak at our lodgings near here, where we awaited the hour you would arise in order to inform you of what had happened."

I fell silent and said no more. But before anyone could speak, Émile approached his beloved Sophie and said, firmly and with greater resolve than I would have expected: "Sophie, you are the arbiter of my fate. You know that well. You can make me die of grief, but do not hope to make me forget the rights of humanity; those rights are more sacred to me than yours; I shall never renounce them for you."

At these words, Sophie, by way of reply, rose, put her arm around his neck, kissed him on the cheek, and, offering him her hand with inimitable grace, said to him: "Émile, take this hand; it is yours. Become my husband and my master whenever you wish, and I shall try to be worthy of the honor."

Scarcely had she kissed him when her delighted father clapped his hands and called out, "Encore, encore!" and Sophie, without further ado, gave Émile two more kisses on the other cheek; but then immediately, afraid of what she had done, she took refuge in her mother's arms and hid her face, burning with shame, in the maternal bosom.

JULIE, OR, THE NEW HÉLOÏSE

As Rousseau relates in the Confessions, *when he was living at the Hermitage in his mid-forties, feeling the advance of age and grieving for the grand romantic passion he had never experienced, he unexpectedly found himself writing a novel. It was told in epistolary form as an exchange of letters between Julie d'Étange, a young woman from the minor Swiss nobility in the Vaud region in Switzerland, and her tutor, who is never explicitly named but who is nicknamed Saint-Preux, with connotations of chivalric prowess. Julie also corresponds with her cousin and best friend, Claire, and Saint-Preux with an English nobleman named Lord Edward Bomston.*

Two of the six parts of the novel, which Rousseau usually referred to as Julie *rather than as* The New Héloïse, *were finished by the time he fell desperately in love with Mme d'Houdetot in the spring of 1757. He acknowledges in the* Confessions *that to a large extent he projected his imaginary heroine's virtues onto her, and as he continued to write, the characterization of Julie was permeated by his feelings for Mme d'Houdetot, but that relationship soon ended and the novel was completed in a mood of retrospective melancholy.*

The lovers are unable to marry, since Saint-Preux is a commoner who would be unacceptable to her parents, but they do sleep together. Julie then gets pregnant, miscarries, has a terrible quarrel with her parents, and commands Saint-Preux to depart on a sea voyage of six years. When he returns, he finds that she has obeyed her father's wishes and married a much older man named Wolmar, who is generous and wise but completely passionless, and she is now a loving mother as well as faithful wife. Wolmar accepts Saint-Preux as a friend and is able to make him understand that the passage of time has altered the former relationship irrevocably. "It's not Julie de Wolmar he's in love with," Wolmar says, "it's Julie d'Étange," a Julie who no longer exists. "He loves her in time past, that's the true key to the enigma. Take away the memory and he'll no longer have the love." Soon Saint-Preux participates gladly in the carefully organized life of the family's patriarchal estate at Clarens on the shore of Lake Geneva, until a fatal accident occurs. Julie tumbles into the lake while rescuing one of her children, falls ill with a dangerous fever, and dies. In the letter she leaves to be read after her death (included below), she reveals that her love for Saint-Preux has never waned, although she vowed successfully never to let him know it. Julie *thus celebrates romantic passion even while it concedes that passion must be neutralized or contained, a double message that made it—to Rousseau's great surprise—the bestselling novel of the entire eighteenth century.*

PART I, LETTER 14:
SAINT-PREUX TO JULIE

From the very beginning, Saint-Preux and Julie acknowl-
edge their feelings for each other, but while her letters are
cautious and restrained, his burn with a passionate rhetoric
that intoxicated many eighteenth-century readers.

What have you done? Ah, what have you done, my Julie? You
wanted to reward me, but you have ruined me. I am drunk, or
rather raving. My senses are disordered, all my faculties shaken
by that fatal kiss. You wanted to assuage my suffering? Cruel
Julie, you have sharpened it. It is poison I have culled from
your lips, poison that is fermenting, inflaming my blood, destroying me. Your pity is killing me.

O immortal memory of that moment of illusion, of delirium
and enchantment, never will you fade from my soul, never, and
as long as Julie's charms are engraved in my soul, as long as my
perturbed heart will fill me with sighs and longings, you will be
the torment and happiness of my life!

Alas, I was steeped in apparent tranquility. Bowing to your
supreme will, I no longer railed at a fate over which you
deigned to preside. I had tamed the impetuous sallies of my
reckless imagination; I had veiled my glances and shackled my
heart; my desires dared express themselves only in inklings,
and I was as content as I was able to be. Then I receive your
note, fly to your cousin, we go to Clarens, I catch sight of you,
and my heart flutters. The sweet sound of your voice agitates it
anew. I draw near you as if transported, in great need of your
cousin's distraction to hide my agitation from your mother. We
walk through the gardens, we dine quietly, you secretly pass me
your letter that I dare not read in the presence of so formidable

a witness. The sun is setting, the three of us flee its last rays into the grove, and my artless simplicity could not picture a condition sweeter than mine.

As we approach the copse I notice, not without secret emotion, your and your cousin's signals of complicity, your smiles and hers, and the heightening flush of your cheeks. As we enter the copse I see with surprise your cousin approach me and with a playfully suppliant air ask me for a kiss. Unable to fathom the mystery of her action I kiss that charming friend, and, so very sweet and pretty as she is, it has never been clearer to me that sensations are simply what the heart makes them to be. But what became of me a moment later, when I felt . . . my hand trembles . . . a sweet shudder . . . your rosy lips . . . Julie's lips . . . touching mine, pressing against them, and my body clasped in your arms? Heaven's flame does not flash brighter or more suddenly than the flame that blazed up within me. Every part of me fused together beneath this exquisite touch. Fire breathed with our sighs from our burning lips, my heart expiring beneath the weight of delight. But suddenly I saw you turn pale, close your beautiful eyes, reach out for your cousin, and fall into a swoon. And so alarm extinguished pleasure, my happiness but a flash.

I barely know what has befallen me since that fatal moment. The powerful impression I received can no longer be extinguished. A favor? . . . No, it is a terrible torment . . . Keep your kisses, I would not be able to bear them . . . they are too bitter, too penetrating, they pierce me, burn me to the marrow . . . they would drive me insane. Just one, just one kiss has cast me into a bewilderment from which I can no longer return. I am no longer the same, and no longer see you as the same. I no longer see you as I used to, strict and severe; but I feel you and touch you constantly, clasped to my breast as you were for an instant.

O Julie! Whatever fate is heralded by a transport of which I am no longer master; whatever treatment your severity destines for me, I can no longer live in the state I am in, and feel that I will at last die at your feet . . . or in your arms.

PART I, LETTER 54:
SAINT-PREUX TO JULIE

I arrive in the grip of an emotion that overcomes me as I enter this inner sanctum. Julie! Here I am in your chamber, here I am in the sanctuary of all that my heart adores. The torch of love led my steps without my being discovered. O enchanting place, O happy place that has seen so many tender glances smothered, so many fiery sighs stifled! O happy place that saw the birth and flaming of the first fires within me, for the second time you will see them crowned! O witness to my undying constancy, behold my happiness, and forever cast a veil over the pleasures of this most faithful and happiest of men.

How this mysterious abode is enchanting! Everything flatters and nourishes the ardor that devours me. O Julie! It is filled with you, and the flame of my desire spreads to every trace of you. All my senses are intoxicated at once. A perfume, I know not what, almost indiscernible, sweeter than the rose and softer than the iris, breathes from everywhere. It is as if I hear the caressing sound of your voice. All your scattered clothing presents to my ardent imagination the parts of you that they shelter. This simple bonnet adorned by the long blond hair that it feigns to cover; this happy scarf, against which at least this time I shall not utter a murmur; this elegant and simple gown that distinguishes so well the taste of her who wears it; these slippers so delicate, which a dainty foot fills with ease; this corset so fine that touches and embraces ... what an enchanting shape ... in front, two slight curves ... O voluptuous sight! ... the whalebone has yielded to the force of your form ... delightful imprints! O to kiss you a thousand times! O ye gods! What will be when ... ah, it is as if I already feel that tender heart beating beneath my happy touch! Julie! My charming Julie! I see you, sense you everywhere, I breathe you in with air that you have breathed; you pervade my whole being! How painful and fiery your room is for me! It inflames my impatience. Oh, come to me, fly, or I am lost!

What luck that I have found some ink and paper! I express what I feel in order to temper its excessiveness; in describing my transports I temper them.

I think I hear a noise. Might it be your cruel father? I do not think myself a coward ... but how terrible death would be at this moment. My despair would be equal to the ardor that consumes me. God in Heaven, grant me one more hour of life and I will gladly relinquish the rest of my existence to Your severity. O desire! O fear! O cruel palpitations! The door is opening! ... Someone is entering! ... It is she! It is she! I catch a glimpse of her, I have seen her, I hear her close the door! O heart, weak heart of mine, you will surely succumb to so much agitation. Find the strength to bear this happiness that is overwhelming you!

PART I, LETTER 55:
SAINT-PREUX TO JULIE

O let us die, my sweet friend! Let us die, beloved of my heart! What use is our insipid youth to us, every delight of which we have exhausted. Explain to me if you can what I felt during that incredible evening; give me a hint that we might spend our life like this, or let me leave this life bereft of everything that I have just experienced with you. I had tasted pleasure, and believed I now understood happiness. Ah, all I felt was an empty dream, and what I imagined was only the happiness of a child. My senses misled my coarse soul. I sought only the highest good in them, but found that their exhausted pleasures were only the beginning of mine. O unique masterpiece of nature! Divine Julie! Exquisite possession for which all the transports of the most ardent love barely suffice! And yet it is not those transports that I yearn for most; indeed not. Withdraw, if you must, those intoxicating favors for which I would give a thousand lives, but return to me everything that was not them but surpassed those favors a thousand times; return to me that intimate union of souls of which you gave me a glimpse, of which you granted me such an enchanting taste; return to me that sweet despondence filled with the effusions of our hearts; return to me that bewitching sleep I found on your breast; return to me those even more delightful waking moments, those intermittent sighs, those sweet tears, those kisses whose voluptuous languor we savored, and those sighs so tender when you pressed to your heart this heart that was created to unite with it.

Tell me, Julie, you who can gauge so well the sensibility of others through your own, do you think that what I felt before was truly love? Do not doubt that my feelings have changed in nature since yesterday; they have taken on something less impetuous, but sweeter, more tender, and more delightful. Do you remember the entire hour we spent talking so serenely about our love and about the obscure and fearsome future, which heightened the present for us even more, that hour which, alas, was all too short, a light touch of sadness making our exchanges so moving? I was at peace, and yet I was in your presence. I was worshipping you, but desiring nothing. I could not even imagine another bliss than feeling your face next to mine, your breath upon my cheek, and your arm around my neck. What tranquility in all my senses! What pure delight, continual, universal! The delight of ecstasy was within my soul. It no longer left it; it endured. What a difference between the frenzies of love and such a tranquil state! This is the first time I have ever experienced it in your presence. And yet, consider the strange change I am undergoing! Of all the hours of my life, this hour is the dearest to me, and the only one I would have wanted to prolong forever.[175]

Julie, tell me then whether I did not love you before, or if now I no longer love you!

If I no longer love you! What a doubt! Have I ceased to exist, and is my life not more in your heart than in mine? I feel . . . I feel you are a thousand times dearer to me than ever, and found in my despondence new strength to cherish you even more tenderly. I have acquired more tranquil feelings for you, it is true, but they are feelings that are more affectionate and of more varied kinds; without growing weaker they have multiplied; the gentle qualities of friendship temper the rages of love, and I cannot possibly imagine any kind of attachment that would not unite me with you. O my enchanting mistress, O my wife, my sister, my sweet friend! How little I will have said about what I feel even after I have exhausted all the names dearest to the heart of man!

I must admit to you a misgiving that I conceived in my shame and humiliation: that you know how to love better than I. Yes, Julie, it is you who are the essence of my life and being; I worship you with all the capacity of my soul, and yet your soul is more loving, love has penetrated it more deeply. One sees it, one feels it; it is your soul that sparks your graces, that

shines in the words you speak, that gives your eyes that penetrating sweetness, your voice such touching sounds. It is your
soul that through your very presence communicates to other
hearts without their knowing the tender emotion of your own.
How far I am from that enchanting condition that is so sufficient unto itself! I seek delight, you seek love; I am given to
transports, you to passion; all my raptures are not worth your
sweet tranquility, and the feeling that nourishes your heart is
the only supreme happiness. It was only yesterday that I first
tasted such pure delight. You have given me something of that
inconceivable charm that is within you, and I believe that with
your sweet breath you breathed into me a new soul. Hasten, I
implore you, to complete what you have begun. Take from my
soul all that remains, and put yours entirely in its place. Angelic beauty, celestial soul! Only feelings like yours can honor
your charms. You alone are worthy to inspire a perfect love,
you alone are able to feel it. O give me your heart, Julie, so I can
love you as you deserve!

PART III, LETTER 7:
CLAIRE TO SAINT-PREUX

Having discovered Julie's letters from Saint-Preux, her
mother has expired with grief and shame, and Claire ex-
presses Rousseau's often-asserted belief that a grand pas-
sion cannot lead to continued happiness.

How could I love you less while having more regard for you
with every passing day? How can I relinquish my former feelings for you when you merit new feelings every day? My dear
and worthy friend, everything that the three of us have been to

each other from our earliest youth, we will be for the rest of our lives. And if our mutual attachment does not increase, it is because it cannot grow any further. The only difference is that I once loved you as a brother but now love you as a son. For although Julie and I are younger than you, and even, in a sense, your disciples, I see you rather as our disciple. While you taught us to think, you learned from us sensitivity, and whatever your English philosopher[176] might say, one way is equal to the other; if it is reason that makes man, it is feeling that guides him.

Do you know why it seemed as if I had changed my manner toward you and Julie? It is not, believe me, because my heart has not remained the same; it is because the situation has changed. I encouraged your flames of passion while there was a ray of hope. But as your insistence on aspiring to Julie can now only make her unhappy, my indulging you would harm you. I prefer to know you less worthy of pity than to make you discontented. When happiness together becomes impossible, is not seeking your happiness in the happiness of the one you love the only recourse in a love that has no hope?

You do more than feel that, my generous friend. You should make the most painful sacrifice a faithful lover has ever made. By renouncing Julie, you are securing her serenity at the price of yours and renouncing yourself for her.

I hardly dare share with you the strange thoughts that come to me about this; but they are consoling, and that emboldens me. First of all, I believe that true love has the same advantage that virtue does, namely that it recompenses everything one sacrifices to it. In a way, one delights in the privations one imposes on oneself through the very feeling of these privations' cost and the reason that leads one to shoulder them. You will attest that Julie was loved by you as she deserved to be, and that you will love her all the more for it and will be the happier. The exquisite amour propre that repays all arduous virtues will blend its charm with that of love. You will say to yourself, *I know how to love,* with a pleasure more lasting and delicate than you would savor by saying, *I possess the one I love.* For the latter diminishes as one delights in it, but the former remains forever, and you would still delight in it even if you no longer loved.

Beyond that, if it is true, as Julie and you have so often assured me, that love is the most exquisite feeling that can enter the human heart, then everything that prolongs and secures it, even at the price of a thousand sufferings, is still good. If love is a desire that is fired by obstacles, as you also used to say, it is not good that it should be at peace; it is better for it to endure and be unhappy than to expire in the midst of pleasures. Your flame, I confess, has withstood the test of possession, of time, of absence, and of every kind of woe; it has overcome every obstacle except the most powerful of all, which is to have no more obstacles to overcome and feed only on itself. The world has never seen a passion withstand this test: What right have you to hope that yours would? Time would have brought together the disaffection of a prolonged possession with advancing age and declining beauty; through separation, time would seem to become fixed in your favor; you would always be for one another in the flower of youth. You would see one another evermore as you did the moment you parted, and your hearts, united to the grave, would prolong your youth along with your love in an exquisite illusion.

If you had not been happy, an insurmountable restlessness might have tormented you, your heart longing for the good it merited, your fiery imagination relentlessly demanding the good you would not have obtained. But love has no delights that it has not heaped upon you, and to speak as you do, you have exhausted within a single year all the pleasures of a lifetime. Remember that letter, so passionate, which you wrote the day after a reckless rendezvous. I read it with an emotion I had never felt before. One sees in that letter no sign of the unwavering condition of a tender soul—only the extreme delirium of a heart burning with love, drunk with pleasure. You yourself judged that one could not experience such transports twice in a lifetime, and that having felt them one had to die. My friend, that was the high point, and whatever fortune and love might have granted you, your flame and your happiness could thereafter only decline. That instant was also the beginning of your misfortunes, and the woman you loved was taken from you the moment you had no more new feelings to relish at her side; as if fate had sought to shield your heart from an inevitable exhaustion, and grant you in the memory of your past pleasures a pleasure sweeter than any you might still enjoy. [. . .]

PART III, LETTER 20:
JULIE TO SAINT-PREUX

When Julie seemed near death with smallpox, she was dimly aware that Saint-Preux came to her bedside, but she believed it to be a delusion until Claire later assured her it was true. He in turn fell ill, and after recovering obeyed Julie's wishes and departed on a six-year voyage. The novel jumps forward to his return, and Julie now writes to explain her commitment to marriage with Wolmar.

You ask whether I am happy. I am touched by this question, and in asking it you help me answer it; for far from seeking to forget, as you say I do, I confess that I could never be happy should you cease to love me. But I am happy in every sense; the only thing lacking to my happiness is yours. If in my previous letter I avoided speaking of Monsieur de Wolmar, I did so out of consideration for you. I know your sensitivity too well not to fear increasing your suffering; but as your concern about my fate compels me to speak about him on whom my fate depends, I can do so only in a manner that is worthy of him, as befits his wife and a friend of truth.

Monsieur de Wolmar is nearly fifty; his life, which is calm, measured, and unperturbed by passions, has preserved in him such a sound constitution and vigorous air that he seems barely forty, and there is no sign of his advancing in years save experience and wisdom. His physiognomy is noble and engaging, his comportment simple and direct, his manner forthright rather than eager. He speaks little, but with much sense and without affecting either overscrupulousness or sententiousness. He is the same toward all, neither seeking out nor avoiding anyone. Reason is his highest priority.

Despite his innate coolness, his heart seconded my father's intentions as he felt that I was suited to him, and for the first time in his life he formed an attachment to another. This moderate but lasting predilection has been so well governed by decorum, and maintained so evenly, that he had no need to change his tone in changing his condition in life, and without hurting conjugal gravity, he has since our marriage maintained toward me the same manner he had before. I have never seen him either cheerful or sad, but always content. He never speaks to me of himself, and rarely of me; he does not seek me out, but is not angered when I turn to him, and he is reluctant to leave me. He does not laugh; he is solemn without constraining others to be; quite the opposite, his serene comportment seems to invite me to cheerfulness, and as the pleasures I enjoy are the only ones to which he seems amenable, one of the attentions I owe him is to seek to be cheerful. In short, he wants me to be happy. He does not tell me this, but I see it; and does not desiring the happiness of one's wife mean that one has achieved her happiness?

However carefully I have observed him, I have not been able to discover in him passion of any kind, except for the one he has for me. And this passion is so tempered and even that one would say he loves only as much as he wants to love, and wants to love only as much as reason will permit him. He is in every sense what Milord Edward believes himself to be, in which I find Monsieur de Wolmar to be quite superior to all us people of sentiment who admire ourselves so; for the heart deceives us in a thousand ways, and acts only on a principle that is always suspect. But reason's sole aim is that which is good; its rules are sound, clear, and straightforward in the conduct of life, and reason only ever errs when it indulges in futile speculation.

Monsieur de Wolmar's foremost inclination is to observe. He likes to judge men's characters, and all the actions he sees. He judges these with profound wisdom and perfect impartiality. If an enemy did him harm, he would discuss the man's motives and means as calmly as if it were a matter of indifference. I do not know how it is that he has heard about you, but he has spoken to me of you several times with much esteem, and I know him to be incapable of dissembling. There were times when I thought I noticed him observing me during these exchanges, but it is quite likely that my apparent noticing was merely the secret reproach of an anxious conscience. Be that as it may, in this matter I have done my duty; neither fear nor shame have led me to be unfairly reserved, and I have done you justice when speaking to him just as I do him justice when speaking to you.

I forgot to tell you about our revenues and how they are

managed. The remnants of Monsieur de Wolmar's estate, united with that of my father, who has reserved only an annuity for himself, afford Monsieur de Wolmar a moderate and respectable fortune of which he makes noble and wise use by not maintaining at home an inconvenient and vain display of luxury, but preferring abundance, the true comforts of life, and providing for the needs of impoverished neighbors. The order he has brought to his house is the image of the order that reigns in the depths of his soul, and seems to imitate in a small household the order established in the hierarchy of the world. One sees here neither that inflexible regularity that is more irksome than beneficial and bearable only to the one who imposes it, nor that disordered confusion which, for possessing too much, renders everything useless. One can always discern in this order the master's hand, but one never feels it. Monsieur de Wolmar has set up the original arrangement so well that everything now runs by itself, and one can enjoy both regulation and freedom at the same time.

That, my dear friend, is an abridged but faithful rendition of Monsieur de Wolmar's character, to the extent that I have come to know it from the time I have lived at his side. As he appeared to me on the first day, he appears to me today without the slightest change, which leads me to hope that I have observed him well, and that nothing more remains for me to discover, since I cannot imagine he could appear otherwise without being diminished.

I hope that this picture will allow you yourself to answer your questions. You would have to have great disdain for me not to think me happy, since I have so much reason for being so.[177] What misled me for a long time, and what perhaps still misleads you, is the idea that love is essential to founding a happy marriage. My friend, this is a mistake; what suffices be-

tween husband and wife is honesty, virtue, particular preferences, and character and humor more than status and age. This
does not prevent a most tender attachment arising from this
union that, though not exactly love, is no less sweet, and yet is
more lasting. Love is accompanied by a constant anxiety of
jealousy or privation and is little suited to marriage, which is a
state of delight and peace. One does not marry in order to think
solely about one another, but in order to fulfill together the duties of civil life, to run the household prudently and raise one's
children well. Lovers never see anyone but themselves; they
are incessantly occupied with no one but themselves, and the
only thing they know to do is love each other. That is not
enough for a married couple, which has so many further duties
to fulfill. There is no passion that gives us such a strong illusion
as love: one mistakes its vehemence for a sign of its enduring.
The heart, flushed with such a sweet feeling, extends love into
the future, so to speak, and for as long as that love lasts, one
believes it will never end. And yet it is its ardor that consumes
it. It expends itself with youth, fades with beauty, and expires
beneath the snows of age; nor have we ever seen, since the beginning of the world, two white-haired lovers sighing for each
other. It is to be assumed, therefore, that sooner or later, lovers
will cease to worship each other; with the idol one served destroyed, each then sees the other as they are. We seek with surprise the one we loved, and no longer finding that person are
vexed by the one we see before us, and often the imagination
now disfigures the once beloved as much as it had formerly
embellished them. There are few people, La Rochefoucauld
says, who are not ashamed of having loved each other once
their love is spent.[178] Is it not therefore very much to be feared
that boredom will follow upon feelings that were too strong,
that the decline of these feelings will not stop at indifference

but will develop into disgust, that in the end the two will find themselves utterly sated with each other, and for having loved each other too much as lovers come to hate each other as spouses? My dear friend, I have always seen you as most amiable—too much so for my innocence and serenity; but I have only ever seen you in love. How am I to know what you would have become once you were no longer in love? Love once spent would still have left you virtue, I admit, but is that enough for happiness within a bond that has to be forged by the heart? And then how many men of virtue are unbearable husbands. As far as all this is concerned, one could say the same for me as well.

As for Monsieur de Wolmar, neither he nor I is under any illusion about the other. We see each other as we are; the feelings that unite us are not the blind transport of passionate hearts, but the steadfast and loyal attachment of two honest and reasonable people who, destined to spend the rest of their days together, are content with their lot and seek to make their condition agreeable for each other. Had we been expressly created in order to be united, I believe it could not have succeeded better. Were Monsieur de Wolmar's heart as tender as mine, it would be impossible to prevent so much sensitivity on both sides from clashing at times, and quarrels would ensue. Were I as even-tempered as he, there would be too much coldness between us, and we would find each other's company less pleasant and warm. If he did not love me at all, we would not live well together; if he loved me too much, I would have found him trying. Each of us is exactly what the other needs. He enlightens me, and I stimulate him. We are worth more united, and it seems that our souls are destined to be one, he being the intellect and I the will. His somewhat advancing years also happen to be to our common advantage, for, with the passion that was tormenting me, it is certain that if he had been younger I would have married him with even more reluctance, and such excessive feeling would perhaps have prevented the happy change that has taken place in me.

My friend, Heaven shines upon the good intentions of fathers and rewards the obedience of children. God forbid that I should intend to slight your distress. It is only my desire to reassure you entirely about my fate that leads me to add what I am about to say. Were I, with the feelings I have had for you in the past and the knowledge I now possess, still free, and with the power to choose a husband, I call upon God who has deigned to enlighten me and who reads the depths of my heart as witness of my sincerity, that it is not you I would choose, but Monsieur de Wolmar.

[. . .]

PART IV, LETTER 17:
SAINT-PREUX TO LORD EDWARD BOMSTON

Saint-Preux and Julie make an excursion by boat to the little hamlet of Meillerie, where long ago he had gazed longingly across the lake at her distant home. He shows her the rocks where in those days he carved her initials and some romantic verses, and he grasps at last that the love they once had is no more. Rousseau captioned the illustration he commissioned for this episode "Monuments of Former Loves."

[. . .]

You know that Madame de Wolmar's house is not far from the lake, and that she loves to go out in a boat. Three days ago, leisure or the absence of her husband, and the beauty of the evening, led us to plan such an outing for the following day.

[...]

You know that after my exile in the Valais, I returned ten years ago to Meillerie to await permission to come back. It is there that I spent such sad and delightful days thinking of nothing but Julie, and it is from there that I wrote her a letter that touched her so. I had always wanted to see once more the isolated retreat that had served as my shelter amidst the ice and snow, where my heart took pleasure in engaging itself with what it held most dear in the world. The opportunity to visit this place, so cherished, during a more pleasant season—and with her whose image had dwelled there with me—was my secret motive in our walk. It would be a joy to show her the past monuments to a constant and unhappy passion.

We reached the place after an hour's walk along winding and cool paths, which, rising gradually between the trees and rocks, were tiresome only to the extent that our walk was long. As we drew near and I recognized the old marks I had left, I almost felt like fainting, but I overcame the feeling, concealed my bewilderment, and we arrived. This solitary place formed a wild and desolate recess, filled with the kind of beauty that is pleasing only to sensitive souls but appears disagreeable to others. Twenty paces from us a torrent, formed by the melting of the snows, was swollen with muddy water, noisily dragging along sediment, sand, and rocks. Behind us a range of inaccessible boulders separated the esplanade where we were standing from the part of the Alps people call glaciers because of the enormous summits of ice that are constantly growing and have covered these mountains since the beginning of the world.[179] Forests of black firs gloomily shaded us to our right. To our left, beyond the torrent, were woods of oak, and below us the immense stretch of water that the lake forms in the heart of the Alps separated us from the verdant shores of the Vaud, with the peak of the majestic Jura crowning the tableau.

In the midst of this superb grandeur, the little spot where we stood displayed every charm of a cheerful and rural retreat. Brooks trickled between the rocks and ran through the meadows in crystalline rivulets. Wild fruit trees bent their heads over ours, and the damp, cool earth was covered with grass and flowers. Comparing so pleasant a retreat with all that surrounded it, one would have thought that this deserted place was meant to be a sanctuary for two lovers, who alone had escaped nature's cataclysm.

After we had reached this place and I had contemplated it for some time, I turned to Julie and, looking at her with tear-filled eyes, exclaimed, "Can it be that your heart tells you nothing here? Do you not feel some secret emotion at the sight of a place that is so filled with you?" Without waiting for an answer, I led her toward the rock and showed her her initials carved in a thousand places, and the lines of Petrarch and Tasso that had reflected the state I was in when I carved them. Seeing them again myself after such a long time, I felt the power with which things can revive the violent feelings that had once seized one in their presence. "O Julie, eternal charm of my heart!" I said to her with some vehemence. "Here are the places where the world's most faithful lover once sighed for you! Here is the place where your beloved image made his happiness, and prepared the happiness you finally granted him. At that time there were neither these fruits nor this shade; flowers and grasses did not carpet these meadows and the courses of these brooks did not mark their boundaries; these birds did not pour forth their songs—only the voracious hawk, the ominous crow, and the terrible eagle of the Alps had made these caverns echo with their cries. Immense ice formations had hung from all these rocks; garlands of snow were the only ornament of these trees. Everything breathed the rigors of winter and the horror of hoarfrost. Only the flame in my heart made this place bearable, and I spent entire days thinking of you. Here is the rock where I sat gazing from afar at your happy abode; on that rock over there I wrote the letter that touched your heart; these sharp stones served as my chisels to carve your initials; here I crossed the icy torrent to retrieve one of your letters that a gust of wind was carrying away; there I reread and kissed a thousand times the last letter you wrote to me; here is the cliff edge where with eager and somber eye I measured the depths of this abyss; and it was here that I came to weep before my sad departure as you lay dying, and to swear that I would not survive you. O maiden loved with so much constancy, you for whom I was born! Must I find myself with you in these same places and grieve for the times I spent mourning your absence? . . ." I was about to continue, but Julie, seeing me approach the edge of the precipice, seized my hand, alarmed, clutching it in silence, and looked at me with tenderness, barely suppressing a sigh; then, suddenly turning her eyes away, she pulled me by the arm. "Let us leave, my friend," she said with feeling, "the air in this place is not good for me." Downcast, I departed with her but did not say anything, and I left forever this sad retreat, my heart as heavy as if I had left Julie herself.

Having walked slowly back to the dock after several detours, we parted for a while. She wanted to remain alone, and I continued my stroll without knowing where I was going. When I returned, the boat not being yet ready nor the water calm enough, we dined with a sad, preoccupied air, our eyes lowered, eating little and speaking even less. After dinner we went to sit by the shore, waiting for the hour when we would depart. The moon rose, the waters became more calm, and Julie suggested we leave. I gave her my hand to help her into the boat, and, seating myself beside her, could no longer relinquish that hand. We sat in deep silence. The even and rhythmic sound of the oars inspired me to dream. The cheerful song of the wood-cocks brought back to me the pleasures of another age, and instead of enlivening me made me sadder. Little by little I felt the melancholy that was overwhelming me increase. A serene sky, the soft moonbeams, the silvery ripples of the water shining around us, the coming together of the most agreeable sensations, the very presence of the beloved object, nothing could chase from my heart a thousand painful reflections.

I began by remembering a similar walk I had once taken with her during the first enchantment of our love. All the exquisite feelings that had then filled my soul gathered to torment it; all the events of our youth, our studies, conversations, letters, meetings, pleasures—*E tanta fede, e si dolci memorie, / E si lungo costume!*[180]—that throng of little things that offered me the image of my former happiness, all came back to heighten my present misery, lodging themselves in my memory. It is over, I said to myself, those times, those happy times, are no more; they have disappeared forever. Alas, they will not return; yet we live and are together, and our hearts are still united! I felt that I would have borne with more fortitude her death or absence, and that I had suffered less during all the time I had spent far away from her. Tormented as I had been by our separation, the hope of seeing her again had relieved my heart. I had dared hope that a mere moment of her presence would erase all my anguish, and I envisioned—at least among possible states—one that was less cruel than mine. But to be at her side; to see her, touch her, speak to her, love her, worship her, and, while nearly possessing her once more, to feel her forever lost to me: this cast me into convulsions of fury and rage that drove me by degrees to the brink of despair. Soon I began to weigh baneful plans in my mind, and in a transport that I recall with a shudder, I was violently tempted to hurl her with me into the waves, and there, in her arms, to put an end to my life and my long torments. This terrible temptation finally became so strong that I was forced to abruptly let go of her hand and move away to the bow of the boat.

There my intense agitation began to take another course; a gentler feeling now slowly crept into my soul, tenderness prevailing over despair; I shed a torrent of tears, and this state, compared to the one from which I was emerging, was not without some pleasure. I wept vehemently and long, and felt relief. When I was fully restored, I returned to Julie's side and took her hand once again. She was holding her handkerchief; I perceived that it was quite moist. "Ah," I said to her softly, "I see that our hearts have never ceased to understand one another!" "It is true," she said, her voice faltering, "but let this be the last time they speak in such a tone." We continued to converse calmly, and after an hour arrived without further incident. When we returned to the house, I noticed in the light that her eyes were red and quite swollen; she cannot have found mine in any better state. After the travails of the day she had great need of rest: she retired, and I went to bed.

My friend, these are the details of the day in my life in which, without exception, I experienced the most powerful emotions. I hope that this is the crisis that will restore me entirely to myself. Furthermore, I avow that this incident has convinced me, more than any discourse, of the freedom of man and the merit of virtue. How many people succumb to the slightest temptation? As for Julie, my eyes saw and my heart felt that she faced on that day the greatest battle a human soul could have faced, yet she triumphed: But what did I do to remain so far from her?

[...]

PART SIX, LETTER 12:
JULIE TO SAINT-PREUX

After giving Saint-Preux a long and sympathetic account of Julie's final hours, Wolmar encloses a letter Julie left to be delivered after her death, which captures both elements that made Julie so popular: her avowal of undying love and her successful resistance to its temptations. She also proposes that Saint-Preux should marry Claire, but this he will never do, remaining faithful to the memory of Julie.

We must give up our plans. Everything has changed, my good friend; let us bear this change without a murmur; it has been dealt us by a power far wiser than we. We were planning to unite: that union would not have been good. It is a blessing that Heaven has prevented it; no doubt it has prevented a calamity.

I have long lived in illusion. That illusion was beneficial for me; it crumbles at the moment when I no longer need it. You believed me cured, and I believed I was. Let us offer thanks to Him who made this misconception endure as long as it was of use; who knows whether seeing myself so near the abyss I would not have lost my reason? Try as I did to suppress that one feeling that made me live, it was rooted too deeply in my heart. There it now awakens, at the moment when it is no longer to be feared. It upholds me as my strength abandons me; it revives me as I lie dying. My friend, I make this confession without shame. This feeling that has prevailed despite myself was involuntary; it did not cost me my innocence. I invested in my duty everything that lay within the power of my will; if my heart, which is not in its power, was yours, that was a torment for me, and not my crime. I did my duty. My virtue remains unblemished, and my love without remorse.

I dare pride myself on the past. But who would have answered for the future? One day more might perhaps have made me sin; to what would a whole life spent with you have led me? What dangers I have risked unawares! To what greater dangers would I have been exposed! No doubt it was for myself that I felt the fears that I thought I was feeling for you. All the trials have been overcome, but they could easily have returned. Have I not lived long enough for happiness and virtue? What else of value has remained for me to draw from life? In taking it from me Heaven takes nothing worth regretting, and places my honor in safety. My friend, I leave at an auspicious moment, happy with you and with myself. I depart with joy, and there is nothing cruel in this departure. After so many sacrifices, I consider a trifle the one left for me to make: it is merely to die one more time.

I foresee your grief, and I feel that grief: your remaining is to be pitied, I know it too well; and the feeling of your grief is the greatest sorrow I take with me. But think of the consolations I am leaving you, and how the obligation you must fulfill toward her whom you cherished makes it your duty to preserve yourself for her! You must still serve her in the better part of herself.[181] You are losing of Julie only what you lost a long time ago. All that was best in her still remains for you. Come and join her family. May her heart remain in your midst. May all she loved gather to bestow on her a new being. Your cares, your pleasures, your friendship will all be her achievement. The knot of your union tied by her will bring her back to life. She will die only with the last of you.

Remember that you still have another Julie, and do not forget what you owe her. Each of you will lose half of your life; unite together to preserve the other half. The only means that remains to the two of you to survive me is to serve my family and my children. I wish I could tie even tighter knots to keep together all that is dear to me. How dear you would be to one another! How this thought should reinforce your mutual attachment! Your objections to this engagement will become new reasons for entering into it. Will you ever be able to talk to each other about me without being touched? No, Claire and Julie will be so well merged into one that it will no longer be possible for your heart to separate them. Her heart will give you everything in return that you felt for her friend; she will be its confidante and its object. You will be happy through her who has remained, without ceasing to be faithful to her whom you have lost; and after so many regrets and sorrows, before the time for living and loving has passed, you will have burned with a legitimate flame and savored an innocent happiness.

It is within this chaste bond that you will be able to occupy yourself with the tasks I leave to you without distractions and without fears; thereafter it will be with ease that you can say what good you have done here below. You know that there is a man worthy of happiness to which he is unable to aspire.[182] This man is your redeemer, the husband of the friend he returned to you. Alone, uninterested in life, without expecting the life to come, without pleasure, without consolation, without hope, he will soon be the most unfortunate of mortals. You must repay him for the efforts he has undertaken for you, and you know what you can undertake to help him. Remember my previous letter. Spend your days with him. Let none of those who loved me abandon him. He gave you back your love of virtue; show him its goal and its worth. Be Christian and so induce him by your example to be one too. Success is closer than you think: he has done his duty; I will do mine; do yours. God is just; my confidence will not deceive me.

I have only a word to say to you about my children. I know

what effort their upbringing will cost you. But I am also certain that you will not find those efforts onerous. In the moments of worry that will necessarily accompany this task, say to yourself that they are Julie's children, and the task will become easy. Monsieur de Wolmar will turn over to you the observations I have made concerning your memoir[183] and the character of my two sons. This writing is merely begun: I am not giving it to you as a set of rules, I submit it to your discernment. Do not make scholars of them, make them into men who are benevolent and just. Speak to them sometimes of their mother . . . you know whether they were dear to her . . . tell Marcellin that I was not sorry to die for him. Tell his brother that it was for him I loved life. Tell them . . . I am tired, I must end this letter. In leaving my children to you, I relinquish them with less sorrow; I feel that I am remaining with them.

Farewell, farewell, my sweet friend . . . Alas! I end my life as I began it. I say too much, perhaps, at this moment when the heart no longer feigns anything . . . Ah, why should I fear expressing all I felt? It is no longer I who am speaking to you; I am already in the arms of death. When you see this letter, worms will be gnawing at your lover's face, and at her heart in which you will no longer be. Yet would my soul exist without you? Without you what happiness would I enjoy? No, I am not leaving you, I shall wait for you. The virtue that has kept us apart on earth will unite us in Eternity. I die in this sweet expectation, so happy to pay with my life for the right to love you forever without guilt, and to tell you so one more time.

CONFESSIONS

Rousseau's Confessions, *like Augustine's whose title he echoes, is one of the most original and influential autobiographies ever written. Previous writers of memoirs took it for granted that readers wanted to hear about their mature achievements, and none of them gave more than a couple of pages to their formative years. Rousseau, who saw early experiences as crucial in the formation of personality, devoted fully two hundred pages to the first twenty years of his life. And whereas other autobiographers usually sought to present a stable, definite character, Rousseau narrated a story of development over time, in which certain events were explored for their unique significance.*

Rather than short excerpts, we give here the first three books in their entirety. These are the richest and deepest, and they crystallize around experiences that commentators have found endlessly suggestive. There is the death of Rousseau's mother at the time of his birth—an all-too-frequent tragedy in an age when the role of infection was not understood—for which he always felt profound guilt. There was his father's disappearance from his life when he was only ten, and his dismissal from his home to the care of a pair of well-meaning strangers. There was the spanking there, which, as he saw with extraordinary insight, was a valuable source of insight into his masochistic relation to women. There was the broken comb for which he was unjustly punished, and later on, the stolen ribbon for which he escaped punishment by implicating an innocent fellow servant. Above all, there was his relationship with Mme de Warens, who would become the mother figure he longed for and who would help him to develop his mind. Without her influence, it is quite possible that we would never have heard of Jean-Jacques Rousseau.

The Confessions *was also a nostalgic exercise in reliving the past, in almost the manner of Proust's* In Search of Lost Time. *Suffering persecution for his writings on government and religion, Rousseau had been driven from his refuge in Switzerland and was living with his common-law wife, Thérèse, in a remote English village, where they barely understood the language and felt alarmingly isolated. "It's the past," he wrote there, "that makes the present bearable." Recalling an idyllic day in the country with two attractive young women, he added, "All the birds in concert were bidding farewell to spring and singing the birth of a fine summer's day, one of those fine days that are never more seen at my age, and have never been seen at all in the gloomy land where I'm now living."*

It should be added that when Rousseau claimed to falsify nothing knowingly, he was telling the truth. His memory was remarkably reliable, and scholars poring through old records have corroborated many details and found few er-

rors. But he also came eventually to see that his feelings in middle age colored the way he remembered his early experiences. In Reveries of the Solitary Walker, *unfinished at the time of his death, he acknowledged that "The 'know thyself' of the temple at Delphi was not such an easy maxim to follow as I believed in my* Confessions.*"*

Intus, et in cute.[184]

BOOK I

I am embarking on an enterprise that has no precedent and whose execution will have no imitator. I intend to present my peers with a man in all the truth of nature. And this man will be me. Myself alone. I feel my heart, and I know mankind. I am not constituted like anyone I have ever encountered. I dare venture that I am not made like anyone else in the world, and though I might be no better, at least I am different. Whether nature has done well or ill in breaking the mold in which she cast me, you will not be able to judge until you have read me.

At the Last Judgment let the trumpet sound when it will! I shall step forward with this book in hand and present myself before the Sovereign Judge. "Here is what I have done," I shall loudly proclaim, "here is what I have thought, here is what I have been. I have revealed the good and the bad with the same frankness. I have not concealed any evil, nor have I added any good, and if I have resorted to this or that trivial embellishment, it was only to fill a gap in my memory. I may have asserted something to be true that I knew might probably be so, but never asserted what I knew to be false. I have presented myself just as I was: contemptible and base when I was that, or good, generous, and noble when I was that. Eternal Being! I have unveiled my inner self as You have seen it. Gather around me the masses of my fellow men, let them hear my confessions, let them shudder at my shameful deeds and blush at my woes, at the foot of Your throne let each of them in turn reveal his heart with the same sincerity, and then let one of them, if he dares, proclaim to You: 'I was a better man than he.'"

I was born in Geneva in 1712, to the citizens Isaac Rousseau and Susanne Bernard.[185] My father had inherited a modest property that had been divided among fifteen children, his own portion being reduced to practically nothing. Consequently, he had nothing to live on but his profession as watchmaker, in which he was truly very skilled. My mother, the daughter of Pastor Bernard,[186] was wealthier, and a woman of wisdom and beauty. My father had not won her without a struggle. Their love had begun almost from the day they were born. By the time they were eight or nine, they were already going on walks every evening through La Treille. By the time they were ten, they could not leave each other's side. Sympathy and the compatibility of their souls strengthened in them the feeling arising from habit. Both, tender and sensitive by nature, were only waiting for the moment when they would find the same disposition in another being; or, rather, the moment was only waiting for them, and they each offered up their hearts to the first one who opened to receive it. Fate, which seemed unfavorable to their love, only fanned it. The young lover, not able to gain his mistress, was consumed by grief. She advised him to set out on travels to forget her. He did so, to no avail, and returned more in love than ever, and found she whom he loved waiting for him, tender and true. After this trial, all they could do was love each other for the rest of their lives. They swore that they would, and Heaven blessed their vow.

Gabriel Bernard, my mother's brother, fell in love with one of my father's sisters, but she refused to marry him unless her brother could marry Gabriel's sister. Love saw to everything, and the two marriages took place on the same day.[187] So my uncle was the husband of my aunt, and their children were my cousins twice over. One child was born right after the marriage and the other a year later, but then the couples were forced to part. My uncle Bernard was an engineer. He went to serve in the Holy Roman Empire and in Hungary under Prince Eugene. He distinguished himself at the siege and battle of Belgrade.[188] My father, after the birth of my only brother, was called to Constantinople, where he became watchmaker to the Sultan. In his absence, my mother's beauty, wit, and accomplishment attracted much admiration.[189] A French gentleman by the name of Monsieur de la Closure was one of the most attentive. His affection for her must have been great, as thirty years later he spoke to me of her with great feeling. But my mother had more than virtue to resist his fervor: she loved her husband most tenderly. She pressed him to return, and he left everything and came back. I was the sad fruit of this return, for I was born ten months later, sickly and weak. I cost my mother her life, and my birth proved to be the first of my misfortunes.

I cannot imagine how my father bore this loss, but I know that he never overcame it. He saw my mother in me, without forgetting that it was I who had robbed him of her. Whenever he kissed me, I felt his sighs and convulsive embraces, and a bitter regret mingled with his caresses, though they were all the more tender. When he would say to me, "Jean-Jacques, let us talk about your mother," I would reply: "So, father, are we going to cry?" And just those words would bring him to tears.

"Ah!" he would say, trembling, "Restore her to me! Console me! Fill the void that she left in my soul! Would I love you so much if my son was all you were?" Forty years after losing her he died in the arms of a second wife, but the name of the first was on his lips, and her image in the depths of his heart.

These were the authors of my existence. Of all the gifts with which Heaven endowed them, the only one they imparted to me was a sensitive heart, which ensured their happiness but caused all the misfortunes of my life.

I was born on the brink of death; there was little hope that I would live. I bore within me the seed of an indisposition that the years have reinforced, which now affords me rare respite from pain only to let me suffer more cruelly in other ways. One of my father's sisters, a kind and wise woman, took such good care of me that I was saved. As I write these words she is still alive, and at eighty years of age caring for a husband younger than she but ravaged by drink. Beloved aunt, I forgive you for having made me live, and it torments me that I cannot offer you at the end of your days the tender care that you lavished on me at the beginning of mine. Jacqueline, my nurse, is also still alive and robust. The hand that opened my eyes when I was born might well close them at my death.

I felt before I thought; this is the common lot of mankind, but I felt more deeply than others. I have no memories of the time before I was five or six.[190] I do not know how I learned to read. I remember only the first things I read and their effect on me. It is the time from which I date an uninterrupted consciousness of my self. My mother had left some novels, and after dinner my father and I took to reading them. At first it was only a matter of my practicing reading with entertaining books, but soon my interest became so fervent that, taking turns, we read incessantly, whole nights at a time. We could never stop until we came to the end of a book. At times my father, hearing the swallows in the morning, ashamed, would say, "Let us go to bed. I am more of a child than you are."

Through this dangerous method I acquired in a short time not only great facility in reading and in understanding myself, but also an insight into passion that was unique for my age. I had no idea about things, but knew all about feelings. I understood nothing; I felt everything. These confused emotions that I experienced one after another did not effect a change in reason, which I did not yet have, but formed within me reason of a different stamp, giving me bizarre and romantic notions of life, of which experience and reflection have never been entirely able to cure me.

We came to an end with the novels in the summer of 1719. The following winter we turned to other things. Once my mother's library was exhausted, we had recourse to the portion of her father's library that had come to us. Fortunately, it contained some good books, which was to be expected, as it had been collected by a pastor who could be said to have been learned, as was the fashion in those times, but who was above all a man of taste and intellect. *The History of the Church and the Empire* by Le Sueur; Bossuet's *Discourse on Universal History; Lives of Famous Men* by Plutarch; *The History of Venice* by Nani; Ovid's *Metamorphoses;* La Bruyère; *The Plurality of Worlds* by Fontenelle and his *Dialogues of the Dead,* and then some volumes of Molière.[191] These volumes were taken into my father's study, and I read them to him every day while he worked.

I acquired a rare and probably unique taste for my years. Plutarch, above all, became my favorite reading. My pleasure at ceaselessly rereading him cured me somewhat of the novels, and soon I preferred Agesilaus, Brutus, and Aristides to Orondates, Artamenes, and Juba.[192] It was from these interesting books and the discussions they occasioned between my father and me that my free republican spirit was formed, the indomitable and proud character intolerant of yoke and servitude that has tormented me all my life in situations least apt to give it wings. I was ceaselessly occupied with Rome and Athens, and living, so to speak, with their great men, myself born a citizen of a republic, the son of a father for whom love of country was his greatest passion and fired by his example. I saw myself as a Greek or Roman, becoming the character whose life I was reading; the stories of their qualities of constancy and fearlessness struck me and made my eyes sparkle and my voice strong. At table one day, when I was narrating the adventure of Scaevola,[193] everyone was alarmed to see me lean forward and hold my hand over the chafing dish to demonstrate his action.

I had a brother, seven years older, who was learning my father's profession. In the face of the profuse affection I was shown, he was somewhat neglected, of which I do not approve. His education was affected by this negligence and he followed a path of dissipation, even before he was old enough to be a true libertine. He was placed under another master, where he continued with the same escapades as in his father's house. I hardly ever saw him, so I cannot really say I knew him, but I did not stop loving him any less tenderly, and he loved me as much as a young scapegrace can love anything. I remember that once, when my father was angrily and harshly chastising him, I impetuously threw myself between them, hugging my brother tight. I covered him with my body, receiving the blows aimed at him, and clung to him so obstinately that my father finally had to pardon him, either disarmed by my cries and tears, or so as not to mistreat me more than him. But my brother turned out so badly that he finally ran away and disappeared entirely. We heard sometime later that he was in Germany. He never wrote once. We had no news after that, which is how I came to be an only son.[194]

If that poor boy was raised with indifference, the same cannot be said of his brother. The children of kings could not be looked after with more ardor than I was during my early years, idolized by everyone around me, and always, which is much rarer, treated as a cherished child, never as a spoiled one. Not once, until I left my father's house, was I permitted to play unattended in the streets with other children, nor was there any need to suppress or satisfy in me those fantastic whims that, though attributed to nature, come entirely from upbringing. I had the faults of my age: I was a chatterbox, a glutton, at times a liar. I would have stolen fruit, candies, and food, but I would never have taken pleasure in harming or attacking anyone, doing damage, or tormenting defenseless animals. Although I do remember once peeing into the cooking pot of one of our neighbors, Madame Clot, while she was in church. I even admit that this memory still makes me laugh, because Madame Clot, though she was on the whole a good woman, was the grouchiest old woman I ever met. This is the brief and truthful summing up of all my childish pranks.

How could I have become bad, when all I ever saw were examples of gentleness, when the people around me were the best people in the world? My father, my aunt, my nurse, my relatives, our friends and neighbors, and all those close to me did not give in to me but loved me, and I loved them in return. My aspirations were so little stimulated and so little opposed that it never occurred to me to have any. I can swear that until my apprenticeship I did not know what a fancy was. Except for the time spent reading or writing beside my father, and when my nurse took me on walks, I was always with my aunt, watching her embroider, hearing her sing, happy as I sat or stood at her side. Her playfulness and gentleness, her charming face, made such a strong impression on me that I can still see her manner, her look, her bearing; I remember the endearing little things she would say, and I could describe how she was dressed and her coiffure, not forgetting the two curls of black hair on her temples, as was the fashion in those days.

I am convinced that it is to her that I owe my taste, or rather my passion, for music, which only fully developed in me a long time afterward. She knew a prodigious number of songs and airs, which she sang in a voice that was light and sweet. This excellent woman's serenity of soul banished melancholy and sadness from her and everything around her. Such was the appeal of her singing for me that not only have many of her songs remained in my memory, but even now that I have lost her, as I grow old, songs I had forgotten since my childhood come back with inexpressible charm. Would one believe that I, an old dotard, worn by sorrows and cares, surprise myself at times by weeping like a child, mumbling these little songs, my voice now trembling and broken? There is one whose tune I remember well, but the words of its second half I simply cannot recall no matter how hard I try, even though the rhymes hazily come back to me. Here is the beginning, and what I remember of the rest:

> *Tircis, je n'ose*
> *Écouter ton Chalumeau*
> *Sous l'Ormeau;*
> *Car on en cause*
> *Déjà dans notre hameau.*
>
> . . .

> *. . . un Berger*
> *. . . s'engager*
> *. . . sans danger;*
> *Et toujours l'épine est sous la rose.*

I do not know where the touching charm my heart finds in this song comes from—it is a whim I am unable to fathom—but I cannot sing it to the end without being stopped by my tears. I intended to write to Paris a hundred times to look for the rest of the words, in case someone might still remember this song. But I am almost certain that my pleasure in remembering it would somehow fade if I had proof that others beside my poor Aunt Suson had sung it.[195]

Such were my earliest emotions. Thus began to form and show itself in me this heart so proud and tender, and my character, so malleable but also indomitable, which, always wavering between weakness and courage, between softness and strength of character, has all my life put me at odds with myself and made abstinence and indulgence, pleasure and prudence, equally elude me.

This course of education was interrupted by an incident whose consequences influenced the rest of my life. My father quarreled with a certain Monsieur Gautier, who was a captain in the French army and apparently had connections to the Council of Geneva. This Gautier was an insolent and cowardly man. During their quarrel his nose began to bleed, and he avenged himself on my father by accusing him of having drawn his sword within the city limits. They wanted to send my father to prison, but he insisted that if that was to be his fate, then according to the law, his accuser had to be imprisoned, too. Unable to prevail, my father preferred to leave Geneva and live in exile for the rest of his life, rather than yield on a matter where he felt his honor and liberty were compromised.[196]

I remained in the care of my uncle Bernard, who at the time was working on the fortifications of Geneva. His oldest daughter had died, but he had a son my own age, also named Bernard, and we were sent to Bossey[197] to board with Pastor Lambercier, to learn, along with Latin, the petty jumble of odds and ends that is considered education.

Two years spent in the village somewhat softened my Roman roughness and restored me to the state of childhood. In Geneva, where nothing had been imposed on me, I had loved reading and study—they had been almost my only amusement. At Bossey, my lessons made me love the games that served as a respite. The countryside was so new for me that I never tired of delighting in it, and I developed a lively pleasure for it that has never paled. Through the years, the memories of the happy days I spent there made me miss those times and their pleasures, until the day that brought me back.[198] Monsieur Lambercier was a man of good sense, who, without neglecting our instruction, did not burden us with onerous tasks. The proof that he did it well is that despite my aversion to discipline, I have never thought back to my hours of study with displeasure. I might not have learned much from Monsieur Lambercier, but what I did learn I learned easily, and I have forgotten nothing.

The simplicity of country life was a boon in opening my heart to friendship. Up to that time I had known only sentiments that were lofty but imaginary. Living with my cousin Bernard in such tranquility brought me close to him, and my feelings for him quickly became even more affectionate than they had been for my brother, and these feelings have never faded. Bernard was a tall boy, extremely thin and lanky, as gentle in spirit as he was weak in body, and he did not abuse overmuch the preference he was shown in the house as my guardian's son. Our studies, our amusements, and our tastes were the same. We were alone, we were the same age, we were both in need of a friend; one could say that to part us would have been to destroy us. Though we had few opportunities to demonstrate our attachment to each other, it was extreme; not only could we not imagine being apart for an instant, we could not imagine ever being separated. We were both of a spirit prone to tenderness, agreeable if we were not being constrained, and so we were always in accord. If, through the preference of those who looked after us, he had some advantage over me, when we were alone I had an advantage over him, which restored the balance. In our studies, I whispered the answers to him when he faltered; when I had finished my lesson I would help him with his, and in our leisure my more active interests always set the pace. Our characters were so well matched, and the friendship that united us so true, that in the more than five years that we were almost inseparable, as much in Bossey as in Geneva, though we often fought, we never had to be separated, and our fights never lasted more than a quarter of an hour; nor did we ever tell on each other. These remarks might be thought childish, but they perhaps provide an example that might be unique ever since there have been children.

My life at Bossey suited me so well that its only fault was that it did not last longer, molding my character completely. Its foundation was feelings that were tender, warmhearted, and peaceful. I believe that no individual of our species has been by nature more free of vanity than I. I raised myself in bursts of energy to sublime heights, only to fall back into my lassitude. To be loved by everyone who approached me was my most passionate desire. I was a gentle boy, as were my cousin and those who tutored us. Throughout those two years I neither witnessed nor fell victim to any angry feeling. Everything nourished the dispositions that my heart had been granted by nature. Nothing was more agreeable to me than to see everyone pleased with me and the world. I will always remember how, if I hesitated in replying to the catechism in church, nothing pained me more than seeing worry and concern in Mademoiselle Lambercier's expression. That alone distressed me more than the shame of failing in public, which affected me acutely, for although only a little sensitive to praise, I was always exceedingly sensitive to shame, and I must say that anticipating Mademoiselle's reproaches distressed me less than the fear of having hurt her.

And yet neither she nor her brother lacked strictness when necessary; but as this strictness was almost always justified and never excessive, I never rebelled against it although it distressed me. I was more vexed by the thought of displeasing them than of being punished, and a sign of dissatisfaction was more cruel to me than corporal punishment. To express myself more directly would be embarrassing, but I must. How we would change our method of dealing with the young if we were more aware of the lasting effects of the way we treat them, often so carelessly and injudiciously! The great lesson one can draw from an example as common as it is baneful makes me resolved to mention it.

Mademoiselle Lambercier loved us as a mother would, but she also wielded a maternal authority, sometimes going so far as to inflict punishment on us when we deserved it, as if we were her children. For a time she would limit herself to threats, and these threats, of a punishment that was so new to me, seemed terrifying. But after the punishment, I found it less terrible than expecting it had been, and what is even stranger is that the punishment drew me even closer to her who had imposed it. It needed all the strength of my affection and all my natural gentleness to keep me from seeking a repetition of the same treatment, and deserving it, for I had found mixed with the pain, and even the shame, a sensuality that left me more desirous than fearful of experiencing it again from the same hand. It is true that blended with it was doubtless some precocious instinct of sexuality, for the same punishment received from her brother would not have seemed pleasant to me in any way. But his nature being what it was, such punishment from him was hardly to be feared, and if I did avoid deserving correction it was only out of fear of angering Mademoiselle Lambercier; so great was the power of benevolence in me—even the power arising from my senses—that it was always the principle that prevailed in my heart.

The repetition of the punishment, which I kept at bay without fear, came about through no fault, or no intentional fault, of mine, so that I can say that I took advantage of it with a clear conscience. But this second time was also the last, for Mademoiselle Lambercier no doubt noticed by some sign that the punishment was not having the desired effect, and she declared that she was giving it up as she found it too tiring. Until then we had slept in her room, and sometimes in winter even in her bed. Two days later we were sent to sleep in another room, and henceforth I had the honor—an honor I would gladly have renounced—of being treated by her as a big boy.

Who would have thought that this punishment of a child, received at the age of eight from a woman of thirty,[199] would set a course for my tastes, my desires, my passions, my whole self, for the rest of my life, a course headed in the opposite direction from what was natural? The moment my senses were aroused, my desires responded so well that, determined by what I had experienced, they never strove to seek anything else. My blood burned with sensuality almost from the moment of my birth, but I preserved myself from stain until the age where the coolest temperaments and the slowest mature. Long tormented without knowing by what, I devoured beautiful women with my ardent eyes. My imagination pictured them incessantly, but only to use them in my fashion and turn them into Mademoiselles Lambercier.

Even after adolescence this strange taste—always persistent to the point of depravity, of madness—preserved in me the good principles one would have expected it to dispel. If ever an upbringing was modest and chaste, mine surely was. My three aunts were women not only of exemplary sagacity, but also of a circumspection no longer found in women of our day. My father, though a man of pleasure, was gallant in the old-fashioned way, and was never heard to speak a word before the ladies he most admired that might make a virgin blush, or before me, as he had the respect owed to children. Monsieur Lambercier was as meticulous on this point as my father, and an excellent maidservant was dismissed for uttering a word in our presence that was a little too racy. It was not only that until my adolescence I had no clear understanding about the union of the sexes, but also the garbled ideas I did have gave rise to dreadful and disgusting images. I had a horror of street women that has never left me. I could never see a libertine without disdain, even dread, so far did my aversion for debauchery go since the time I went to Sacconex along a sunken path and saw on either side holes in the earth where, I was told, such people did their coupling. What I had seen dogs do also came to my mind whenever I imagined others in the act, and that memory alone made me sick to my stomach.

These prejudices of my upbringing, by themselves fit to delay the first explosions of an ardent temperament, were reinforced, as I have said, by the wrong path on which the first awakening of my sensuality had set me. I was only able to imagine what I had experienced, and despite the troubling arousal of my senses, I could only fulfill my desires through the kind of pleasure I had known. I could not turn to other pleasures that had been rendered detestable to me, and which I did not suspect of being so close to mine. In my crazed fantasies, my erotic furies, in the extravagant acts to which these at times drove me, I had recourse in my imagination to being rescued by the opposite sex. It never occurred to me that the opposite sex might be suited to some other use than the one that I was burning to draw from it.

Thus, in spite of an extremely ardent, lascivious, and precocious temperament, I passed the age of puberty without desiring or knowing other pleasures than those for which Mademoiselle Lambercier had so innocently given me the idea. But when the passing of years made me a man, it was again the case that that which ought to have ruined me proved to be my salvation. My childhood proclivity, instead of disappearing, became so associated with these other pleasures that I could never push it away from the desires sparked by my senses. And that folly, together with my natural timidity, always made me extremely unenterprising with women, either through not daring to say everything I wanted, or not being able to do it. The kind of pleasure of which the other is for me the final goal cannot be attained by him who desires it, nor guessed at by her who could accord it. Consequently I have spent my life coveting but keeping silent before the women I have loved most. Never daring to declare my proclivity, I have at least fanned it through relationships that preserved the idea within me. Kneeling before an imperious mistress, obeying her orders, and having to ask her forgiveness was for me the sweetest pleasure, and the more my lively imagination inflamed my blood, the more I had the air of a fainthearted lover. As one can imagine, this manner of making love does not lead to rapid progress, and is not a particular danger to the virtue of the ladies who are its object. Thus I have possessed very few women, but have not held back from enjoying many in my fashion; that is, in my imagination. This is how my senses, in accord with my timid disposition, and my romantic spirit, have kept my feelings pure and my morals honest. But with a little more impudence, the same proclivity would perhaps have plunged me into the most brutal sensuality.

I have taken the first and most painful step in this dark and mired labyrinth of my confessions. What is hardest to recount is not what is criminal, but what is shameful and ridiculous. From now on, I am sure of myself; after what I have just dared to tell, nothing can stop me. One can judge what such disclosures have cost me throughout my life. Drawn at times to women by the tumults of a passion that deprived me of sight and hearing, insensate, a passion that threw my body into convulsive shivers, I still could not bring myself to declare my folly to them, to implore them in moments of the most intimate familiarity for the only favor lacking among all the others. I was granted this favor only once, while I was still a child, by a girl of my own age. What is more, she was the one who suggested it.

Returning in this way to the first traces of my sentient being along this path, I find aspects that at times seem incompatible, but that unite in order to produce a strong, simple, uniform effect. And I find other aspects that appear to be the same, but have through the confluence of certain circumstances formed such different combinations that one would never imagine any connection between them. Who would believe, for instance, that the essence of the most vigorous impulses of my soul would be immersed in the same spring from which lust and indolence flowed into my blood? Without abandoning the subject of which I have just spoken, one will see a very different impression emerging.

One day I was studying alone in the room next to the kitchen. The maid had placed Mademoiselle Lambercier's combs to dry on a stand next to the fireplace. When she came back to get them, she found that in one of them a whole row of teeth were broken. Who was to blame for this? No one but me had entered the room. I was questioned. I denied touching the comb. Monsieur and Mademoiselle Lambercier joined forces: they exhorted me, pressed me, and threatened me, but I persisted in my stubborn denials. Yet the proof against me was too strong and prevailed over all my protestations, though it was the first time I was found to be so audacious in my lies. The matter was regarded as very serious, which indeed it was. The wickedness, the lie, the obstinacy, all seemed equally worthy of punishment. But this time it was not Mademoiselle who inflicted it. A letter was sent to my Uncle Bernard, who came. My poor cousin also happened to be charged with an equally serious misdeed, and we were both given the same punishment. It was terrible. If they had sought to deaden my depraved senses by seeking the remedy in the ill, they could not have done better. Thus my senses left me in peace for a long time.

They did not manage to force from me the confession they wanted. I was repeatedly reprimanded and reduced to a most terrible state but remained unshakable. I would rather have suffered death, and was resolved to do so. Even force had to cede before a child's diabolical obstinacy, which is what they called my steadfastness. I finally emerged from this cruel trial shattered but triumphant.

Some fifty years have passed since this event, but today I would not shrink from facing punishment all over again for the same incident. As God is my witness, I was innocent. I had neither touched nor broken the comb. I had not gone anywhere near the fireplace; it had not even crossed my mind to do so. Do not ask me how the damage occurred. I have no idea, and I cannot understand it. The one thing I know for certain is that I was innocent.

Imagine a temperament that is timid and docile in everyday life, but ardent, proud, and indomitable in passion; a child always governed by the voice of reason, and always treated with gentleness, fairness, and kindness, who has not the slightest idea of injustice and who, for the first time, experiences an injustice so terrible, coming from the people he most cherishes and respects. What an upheaval in his thoughts! What turmoil in his feelings, his heart, his mind, in all his young intelligent and moral being! Imagine all this, if you can. As for myself, I am incapable of untangling and making sense of even a trace of what was happening inside me.

I did not yet have enough reason to understand how appearances condemned me, or to see things from other people's point of view. I remained stubborn, and all I felt was the harshness of a terrible punishment for a crime I had not committed. I little minded the physical pain, though it was acute: all I felt was indignation, rage, and desperation. My cousin was in a somewhat similar predicament, punished for an involuntary error as if he had done it on purpose. Spurred on by my example he flew into a rage, demonstrating, one might say, solidarity with me. In our bed we hugged and sobbed convulsively, and when our young hearts had settled a little and we were able to express our anger, we sat up and began to shout together a hundred times at the top of our voices: *Carnifex! Carnifex! Carnifex!*[200]

As I write this I feel my pulse once again beating faster. If I were to live a thousand years, these moments would always be present to me. That first feeling of violence and injustice has remained so deeply engraved in my soul that all the ideas associated with it bring back my emotion at the time; and this feeling, as it relates to me in its origin, has taken on such a life of its own, and is so detached from all personal interest, that my heart flares up as if I were the victim when I see or hear of any unjust action, whatever its object and wherever it may be committed. When I read of the cruelty of a ferocious tyrant, or the subtle machinations of a treacherous priest, I would gladly set out to stab those wretches to the heart, even if I were to perish a hundred times. Drenched in sweat, I have often run after and thrown stones at a rooster, a cow, or a dog, when I have seen one animal tormenting another just because it felt superior in strength. This urge may be inherent in me, and I believe it is; but the lasting memory of that first injustice I suffered has been too long and too strongly tied to that experience not to have greatly strengthened this urge.

That was the end of the serenity of my childhood days. From that moment on I no longer enjoyed pure happiness. Even today I still feel that the memory of those happy days ended there. We remained at Bossey for a few more months. We were living as we are told the first man lived in his earthly paradise, but we were no longer enjoying it. In appearance nothing had changed, but in fact everything was now entirely different. The bonds of affection, respect, intimacy, and trust no longer linked us pupils to our guides. We no longer perceived them as gods who could read our hearts; we were less ashamed of doing wrong than we were frightened of being accused. We became furtive, unruly, and mendacious. All the vices of our age corrupted our innocence and tainted our games. In our eyes even the countryside lost its attraction of sweetness and simplicity that goes to the heart; it now seemed to us deserted and somber. It was as if it had donned a veil that hid its beauties from us. We ceased cultivating our little gardens, planting herbs and flowers, digging about in the soil, crying out with delight whenever we saw a seed we had planted sprouting. We disliked our life at Bossey, and we were disliked. Our uncle took us away and we parted from Monsieur and Mademoiselle Lambercier, each side having had enough of the other, and little regretting the separation.

Almost thirty years have passed since I left Bossey, without my ever gathering my scattered memories in a particularly agreeable manner. But since I have passed my prime and am declining toward old age, I feel that while other memories fade these are reborn, engraving themselves on my memory, their charm and strength increasing with every day. It is as if, feeling that life is slipping away, I seek to grasp it again in its beginnings. The most negligible incidents from those times please me simply because they are from those times. I remember every circumstance of people, places, and hours. I see the maid or the servant busy in the room, a swallow coming through the window, a fly settling on my hand while I recite my lesson. I clearly see the arrangement of the room in which we were. Monsieur Lambercier's study to the right, an engraving showing all the popes, a barometer, a large calendar. The garden into which the back of the house was built being quite high, raspberry bushes shaded the window, even spilling over into the room. I am aware that the reader might not need to know all this, but I have the need to tell it. If only I dared tell in the same way all the little stories of that happy time that still make me shiver with pleasure when I remember them! There are five or six in particular—but let us compromise. I will spare you five of them but will insist on telling you one, just one: provided that you let me tell it at length as I want to, so that I can savor my pleasure. If I were seeking only your pleasure, I could choose to tell you the story about Mademoiselle Lambercier's bottom, which as a result of an unfortunate tumble at the edge of the meadow was exposed in full view of the King of Sardinia as he was marching by.[201] But the story about the walnut tree on the terrace amuses me more, since I was an actor and not merely a spectator, as I had been in the case of Mademoiselle Lambercier's tumble.

O reader, curious to hear the grand tale of the walnut tree on the terrace, listen to the terrible tragedy, and refrain from a shudder if you can!

Outside the courtyard gate, to the left as one entered, there was a terrace where we often sat in the afternoon, but which had no shade. So that there would be some shade, Monsieur Lambercier had a walnut tree planted there. The planting of the tree was performed with much ceremony. My cousin and I were the tree's godfathers, and we each held the tree with one hand, singing songs of celebration, as the tree was planted. A sort of basin was dug around its foot so it could be watered. We were ardent spectators of the daily watering, and my cousin and I professed that it was much finer to plant a tree on a terrace than a flag of victory in the breach. We resolved to seek this glory for ourselves, without sharing it with anyone else.

We took a cutting from a young willow and planted it on the terrace, some eight to ten feet away from the noble walnut tree. We did not forget to dig a basin around our tree, too, the only difficulty being that we had trouble filling it with water. The well was quite far away, and we were not allowed to go there. And yet water was absolutely necessary for our willow, so for a few days we resorted to all kinds of ruses to get some, and were so successful that we saw our tree bud and sprout little leaves whose growth we measured from hour to hour, convinced that although it was not yet a foot high, it would not be long before it gave us shade.

As our tree occupied all our attention, we were incapable of applying ourselves to anything else, including our studies. We were in a kind of delirium, and as our tutors did not know what had got into us, we were kept on a shorter leash than before. We foresaw the fatal moment when we would run out of water and were downcast, expecting to see our tree shrivel and die. Finally necessity, the mother of invention, suggested a solution that would assure that the tree, and we with it, would escape certain death. Our idea was to dig an underground channel that would secretly divert some of the walnut tree's water to the willow. This enterprise, though executed with ardor, did not at first succeed. We so miscalculated the incline that no water flowed. The earth crumbled and blocked the channel, its opening filling with dirt. Everything went wrong, but nothing could discourage us. *Omnia vincit labor improbus.*[202] We dug the basin and our channel deeper so the water could flow; we cut the bottoms of boxes into small narrow boards, placing some flat and the others at an angle on the two sides, forming a triangular conduit for our channel. At its opening we stuck thin sticks into the ground, creating a kind of grille or lattice that kept out the mud and stones without blocking the water. We carefully pressed down the earth covering our creation, and the day it was ready we waited, trembling with hope and fear, for the hour when the walnut tree would be watered. We waited for centuries, but the moment finally arrived. Monsieur Lambercier, as was his custom, also came to oversee the operation, and we both stood behind him in order to hide our tree, to which, luckily enough, he kept his back turned.

The first bucket of water had barely been poured when we

saw it beginning to flow into our basin. At the sight we abandoned all caution, emitting shouts of joy that made Monsieur Lambercier turn around. This was most unfortunate, because he had been taking great pleasure in seeing that the earth around the walnut tree was such good soil, avidly drinking all the water. Stunned at seeing the water shared by two basins, it was his turn to shout. He looked, saw the trickery, called brusquely for a pickax, and with a blow, the splinters of our boards flying through the air, he shouted at the top of his lungs, "An aqueduct, an aqueduct!" He struck pitiless blows in all directions, each blow striking our hearts. In a moment the boards, the channel, the basin, the willow were all torn up, all destroyed. Throughout the terrible onslaught no other word was uttered but "aqueduct," which he repeated over and over. "An aqueduct!" he shouted, as he smashed everything. "An aqueduct! An aqueduct!"

One might think that the incident would have ended badly for the little architects, but one would be mistaken. Monsieur Lambercier did not utter a single word of reproach, nor did he in any way frown or ever speak of the matter. Some time later we even heard him laughing at the top of his voice when he was talking to his sister, for the laughter of Monsieur Lambercier could always be heard from a distance; and what was even more astonishing is that after our initial shock, we ourselves were not particularly upset. We planted another tree elsewhere, and often talked about the catastrophe of the first, repeating over and over, "An aqueduct! An aqueduct!" Before, I had suffered bouts of pride, imagining myself an Aristides or Brutus.[203] But this was my first indisputable fit of vanity. To have managed to build an aqueduct with our own hands, to have put a sapling in competition with a large tree, seemed to me the height of glory. At ten I was cleverer than Caesar at thirty.

The idea of the walnut tree and the little tale connected with it has remained in my memory, or come back to me, so clearly, that one of the most pleasant anticipations of my traveling to Geneva in 1754 had been to go to Bossey to see again the landmarks of my childhood games, most of all the dear walnut tree that must already be a third of a century old. But I was so constantly overwhelmed with work, so little my own master, that I could not find a moment to carry out my intention. It seems unlikely that another occasion will ever present itself, but I have not lost the desire and the hope, and I am almost certain that if ever I return to that beloved place and find my dear walnut tree still standing, I would water it with my tears.

Returning to Geneva, I spent two or three years in my uncle's house waiting for a decision to be made about what was to be done with me.[204] As my uncle intended that his son become an engineer, he had him study a little drawing and taught him the elements of Euclid. I studied all this along with him to keep him company and acquired a taste for it, especially for drawing. In the meantime the family was deliberating whether I was to become a watchmaker, a barrister, or a pastor. I liked the idea of pastor best, as I was quite fond of preaching. But the small income from my mother's property, which was divided between my brother and myself, was not enough to further my studies. As my age at the time did not yet make the decision pressing, I sat around at my uncle's more or less wasting my time, but still paying, as was fair enough, a quite substantial sum for my room and board.

My uncle, like my father, was a man of pleasure, but unlike my father did not put duty first, and so barely bothered with us. My aunt was a devout woman, even pietistic, who preferred singing psalms to supervising our education. Consequently we were almost entirely left to run free, a state we never abused.

My cousin and I were always inseparable and had no need of anybody else, and so were not tempted to seek the company of young rascals our own age. We did not adopt any of the dissolute habits that idleness might have inspired in us. Not that we were idle—in fact we had never been less idle in our lives, and, happily, all the amusements we eagerly embraced kept us occupied in the house, without our ever being tempted to go out into the street. We built and assembled cages, flutes, kites, drums, huts, water pistols, and crossbows. We ruined my dear old grandfather's tools to make watches as he had done.[205] What we liked above all was to scribble on paper, to draw, paint, fill in figures, or create a mess of colors. An Italian mountebank by the name of Gamba-Corta came to Geneva with his puppets. We went to see him perform, and though we did not want to go again, we set about making puppets of our own. His puppets had performed theatrical pieces, and so we invented some for our puppets, too. Not having any experience, we mimicked the throaty voice of Punchinello as we performed the charming comedies, which our poor relatives had the patience to sit through. But one day my uncle Bernard read out to the assembled family a very fine sermon he had composed, and we abandoned our comedies and began writing sermons. I admit that these details are not particularly interesting, but they show the extent to which our early education must have been well managed, since now, left to ourselves almost entirely at such a tender age, we were so little tempted to waste our time. We felt such little need to make friends that we neglected doing so. When we went on walks, we glanced at the games other children played without the least thought of joining in. Our friendship so filled our hearts that it was enough for us to be together for the simplest pleasures to be a delight.

But by being so inseparable my cousin and I attracted attention, especially since Bernard was very tall and I very short. This made us an odd pair. His long, lanky body, his small face that looked like a baked apple, his gentle ways, his slovenly manner, encouraged the other children to mock him. They called him Barna Bredanna in their local dialect.[206] As soon as we left the house, all we heard was "Barna Bredanna!"

He bore this more calmly than I did. I was furious and wanted to fight, which is exactly what the little roughnecks were hoping. I struck out at them and was beaten up. My poor cousin tried to defend me as best he could, but he was weak and was knocked down with a single blow. I flared up, and though I took many punches, it was not me they were after but Barna Bredanna. Yet my fit of anger only poured oil on the fire, so that we no longer dared leave the house except during the hours when the roughnecks were at school, out of fear of being hooted at and followed.

So I was already a righter of wrongs. The only thing lacking for me to be a true heroic knight was a lady. And I was to have two. From time to time I went to visit my father in Nyon, a small town in the province of Vaud, where he had settled. He was much loved there, and I, as his son, benefited from everyone's goodwill. During my short stays, everyone feted me. A certain Madame Vulson in particular made a great fuss over me, and, to crown the matter, her daughter chose me as her beau. One can imagine what a beau of eleven years of age can offer a young woman of twenty-two; but all those roguish girls like to parade little dolls in order to conceal bigger ones, or to tempt the bigger ones by playing a game they know how to make seductive. I, who saw no disparity between Mademoiselle Vulson and myself, took the matter seriously. I abandoned myself with all my heart, or rather all my head, as it was only in my head that I was in love—even though I was in love to distraction—my raptures, outbursts, and fits of rage giving rise to hilarious scenes.

I have known two types of love that are very distinct and real, and though they have almost nothing in common they are both intense, and both differ from tender friendship. The whole course of my life has been divided between these two kinds of love that are so different in nature. I have even experienced them both at the same time, as for example in the period I am discussing: while I took Mademoiselle de Vulson by storm so publicly and so tyrannically that I was unable to bear any man's approaching her, I was also having short but lively tête-à-têtes with a little Mademoiselle Goton,[207] in which she deigned to play the schoolmistress, but that was all. Yet that "all" was all to me, and seemed to me supreme bliss, and though I was still only a child, I already sensed the value of secrecy as I set out to pay Mademoiselle de Vulson back—who was scarcely aware of any of this—for the pains she took in using me to conceal her other loves. But to my chagrin my secret was discovered, or less well concealed by my little schoolmistress than it was by me, for we were quickly separated, and back in Geneva sometime later when I was on my way to Coutance, I heard some little girls calling out, "Goton slappety-slaps Rousseau!"

Little Mademoiselle Goton was indeed a remarkable person. She was not pretty, but she had a face that was difficult to forget, and I still think of her often, too often for an old fool. Her eyes, above all, were not those of a little girl, nor was her figure or her comportment. Her manner was imposing and proud, which fit her role perfectly and had sparked the idea of her playing my schoolmistress. But what was most bizarre about her was a mixture of audaciousness and reserve that is difficult to explain. She allowed herself to take every liberty with me, without ever allowing me to take any liberty with her.

She treated me exactly like a child, which leads me to believe that either she had already stopped being one, or the opposite: that she was still so much of a child that she thought the danger to which she was exposing herself was only a game.

I belonged, so to speak, completely to each of them, so that whenever I was with one, I never had a thought of the other. But beyond that, the feelings each aroused in me had nothing in common. I could have spent my entire life at Mademoiselle de Vulson's side without dreaming of leaving her, but when I was with her my joy was calm, never spilling over into emotion. I loved her particularly at big affairs, with all the banter and flirting; I even found the jealousy interesting and appealing. I felt triumphant that she preferred me to my formidable rivals, whom she appeared to mistreat. I was tormented, but I loved the torment. The applause, the encouragement, the laughter, excited me and goaded me on. I had fits of passion, bursts of wit. In company I was transported by love; had I been left alone with her, I would have been awkward, cool, perhaps even bored. Nevertheless, my feelings for her were most tender. I suffered when she was unwell; I would have given my health to bring back hers, and it must be remembered that I knew through experience what sickness and health were. When we were apart I thought of her and missed her. In her presence her caresses were sweet to my heart but not to my senses. I was familiar with her with impunity; my imagination did not ask for anything but what she gave me. And yet I would not have been able to bear seeing her do the same for another. I loved her like a brother but was jealous like a lover.

As for Mademoiselle Goton, I would have been a Turk, a madman, or a tiger had I for an instant imagined that she would give another the same treatment she accorded me, for it was, after all, a grace that had to be begged for on bended knee. I approached Mademoiselle de Vulson with lively pleasure but without agitation, while in seeing Mademoiselle Goton I could see nothing else; all my senses were in turmoil. I was familiar with the former without real familiarity, while with Mademoiselle Goton I was both trembling and agitated, even during our most intimate moments. I believe that had I stayed too long with her I would not have survived; palpitations would have suffocated me. I was equally afraid of displeasing either of them, but was more complaisant with the one, and more obedient with the other. I would not have wanted to vex Mademoiselle de Vulson for anything in the world, and yet had Mademoiselle Goton ordered me to throw myself into a fire, I believe I would have obeyed instantly.

Fortunately for her and for me, my trysts, or rather my meetings, with Mademoiselle Goton were brief. My liaison with Mademoiselle de Vulson, on the other hand, though it did not present the same danger, might also have led to catastrophe if it had lasted longer. The ending of such affairs should always have a romantic touch and a wringing of hands. Though my involvement with Mademoiselle de Vulson was less animated, it was perhaps closer. Our separations never took place without tears, and the devastating void I was plunged into after our parting was extraordinary: I could speak only of her, think only of her, and my sorrow was genuine and deep; but I believe that deep down my heroic lamentations were not entirely for her, but that without my being aware of it, the amusements of which she was the center also played an important role. To temper the pain of absence, we wrote letters of a pathos fiery enough to melt stone. Finally I triumphed in that she could no longer bear our separation and came to see me in Geneva. Now I really lost my head. I was crazed and intoxicated for the two days she stayed. When she left, I wanted to throw myself into the lake after her, and my cries rent the air for a long time. A week later she sent me some bonbons and a pair of gloves, which would have struck me as a most romantic gesture had I not learned at the same time that she was now married, and that the journey with which she had deigned to honor me had been undertaken in order to buy a wedding dress. I will not describe my rage, but it can be imagined. In my noble wrath I swore I would never again speak to the perfidious woman, imagining for her no more terrible punishment. And yet she did not succumb, as twenty years later, during an outing on the lake with my father, we saw a boat near ours with some ladies; when I asked my father who they might be, he replied with a smile, "What? Can it be that your heart does not tell you? It is none other than your former love, Madame Cristin, who was Mademoiselle de Vulson." I shuddered at this name I had almost forgotten, but I still told our boatman to change course, for though this would have offered an excellent opportunity to take revenge, I did not feel it worth breaking my vow never to speak to her again, and to renew a twenty-year-old quarrel with a woman of forty.

Thus the most precious time of my boyhood was wasted on trifles, while my family had still not made a decision concerning my future career. After long deliberations to assess where my natural disposition lay, they finally decided upon a career to which I was least disposed, and placed me with Monsieur Masseron, the town clerk, to learn, as my uncle Bernard put it, the useful trade of *money-grubber*. This epithet was most unpleasant to me: the prospect of gaining a large pile of crowns by base means little flattered my lofty sentiments. The job struck me as boring and unbearable, the assiduity and subservience it required repelled me, and I never entered the clerk's office without feeling a horror that grew with every day. Monsieur

Masseron, for his part, was little pleased with me, treating me with contempt, ceaselessly reproaching me for my torpor and stupidity, never tiring of repeating that my uncle had assured him that I knew what was what, while in fact I knew nothing; that he had been promised a clever boy but had been given a dunce. In the end I was ignominiously dismissed for ineptitude, and Monsieur Masseron's clerks were of the opinion that I would do better with a file and chisel.

My vocation thus determined, I was made an apprentice—not to a watchmaker, but to an engraver. As the clerks' contempt had humiliated me beyond measure, I obeyed without a murmur. My master, Monsieur Ducommun, was a violent, uncouth young man,[208] who in a very short time managed to dull the sparkle of my youth and blunt my lively, loving nature, and cut me down in spirit and circumstance to the station of a mere apprentice. My Latin, my knowledge of the classics and of history, were to be forgotten for a long time. I did not even remember that the Romans had ever existed. When I went to visit my father, he no longer saw me as his idol; for the ladies I was no longer the gallant Jean-Jacques, and I felt so certain that Monsieur and Mademoiselle Lambercier would not have recognized their former pupil that I was ashamed of presenting myself to them, and so never saw them again thereafter. The most vile and base behavior replaced my charming amusements, of which not the slightest trace remained. In spite of the sound education I had been given I must have had a strong penchant for dissoluteness, because this all happened very quickly without the slightest difficulty; never did such a precocious Caesar turn so quickly into a Laridon.[209]

I did not dislike my trade as such. I had a lively interest in drawing; I enjoyed playing with engraving tools well enough, and, as the art of the watch engraver is quite limited, I had every hope of excelling. And I might have, had not my master's brutality and the never-ending abuse made the work repellent. I cheated my master of my time, using it, however, to engrave other things, which had for me the appeal of liberty. I began engraving medals that my friends and I could use as chivalric orders. My master surprised me in this contraband work and gave me a thorough beating, accusing me of trying to forge money, because our medals bore the arms of the republic. I can swear that I had no idea of counterfeit money, and little enough idea of the real thing. I knew better how a Roman *A* was to be drawn than what a three-sou coin might look like.

My master's tyranny led to making unbearable a trade I might have loved, and instilling vices in me—such as lying, idleness, and thievery—that I ought otherwise to have hated. Nothing better taught me the difference between filial dependence and utter servitude than the memory of the change that this period brought about in me. Naturally timid and shy, no fault was more alien to me than impudence. But I had enjoyed an honest freedom that until then had been reduced only by degrees, and that now disappeared entirely. I had been bold in my father's house, free at Monsieur Lambercier's, and discreet at my uncle's. But under my master I became fearful, and from then on I was lost. Accustomed to utter equality with my superiors in manner of living, no pleasure had been beyond my reach; there was not a single dish I could not share, no desire I could not state, no impulse of my heart that I could not voice; hence it is easy to judge what I was destined to become in a house where I did not dare open my mouth, where I had to leave the table not halfway through the meal, and leave the room the instant I was no longer needed, or was ceaselessly chained to my work. I saw only objects of enjoyment for others and privations for myself; the sight of the freedom of my master and his journeymen augmented the oppression of my sub-jugation. In debates on matters about which I knew more than they, I did not dare say a word. And finally, whatever I saw I coveted simply because I was deprived of everything. Farewell to ease, to gaiety, to witty words that in the past had often helped me escape punishment when I had done wrong! I have to laugh when I remember how one evening my father sent me to bed without supper for some prank, and passing by the kitchen with my sad piece of bread, I saw the roast turning on the spit. Everyone was sitting by the fire, and, as I was passing by, I had to greet them. When I had made the round, peering from the corner of my eye at the roast that looked and smelled so good, I could not resist bowing to it as well and saying in a piteous tone, "Goodnight, roast!" That naive sally struck the company as so witty that they let me stay for supper. Such wit might have had the same luck at my master's, but it certainly would not have occurred to me there, or if it had I would not have dared utter it.

That was how I learned to covet in silence, to hide myself, to dissemble, to lie, and even to steal, an idea that would never have occurred to me before, and of which since then I have never quite been able to cure myself. Coveting and powerless-ness always lead to theft, which is why servants are such rascals, and apprentices often, too. If young apprentices were treated fairly and with less severity, and could have anything they would otherwise steal, they would lose this shameful penchant as they grew up. I had not had that advantage, and so did not profit from it.

It is almost always impulses that are good but misdirected that make children take the first step toward evil. Despite the constant temptations and privations, I remained more than a year in my master's service without resolving to take anything,

not even food. My first theft was committed as a favor to someone else, but it opened the door to other thefts that had a less
worthy aim.

My master had a journeyman called Monsieur Verrat whose
house, though nearby, had a garden some distance away. There
his mother grew some wonderful asparagus. Verrat was short of
money, and he came up with the idea of stealing the ripest of
her asparagus in order to sell it so that he could enjoy a few
good meals. As he did not want to compromise himself and was
somewhat lacking in agility, he chose me for the undertaking.
He won me over after some coaxing, especially as I was unaware of what he had in mind, and he suggested the idea to me
as if it had just occurred to him. I vehemently refused, but he
insisted. As I could never resist flattery, I gave in, and went
every morning to pick the best asparagus, which I took to
Molard, where a market woman, who knew right away that I
had stolen them, told me as much so that I would give her the
asparagus more cheaply. I was afraid, and accepted whatever
money she gave me and took it to Monsieur Verrat, who
promptly changed it into a good meal of which I was the pur-
veyor but which he shared with a comrade of his. I was happy
enough to receive a few scraps from their table but did not get
any wine.

This little arrangement lasted several days, without its ever
crossing my mind to rob the robber, exacting a levy on the pro-
ceeds of his asparagus from Monsieur Verrat. I conducted my
mischief with the greatest loyalty, my only motive being to
please. And yet, had I been caught, what beatings, what abuse,
what cruelty I would have had to endure. The wretch would
have denounced me and would have been taken at his word,
while I would have been punished twice over for daring, as a
mere apprentice, to accuse a journeyman. This is how every

time the powerful who are guilty save themselves at the expense of the weak who are innocent.

Thus I learned that stealing was not as terrible as I had thought, and quickly turned my skill to such good use that nothing I coveted was safe from my reach. My master did not actually starve me, and sobriety would not have been so difficult for me had my master not indulged so excessively, but the custom of sending the young from the table just as the most tempting dishes are being served strikes me as an ideal way of turning the young into gluttons and rogues; and soon enough I became both, generally faring very well, though sometimes, when I was caught, very badly.

A memory that still makes me shudder and laugh at the same time is a foray for apples that cost me dearly. These apples were at the bottom of a pantry that received light from the kitchen through a high shuttered window. One day, alone in the house, I climbed onto a kneading trough to peek into this garden of the Hesperides where lay the precious fruit that I could not reach.[210] I went to get a roasting spit to see if I could reach it, but it was too short. I lengthened it with a shorter spit used for roasting small game, as my master liked hunting. I stabbed at the apples a number of times, but to no avail. Finally, to my joy, I speared one. I pulled it in very gently; the apple was already touching the shutters, it was just within reach, when—who can describe my despair!—the apple was too big to fit through the gap. What machinations I resorted to in my attempts to pull it through! I had to find supports to keep the spit in place, a knife long enough to slice the apple in two, a slat to support it. Through application and time I managed to cut it in two, hoping to draw in the pieces one after the other, but no sooner had the apple been sliced than the pieces fell back down into the pantry. Imagine my distress, compassionate reader!

I had lost none of my courage, but I had lost much time. I was afraid of being surprised. I hoped for a more successful attempt the next day, and returned to work as calmly as if nothing had happened, without giving thought to the two indiscreet witnesses down in the pantry that gave evidence against me.

The following day, finding the occasion again favorable, I made another attempt. I climbed onto my trestle, reached out with the spit, aimed it, and was about to spear the apple . . . but to my misfortune, the dragon was not sleeping. The pantry door suddenly flew open, my master came out, crossed his arms, looked me in the eye, and said, "Courage . . ." The pen with which I am writing falls from my hand.

Soon enough, the ill treatment I was subjected to made me less sensitive. In a way it seemed to me a kind of payment for my thievery that gave me the right to continue stealing. Instead of looking back and thinking about the punishment, I looked forward and was thinking about revenge. I felt that if I was going to be beaten like a rascal, I had every right to behave like one. I felt that stealing and being beaten went together, that they constituted a kind of fixed relationship, in which I, playing my own part, could leave the other part to my master. With this idea, I set out to steal with a greater ease of mind than before. I said to myself, "What will come of it? I will be beaten. So be it. That is what I was made for."

I like eating, but I am not greedy. I am sensual, not a glutton. Too many other tastes distract me from that one. I never thought about my palate except when my heart was idle, and that happened so rarely in my life that I barely had any time to think about tasty morsels. This was why I did not for long limit my thieving to food, soon extending it to anything that tempted me, and if I did not become a bona fide thief, it is because I was never very tempted by money.

Within my master's larger workshop was a separate one that could be locked. I found a way to unlock it and to relock it without anyone noticing. Inside, I made use of my master's best tools, his finest drawings, prints, and anything else that caught my fancy, in short all the things he took pains to keep away from me. At bottom, these thefts were innocent, as they were committed only to be used in his service. But I was transported with joy at having these trifles in my power. I believed that with his creations I was appropriating his talent. Furthermore, he had boxes of gold and silver filings, small jewels and more valuable jewelry, and coins. I never had more than four sous in my pocket, and yet I touched none of these things, and do not even remember casting a coveting glance in their direction. I looked at them more with fear than pleasure. I believe that my horror of stealing money, and the consequences, was to a large extent the product of my education; mingled with this were vague ideas of infamy, prison, punishment, and the gallows that would have made me shudder if I had tried. My thefts, on the other hand, seemed to me only a little bit of mischief and were in fact nothing more. All this would not bring me more than a caning by my master, but I had prepared myself for that in advance.

And yet I will stress again: I did not even covet anything enough to have to abstain. I had no need to fight the urge. A single sheet of good paper to draw on was a greater temptation than money to pay for a whole stack. This peculiarity rests on one of the aspects of my character. It has so much influence on my conduct that it is important for me to explain it.

My passions are most ardent, and while I am in their grip my impetuousness knows no bounds. I no longer know either circumspection, respect, fear, or propriety. I am cynical, brazen, violent, and bold. No shame will stop me, no danger frighten me. Beyond the one thing that is preoccupying me, the universe means nothing. But all this lasts only for a moment, and the moment that follows annihilates me. If you come upon me in a state of calm, I am indolence and timidity in person; everything frightens me, everything cows me, I am afraid of a buzzing fly. Saying a word, making a gesture, rattles my torpor, and fear and shame subjugate me to such an extent that I want to eclipse myself in the eyes of all mortals. If I have to act, I do not know what to do; if I have to speak, I do not know what to say; if someone looks at me, I am disconcerted. But often when I am in the grip of passion I know just what to say; and yet in normal conversation I find nothing to say, nothing at all. These conversations are unbearable to me for the simple reason that I am obliged to speak.

Furthermore, none of my dominant tastes consists of things that can be bought. I need only pure pleasures, and money poisons them all. I love, for instance, the pleasure of the table, but I can bear neither the boredom of good company nor the rowdiness of the tavern. I enjoy these pleasures only with a friend, for I cannot do so alone, but then my imagination is occupied by other things and I cannot enjoy eating. If my aroused blood craves women, my moved heart craves love even more. Women who can be bought lose for me all their charm. I doubt I even have it in me to take advantage of them. It is the same with all the pleasures within my reach: if they are not free, I find them insipid. I like only goods that belong to no one but the first who knows how to savor them.

Money never struck me as a thing that is as precious as people think; moreover, it has never even seemed to me a particular convenience. In itself, it is useless; you must transform it in order to make use of it. You buy, barter, are often cheated, pay much, and are badly served. If I want something of good quality, I can be sure that my money will get me something bad. I pay dearly for a fresh egg, but the egg is old; for a ripe fruit, but the fruit is green; for a girl, but the girl is tainted. I like a good wine—but where can I get some? At a wine merchant's? Whatever I do, he will poison me. If I really want to be well served, how much trouble and difficulty it entails! Having connections, knowing people, placing orders, writing, going, coming, waiting, and often ending up duped. My money causes me nothing but trouble. I fear it more than I like good wine.

Countless times during my apprenticeship and since, I have gone out with the intention of buying some tasty morsel: I approach a pastry shop, I see the women at the counter, and I imagine that among themselves they are mocking me, making fun of the little glutton. I walk past a fruit stand, and out of the corner of my eye see the beautiful pears; their aroma allures me, but two or three young men nearby are eyeing me, or a man I know is standing in front of his shop, or I see from a distance a girl approaching: isn't it our housemaid? My nearsightedness causes a thousand illusions. I mistake everyone passing me in the street for an acquaintance. I am intimidated from every side, restrained by some obstacle. My desire grows with my shame, and finally I go back home like a fool, devoured by my covetousness, with enough money in my pocket to satisfy it, but not having dared to buy anything.

I would have to launch into the most tedious details if I were to dwell on the embarrassment, shame, repugnance, and inconvenience of every kind that I feel when I or others spend my money. But as the reader follows my life he will understand my disposition, and will feel all this without my having to go out of my way to sum it up. Once he has grasped this, he will understand without difficulty the seeming contradiction in my nature: an almost sordid miserliness linked to the greatest disdain for money. Money is a passing asset that is of so little interest to me that longing for it when I have none will not even occur to me; and when I do have money, I hold on to it for a long time without spending it, for want of knowing how to use it according to my whim. But if an agreeable occasion arises, I make such good use of my money that my purse is empty before I know it. And yet you will not find in me the foible of the miser who spends for ostentation, quite the opposite; I spend in secret and for pleasure. Far from glorying in my spending, I conceal it. I feel so strongly that money is of no use to me that I am almost ashamed to have any, and even more ashamed to make use of it. Had I ever sufficient income to live comfortably I would never have been tempted to be a miser; of this I am very sure. I would spend all my income without seeking to increase it. But my precarious situation keeps me always fearful. I love freedom; I abhor poverty, trouble, and being constrained. As long as the money in my purse lasts, my independence is ensured. I am spared from scheming to find more, a necessity I have always dreaded. But the fear of seeing my money come to an end makes me coddle it. The money one possesses is the instrument of freedom—the money one pursues, the instrument of servitude. That is the reason I hold on to what I have and covet nothing.

Hence my disinterestedness is simply laziness; the pleasure of having is not worth the pain of acquisition. And my extravagance is simply laziness, too. When the occasion to spend with pleasure arises, one must make the most of it. I am less tempted by money than by things, because between money and the desired possession there is always something intermediary, while between the object itself and its enjoyment there is none. I see a thing, it tempts me. If I see only the method of acquiring it, I am not tempted. So I have been a rogue in the past, and sometimes still am with trifles small or large that tempt me and that I would rather take than ask for. But I do not recall ever having taken a sou from anyone, except for one time, some fifteen years ago, when I stole seven francs and ten sous. The incident is worth relating, as it contains a priceless combination of effrontery and foolishness that I would be hard pressed to believe if it concerned anyone but me.

It happened in Paris. I was strolling with Monsieur de Francueil[211] at the Palais Royal around five o'clock. He took out his watch, looked at it, and said, "Let's go to the opera." I assented, and we went. He bought two tickets for the parterre, gave one to me, and went on ahead with the other. I followed him as he went in, and entering after him I saw a crowd around the doors. I looked in, and, seeing that everyone was still standing about, concluded that one could plausibly get lost in such a crowd, or at least lead Monsieur de Francueil to believe that I was lost. I went outside, had my ticket refunded, and left the theater, without thinking that by the time I left, everyone would have been seated and it would have been clear to Monsieur de Francueil that I was no longer there.

As there is nothing more foreign to my disposition than such a deed, I note it to show that there can be at moments a kind of delirium, where one must not judge a man by his actions. I was not so much stealing this money as I was stealing the use to which it had been put; which might make it less of a theft but more of a disgrace.

The details would be interminable if I attempted to follow all the paths over which I passed during my apprenticeship, from the sublimity of heroism to the baseness of a good-for-nothing. Nevertheless, though I did embrace the vices of my station in life, I could not entirely embrace its tastes. The amusements of my fellow apprentices bored me; and after my master's excessive oppression had also turned me against the work, everything bored me. This revived my taste for reading, which I had lost a long time before. The reading that I now did during my work became a new crime, which again brought new punishment. This taste, heightened by being forbidden, turned into a passion, and soon enough an infatuation. La Tribu, the famous book lender, furnished me with every kind of book; good and bad, I liked them all. I was not discerning and read everything with equal avidity. I read at my workbench, I read while I went on errands, I read in the privy, and lost myself in reading for hours at a time. Reading turned my head, I no longer did anything else. My master spied on me, caught me in the act, beat me, and took away my books. How many volumes were torn to shreds, burned, hurled out the window! How many volumes in La Tribu's collection were rendered incomplete! When I no longer had the money to pay her, I gave her my shirts, my ties, my clothes. I regularly handed her the three sous pocket money I received every Sunday.

Hence, one might be led to believe, money had become necessary. It had, but now reading had deprived me of all other activity. Entirely delivered up to my new passion, I no longer did anything but read. I no longer stole. This is another of my peculiar characteristics: in the intensity of a certain way of being, a trifle will distract me, change me, rivet me, finally impassion me, and I forget everything else. I no longer think of anything except the new thing that preoccupies me. My heart would beat with impatience to leaf through the new book that I had in my pocket. I would take it out the moment I was alone, and no longer gave thought to rummaging through my master's office. I can scarcely believe that I would have stolen, even if I had had more expensive passions. Caught up in the present, I was incapable of scheming for the future. La Tribu extended me credit. The advances were small, and once I had a book in my pocket, I could not think of anything else. Any money I earned made its way to her, and when she insisted I pay my debts, the closest things at hand were my own belongings. To steal in advance was thinking too far ahead, and stealing to pay her was not even a temptation.

As a result of the ensuing quarrels, beatings, and the furtive, haphazard reading, I became taciturn and unruly, and my thoughts took a turn for the worse. I was living as a true wild man. If my taste did not preserve me from dull and insipid books, my good fortune kept me from licentious and obscene ones, not that La Tribu, a most accommodating woman in every sense, would have had any scruples about lending them to me; indeed, she pressed them on me, referring to them with an air of mystery, which was what led me to turn them down, as much from distaste as from shame. Chance furthered my prudish disposition to such an extent that I was over thirty before I even glanced at one of the dangerous books that a certain fine lady of the world has called inconvenient, because one can read it only with one hand.

In less than a year I had exhausted La Tribu's meager collection and found myself cruelly unoccupied during my free hours. I was cured of childish and roguish predilections by my taste for reading, and even by what I read, which, though indiscriminate and often bad, sparked more noble sentiments in my heart than those my station would have afforded me; disgusted by everything around me, and feeling that anything that might tempt me was beyond my reach, I saw nothing to beguile my heart. My aroused senses had for a long time been seeking a satisfaction whose object I could not even imagine. I was as far from this object as if I were sexless; I was already pubescent and receptive, sometimes dwelling on my crazed fantasies, but I could see nothing beyond them. In this strange state my restless imagination took a path that saved me from myself and calmed my budding sensuality, which was nourishing itself on situations that had caught my interest in the books I read. I would remember them, vary them, and combine them, appropriating them to such an extent that I became one of the figures I imagined, always picturing myself in situations that were most agreeable to my taste; so much so, that the fictitious state I put myself in made me forget the real state with which I was so discontented. My love of imaginary objects, and my facility in occupying myself with them, made me utterly disgusted with everything around me, and determined the taste for solitude that has remained with me ever since. The bizarre effects of this disposition will come to the fore more than once in the course of what I shall relate. It is a disposition that might appear gloomy and misanthropic, but it comes from a heart that is too affectionate, loving, and tender; a heart that, unable to find any others who resemble it in the real world, has to feed on fiction. It suffices at present to have pointed out the origin and initial cause of a tendency that has affected all my passions, and which, from the effort of restraining them, has always made me slow to act through designing with too much ardor.

And so I reached my sixteenth year, restless, discontented with myself and everything, without the tastes appropriate to my station in life, without the pleasures of my age, devoured by desires whose object I did not know; weeping without cause for tears, sighing without knowing why, tenderly indulging in fantasies for lack of anything around me worthy of them. On Sundays the other apprentices would come by after the church service to take me along on their jaunts. I would have gladly avoided them if I could, but once I got caught up in their games I became more ardent than they and went further than any of them. It was as difficult to get me involved as it was then to restrain me. This has always been my way. In our hikes outside the town, I always walked ahead, never thinking about returning unless someone else thought it for me. I was caught twice: the city gates were locked before I could get back. One can imagine how I was treated the following day, and the second time this happened I was promised such a reception should it occur a third time that I resolved not to run the risk. However, the much-feared third time did occur. My alertness was foiled by an accursed Captain Minutoli, who always closed the gate where he was standing guard half an hour before any of the others did. I was returning with two comrades when, just a mile out of town, I heard the retreat being sounded. I doubled my pace, heard the tattoo starting, began to run as fast as I could, and reached the gate out of breath, drenched in sweat, my heart pounding, and saw from a distance the soldiers standing at their post. I ran toward them, calling out in a faltering voice. But it was too late. Some twenty paces away from the advance guard I saw the first drawbridge being raised. I shuddered at the sight of those terrible, sinister horns rising into the air like a fatal sign of the inevitable destiny that at that moment was descending upon me.

In the first transport of despair I flung myself onto the embankment and buried my face in the dirt. My comrades laughed at their misfortune and resolved to make the best of it. So did I, but in a different way. Then and there I swore never to return to my master; and the following morning, when the others went back into town after the gates were opened, I bade them farewell forever, begging them only to inform my cousin Bernard secretly of my resolution, and to tell him where he should come if he wanted to see me again.

Since I had begun my apprenticeship we had been separated, and I saw him less. For a time we did meet on Sundays, but gradually we formed other habits and grew apart. I have a feeling that his mother had much to do with this. He was, after all, a boy from the upper town, while I was a wretched apprentice, a child of Saint-Gervais. We were no longer equals despite our birth; it was unseemly for him to keep company with me. And yet our connection had not ceased entirely, and as he was a good-natured boy he sometimes followed his heart despite his mother's orders. When he heard of my resolution he came running to see me; not to dissuade or join me, but to make my flight somewhat more agreeable with little presents, as my own resources would not have got me very far. He gave me among other things a little sword that I was very taken by, and which I carried with me all the way to Turin, where necessity, stabbing me to the heart, as one might say, forced me to part with it. But over the years, the more I have thought about the manner in which he comported himself during this critical moment, the more I am persuaded that he had only been following his mother's instructions—perhaps even his father's—for it is not possible that he would not have made some effort to stop me of his own accord, or that he might have been tempted to follow me, but did not. He encouraged me in my plan rather than holding me back, for seeing me resolved to go, he left me without too many tears. It is a pity, but we were never to write or see one another again. His character was essentially good; we had been made to love each other.

Before abandoning myself to the fatality of my destiny, allow me to turn for a moment to what would have awaited me as a matter of course if I had fallen into the hands of a better master. Nothing would have been more agreeable to my nature, or more capable of rendering me happy, than the tranquility and obscurity of a respectable artisan's life, especially of the kind led by the engravers of Geneva. It would have been lucrative enough to afford a modest life of comfort but not lucrative enough to lead to a fortune. It would have limited my ambitions for the rest of my days, leaving me sufficient hours of honest leisure in which to cultivate moderate tastes. It would have confined me in my sphere without offering any means of escape. As I have an imagination rich enough to adorn any station in life with these fantasies, and strong enough to transport me at will, so to speak, from one station to another, it would have mattered little which station I was actually in. The most magnificent castle in the air would not have been so out of reach that I would not be able to settle into it with ease. It follows from this alone that the simplest station in life, one that would have afforded me the least worry and care and allowed my spirit more freedom, would have been the station most suitable for me. And that was precisely my situation. I could have lived a pleasant, peaceful life in the bosom of my religion, my country, and my family and friends, lived a calm and peaceful life suited to my nature in the routine of agreeable work, and in a society after my own heart. I would have been a good Christian, a good citizen, a good family man, friend, worker; a good man in every way. I would have loved my station in life, perhaps even honored it. And after a life that was obscure and simple, but calm and serene, I should have died peacefully in the bosom of my family. Though no doubt soon forgotten, I would at least have been mourned for as long as I was remembered.

Instead of which . . . what a picture I shall paint! But let us not anticipate the sorrows of my life. I will be involving my readers only too much in this sad subject.

BOOK II

As sad as the moment had seemed when fear suggested the idea
of flight, the moment I fled seemed delightful. Still a child, I
was leaving my country, my relatives, my means of support,
and my resources, abandoning my apprenticeship halfway
without knowing my profession well enough to survive. I was
offering myself up to the horrors of poverty without seeing a
means of escape, exposing myself at a tender and innocent age
to every temptation of vice and despair; in distant lands I was
seeking out evils, sins, snares, enslavement, and death under a
yoke considerably harsher than the one I had not been able to
bear. That was what was awaiting me, those were the prospects
I ought to have foreseen. How different from the prospects I
envisioned! The independence I thought I had acquired was
the only feeling that gripped me. Free and my own master, I
believed I could do anything, accomplish anything; I had only
to leap into the air to soar up high. I entered the vast world
with confidence, a world that I would fill with my accomplishments. At every step I would find feasts, treasures, romances,

friends ready to serve me, and mistresses eager to please me. I had but to show myself to draw the attention of the whole universe—perhaps not in its entirety. I could dispense with some of it, for my needs were modest: a charming social circle would suffice without my giving too much thought to the rest. My diffidence would bring me into a sphere that was narrow but delightfully select, where I would be assured of reigning supreme. A single castle would satisfy my ambition. I would be the favorite of the lord and lady, the lover of the damsel, the brother's friend, and the protector of the common folk. I would be content; I would need nothing more. While waiting for this modest future, I wandered about for a few days outside the town, lodging with peasants I knew, all of whom received me with more kindness than I could have expected from the townsfolk. They took me in, gave me a bed for the night, fed me with too much kindness to make me feel obligated. It could not be called alms, as they did not assume the required air of superiority.

Wandering about in this manner I reached Confignon in the State of Savoy, some two leagues from Geneva. There was a curate there by the name of Pontverre. That name, so famous in the history of the Republic of Geneva, took me aback. I was curious to see what the descendants of the Knights of the Spoon might look like.[212] I visited Monsieur de Pontverre, who welcomed me warmly, spoke to me of Geneva's heresy, of the authority of the Holy Mother Church, and invited me to dinner. I found I had little with which to counter arguments that ended in this way, and concluded that curates with whom one could dine so well were worth at least as much as our men of the Church. My learning was definitely sounder than Monsieur de Pontverre's, despite his being a gentleman. But I was too good a guest to be a good theologian, and his wine from

Frangi, which struck me as excellent, argued so victoriously for him that I would have blushed to contradict such a fine host. So I ceded, or at least did not openly disagree with him. Considering the tact I employed, one might have thought me false; but one would have been mistaken. I was most honest, that is certain. Flattery, or rather condescension, is not always a vice: it is more often a virtue, particularly in the young. The kindness with which a man treats you draws you to him; you yield not in order to deceive him but in order not to upset him, not to use him badly in return for his goodness. What was it that led Monsieur de Pontverre to receive me, treat me with kindness, and want to convince me? Nothing but my best interest. My young heart told me that, and I was touched with gratitude and respect. I sensed my superiority, but did not want to offend the priest in recompense for his hospitality. There was no hypocrisy at all in my attitude. I had no intention of changing my religion, and far from embracing this idea so quickly, I envisioned it with a horror that was to keep me from doing so for a long time; I just did not want to vex those who were being so kind in the hope of converting me. I wished to cultivate their benevolence, and leave them hope of success by appearing less effectively armed than I really was. My fault in this matter resembled the coquetry of respectable women who sometimes, to gain their ends, are adept at exciting hope for more than they intend to grant, but without permitting or promising anything.

Reason, pity, and love for order would surely have demanded that, far from encouraging the folly of my escape, Monsieur de Pontverre would have deterred me from the ruin toward which I was hastening and sent me back to my family. That is what any man of principle would have done or striven to do. But although he was a good man, he was certainly not a man of principle. Quite the opposite. He was a zealot who knew no other virtue than adoring images and praying the rosary. He was the kind of missionary who could not imagine anything better for his faith than launching libels against the ministers of Geneva. Far from thinking of sending me back home, he took advantage of my desire to flee from it, in order to make it impossible for me to return even if I had wanted to. The chances were that he would be sending me to perish in misery or become a good-for-nothing. But that was not what he saw; he saw a soul saved from heresy and returned to the Church. What did it matter whether I was an honest man or a good-for-nothing, as long as I went to Mass. Not that this way of thinking was particular to Catholics; it is the way of all dogmatic religions where faith is essential, not deeds.

"God is summoning you," Monsieur de Pontverre said to me. "Go to Annecy. There you will find a good woman who is most charitable. Through the generosity of the king she is able to rescue other souls from the sin she herself escaped." The lady in question was Madame de Warens, a new convert whom the priests were in effect forcing to share with all the riffraff that came to sell their faith a pension of two thousand francs that the King of Sardinia had bestowed on her.[213] I felt quite humiliated that I would be depending on the charity of a good and bountiful lady. I would have been delighted to be granted all I needed, though not in the form of alms, nor from a pious convert. But urged on by Monsieur de Pontverre and tormenting hunger—and excited at the prospect of a journey and a goal—I agreed, although with some misgivings, and set out for Annecy. I could easily have been there in a day, but did not hurry, and took three.[214]

At every estate I passed along the way I sought the romance that I was certain awaited me. Not that I dared enter or even knocked at their doors, for I was quite timid; but I sang beneath

the window that looked most promising, and was quite surprised, after singing at the top of my lungs, that no lady or
damsel appeared, drawn by the beauty of my voice or the fire
of my song, for I knew some excellent tunes that my comrades
had taught me and that I could sing admirably.

At last I arrived and saw Madame de Warens. This was the
period of my life that decided my character, and I cannot bring
myself to pass over it lightly. I was in my sixteenth year. Without being what one might call a handsome boy, I was slender
and well formed. I had a shapely foot, a fine leg, an easy air, and
lively features. My lips were delicate, my hair and eyebrows
dark; my eyes were small, even deep-set, but were as fiery and
passionate as my blood. Unfortunately I knew nothing of all
that, and have never in my life given thought to my appearance, except when it was too late to put it to use. Thus, along
with a natural and loving disposition, I also had the timidity of
my age and was always troubled by the fear of displeasing
others. Furthermore, though my mind was sufficiently cultivated, I had never been in society and was entirely lacking in
manners, and my knowledge, far from supplying them, served
only to intimidate me even more by making me feel how far I
fell short.

Thus fearing that a first impression of me could not be favorable, I tried to gain an advantage by writing a fine letter in
rhetorical style, stitching together phrases from books along
with apprentices' expressions, deploying all my eloquence to
gain Madame de Warens's good will. I enclosed Monsieur de
Pontverre's letter with mine and set out for the terrible audience. Madame de Warens was not at home; I was told she had
just left for church. It was Palm Sunday of 1728. I run to catch
up with her, see her, reach her, speak to her . . . I must recall the
place. I have often since wet it with my tears and covered it

with my kisses. If only I could surround that happy place with a golden balustrade![215] If only I could bring to it the homage of all the world! Whoever is drawn to honor monuments to the salvation of man should approach this spot on his knees.

The place was a passageway behind her house, between a brook on the right that separated the house from the garden, and the wall of the court on the left. It led to a hidden door to the Franciscan church. Just as she was about to enter that door, Madame de Warens heard my voice and turned around.

I was utterly overcome! I had imagined a grim, pious woman of advancing years—what else could Monsieur de Pontverre's pious lady be? But what I saw was a face full of charm, beautiful blue eyes full of gentleness, a radiant complexion, and the outline of an enchanting breast. Nothing escaped the swift glance of the young proselyte. At that moment I became hers, certain that a religion preached by such a missionary could not fail to lead to paradise. With a smile, she took the letter that I had given her with my trembling hand, opened it, glanced at Monsieur de Pontverre's letter, and returned to mine, which she read carefully and would have read again if her servant had not reminded her that it was time to enter the church.

"Ah, my child," she said in a tone that made me tremble, "you are very young to be wandering alone in the world. It is such a pity!" Then, without waiting for a reply, she added, "Wait for me at my house. Tell them to give you some breakfast. After Mass I will come and talk to you."

Louise-Éléonore de Warens was a daughter of the ancient and noble de la Tour de Pil family from Vevay in the Vaud. At a very young age she had married Monsieur de Warens of the House of Loys, the oldest son of Monsieur de Villardin of Lausanne. The marriage, which remained childless, was not a happy one, and Madame de Warens, prompted by some domestic trouble, chose the moment when King Victor-Amédée was visiting Evian to cross the lake and throw herself on the prince's mercy. Thus she abandoned her husband, her family, and her country in a rash moment, not unlike what I had done, a moment that she, too, had had occasion to regret.[216] The king, who liked to play the pious Catholic, took her under his protection, granted her a pension of fifteen hundred Piedmont francs, a significant sum for a prince not known for his largesse, and, realizing that people would think he was enamored of her, sent her to Annecy escorted by a detachment of his guards. There, under the direction of Michel-Gabriel de Bernex, the titular bishop of Geneva, she abjured the Protestant faith at the Convent of the Visitation.

She had lived in Annecy for six years when I arrived, and was now twenty-eight, having been born with the century. She had a beauty that endures, as it was more a beauty of physiognomy than one of traits, and it was also in its first radiance. She had a tender and caressing manner, a gentle look, an angelic smile, and a mouth not unlike mine. Her ash blond hair was uncommonly beautiful and she wore it negligently, which made it very piquant. She was small in stature, even short, and somewhat plump around the waist, though not in an unshapely way. And yet nowhere would you ever find a prettier head, a more beauteous breast, more delicate hands and arms.

Her education had been desultory. She, too, like me, had lost her mother at birth and, having received haphazard instruction, learned very little from her governess, her father, and her tutors, and a great deal from her lovers, particularly from a Monsieur de Tavel, a man of taste and knowledge who lavished both on the woman he loved. But so many different fragments of learning only got in one another's way, and the little order she imposed on her sundry studies prevented her natural soundness of mind from blossoming. Consequently, although she was familiar with some of the principles of philosophy and physics, she also embraced her father's taste for empirical medicine and alchemy. She concocted elixirs, tinctures, salves, and precipitates, and claimed to have secret knowledge. Charlatans took advantage of her weakness, besieging and ruining her, and among potions and crucibles consumed her spirit, talents, and grace that would have adorned the best society.

Though these vile rogues took advantage of her erratic education to cloud her reason, her good heart remained firm and unwavering: her gentle, loving nature, her sympathy for the unfortunate, her inexhaustible kindness, and her cheerful and frank humor never changed. Even with the approach of old age, when she was plagued by poverty and dire troubles, the serenity of her beautiful spirit retained all the cheerfulness of her best days to the end of her life.

Her mistakes came from an inexhaustible fountain of energy that constantly sought activity. She was drawn not to feminine intrigue but enterprises that allowed her to act and direct. She was born for great affairs. In her place, Madame de Longueville[217] would have been a mere busybody, while in Madame de Longueville's place she would have ruled the state. Her talents were wasted, and what in a more elevated position would have brought her glory, in the situation she was in brought her ruin. In whatever was within reach, she always enlarged the plan in her mind, always seeing it on a grand scale. As a result, she chose means that were more in accord with her ideas than with her capacities, failing through the fault of others. And when her enterprises failed, she was ruined where others would have lost but a trifle. This predilection for involving herself, which brought her so much harm, at least had the benefit of freeing her from the monastic retreat in which she might otherwise have been tempted to remain for the rest of her days. The placid and simple life of the nuns, the tittle-tattle of their parlor, could not gratify a spirit always on the move, forming new plans every day and needing the liberty to pursue them. The good Bishop of Bernex, though not as clever as François de Sales, resembled him in a many ways, and Madame de Warens, whom he called his daughter and who resembled Madame de Chantal[218] in a number of other respects, could also have resembled her in her life of seclusion if the idleness of the convent had been to her taste. It was certainly not lack of zeal that kept this admirable woman from delivering herself over to the trivial acts of devotion that were expected in a new convert living under the guidance of a prelate. Whatever her motive had been to change her religion, she embraced her new faith with sincerity. She perhaps regretted her conversion, but did not wish to return to her old religion. And yet she not only died a good Catholic, but lived as one in good faith, and I dare affirm that I, who believe I have looked deep into her soul, am certain it was only her aversion for affectation that kept her from a public display of her piety. Her piety was too profound for her to affect devotion. But this is not the place for me to expand on her principles; I will have other occasions to speak of them.

Let those who deny a sympathy between souls explain, if they can, how from that first interview, from the first word, the first glance, Madame de Warens inspired in me not only the most lively attachment, but also a perfect trust that has never failed. Let us suppose that what I felt for her was in fact love, which will seem doubtful to whoever follows the story of our relations. How could it be that this passion was accompanied from the beginning by feelings that it ought to inspire least: a tranquil heart, calm, serenity, confidence, and trust? How, in approaching for the first time an amiable, refined, and radiant woman, a lady of a higher condition than mine, the likes of whom I had never before addressed, in whose hands one could say my fate rested, depending on how much interest she might take in it—how is it, I ask, that I instantly found myself as free and at ease as if I were perfectly sure that she would like me? How was it that I had not a moment of embarrassment, timidity, or awkwardness? I was by nature shy and unsure of myself, knew nothing of the world—is it not remarkable that from the first day, the first moment, I adopted the same easy manner, tender words, and familiar tone that I was still to have ten years later, when the greatest intimacy made it natural? Can love exist, I will not say without desire, for I did desire, but without anxiety, without jealousy? Does one not want at least to learn from one's object of love if one is loved? It is a question that never occurred to me to ask her, any more than I would have asked myself if I loved myself. Nor did she ever ask it of me. But there was certainly something unique in my feelings for this charming woman, of which the reader will subsequently find surprising and unexpected examples.

The question was what was to become of me, and to discuss the matter she asked me to stay for dinner. It was the first meal in my life at which I had no appetite, and the maid who served us remarked that she had never before seen a traveler of my age and kind without appetite. That remark, which did not lower me in her mistress's esteem, was aimed rather at a loutish fellow who was dining with us and singlehandedly devouring a dinner for six. As for me, I was in a state of rapture that did not permit me to eat. My heart was feeding on an entirely new feeling that had seized my whole being, and left me no spirit for anything else.

Madame de Warens wanted to know the details of my modest story. In telling it I regained all the fire I had lost during the apprenticeship to my master. The more I interested this excellent soul in my favor, the more she lamented the fate to which I was going to expose myself. Her tender compassion expressed itself in her air, her look, her gestures. She did not dare press me to return to Geneva; in her position that would have been a crime against the Catholic faith, and she was aware of how carefully she was being watched, her every word weighed. But she spoke to me so touchingly in regard to my father's predicament, that it was clear she would have approved of my going to console him. She did not know how much she was unwittingly pleading against herself. Not only was my mind made up, as I believe I have already said, but the more eloquently and persuasively she argued and the more her arguments touched my heart, the less could I bring myself to part from her. I felt that returning to Geneva would have put a barrier between us that was almost insurmountable, unless I were to repeat the step I had just taken, a step by which it would be better now to abide. So I remained steadfast. Seeing that her efforts were in vain, Madame de Warens did not insist to the point of compromising her duty to her faith. But with a look of commiseration she said to me, "Poor boy, you must go to where God calls you. But when you are grown up you will remember me." I think that she herself did not realize how cruelly her prediction was to come true.

But the difficulty was still there. How was I, at such a young age, to survive away from my country? With my apprenticeship less than half completed I was far from mastering my trade, and even if I had mastered it, I could not have made a living in Savoy, which was too poor a country to support such crafts. The lout who was eating enough for all of us, compelled to pause for an instant to give his jaws a rest, put forth a proposition that he said was inspired by Heaven, but that, judging by what was to come later, was inspired by the opposite place. He proposed that I should go to Turin, where there was a hospice established for the instruction of catechumens. There, he said, I would be offered both a temporal and spiritual life until I entered the bosom of the Church and through the charity of good people found a suitable position. "As for the expense of the journey," the fellow continued, "His Eminence Monseigneur the Bishop will most certainly not fail to provide for it, if Madame proposes this saintly act, and Madame Baroness, who is so charitable," he said, bowing over his plate, "would surely be pleased to contribute as well."

I found all this charity difficult to bear; my heart was heavy and I remained silent, while Madame de Warens, without taking up the suggestion as ardently as it was offered, simply said that everyone had to contribute to a good deed to the extent that they could, and that she would speak to His Eminence. But that devil of a man was worried that she would not speak to the bishop in a way that suited his desires, and having his own interests at heart hurried off to alert the almoners. He worked upon the good priests so well that when Madame de Warens, afraid for my safety on such a journey, approached the bishop to discuss the matter, she found that everything had already been arranged, and he immediately handed her the money for my travel. She did not dare insist that I stay, as I was approaching the age where it would not be proper for a woman of her age, in all propriety, to wish to keep me at her side.[219]

With my journey thus arranged by those who had taken me into their care, I had to acquiesce, and in fact did so without much hesitation. Though Turin was further away than Geneva, I felt that as the capital of Savoy, Turin would be a better connection to Annecy than Geneva, a town of a different faith and in a different country. Furthermore, as I was obeying Madame de Warens's wishes by setting out for Turin, I saw myself as still living under her direction, which was better than merely living in her vicinity. Finally, the idea of a great voyage appealed to my passion for walking, which had already begun to manifest itself. It struck me as a fine thing to cross the mountains at my age, and thus to elevate myself above my comrades by the entire height of the Alps. To see other countries is a temptation that few Genevans can resist, and so I agreed to the venture. The lout was to set out in two days with his wife, and I was placed in their care. They were handed my traveling funds, which Madame de Warens had augmented—also giving me a small sum of my own along with much advice—and we set out on the Wednesday of Holy Week.

The day after my departure, my father arrived in Annecy, having followed my trail with his friend Monsieur Rival, who was a watchmaker like him and a man of wit, even of great wit. He wrote poems better than La Motte,[220] and spoke almost as well as he—an honorable man, but whose misguided taste in literature led to one of his sons becoming an actor.

My father and his friend met Madame de Warens, and they contented themselves with lamenting my fate with her instead of following and catching up with me, which they could have done easily enough, as they were on horseback and I was on foot. The same thing happened with my Uncle Bernard. He had come to Confignon, and though he knew I was in Annecy, he returned to Geneva. It seemed that those closest to me were conspiring with my ill-fated star to deliver me to the destiny that was awaiting me.[221] My brother had been lost through similar negligence, so much so that we never found out what happened to him.

My father was a man not only of honor, but also of great probity. He had great moral convictions. And he was also a good father, particularly to me. He loved me tenderly, but also loved his pleasures. Since I had lived apart from him, new tastes had somewhat cooled his paternal affection for me. He had remarried in Nyon, and though his wife was past the age of providing me with brothers, she had relatives. This created another family, other aims, a new state of affairs that no longer called me so often to mind. My father was growing old, and he had no fortune to rely on in his old age. My brother and I had inherited a small property of my mother, the revenue from which could be claimed by my father while we were absent. That idea had not come to him directly, and did not hamper him from doing his duty, but it acted on him silently without his noticing it, sometimes diminishing his zeal, which might otherwise have gone further. That, I believe, was the reason he pursued me to Annecy but did not follow me as far as Chambéry, where he would have been morally certain to find me. This was also why whenever I visited him after my flight, he was always as warm to me as a father could be, but without making much of an effort to keep me.[222]

This behavior from a father whose tenderness and merit I had known made me reflect on myself in ways that contributed not a little to keeping my heart sound. I learned from it a great moral principle, perhaps the only one that can be of practical value: to avoid situations that put our duties in conflict with our interests, situations that benefit us at the expense of another. For it is certain that in such situations, sincere as our love of virtue might be, one will sooner or later grow weak without realizing it, becoming unjust and evil in deed while not ceasing to be just and good in one's heart.

This principle, put into practice from the bottom of my heart in everything I did, albeit somewhat later, is one of the principles that have made me appear bizarre and foolish both in public and among my acquaintances. I have been accused of wanting to be original and of acting differently from everyone, while in fact I never thought of acting either like or unlike anyone else. I sincerely wanted to do what was good. I did my utmost to avoid situations that would be to my advantage but to another's detriment and consequently produce a secret, if involuntary, desire for the other's harm.

Two years ago Lord Marshal desired to put me in his will.[223] I opposed this with all my strength. I made it clear to him that the last thing in the world I wanted was to be in anybody's will, least of all his. He acquiesced but insisted on giving me a pension for life, which I did not oppose. It could be said that this is more to my advantage, which might well be. But O my benefactor, you who are like a father to me! If I have the misfortune of surviving you, I know that in losing you I will lose everything and gain nothing.

This, in my opinion, is a sound philosophy, the only one truly suited to the human heart. With every passing day I am more convinced of its profound truth, and in all my recent works I have come back to it in different ways; but the public, ever frivolous, has not noticed this. If I live long enough after finishing this enterprise to undertake another, I intend to give, in a sequel to *Émile*, such a charming and striking example of this principle that my reader will be compelled to notice it. But enough reflections for a traveler—it is time to resume my journey.

I did so, and much more pleasantly than I would have expected, as the loutish fellow was not as much of a lout as he had seemed. He was a man of middle years who wore his graying hair in a pigtail. He had the air of a grenadier, a strong voice, was cheerful, walked well, ate better, and was a jack-of-all-trades but master of none. He intended, I believe, to set up some sort of factory in Annecy, and Madame de Warens had not failed to support the enterprise. Well provided with funds, he was now traveling to Turin for the purpose of obtaining the minister's approval. This man had a talent for intrigue and schemes; he was always hobnobbing with priests, and in his bowing and scraping had picked up a pious gibberish of which he ceaselessly made use, fancying himself a great preacher. He even knew a passage from the Bible in Latin, and it was as if he knew a thousand, for he repeated it a thousand times a day. He rarely lacked money when he sniffed it in the pocket of another, though he was more wily than knavish, and when he began his religious tirades he resembled Peter the Hermit, sword at his side, preaching the Crusade.

As for his wife, Madame Sabran, she was a good enough woman, though more restrained during the day than she was during the night. As I always slept in their room, their noisy bouts of insomnia often woke me, and would have done so even more had I known what was happening. But I had no inkling, and in this matter I was such a fool that my instruction was entirely left to nature.

I cheerfully continued along the road with my pious guide and his feisty companion. No mishap marred our journey. I was happier in body and mind than I had ever been. Young and vigorous, bursting with health, certainty, and confidence in myself and others, I was at that brief but precious moment in life where its expansive richness extends our being, so to speak, though all our sensations, embellishing nature with the charm of our existence. My sweet restiveness had an object that rendered it less wayward and steadied my imagination, for I saw myself as the creation, the pupil, the friend, almost the lover of Madame de Warens. The kind things she had said to me, her small attentions, the tender interest she seemed to take in me, her charming looks that struck me as being so full of love because they inspired love in me, all this nourished my ideas during the journey and filled me with delightful reveries, untroubled by fears or worries of what might become of me. In sending me to Turin she was, in my view, seeing to it that I would have a livelihood, that I would find a suitable situation. I was no longer worried about myself, for others had taken on that burden. And so I walked with a light step, relieved of this weight. My soul was filled with young desires, enchanting hope, and brilliant projects. Everything I saw struck me as a guarantee of future happiness. I imagined bucolic feasts in all the houses, in all the meadows playful frolicking; along the riverbanks bathing, strolling, and fishing; delicious fruit on all the trees, in their shade voluptuous trysts; pails of milk and cream on the mountain slopes. There was a charming kind of idleness, peace, simplicity, and the joy of walking without aim. Nothing caught my eye that did not fill my heart with pleasurable attraction. The grandeur, variety, and beauty of the scenery rendered that attraction worthy of reason. Even vanity entered into it: I felt that being so young and going to Italy, seeing so many countries, crossing the Alps in Hannibal's footsteps, was glory well beyond my years. And then there were frequent stops at fine inns, and a healthy appetite with ample food to still it. For indeed it made no sense to deny myself anything, and my portions of food, in comparison to those of Monsieur Sabran, seemed paltry.

I do not remember having had in all my life a time more perfectly free of worry and trouble than the seven or eight days we spent on this journey, for Madame Sabran's pace, to which we had to keep our own, turned it into a lengthy tour. This memory has left me with a lively taste for everything connected with this journey, particularly the mountains and traveling on foot. In my younger days I traveled only on foot, and always with great delight, but soon duties, business, and the baggage I had to carry forced me to play the gentleman and take carriages, with gnawing worries, difficulties, and inconvenience as traveling companions. Since then, I no longer feel as before the pleasure of setting out—I only feel the need of arriving. In Paris, I had sought endlessly for two traveling companions who might share my taste, who might want to devote fifty louis from their purse and a year of their time to join me in a walking tour of Italy with nothing but a boy to carry a small bag. Many declared themselves enchanted by the prospect, but only in appearance; for them it was only a castle in the air. I remember discussing this project so passionately with Diderot and Grimm[224] that I was certain I had fired their imaginations. I thought everything was settled, but it turned out that theirs was to be a journey on paper. Grimm thought nothing so amusing as to imagine goading Diderot into uttering a string of impieties and then having me dragged off by the Inquisition in his stead.

My regret at arriving so quickly in Turin was tempered by my pleasure at seeing a large city and by the hope of soon cutting a figure worthy of myself. Already the fumes of ambition were rising to my head, and I could see myself rising infinitely above my former station of apprentice, and I was far from predicting that in a short while I would be falling far beneath it.

Before going further, I owe the reader an excuse or justification for both the minute details I have just dwelt on and also for those on which I am about to dwell, which details can be of no interest to him. In the enterprise that I have embarked upon to show myself without reserve to the public, it is important that nothing of me remain hidden or obscure. I must hold myself before the reader's gaze so that he can follow me in all the peregrinations of my heart, into all the corners of my life, so that he does not lose me from sight for a single instant; for I fear that if the reader finds the slightest gap, the slightest omission, and asks himself what the young man was doing during that time, the reader might accuse me of not wanting to reveal everything. By my writings I am sufficiently laying myself open to the malice of men, without wanting to expose myself further through silence.

My meager savings were gone. I had let slip that I had some money on me, and my lack of discretion was to my guardians' profit. Madame Sabran found a way to snatch away even the ribbon frosted with silver that Madame de Warens had given me for my little sword, and that I regretted giving up more than all the rest. Even the sword would have ended up in their hands had I been less obstinate. They had faithfully met my expenses during the journey, but now they left me with nothing. I arrived in Turin without clothes, money, or linen, with nothing left to rely on but my merits for the honor and fortune I was going to achieve.

I was carrying some letters of introduction, which I delivered, and was immediately taken to the hospice of the catechumens to be instructed in religion in exchange for which I was to be given sustenance. As I entered, I saw a large gate with iron crossbars that was immediately pulled shut and double-locked behind me. This beginning struck me as more imposing than pleasant and I was having second thoughts, when I was led into a large chamber. The only furniture I saw was a wooden altar at the far end on which stood a large crucifix, and four or five chairs that were also of wood and looked well waxed, though they were in fact merely shiny from rubbing and wear of use. There were five or six frightening villains in the chamber, my fellow pupils, who seemed more like the Devil's henchmen than those aspiring to become the children of God. Two of the ruffians were Slavs who claimed to be Jewish Moors. They admitted to me that they spent their lives traveling around Spain and Italy embracing Christianity and having themselves baptized wherever the profit was worth the trouble. Another iron gate was opened, which divided a large balcony overlooking the central court, and through this gate our sister catechumens entered. Like me, they were to be reborn not by baptism but by solemn abjuration. They were without doubt the greatest sluts and vilest hussies ever to soil the Lord's flock. Only one struck me as pretty and quite interesting. She was more or less my age, perhaps a year or two older, and had a mischievous eye that at times caught mine. This inspired in me a desire to meet her, but throughout the almost two months she remained at the hospice—in which she had already been for three—I found it impossible to approach her, so strict was the guard of the old woman who was our jailer, and so vigilant the jealous eye of the holy father who labored with more zeal than diligence over the girl's conversion. She must have been very slow-witted, even though she did not appear to be, for no one else ever received as much instruction as she did. But her reverend tutor still did not find her quite ready to abjure. She was becoming restless at being locked up, and said she wanted to leave, Christian or not. They finally had to take her at her word while she was still prepared to convert, out of fear she might rebel and refuse to do so.

The small community was gathered together in my honor as a newcomer. There was a brief exhortation during which I was directed to accept the grace God was granting me, and the others were asked to offer me their prayers and to edify me by their example, after which, the demure virgins having returned to their cloister, I had the leisure to marvel at the situation in which I found myself.

The next morning we were again brought together to receive instruction, and it was then that I began for the first time to reflect on the step I was about to take and the events that had led me to it.

I have said, and I repeat, and will probably repeat again, something of which I am increasingly certain with every passing day, that if ever a child received a reasonable and sane education, it was I. Born into a family distinguished from the common people by its moral principles, I received only lessons of wisdom and examples of honor from all my relatives. My father, though a man of pleasure, not only had sound integrity, but was quite religious, too. A gallant man in the world and a Christian within, he inspired in me in my youngest years the sentiments with which he was filled. Of my three aunts—all virtuous and sensible women—the two elder were pious, while the youngest was a woman of grace, wit, and sense, and was probably more pious than her sisters, though with less ostentation. From the bosom of such a worthy family I was passed on to Monsieur Lambercier, who, despite being a man of the Church and a preacher, was indeed a man of sound belief and almost always practiced what he preached. With gentle and judicious instruction he and his sister cultivated in me the principles of piety that they found in my heart. To achieve such ends, these worthy people employed means that were so correct, discreet, and sensible, that far from boring me with sermons, I never left their lessons without being deeply moved and resolved to act correctly, which, consciously, I rarely failed to do. I found my aunt Bernard's piousness more exasperating because she made a profession of it. At my master's, I rarely thought of religion anymore, without, however, changing my principles. I had no young friends who led me astray. I became a rogue but not a libertine.

I consequently had as much religion as a child of my age

could have—perhaps more, for why should I disguise my thoughts here? My childhood was not that of a child. I always thought and felt like an adult. It was only in growing up that I rejoined the class of ordinary men, which I had left upon being born. The reader will laugh at my modesty in presenting myself as a prodigy. So be it. But when he has finished laughing, I will ask him to find me a child of six who is so drawn to novels, transported to the point of hot tears; find me such a child and I will admit that my vanity is ridiculous and that I am wrong.

Consequently, when I said that one should not speak to children of religion if one wants them to be religious one day, and that they are incapable of knowing God, even in our way, I came to this view from my observation, not from experience. I knew that others would not understand. Find some six-year-old J. J. Rousseaus, speak to them of God at seven, and I assure you that you will be running no risk.

The general view, I believe, is that for a child, or even a man, to have a faith means to follow the faith into which he was born. Sometimes one's faith weakens—only rarely does it increase. Dogmatic faith is a product of upbringing. Beyond this general principle that attached me to the religion of my fathers, I also had the aversion to Catholicism particular to our city. We were taught it was abominable idolatry, its clergy portrayed in the blackest hues. With me this feeling initially went so far that I could never look inside a Catholic church, never cross the path of a priest in a surplice, never hear the bell of a procession, without a shudder of terror that quickly left me when I was in a city but often seized me when I was in a country parish similar to those in which I first had this feeling. It is true that this impression stands in marked contrast to the memory of the kindnesses that the priests in the region around Geneva bestowed upon the children of that city. While the bell of the viaticum frightened me, the Mass and Vespers bell reminded me of breakfast, a pleasant snack, fruit, fresh butter and cream.[225] Monsieur de Pontverre's fine dinner had also made a great impression on me. I was easily intoxicated by all this. Merely envisioning Catholicism by way of its connection to amusements and fine food, I had accustomed myself to living under it without too much difficulty. But the idea of solemnly embracing that religion had only crossed my mind, as a possibility in some distant future. But now I could no longer deceive myself. I saw with the liveliest horror the kind of commitment I had made and its inevitable course. The future neophytes who surrounded me were not of the kind to sustain my courage by their example, and I could not dissimulate that the holy work I was going to perform was not at bottom the action of a rogue. But despite my youth, I felt that whichever of the two was the true religion, I was going to betray mine, and that even if my choice were the right one, I would, in my heart, be lying to the Holy Spirit and deserving the scorn of man. The more I thought of it, the more indignant I became with myself, and I lamented the fate that had brought me to this point as if none of this had been my own doing. There were moments when such thoughts became so strong that, had I found a door open for an instant, I would certainly have fled. But it proved impossible, and my resolution weakened with time.

Too many secret desires fought against my resolution for it to stand. Furthermore, I was stubbornly resolved not to return to Geneva. The shame, the difficulty of crossing the mountains again, the distress of being far from home without friends, without means—all that drove me to view the remorse of my conscience as a belated repentance. I pretended to reproach myself for what I had done in order to excuse what I was going to do. In exaggerating the sins of my past, I viewed the future as a necessary outcome. I did not tell myself, "Nothing is yet settled, you can still choose the path of innocence if you want." Instead I said to myself, "Lament the crime of which you have made yourself guilty, and which you have made it necessary to carry out."

What strength of spirit it would have taken, at my tender age, to go back on everything that up till then I may have promised or allowed others to hope for, and to break the fetters with which I had chained myself, boldly declaring that I wanted to keep the faith of my forefathers regardless of the consequences. I was too young for such resoluteness, and it is doubtful that it would have prevailed. Matters had progressed too far for me to be able to stop them, and the greater my resistance, the more resolute the priests would have been in their seeking to overcome it one way or another.

The sophism that proved my undoing was that of most men who complain of their lack of strength when it is already too late to make use of it. Courage comes at a great cost only through our own fault, for if we were always sensible, we would have no need to be courageous. But inclinations that could be easily overcome carry us away without resistance, and we give in to minor temptations whose dangers we scoff at. Imperceptibly we fall into perilous situations that we could easily have avoided but from which we can no longer extract ourselves without heroic efforts that intimidate us, and we finally fall into the abyss, asking God why He has made us so weak. Yet He does not reply to us but to our conscience: "I made you too weak to escape the abyss, because I have made you strong enough not to fall into it."

I did not exactly resolve to become Catholic, but seeing the moment still far away I took my time accustoming myself to the idea, and as I waited I imagined that some unforeseen event would save me from this quandary. In an attempt to gain time, I was resolved to put up the best resistance I could. But soon enough my vanity absolved me from thinking of my resolution, for once I noticed that at times I was managing to fluster those seeking to instruct me, I soon sought to overwhelm them entirely. I set about this with a zeal bordering on the ridiculous: as they worked on me I sought to work on them, believing that all it would take for them to embrace the Protestant faith was for me to talk them into it.

Hence they did not find me quite as pliable as they had expected, neither in knowledge nor willingness. Protestants are generally better educated than Catholics, which is as it should be, for the doctrine of the Protestants demands discussion, while that of the Catholics demands submission. A Catholic must accept the decision he is proffered, while a Protestant must learn to decide for himself. The instructors were aware of that, but as men of experience they did not expect to encounter great difficulties from someone of my age and background. Besides, I had not yet received my first communion, nor the instruction connected with it. That, too, they knew. But they were not aware that I had received a sound education from Monsieur Lambercier, and that I had recourse to a pamphlet that was most inconvenient to these gentlemen, titled *History of the Church and the Empire*.[226] I had learned it almost by heart when I was still living with my father, and though I had almost forgotten it since, it now came back to me all the more clearly as the debate grew more heated.

An old priest, a small but venerable man, assembled us for our first lecture. For my companions this was more of a catechism than a dispute over points of faith, but he strove to instruct them, not to counter their objections. I saw the matter differently. When my turn came, I stopped the priest on every point, and would not spare him a single difficulty I could put in his path. This made the lecture long and tedious for the participants. Our old priest spoke profusely, became heated, lost the thread, and could extricate himself only by claiming that he did not understand French well enough. The following day, out of fear that my outspoken objections might have unsettled my companions, I was put alone in another chamber with a different priest, who was younger, eloquent—in other words, a weaver of long sentences—and as self-satisfied as a scholar could be. I did not, however, allow myself to be too intimidated by his imposing manner. Feeling that after all I was doing my duty, I set about answering him with some confidence, while launching attacks whenever I could. He thought he could vanquish me with Saint Augustine, Saint Gregory, and other fathers of the Church, but to his utter amazement he found that I could handle those fathers with almost as much ease as he. Not that I had ever read them, nor had he, perhaps, but I had retained many passages from my Le Sueur, and the moment he cited one, I would immediately cite one back, often to his great embarrassment. In the end he prevailed, for two reasons. First, because he was more powerful than I, and I, feeling myself so to speak at his mercy, judged that despite my youth I should not push him to the limit, since it had been clear enough that the day before, the little old priest had not taken a liking to either my erudition or to me. The second reason was that the young priest had studied, while I had not. Consequently he used a method of debate that I could not counter, and the moment he felt challenged by an unexpected question, he would postpone it to the following day, saying that I was digressing. At times he even rejected all my quotations, claiming that they were wrong. He offered to fetch the volume in question, defying me to find the passages I was quoting. He knew that in doing this he was not risking much, for with my borrowed erudition I had little practice in looking things up and was too weak in Latin to be able to find a passage in a thick tome, though I was certain it was there. I even suspect that he used the same trickery he accused our priests of using, sometimes fabricating passages to extricate himself from an inconvenient objection.

While our squabbling continued and we spent our days in argument, mumbled prayers, and idleness, there was a rather disgusting incident that might have turned out quite badly for me.

There is no soul too base or heart too barbarous not to be susceptible to some kind of attraction. One of the two ruffians who were posing as Moors had taken a liking to me. He would seek me out whenever he could, chat with me in his gibberish, do me little favors, give me some of his food at dinner, and at every opportunity kiss me with a fervor I found most irksome. Despite my natural fear of his dark face, adorned with a long scar, and his fiery eyes that seemed more crazed than tender, I endured his kisses, telling myself, "The poor man feels a strong friendship toward me. It would be wrong for me to push him away." He then became freer with me, at times making such strange suggestions that I thought he had lost his mind. One night he wanted to sleep with me. I refused, saying that my bed was too small. Then he insisted I come to his. I still refused, for the wretch was so dirty, and reeked so much of chewed tobacco, that it turned my stomach.

The next day, quite early in the morning, he and I happened to be alone in the assembly chamber. Again he began caressing me, but now with fierce and rough motions that frightened me. He proceeded to take shocking liberties, and forced my hand to do the same. I recoiled, crying out and jumping away, without indignation or anger, for I had no idea what he was doing. I expressed my surprise and disgust so energetically that he let go of me, but as he finished thrashing about I saw something white and sticky spurt toward the fireplace and fall on the ground that made me sick to my stomach. I fled onto the balcony more agitated, troubled, and frightened than I had ever been in my life.

I could not understand what was wrong with the poor wretch. I thought he must have had an epileptic fit, or some other frenzy even more terrible. Indeed I know of no sight more hideous than coldly watching such obscene and dirty actions and the repugnant face burning with the most brutal lust. I have never again seen a man in such a state, but if that is how we look at the height of our passion with women, then their eyes must be bewitched not to be horrified by us.

I hurried away to tell everyone what had just happened. Our old matron told me to hold my tongue, but I could see that she was greatly troubled by the incident, and I heard her mumbling, *"Can maledet! Brutta bestia!"*[227] As I could not understand why I should keep quiet, I went on talking about it despite her admonition, and I spoke at such length that the following day one of the overseers came to see me early in the morning and gave me a lively scolding, accusing me of making much ado about nothing and compromising the honor of a holy sanctuary.

He continued with his censure, clarifying many things that I had not known, but of which he thought I was aware. He was under the impression that I had pushed the man away knowing what he wanted of me but refusing to consent. The overseer told me gravely that what the man had done was prohibited, like all lewdness, but that it was not a sin for the person who was the object of such attentions, and that there was no cause to be angry simply because someone had found me appealing. He told me in no uncertain terms that in his youth he, too, had been subjected to the same *honor*, and, having been taken by surprise, not been able to put up resistance, but that he had found nothing about it that was particularly cruel. He was brazen enough to describe it in plain words, and, believing that my resistance had been from fear of pain, assured me that there was no cause for alarm.

I listened to this treacherous man with an astonishment that was all the greater as his intention was to instruct me for my benefit, and not for some benefit of his own. The matter seemed so innocent that he did not even pull me aside to speak to me in private, and a priest who was following our conversation seemed just as unconcerned. Their casual air made such an impression on me that I came to believe that the incident was without doubt an accepted custom in society of which I had somehow not been informed. And so I listened without anger, but not without disgust. The image of what had happened to me, particularly what I had seen, was so firmly imprinted on my memory that I still feel sick to my stomach when I think of it. Without my being aware of it, my disgust for the act extended to disgust for the apologist, and I could not constrain myself enough to hide from him the bad effect that his lessons were having on me. He gave me a cold look, and from that point on went to great lengths to make my stay at the hospice disagreeable. He was so successful in this that I saw only one route of escape and did my best to take it, even though until then I had done my best to avoid it.

The adventure did much to protect me from advances by other knights of the cuff,[228] and the mere sight of anyone who looked as if he might be one made me recall the manner and gestures of the frightening Moor, inspiring such horror in me that I had trouble concealing it. Women, on the other hand, rose much in my esteem from this comparison, for I felt that I owed them reparations in tenderness and homage to make up for the offenses of my sex. In my eyes, when I remembered the counterfeit African, the ugliest wench became an object of adoration. As for him, I do not know what they might have told him. It did not seem to me that with the exception of Madame Lorenza anybody looked upon him with more disdain than before. But he no longer approached me or spoke to me. A week later he was baptized with great ceremony and was dressed in white from head to foot to demonstrate the purity of his reborn soul. The next day he left the hospice, and I never saw him again.

My turn came a month later, for I needed that much time to grant my directors the honor of a difficult conversion, and they made me recite all the dogmas so that they could exult in my new docility.[229]

Finally, sufficiently instructed and well disposed for my masters' purpose, I was led in a procession to the Metropolitan Church of St. John to make a solemn abjuration of my faith and to receive the accessories of baptism, even though they were not really baptizing me. But as these ceremonies for converting Jews and Protestants are almost the same, the solemnities serve to persuade the people that Protestants are not Christian. I was dressed in a gray robe with white frogging that was used for these kinds of occasions. Two men, one in front of me and one behind, carried copper basins they kept striking with a key, into which everyone could throw alms according to his piety or his interest in the new convert. Nothing of Catholic pomp was omitted to render the ceremony as edifying as possible to the congregation, and as humiliating as possible to me. The only thing lacking was the white robe, which would have been good to have, but which they would not grant me as they had granted the Moor, since I did not have the honor of being a Jew.

This was not all. I now had to go to the Inquisition to receive absolution for the crime of heresy, and return to the bosom of the Church with the same solemnity to which Henry IV had been subjected by his ambassador.[230] The air and manner of the most reverend Father Inquisitor were not designed to dissipate the secret terror that seized me as I entered. After several questions about my faith, my station in life, and my family, he asked me roughly whether my mother had been damned. The shock made me stifle the first flush of my indignation, and I simply replied that I would hope she had not been damned, and that God might have enlightened her in her final hour. The monk was silent, but made a grimace in which I saw no sign of approbation.

When this was over, at the moment when I thought I might be positioned in life according to my hopes, they dismissed me with little more than the twenty francs in coins that the collection had gathered. I was told to live as a good Christian and be faithful to God's grace. They wished me good fortune, closed the door on me, and that was that.

Thus in an instant all my great hopes were shattered, and all that remained of the step I had taken in my self-interest was the realization that I had been both an apostate and a dupe. It is easy to imagine the sudden turmoil that gripped my thoughts when I saw myself plunging from my shining projects of great fortune to utter and complete poverty, and that after pondering that morning my choice of palaces I saw myself reduced to sleeping in the streets. One might think that I would have given way to a despair made all the more cruel through lamenting my errors, which was increased by the reproach that my misfortune was my own doing. But nothing of the kind. For the first time in my life, I had been locked away for more than two months. The first joyful feeling I experienced was my newfound freedom. After a long period of slavery, once more master of myself and my actions, I found myself in a big town abounding in resources, filled with people of station who would welcome me as soon as they recognized my talents and merits. Furthermore, I had plenty of time on my hands, and the twenty francs in my pocket seemed to me an inexhaustible treasure; I could dispose of it as I pleased without having to answer to anyone. It was the first time I considered myself so rich. Far from abandoning myself to dejection and tears, I simply changed my expectations, and my self-confidence was not diminished. Never had I felt such assurance and security. I was certain that my fortune was already made, and pleased that I had nobody but myself to thank for it.

The first thing I did was to satisfy my curiosity and stroll through the whole city, though this might just have been an act of declaring my freedom. I went to see the changing of the guard, as I am very fond of military bands. I followed the processions, and liked the chanting of the priests. I went to see the king's palace, approaching it with apprehension, but on seeing other people enter I did as they did and was let through. Perhaps this was because of a little package that I had under my arm. Be that as it may, I had a high opinion of myself once I was within the palace, already almost seeing myself a resident. Finally I began to tire of walking around. I was hungry and the day was hot. I entered a milk shop and was given some *giuncà*, curdled milk, with two *grisses* of that excellent Piedmont bread that I love above all others, and so for five or six sous had one of the best dinners I've ever had.

I had to look for a place to stay. As I already knew enough Piedmontese to make myself understood, lodgings were easy enough to find, and I was prudent enough to choose a place more in keeping with my purse than with my taste. I was told that in the Rue du Pô the wife of a soldier took in out-of-work servants at one sou a night. She had an empty pallet for me, and I moved in. She was young and newly married, though she already had five or six children. All of us—mother, children, and guests—slept in the same room, which we did throughout the time I stayed there. All in all, she was a good woman, who swore like a carter, was always disheveled and untidy, but was kindhearted and obliging. She proved a friend to me, and in fact even helped me.

I spent several days abandoning myself entirely to the pleasures of independence and curiosity. I wandered around through the town and its outskirts, looking at the sights and visiting all the places that struck me as new and interesting, which it all was for a young man who had left his milieu and had never before been in a capital city. I was above all meticulous about visiting the palace, and attending the royal Mass every morning. I felt that it was a fine thing to find myself in the same chapel as the king and his retinue, but my passion for music, which was beginning to declare itself, played a larger role in my diligence than the pomp of the court, which once seen never changes, and so is not striking for long. In those days, the King of Sardinia had the best music in all Europe. Somis, Desjardins, and the Bezuzzis all shone there in turn. It did not take much to fascinate a young man, transported with delight by the least instrument provided it was played in tune. For the rest, I had only a dull admiration, without coveting the magnificence I saw. The one thing that interested me in all the brilliance of the court was to see if there were not some young princess who might merit my homage, and with whom I might embark on a romance.

I almost did embark on one in a less resplendent ambiance, though, had I carried it through, I could have found pleasures a thousand times more delightful.

Although I was living frugally, my purse, without my noticing it, was gradually becoming empty. This frugality, however, was less the result of prudence than simplicity of taste, which even today my custom of dining with the rich has not changed. For me there has never been better fare than a rustic meal. One can be certain to entertain me well with butter and cream, eggs, cheese, vegetables, brown bread, and passable wine. My good appetite will do the rest, as long as I am not put off by the annoying sight of butlers and servants bustling around. I had much better meals for six or seven sous at that time than I have since had for six or seven francs. Hence it was a lack of temptation that kept me in check; and yet I did not deny myself, since I added every possible sensual taste to my meals. I was the happiest gourmand enjoying pears, *giuncà*, the cheese and the Piedmontese bread, and a few glasses of Montferrat wine, which was so hearty one could cut it with a knife. But despite all this the end of my twenty francs was in sight, a truth I perceived more acutely with every passing day. In spite of the insouciance of youth, my anxiety for the future soon turned into fear. Of all my castles in the air, the only one that remained was to find an occupation that would provide me with a livelihood, which was itself no easy task. I considered plying my former trade, but did not know it well enough to work for a master, and there were few enough masters in Turin. So as I waited for something better I went from shop to shop, offering to engrave initials or coats-of-arms on dishes, hoping to tempt the shopkeepers with a low price, which I left up to them. This expedient, however, was not particularly successful. Almost everywhere I went I was shown the door, and the work I found was so negligible that I barely gained a few meals from it. One day, however, as I was walking early in the morning through the Contrà Nova, I saw through a shop window a young saleswoman who was so attractive and pretty that despite my timidity in front of ladies I did not hesitate to enter and offer her my modest talent. She did not send me away, but had me sit down and tell her my sad little tale, pitied me, told me to have courage and that good Christians would surely stand by me. Then, as she sent to a goldsmith in the neighborhood for the tools I told her I needed, she herself went upstairs to her kitchen and brought me some breakfast. This beginning struck me as auspicious, as did what followed. She seemed pleased with my work, and even more pleased with my conversation once I felt a little more confident, for she was splendid and well dressed, and, despite her gracious manner, her appearance overawed me. But the kind way she received me soon put me at ease, as did her compassionate tone and her warm and gentle manner. I could see I was succeeding, and that made me succeed more. But though she was Italian, and too pretty not to be slightly coquettish, she was modest, and I was too timid for matters to progress swiftly. We were not given enough time to finish the romance. This only increased in my memory the delight in the few moments I spent near her, and I can say that in these moments I tasted the sweetest and also the purest pleasures of love.

She was a spirited brunette whose unaffected nature radiated in her pretty face, which made her vivacity touching. Her name was Madame Basile. Her husband, older than she and more than a little jealous, would leave her, whenever he was traveling, in the care of a clerk who was too glum to be seductive but not without pretensions of his own, which expressed themselves through his ill temper. He took a great dislike to me, even though I enjoyed listening to him play the flute, which he did quite well. This new Aegisthus[231] always grumbled when he saw me enter his mistress's house, treating me with a disdain for which she paid him back in full. It even seemed that she enjoyed making a fuss over me in his presence to torment him. This form of vengeance, though very much to my taste, would have been even more delightful in a tête-à-tête. But she never took matters that far, or at least not in the same way. Whether she found me too young, or did not know how to make advances, or perhaps did not want to act improperly, she always kept a kind of reserve that did not push me away, but which intimidated me without my knowing why. I did not feel for her the true, tender respect I felt for Madame de Warens, but felt more awe and much less familiarity. I was confused and wavering. I did not dare look at her, did not dare breathe in her presence. And yet I feared leaving her more than I feared death. With a hungry eye I devoured everything I could see without being noticed: the flowers in her dress, the tip of her pretty foot, her firm white arm in the gap between her glove and her sleeve, and the gap that appeared at times between her décolleté and her scarf. Every part heightened the impression of the others. From gazing at what I could see and even beyond, my eyes became clouded, my chest heavy, my breath more and more labored and harder to control, and all I could do was to emit quiet, troubling sighs in the silence we often fell into. Luckily, Madame Basile, busy with her needlework, did not notice, or so it seemed to me. And yet I sometimes saw her scarf shudder with sympathy. This dangerous sight completed my ruin, but just as I was ready to give in to my rapture she would say something to me in her calm voice, which instantly brought me back to myself.

I saw her alone in this manner several times, without ever a word, a gesture, or an eloquent glance hinting at the least understanding between us. This state, which was a great torment to me, was also a great delight, and in the simplicity of my heart I could barely imagine why I was so tormented. It appeared that our little private meetings were not unpleasant to her either—at least she quite frequently brought them about—surely a gratuitous endeavor on her part, considering the use she made of them, or allowed me to make.

One day, bored by the clerk's foolish talk, she went up to her room, and I hastily finished the little job I was doing in the back room of the shop and followed her. Her door stood ajar, and I entered unperceived. She sat embroidering by the window, with her back to the door. She could not have seen me enter, nor could she have heard me through the clattering of wagons in the street. She always dressed well, on that day almost coquettishly. She was sitting gracefully, her head slightly lowered, revealing the whiteness of her neck. Her hair, elegantly pinned up, was decorated with flowers. Her whole form exuded a charm that I had time to consider, and this made me lose my head. At the door to her room I threw myself on my knees, passionately reaching out to her, convinced that she could not hear me, and thinking she could not see me. But there was a mirror on the mantelpiece that betrayed me. I do not know what effect my rapture had on her: she neither looked at me nor spoke to me, but half-turning her head, pointed with a simple movement of her finger to the straw mat at her feet. I shuddered, emitted a cry, and in an instant had thrown myself at the place to which she had pointed; but what one might find difficult to believe is that once there I did not dare take the matter any further, or say a single word, or raise my eyes to hers—not even to touch her or steady myself on her knee, as I was crouching so awkwardly. I was silent, stock-still, but certainly not calm. Everything demonstrated my agitation, my joy, my gratitude, the ardent desires that were so uncertain of their object and constrained by the fear of displeasing, in which my young heart could not be assuaged.

She seemed neither more calm nor less timid than I was. Troubled to see me there, perturbed that she had drawn me to her room, and beginning to feel the whole consequence of a sign she had given doubtless without reflection, she neither welcomed me nor pushed me away. She did not raise her eyes from her work, and tried to act as if she did not notice me at her feet; but all my foolishness did not hinder me from understanding that she shared my confusion, perhaps even my desires, and that she was held back by a shame similar to mine, without this giving me the strength to overcome it. The five or six years that she was older than I, I felt, should place all the boldness on her side, and I told myself that as she did nothing to spark my boldness, she must not want me to show any. Even today I believe I was right, and certainly she was too clever not to see that a novice, such as I was, needed not only encouragement but also instruction.

I do not know how this mute, lively scene would have ended, nor for how long I would have remained immobile in that ridiculous and delightful position, had we not been interrupted. At the height of my agitation I heard the opening of the door to the kitchen next to the room in which we were, and Madame Basile, alarmed, motioned me with quick words and gestures, "Get up, Rosina is here!" Jumping up hastily, I seized her outstretched hand, and with burning lips kissed it twice. With the second kiss I felt her charming hand press slightly against my lips. This was the sweetest moment in all my life, but the opportunity I had lost did not return, and our young love went no further.

This is also perhaps why the image of this lovely woman has

remained preserved with such charming contours in the depths of my heart. This image has even grown in beauty the more I have come to know the world and women. Had she had a little more experience, she would have gone differently about encouraging a young boy; but though her heart might have been weak, it was honest, and she was giving way involuntarily to the inclination that was transporting her. From all appearances this was her first infidelity, and I probably would have had a harder task overcoming her scruples than my own. In those moments with her I tasted an inexpressible sweetness. None of the delights of possessing a woman can compare with the two minutes I spent at her feet without so much as daring to touch her dress. No, there are no pleasures like those an honest woman one loves can bestow. Everything she grants is a favor. A light stir of her finger, her hand pressed gently against my lips, were the only favors I ever received from Madame Basile, and the memory of these trifling favors still transports me when I think back on them.

For the next two days I waited impatiently for a new tête-à-tête in vain. It was impossible for me to find an opportunity to arrange one, nor did I notice any attempt on her part. Her manner, though not colder, was now more reserved, and I believe she avoided my glances from fear that she could not sufficiently control hers. Her confounded clerk was more irritating than ever. He even began to ridicule and mock me, telling me that he could see I would do well with the ladies. I was mortified that I might have committed some indiscretion, and, seeing myself as already having reached an understanding with Madame Basile, was eager to cloak feelings that until then had needed no concealment. This made me more careful about seizing the opportunity to satisfy them, and as I wanted those occasions to be discreet, I did not find any opportunity at all.

This is another romantic foible of which I have never been

able to cure myself, and which, coupled with my natural timidity, has done much to disprove the clerk's predictions. I have, if I may venture to say so, always loved too sincerely, too perfectly for me to be able to boast of easy success. No passion has ever been more alive and pure than mine, no love more tender and more true, or more disinterested. I would have sacrificed my happiness a thousand times to that of the person I loved. Her reputation was dearer to me than my life, and never, for all the pleasures of delight, would I have wanted for a single moment to compromise her peace of mind. This has made me so careful, so cautious and secretive in my ventures that none has ever succeeded. The little success I have had with women has always come from my loving them too much.

To return to Aegisthus the flute player, what was peculiar was that the more unbearable this traitor was, the more amiable he became. From the first day that his mistress had taken a liking to me, she had thought of making me useful in the shop. I was passably good at arithmetic, and she had suggested to him that he teach me to keep the books. The boor, however, took this suggestion very badly, fearing perhaps that I might supplant him. Consequently, the only work I did with the fellow was to copy out a few bills and notes, clean up a few books, and translate a few business letters from Italian into French. But suddenly he decided to take up the suggestion that Madame Basile had made and he had rejected, and announced that he would teach me double-entry bookkeeping so that I could be of service to Monsieur Basile on his return. There was in his tone and manner something false, mean-spirited, and mocking that inspired little confidence in me. Without waiting for my answer, Madame Basile told him coldly that I would certainly be grateful to him for his offer, but that she hoped Fortune would favor my merit, and that it would be a great pity were I, with so much talent, to end up a mere clerk.

She had told me on several occasions that she wanted to introduce me to someone who could be useful to me. She was wise enough to feel that the time had come to distance herself from me. Our silent declarations had been made on Thursday, and on Sunday she held a dinner I attended at which there was also a Jacobin monk, a man of handsome aspect, to whom she introduced me. The monk treated me warmly, complimented me on my conversion, and mentioned a number of things regarding my story that indicated she had spoken to him about me. Then he patted me twice on the cheek and told me to be a virtuous young man, to have courage, and to come and see him so we could talk further at leisure. I could tell by the respect everyone showed him that he was a man of standing, and, judging by his paternal tone to Madame Basile, that he was also her confessor. I remember well that his courteous familiarity toward her was marked by esteem and even respect for his penitent, which at the time made less of an impression on me than it does today. Had I been more clever, how touched I would have been at having stirred the feelings of a young woman so respected by her confessor!

As the dining table was not large enough for the number of people present, a smaller table was set up where I was to delight in the company of the clerk. Not that I was deprived of any attentions or good food. Quite a number of plates were sent to the little table that were clearly not meant for him. Everything had gone very well until now; the ladies were vivacious, the gentlemen gallant, and Madame Basile did the honors with charming grace. As we were dining, a carriage pulled up at the door, and footsteps were heard coming up the staircase. It was Monsieur Basile. I can see him as if he were entering the room this instant in his red coat with gold buttons, a color for which I have had an aversion ever since. Monsieur Basile was a tall, handsome man with an imposing presence. He burst into the room as if he were catching the company red-handed, though only his friends were present. His wife rushed to embrace him, clasped his hands, and lavished caresses on him, which he did not return. He greeted the company and was given a setting. He ate. He had barely begun talking about his voyage when he glanced over at our little table and asked in a severe tone who the boy he saw there might be. Madame Basile told him quite straightforwardly. He asked whether I was living in his house, and when he was told I was not, asked gruffly, "And why not? If he is here all day, he might as well stay here all night as well." The monk intervened, and after sincere words of praise for Madame Basile, he praised me, too, in a few words, adding that Monsieur Basile would do well to partake of his wife's pious charity instead of condemning it, as no boundaries of discretion had been crossed. The husband mumbled a surly reply under his breath, held in check by the presence of the monk, but which gave me to understand that the clerk had informed him about me, and thus was paying me back in his own way.

We had barely risen from the table when the clerk, dispatched by his master, triumphantly came to inform me that I was to leave the house this instant and never set foot in it again. The clerk seasoned his commission with everything that could render it insulting and cruel. I left without a word, but my heart was crushed, less for leaving this charming woman than for leaving her prey to her husband's brutality. He was without doubt right in not wishing his wife to be unfaithful, but although she was virtuous and of good family, she was Italian, that is to say, quick to take offense and vindictive. He had made a mistake, in my view, to take the measures he took with her, which were just the kind that would bring on the misfortune he feared.

Such was the success of my first romance. On two or three occasions I tried walking back and forth in the street in the hope of at least seeing the woman for whom my heart ceaselessly yearned. Instead I saw only her husband and the watchful clerk, who, on seeing me, approached me with the shop's yardstick, his mien more expressive than welcoming. Seeing that I was closely watched, I lost heart and stopped going there. But I wanted to at least meet the patron she had secured for me. Unfortunately, I did not know his name. I wandered around the monastery several times in the hope of seeing him, but to no avail. Finally other events effaced the charming memories of Madame Basile, and soon I had forgotten her so completely that I became once again as guileless and as much of a novice as I had been before, not even attracted to beautiful women.

Her generosity, however, had somewhat refurbished my scanty wardrobe, if modestly and with the foresight of a practical woman more concerned with decent apparel than with show, and who sought to make me presentable and not to make me shine. The clothes I had brought with me from Geneva were still holding up well; she had added only a hat and some linen. I had no cuffs and she did not want to give me any, even though I would very much have liked some. She was content to keep me presentable, something I did not need reminding of whenever I was in her presence.

A few days after the catastrophe, my landlady, who, as I have mentioned, had taken a liking to me, told me that she had perhaps found a place for me, and that a lady of quality wanted to see me. On hearing this I immediately saw myself plunged into a great adventure, as my mind always returned to that. This adventure, however, turned out not to be as brilliant as I imagined. I went to visit the lady with one of her servants who had spoken about me to her. The lady asked me some questions, looked me over, seemed satisfied enough, and I immediately was taken into her service—not as a favorite, but as a lackey. I was dressed in her livery, my only distinction being that while the others wore aiguillettes, I was not given any. As her livery had no gold braid, it looked more or less like a townsman's dress. Such was the unexpected end of all my great hopes.

The Countess de Vercellis, into whose service I entered, was a widow without children. Her husband had been from Piedmont, though I believed her to be from Savoy, as I could not imagine that anyone from Piedmont could speak French as well as she did, and with such a pure accent. She was in her middle years, had a noble countenance, a cultivated mind, and a great love for French literature, which she knew well. She wrote a great deal, and always in French. Her letters had the turn, and almost the grace, of those of Madame de Sévigné;[232] indeed, one could have mistaken some of them for hers. My main task, which did not displease me, was to write them from her dictation, since a cancer in her breast that caused her much suffering prevented her from any longer being able to write.

Madame de Vercellis not only had great intelligence but also was a strong and lofty soul. I followed her in her final illness, and saw her suffer and die without showing a moment of weakness, without the slightest effort at constraint, without ever abandoning her role as woman, and without suspecting that there was in this any philosophy, a word that had not yet come into vogue, and that she did not even know in the sense in which it is used today. This strength of character sometimes bordered on coldness. She always struck me as being as little sensitive to others as she was to herself, and when she helped those in need, she did so because it was good in itself, rather than out of real sympathy. I felt something of that coldness during my three months in her service. It was natural that she would take a liking to a young man of some promise who was always in her presence, and, knowing that she was dying, that he would need help and support after she was gone. But either because she did not judge me worthy of particular attention, or because the people besetting her would not allow her to think of anybody but them, she did nothing for me.

And yet I remember well that she had shown some interest in me. She would sometimes ask me questions, and she liked me to show her the letters I was writing to Madame de Warens and to hear about my feelings. But she did not go about getting to know these feelings in the best way, since she never revealed her own to me. I loved to pour out my heart, as long as I felt another heart open to receive it. A cold and dry questioning, without a sign of approval or displeasure at my responses, robbed me of confidence. When nothing indicated that my words were pleasing or displeasing I would always become fearful, seeking less to show what I thought than to be silent about anything that might be to my disadvantage. I have noticed since that this dry manner of questioning people to get to know them is quite common among women who pride themselves on their intelligence. They imagine that in not letting any of their feelings show they will be more successful in penetrating yours. But they do not see that by doing this they deprive you of the courage to show your feelings. This alone will lead a man who is questioned in this way to put up his guard, and if he thinks that the woman is simply trying to have him talk without taking any real interest in him, he will lie or be silent, or double his guard, preferring to pass for a fool than to be duped by her curiosity. It is invariably a bad way of attempting to read the heart of another when one affects concealment of one's own.

Madame de Vercellis never spoke to me a word tinged with

affection, pity, or benevolence. She questioned me coldly, and I replied with reserve. My answers were so timid that she must have found them commonplace and was bored. In the end, she stopped asking me about myself and no longer spoke to me, except in matters of service. She judged me less on what I was than on what she had made of me, and, seeing me as nothing but a lackey, prevented me from appearing to her as anything else.

I believe that from this time on I was to experience the malicious sport of hidden interests that has crossed me all my life and given me a real aversion for the apparent order that produces them. Having no children, Madame de Vercellis had as her heir her nephew, the Count de la Roque, who paid court to her assiduously. Furthermore, her principal servants, knowing her end was approaching, saw to their own interests, and she was surrounded by so much bustle that it would have been difficult for her to have a moment to think of me. Her household was run by a certain Monsieur Lorenzi, a wily man, whose wife was even wilier and had so insinuated herself into the good graces of her mistress that she had achieved the rank of a friend rather than of a maid in her service. Madame Lorenzi had persuaded Madame de Vercellis to take on as chambermaid her niece, Mademoiselle Pontal, a devious schemer who had adopted the airs of a lady-in-waiting and had so successfully helped her aunt ingratiate herself with their mistress that Madame de Vercellis saw only through their eyes and acted through their hands. I did not have the good fortune to be looked on with favor by these three. I obeyed them but would not serve them, as I did not feel that beyond serving our mistress I should also be the lackey of her lackeys. Furthermore, I was in a sense an unsettling person for them. They could clearly see that in the household I was not in the position I merited, and they were worried that Madame would see this, too, and that were Madame to make amends this might diminish their inheritance; this type of people, too greedy to be just, saw any legacy to others as a loss to their own. Consequently they joined forces to keep me out of her sight. She liked to write letters, in her condition one of the few pleasures she had left, but they turned her against it, convincing the doctor to persuade her that it was too tiring. On the pretext that I was inexperienced, they employed instead two fat louts to carry her about in a chair. Their efforts proved so successful that when she wrote her will, I had not entered her room in a week. It is true that afterward I was allowed to enter as before, and was even more attentive than anyone else, for the poor woman's pain was heartrending. The fortitude with which she bore her suffering made me respect and cherish her, and I shed genuine tears in her room that neither she nor anyone else saw.

We finally lost her. I saw her expire. Her life had been that of a woman of wit and sense, her death that of a sage. I can say she made the Catholic faith dear to me, fulfilling its duties with a serenity of spirit, conscientiously and without affectation. She was of a serious nature. Toward the end of her illness she assumed a cheerfulness that was too calm to be feigned, and which was merely a counterweight that reason granted her against the sadness of her condition. She remained in bed only for her final two days, continuing to converse serenely with those around her. Finally, speaking no more and in the throes of death, she farted loudly. "Good," she said, turning to the other side. "A woman who farts is not dead." Those were her last words.

She had bequeathed a year's wages to each of her menial servants, but as I was not even recorded on the list of her estate, I was left nothing. Count de la Roque nevertheless gave me thirty francs and allowed me to keep the new livery I was wearing, which Monsieur Lorenzi had wanted to take from me.[233] The count even promised to try to secure another position for me, and told me to come and see him. I went two or three times, but was not able to speak to him. I was easily deterred, and so did not go again, a mistake, as it turned out.

If only this were all I had to say about my stay with Madame Vercellis! But even though I outwardly remained the same, I did not leave the house as I had entered it. I took with me the enduring memory of a crime and the unbearable weight of remorse that after forty years still burden my conscience, and the bitterness of the feeling, far from growing weaker, grows stronger as I age. Who would believe that the error of a child could have such cruel consequences? It is because of these all too probable consequences that my heart cannot console itself. I most likely caused a charming, honest, and admirable girl, who was certainly a far worthier person than I, to perish in disgrace and misery.

It is to be expected that the dispersal of a household will lead to some confusion and that a number of things will get lost. Nevertheless, the servants were so faithful, and Monsieur and Madame Lorenzi so vigilant, that nothing was found to be missing from the inventory. It was only Mademoiselle Pontal who was missing an old pink and silver ribbon. There were many better things that would have been within my reach, but this ribbon alone tempted me and I stole it, and as I did not go out of my way to hide it, it was quickly found. They asked me where I had got it. I became flustered, stuttered, and finally, blushing, said that Marion had given it to me. Marion was a young girl from Maurienne whom Madame de Vercellis had hired to cook for her when she could no longer give dinners and had dismissed her old cook, as all she needed was good soups rather than rich stews. Not only was Marion pretty, but she had the fresh complexion one finds only in the mountains. Above all, she had an air of modesty and sweetness that won the hearts of everyone who set eyes on her. She was, furthermore, a good girl, well behaved and absolutely honest. That is why they were so surprised when I named her. She and I were equally trusted, and consequently they thought it vital to ascertain which of us was the thief. She was summoned. There were many people present, the Count de la Roque as well. She came in and was shown the ribbon, and I boldly accused her. Taken aback, she did not utter a word, but looked at me with eyes that could have disarmed the Devil, but not my barbarous heart. She finally denied the deed resolutely but without anger, reproached me, exhorting me to return to my senses and not to dishonor an innocent girl who had never done me wrong. But with hellish impudence I repeated my accusation, and asserted before her that she had given me the ribbon. The poor girl began to weep, saying to me only, "Ah, Rousseau, I thought you were a good person. You are making me terribly unhappy, but I would not want to be in your place." That was all. She continued to defend herself with simplicity and firmness, but without a single sharp word against me.

This moderation, compared to my resolute tone, worked against her. It did not seem natural to assume such a diabolical audacity on one side and such angelic sweetness on the other. They did not seem able to decide either way, but appeared prejudiced in my favor. In all the upheaval of the household, they did not take time to look deeper into the matter, and Count de la Roque dismissed both of us, saying only that the conscience of the guilty one would seek vengeance for the innocent. His prediction was not in vain. Not a single day passes that it does not fulfill itself.

I do not know what became of the victim of my slander, but it is unlikely that after that she would have easily found a good position, for there was a stain on her honor that was cruel in every way. The theft had been a trifle, but it was a theft, and, what was worse, a theft committed with the aim of seducing a young man. Finally, lying and obstinacy left nothing to hope for from one in whom so many vices were joined. I do not even consider poverty and destitution as the greatest dangers to which I had exposed her. Who knows, at her age, where the discouragement of injured innocence might have led her! Ah, if my remorse at having made her wretched is unbearable, one may judge my remorse at having made her worse than myself!

This cruel memory sometimes troubles me, upsetting me to the point of seeing the poor girl in my sleepless nights coming to reproach me for my crime as if I had committed it only yesterday. Whenever I have lived quietly it has tormented me less, but in the midst of a stormy life it robs me of my sweetest consolation of persecuted innocence, and it makes me feel what I believe I have said in one of my books: that remorse slumbers during prosperous times but becomes severe in adversity. And yet I have never been able to bring myself to unburden my heart of this confession to a friend. The closest intimacy has not driven me to confess to anyone, even Madame de Warens. I could only bring myself to avow that there was an atrocious act for which I had to reproach myself, but I never divulged what this act was. Thus the weight has remained on my conscience without respite, and I can say that the desire to deliver myself of it in some way has contributed much to my resolve in writing my confessions.

I have been in every way sincere in the admission I have just made, and one will surely find that I have not attempted to whiten the blackness of my deed. But I would never fulfill the

aim of this book if I did not at the same time reveal my inner
dispositions, and that I might fear to excuse myself by saying
what is strictly true. What is true is that never have wicked intentions been further from my heart than at that cruel moment,
and when I accused the unfortunate girl—this is bizarre but
true—my friendship for her was the cause. I had been thinking
about her, and I used the first object at hand as an excuse. I accused her of having done what I had wanted to do, of giving me
the ribbon, because I had intended to give it to her. When she
appeared afterward my heart was crushed, but the presence of
so many people was stronger than my repentance. I was not so
much afraid of punishment, but very much afraid of shame. I
feared it more than death, more than crime, more than anything in the world. I would have wanted to bury myself, to sink
deep into the earth. Invincible shame overcame everything.
Shame alone caused my impudence, and the more criminal I
became, the more the terror of admitting it made me fearless.
All I could see was the horror of being found out, publicly denounced, called a thief, a liar, a slanderer. An utter mortification deprived me of all other feelings. If they had let me come
back to my senses, I would without fail have admitted everything. Had Monsieur de la Roque taken me aside and said—
"Do not ruin this poor girl. If you are guilty, confess it to
me!"—I would have instantly thrown myself at his feet, of that
I am quite certain. But instead of giving me courage they intimidated me. My age must also be taken into account; I had
barely left childhood, or rather I was still a child. True wickedness is even more criminal in a young person than it is in those
of maturer years, but what is merely weakness is much less
criminal, and at bottom my crime was hardly anything else.
Hence the memory afflicts me more because of the evil it must
have caused than because of the evil itself. The terrible im-

pression that has remained of the only crime I have ever committed has had the benefit of protecting me for the rest of my life from any act tending to crime, and I believe that my aversion to lying is, to a large extent, regret at the horror that I could have lied in such a heinous fashion. If this is a crime that can be expiated, as I dare believe it can be, it ought to be expiated by the many evils that are overwhelming the final years of my life, and by forty years of honor and decency in difficult circumstances. Poor Marion has found so many avengers in this world that however great my offense against her, I have little fear of having to carry my guilt to the grave. This is all I have to say on this matter. May I be permitted never to speak of it again.

Book III

I left Madame de Vercellis's household in almost the same condition as I had entered it, and returned to my former landlady. I stayed with her for five or six weeks, during which time good health, youth, and idleness often made my temperament fickle. I was anxious, preoccupied, and dreamy; I wept, sighed, and longed for a happiness I could not picture but that I felt to be lacking. It is impossible to describe this state, and few men can even imagine it, for most have anticipated this plenitude of life, both so tormenting and so delicious, which gives a foretaste of enjoyment in the intoxication of pleasure. My blood was inflamed, incessantly filling my mind with girls and women, but since I was unaware of their true purpose, I used them in my thoughts and fantasies in bizarre ways without knowing what else to do with them. And these fantasies kept my senses in a state of perturbed turmoil, from which, fortunately, they did not teach me to deliver myself. I would have given my life to relive fifteen minutes with another Mademoiselle Goton, but I was beyond the age where the games of childhood could be led there as if of their own accord. Shame, the companion of an awareness of vice, had come with the years. It had increased my natural timidity to the point of rendering it insurmountable, and never, neither in those days nor since, have I been able to bring myself to make an indecent proposal, unless the woman by her advances forced me in some way to do so, even when I knew that she was unscrupulous and would almost certainly accept.

My agitation grew to the point that, unable to satisfy my desires, I fanned them in the most extreme ways. I sought out dark alleys and hidden nooks where at a distance I could expose myself to women in the condition in which I would have liked to be while in their company. What they saw was not an obscene object—something I did not even dream of—it was simply a ridiculous one.[234] The foolish pleasure I derived from displaying it before their eyes cannot be described. There was but one more step to take to receive the treatment I longed for, and I do not doubt that some bold woman would have afforded me this pleasure in passing, had I had the audacity to wait. This folly ended in a disaster that was almost comical but somewhat unpleasant for me.

One day I took a position at the far end of a courtyard in which there was a well where the girls of the house often came to fetch water. At the back of that courtyard were stairs leading down to some cellars by a number of passageways. I explored these subterranean passages in the darkness, and, seeing that they were long and probably endless, felt that should I be seen and need to flee they would make for a good refuge. Now confident, I offered the girls who came to the well a spectacle that was more laughable than seductive. The more sensible girls acted as if they had not seen anything, while others burst out laughing, and others again felt insulted and made a big fuss. I escaped into my retreat, but was followed. I heard a man's voice, something I had not bargained for and which alarmed me. At the risk of getting lost I plunged deep into the passageways—the noise, the voices, the man calling out, were all coming after me. I had counted on darkness, but now saw light. I shuddered and plunged deeper into the cellars. Then I was stopped by a wall, and, unable to go any further, stood awaiting my fate. A moment later I was seized by a big man with a big mustache, a big hat, and a big sword, flanked by four or five old women, each armed with a broomstick, and among them the little hussy who had betrayed me and who, doubtless, wanted to look me in the face.

The man with the sword grabbed me by the arm and asked me roughly what I was doing there. As one might imagine, I did not have an answer, but, quickly recovering my wits, in an act of desperation, invented a romantic tale that proved successful. In an abject tone I begged the man to have pity on my young years and condition: I was a foreign youth of high birth who was beset by madness, and had run away from my ancestral home because they wanted to lock me up. If he gave me away I would be lost, but if he let me go I might one day be able to repay his kindness. Against all expectation, my tale and manner had the desired effect. The menacing man was touched, and after a brief reprimand he gently let me go without questioning me any further. Judging by the looks that the young girl and the old women gave me as I left, I felt that the man I had so feared had done me a great service, and that had I been left to the women I would not have come away so cheaply. I heard them murmuring something, but I hardly cared what, for as long as the sword and the man were not involved, I was certain that, nimble and vigorous as I was, I would be able to flee them and their cudgels.

A few days later, walking down a street with a young priest who was my neighbor, I ran straight into the man with the sword. He recognized me, and mimicking me in a mocking tone, called out, "I am a prince, a prince, and a coward, too! But His Highness had better not dare show his face again!" He did not say any more, and I stole away, hanging my head, thanking him in my heart for his discretion. The horrible old women had probably shamed him for his credulity. However that may be, he was a good man despite being Piedmontese, and I never think of him without gratitude, for the story was so amusing that someone else in his place would have disgraced me publicly just for a laugh. Though this incident did not have the consequences I might have feared, it did not fail to keep me well behaved for quite a while.

During my time with Madame de Vercellis I had made a few acquaintances whom I cultivated in the hope of their proving useful to me. Among others I sometimes visited a priest from Savoy by the name of Monsieur Gaime, who was the tutor of the Count de Mellarède's children.[235] The priest was still young and had not been much in society but was a man of good sense, decency, and intelligence, and one of the most honest men I have ever met. As he did not have enough influence to secure me a position, he could be of no help in the cause for which I had originally cultivated him, but I found in his company benefits that were more precious, and from which I have profited all my life: principles of sound morality and good reason. In the shifting sequence of my tastes and ideas I had always positioned myself either too high or too low, an Achilles or a Thersites,[236] sometimes a hero, at other times a good-for-nothing. Monsieur Gaime took pains to restore me to my proper place and show me to myself without sparing me, but without discouraging me, either. He spoke to me in a forthright manner about my natural gifts and talents, but added that he saw emerging possible barriers that might stop me from putting them to best use; so that my talent, in his view, was less likely to serve me as steps leading to fortune than as a resource that would help me do without it. He painted a true picture of life, of which I had such false ideas. He taught me that in times of adverse fortune a wise man could always strive for happiness and sail close to the wind to reach it—that there is no true happiness without wisdom, and there is wisdom in every station in life. He curbed my fascination with grandeur, proving that those who rule others are neither wiser nor happier than those they rule. He told me something I have often remembered: that if every man could look into the hearts of others, there would be more people seeking to descend in the world than to rise. This thought, whose truth is striking and not in the least exaggerated, has been of great help to me throughout my life in resigning myself to my place. He taught me the meaning of honesty, which my inflated genius had grasped only in its excesses. He taught me that enthusiasm for sublime virtues was of little use in society; that the higher one soared, the greater the danger of falling, and that the consistent performance of small duties well executed required no less effort than heroic actions and was a surer path to honor and happiness. He showed me that it was infinitely better to have the respect of men at all times than to have their admiration only some of the time.

To establish the duties of man one had to return to his origin. Furthermore, the conversion I had just undertaken and of which my present condition was the result, led us to discuss religion. The reader will already have guessed that Monsieur Gaime served to a large extent as a model for the Savoyard Vicar. As prudence obliged him to speak with some reserve, on certain points he expressed himself less openly, but otherwise his principles, feelings, and points of view, as well as his advice that I return to my country, were the same as those of my Savoyard Vicar. It was all as I have since presented it to the public. Thus I shall not expand on conversations that can be read elsewhere, and will only say that his lessons, wise but initially without effect, planted in my heart a seed of virtue and religion that has never been stifled, and that needed only the care of a more beloved hand to flower.

Although my conversion at the time had not quite struck root, I was nonetheless moved. Far from being bored by his lessons, I took pleasure in them because of their clarity and simplicity, and above all because of a certain warm interest in me with which I sensed they were filled. I have a loving soul, and am always drawn to people less in proportion to the good they have done me than the good they have wished me. In this my intuition has rarely been wrong. I also became truly fond of Monsieur Gaime. I was, so to speak, his second pupil, and that even provided me for the time being the inestimable benefit of turning me away from the penchant for vice to which my idleness had led me.

One day, when I least expected it, the Count de la Roque sent for me. Annoyed at having gone to see him several times without managing to speak to him, I had given up. I thought he had forgotten me, or that he had retained a bad impression of me. I was mistaken. He had more than once witnessed the pleasure with which I had attended his aunt. He had even spoken to her about it, and mentioned it to me after I was no longer giving it any thought. He received me well, told me that he had not wanted to fan my hopes with vague promises but had been looking for a position for me and found one, that he was putting me on a path to making something of myself and that it would be up to me to do the rest. The house in which he was placing me, he said, was powerful and respected; I would not need other patrons for my advancement, and though I would initially be treated as a mere servant, as I had been in Madame de Vercellis's house, I could rest assured that if my actions and disposition were to be judged beyond that station, they would be disposed to advance me. The ending of his speech cruelly contradicted the shining hope that the beginning had given me. "What? Am I still to be a lackey?" I thought to myself with bitter scorn, which confidence, however, soon effaced, as I felt that I was not made for such a position and consequently need not fear being left in it.

He took me to the Count de Gouvon, First Equerry to the Queen and head of the illustrious house of Solar. The venerable old man's dignity rendered the affability of his welcome even more touching. He asked me about myself with interest, and I answered with sincerity. He said to the Count de la Roque that I had a pleasant physiognomy that bespoke intelligence, of which he believed I had a good deal, but that intelligence was not everything, and that we would have to wait and see about the rest. Then he turned to me. "My child," he said, "a beginning is always difficult, but your beginning here will probably not be so hard. Behave yourself and try to please everyone. That is all you need do for the present. As for the rest, take heart; we will look after you." He immediately took me to his daughter-in-law, the Marquise de Breil, and presented me to her, and then to his son, the Abbé de Gouvon. This beginning augured well, for I already knew enough to be aware that one did not make such introductions for a lackey. And I was not, in fact, treated as one. I dined at the head steward's table and was not given livery to wear, and when the Count de Favria, a frivolous young man, wanted to have me ride on the back of his carriage, his grandfather forbade me to ride on the back of any carriage, or to follow anyone in attendance outside the house. I did, however, serve at table, and in practice did most of the chores of a lackey inside the house, but I did so freely, and was not overtly attached to anyone. With the exception of a few letters that I took in dictation, and a few figurines that the Count de Favria had me carve, I was almost master of my own time the entire day. This trial, which I did not realize was one, was assuredly most dangerous and not even very humane, for this excessive amount of idleness could have led me to vices that I would otherwise not have adopted.

But fortunately that did not happen. Monsieur Gaime's lessons had made an impression on my heart, and I had grown so fond of them that I sometimes stole away to listen to them again. I believe that those who saw me leave furtively would never have guessed where I was going. Nothing could have been more sensible than the advice that Monsieur Gaime had given me on how I should conduct myself. I began admirably. I was diligent, attentive, and full of zeal, and everyone was charmed. Monsieur Gaime had wisely advised me to temper my initial fervor from fear that it might abate, which people would notice. "The way you begin," he had told me, "will be the norm to which you will be held. Endeavor to do more in the future, but beware of doing less."

Since no one had troubled to inquire what accomplishments I might have, supposing that I had only those that nature had granted me, it did not seem as if they intended to make any use of me, despite what the Count de Gouvon had initially told me. Other matters intervened, and I was more or less forgotten. The Marquis de Breil, the son of the Count de Gouvon, was at the time ambassador to Vienna. There had been an upheaval at court that had affected the family, and for several weeks there was so much agitation in the house that nobody had time to give any thought to me. Nevertheless, until then I had not slackened in my efforts. There was one thing, however, that did me both good and harm, keeping me from external temptations but making me somewhat more distracted in my duties.

Mademoiselle de Breil was a young woman of about my age, well formed, quite pretty, with a very fair complexion and very black hair, despite which her face had that air of softness that blond women have, which my heart has never been able to resist. The court dress, so attractive on young women, accentuated her pretty waist and left her bust and shoulders free, and as the court wore mourning, it rendered her complexion even more dazzling. One will say that it is not for a servant to take note of such things, and I was doubtless wrong to do so. But I noticed them all the same—nor was I the only one. The head steward and the servants sometimes spoke of it at table, with a crudeness that made me suffer cruelly. I did not, however, lose my head enough to have altogether fallen in love with her; I did not forget myself. I kept to my station and did not even let my thoughts roam free. I liked to look at Mademoiselle de Breil, to hear her speak a few words that marked her wit, good sense, and sincerity. My ambition, limited to the pleasure of serving her, never went beyond my duties. At table I watched for opportunities to put them into practice. If her servant left her chair for a moment, I immediately went and stood behind it myself. Otherwise, I stood across from her. I tried to read in her eyes what she was going to ask for, and I lay in wait for the moment to change her plate. What would I not have done for her condescending to order me to do something, to look at me, to say a single word! But no. I had to bear the mortification of being nothing at all to her; she did not even notice that I was there. And yet when her brother, who sometimes addressed me at table, said something ungracious to me and I answered with a few elegant words, she would notice and glance at me. That glance, fleeting as it was, did not fail to enchant me. The following day the opportunity for a second glance presented itself, and I took advantage of it. A great dinner was being given, where I saw to my astonishment the head steward for the first time serving with a sword at his side and a hat on his head. By chance, the conversation turned to the motto of the House of Solar, which appeared on a tapestry with the family's coat of arms. *Tel fiert qui ne tue pas.*[237] As the Piedmontese are not usually accomplished in the French language, someone thought they saw a spelling error in the motto, saying that the word *fiert* should not have a final *t.*

The old Count de Gouvon was about to reply, but he noticed that I was smiling without daring to say anything, and ordered me to speak. So I said that I did not believe that the *t* was a mistake, that *fiert* was an old French word that did not come from *ferus,* "proud" or "threatens," but from the verb *ferit,* "he strikes" or "he wounds." Thus the motto did not appear to me to be saying "he threatens who does not kill," but "he wounds who does not kill."

Everyone stared at me and at each other in silence. Never had a party been more thunderstruck. But what pleased me even more was to see a definite air of pleasure on Mademoiselle de Breil's face. This girl, who was so disdainful, deigned to cast a second glance at me, which was worth almost as much as the first. Then, turning to her grandfather, she seemed to be waiting with some impatience for the praise he owed me, and which he gave me so fully and completely, and with such delight, that the whole table hastened to join in. The moment was brief but delightful in every way. It was one of those all too fleeting moments that put things back in their rightful order and that avenge the unmerited strokes of Fortune's outrages. A few minutes later, Mademoiselle de Breil again raised her eyes to me and asked in a voice that was as demure as it was friendly to pour her some water. As one can imagine, I did not keep her waiting. But drawing near I was gripped by such a fit of trembling that I poured too much into the glass, some of the water splashing onto her plate and even onto her. Her brother in his boorish way asked me why I was shaking so much—a question that did little to reassure me, and made Mademoiselle de Breil blush a bright red.

Here ended the romance in which, the reader will observe, as with Madame Basile and throughout my life, I have been unlucky in the conclusion of my loves. I devoted myself to Madame de Breil's antechamber in vain; I was never again to receive a mark of attention from her daughter. She came and went without a single glance in my direction, and I barely dared to glance at her. I was even so foolish and clumsy that one day when she dropped her glove as she walked past me, instead of throwing myself on the glove, which I wanted to cover with kisses, I dared not move, allowing a fat lout of a lackey whom I would have gladly crushed to pick up the glove. To complete my discomfort, I soon noted that I did not have the good fortune of Madame de Breil looking upon me with favor. Not only did she never have me perform any task, but she never accepted my services, either, and on two occasions, finding me in her antechamber, she asked me coldly whether I was not needed elsewhere. I had to give up this dear antechamber. At first it upset me, but other distractions intervened and soon I no longer gave it any thought.

However, I found consolation for Madame de Breil's disdain in the kindness of her father-in-law, who at last noticed my presence. On the evening of the dinner I have just spoken of, he and I had a conversation that lasted for half an hour, with which he seemed pleased and with which I was enchanted. This kind, elderly gentleman was a man of intelligence, and though less so than Madame de Vercellis had been, he had more heart, and I proved more successful with him. He told me to attach myself to his son, the Abbé de Gouvon, who had taken a liking to me, and that it might prove to my advantage if I made good use of it and could acquire what I lacked for the prospects they had in view for me. I hurried to the Abbé the very next morning, and far from receiving me as a servant, he had me sit by the fire and questioned me with the greatest kindness. He quickly saw that my education, which had been commenced in many subjects, had not been completed in any. Noting above all that I had very little Latin, he undertook to teach me more. It was decided that I would come to him every morning, and I began the following day. Thus by one of those strange coincidences that have been so characteristic of my life I found myself both above and below my station, both pupil and servant in the same house, and, though merely a servant, having a tutor whose birth could match that of a king's son.

The Abbé de Gouvon was a younger son destined by his family for a bishopric, which was why his education had been furthered more than is usual for children of the nobility. He had been sent to the university of Siena, where he had remained for several years and from which he had brought back a strong dosage of Cruscantism, so that at Turin he was almost what the Abbé de Dangeau had been at Paris.[238] A distaste for theology had made him turn to literature, which is not unusual in Italy among those pursuing a career in the prelacy. He knew the poets well, and he composed passable verse in Latin and Italian. In a word, he had the taste necessary to form mine, and to introduce some discernment into the jumble with which I had filled my head. But either because my prattle had misled him about the extent of my knowledge, or because he could not bear the boredom of elementary Latin, we began with lessons that were too advanced, and no sooner had he made me translate a few fables from Phaedrus than he plunged me into Virgil, where I barely understood a thing. I was destined, as will subsequently be seen, to relearn Latin quite often without actually learning it. Nevertheless I worked with zeal, and the Abbé lavished his attention on me with a kindness the remembrance of which still moves me. I spent a good part of every morning with him, as much for my instruction as for service; though not to serve him, as he would not accept that, but in order to take dictation and to make fair copies. My duty as secretary proved more useful to me than that of pupil, as not only did I learn Italian in all its purity, but I developed a taste for literature and some knowledge of good books, something that was not to be acquired at La Tribu and which was of much use to me later when I began to work on my own.

This was the period in my life when, not being involved in romantic schemes, I could most reasonably abandon myself to the hope of success. The Abbé was pleased with me and told everyone so. His father had taken such a liking to me, that—as the Count de Favria told me—he had even spoken to the King about me. Madame de Breil, too, had discarded her air of contempt. In short, I became a kind of favorite in the house, to the great jealousy of the other servants, who, seeing me honored by being given lessons by the master's son, felt that I was not intended to remain their equal for long.

As far as I was able to judge the prospects being planned for me from a few casual remarks I heard in passing, and to which I gave thought only afterward, I gathered that the House of Solar intended to pursue ambassadorships, and later perhaps even governmental ministries, and intended to educate in advance someone with merit and talent who was entirely dependent on the family and who, having their full trust, would be of much use and service. This plan of the Count de Gouvon was noble, judicious, magnanimous, and truly worthy of a farsighted and beneficent nobleman. But I could not at the time see the full scope of the project, which was too reasonable for my temperament and required too long a period of subjection. My mad ambition sought fortune only through romantic adventure, and, not seeing a woman in any of this, I found this means of success slow, laborious, and gloomy, while I ought to have found it more honorable and certain since no women would be involved, and the kind of merit women can further is surely in no way comparable to that which the House of Solar ascribed to me.

Everything was proceeding wonderfully. I had secured everyone's esteem, almost taken it by storm. My trial period was over and I was generally considered a young man of great promise who was below his true station, but whom everyone expected to see reach it. But my station was not one that had been assigned to me by men, and I had to attain it in a very different way. I will now touch on a characteristic trait of mine, which it will suffice to present to the reader without comment.

Though there were many new converts of my kind in Turin I did not like them and never wanted to see any of them. But I had met some Genevans who were not converts, among others a Monsieur Mussard, nicknamed Tord-Gueule,[239] who was a painter of miniatures and a distant relative of mine. This Monsieur Mussard found out that I was living at the Count de Gouvon's and came to see me with another Genevan by the name of Bâcle, with whom I had been friends during my apprenticeship. Bâcle was an amusing fellow, a clown who was lively and full of wit, which his young years rendered agreeable. I suddenly became infatuated with him, to the point of wanting to be with him all the time. He was to return to Geneva soon; what a loss this would be! I realized its full extent, and in order at least to take advantage of the time remaining to us I no longer left his side, or rather he did not leave mine, as initially I did not lose my head to the point of spending the entire day with him outside the house without leave. But soon, when the masters saw that I was completely obsessed with him, they forbade him the house, and I became so angry that, forgetting everything beside my friend Bâcle, I no longer went to the Abbé or the Count, and was no longer seen in the house. I was reprimanded, but to no avail. They threatened to dismiss me, a threat that proved my undoing; it made me realize that my friend Bâcle need not leave alone. From that moment on I saw no other pleasure, no other fate or happiness, than that of embarking on such a journey, and in it I saw only the indescribable bliss of a voyage at the end of which I glimpsed Madame de Warens, though at a great distance; for I never considered actually returning to Geneva. The mountains, the fields, the woods, the streams, and the villages succeeded each other endlessly with ever-new charms. I saw this blissful journey absorbing my whole life. I remembered with delight how charming this same voyage had appeared to me on my way here. How much more charming it would be if, added to all the appeal of independence, there was the pleasure of traveling with a lighthearted companion of my own age and taste, freed from all worries and duties, without constraint, without being obliged to stay or go anywhere but where we pleased. One would have to be mad to sacrifice such good fortune to aspiring ambitions whose fulfillment would be slow, difficult, and uncertain, ambitions that, supposing they were realized someday, would in all their luster not be worth a quarter of an hour of the true pleasure and freedom of youth.

In the grasp of such whimsical wisdom I behaved so well

that I finally had myself thrown out, which was not an easy accomplishment. One evening, on returning to the house, the head steward, on behalf of the count, informed me of my dismissal. This was exactly what I had wanted, for, feeling in spite of myself that my conduct was excessive, I added injustice and ingratitude as an excuse for my behavior, believing that in this way I could lay the blame on others and justify to myself that necessity had forced me to make this decision. I was told that the Count de Favria wished to speak to me the following morning before I left, and, as they saw that I had completely lost my head and might not do so, the steward put off paying me some money that had been set aside for me but which I had certainly not earned; intending to promote me above the station of servant, they had not yet fixed my wages.

The Count de Favria, young and foolish though he was, spoke to me on that occasion in the most sensible, and I would almost dare say tender, words, laying before me in a flattering and touching manner his uncle's interest in me and his grandfather's intentions. Finally, after having vividly portrayed everything I was sacrificing as I rushed to my ruin, he offered to reinstate me, the only condition being that I never again see the wretch who had led me astray.

It was quite clear that the Count de Favria was not saying all this of his own accord, and despite my blind folly I was touched, sensing all the kindness of my old master. But the vision of the journey was too deeply imprinted on my imagination for anything to be able to outweigh its charm. I was completely out of my mind. Callous and proud, I arrogantly replied that I had been given my dismissal and had accepted it, that what was done was done, and that whatever my fate, it would certainly not entail being sent away twice from the same house. At which the young Count, justly incensed, called me all the names I deserved, grabbed me by the shoulders, thrust me out of the room, and slammed the door after me. I marched out triumphantly as if I had just won the greatest victory, but, afraid of having to wage a second battle, I was contemptible enough to leave without thanking the Abbé for all his kindness.

In order to comprehend how far my delirium carried me at that moment, one must understand how readily my heart will passionately blaze up at the slightest thing, and with what force it will plunge into imagining the object that fires it, however worthless this object might sometimes be. The most bizarre, childish, and foolish plans will come to flatter an idea I am fixed on, convincing me how plausible it is to abandon myself to it. Could one believe that a young man of almost nineteen might plan to live the rest of his life off an empty water bottle? I will explain.

A few weeks earlier the Abbé de Gouvon had given me as a present a most beautiful little Hero water fountain that had enchanted me.[240] Wise Bâcle and I made the fountain play so much while we were discussing our journey that we came upon the idea that the fountain could prove useful to our trip, and even prolong it. Was there anything in the world as curious as a Hero Fountain? On this principle we built the entire edifice of our fortune. All we had to do was in every village to gather the peasants around our fountain, and food and good cheer would come raining down upon us with all the more abundance as we were both persuaded that the earth's bounty did not cost anything to those who gathered it, and that if these peasants did not heap food on passersby, it was purely out of malice. We imagined feasts and weddings everywhere, and deemed that without spending anything but the air in our lungs and the water of our fountain, we could cover all our costs in Piedmont, Savoy, France, and the rest of the world. We planned endless journeys, and first set out to the north, more for the pleasure of crossing the Alps than from the necessity of getting to a particular place.

Such was the plan on which I set out, abandoning without regret my protector, my tutor, my studies, my hopes, and the expectation of an almost assured fortune in order to embrace the life of a true vagabond, bidding farewell to the capital, farewell to the royal court, to ambition, vanity, love, beautiful women, and all the hope for romantic adventures that had brought me this far the year before. I set out with my fountain and my friend Bâcle, my purse lightly garnished but my heart saturated with joy, not thinking of anything except delighting in the roving happiness to which I had so quickly reduced my illustrious plans.

This extravagant journey turned out to be almost as pleasant as I had imagined it would be, but not quite in the same way, for though our fountain briefly amused the landladies and their maids in the taverns, we still had to pay as we left. But that hardly worried us, and we resolved to make use of this resource only when we ran out of money. An accident spared us the trouble, for near Bramans the fountain broke, and none too soon, for though we did not dare admit it to each other it was beginning to bore us. This disaster made us even more cheerful than we had already been, and we laughed a lot at our flightiness at not having foreseen that our clothes and shoes would wear out, or thinking that by demonstrating our fountain we could replace them. We continued our journey as merrily as we had embarked on it, but heading a little more directly toward our destination that our dwindling funds were now compelling us to reach.

At Chambéry I became pensive; not about the folly I had committed—for no man ever came to terms so rapidly or so completely with what is past—but about the reception that might await me at Madame de Warens's, for in my eyes her house was as much my home as my father's house. I had written her of being taken into the Count de Gouvon's household. She knew my position there and, congratulating me, had given me some very sound advice on the manner in which I ought to respond to the kindness I was being shown. She thought my fortune assured, as long as I did not ruin things. What would she say now on seeing me return? I did not for a moment think that she might close her doors to me, but I feared the disappointment I would cause her and her reproaches, which would be harsher for me than the greatest privation. I resolved to endure everything in silence and do anything to appease her. For me she was the only person in the universe; to live in her disfavor was impossible. But what worried me most was my traveling companion, with whom I did not want to burden her, but of whom I might have difficulty ridding myself. I prepared for our separation by acting coldly toward him on that last day. Bâcle understood me; he was crazy, not foolish. I thought he would be hurt by my fickleness, but I was wrong. Nothing could hurt my friend Bâcle. We had barely set foot in Annecy when he said, "Well, you're home now!" kissed me, said good-bye, turned on his heel, and disappeared. That was the last I ever saw or heard of him. Our acquaintance and friendship had lasted altogether about six weeks, but the consequences will last as long as I do.

How my heart beat as I approached the house of Madame de Warens! My legs were shaking beneath me, and I felt as if my eyes were covered by a veil. I saw nothing, heard nothing, nor would I have recognized a soul. I was forced to stop several times to catch my breath and recover my senses. Was it the fear of not being given the help I needed that worried me so? Would the fear of dying of hunger cause such alarm in a boy my age?

No! And I can say with as much truthfulness as pride that never in my life has selfishness or indigence caused me to either open or shut my heart. In a life uneven and marked by vicissitudes, often without bread or shelter, I have always looked upon opulence and poverty with the same eye. In times of need I was as capable of begging or stealing as the next man, but not of feeling grieved at having been reduced to it. Few men have borne as much pain as I, few have wept as many tears, but never has poverty or the fear of falling into it caused me to breathe a single sigh or shed a tear. My soul, in defiance of Fortune, has known neither true good nor true ill, except for that which does not depend on Fortune: it is when I have not lacked for anything that I have felt myself the most unfortunate of mortals.

No sooner did I appear before Madame de Warens than her manner reassured me. At the first sound of her voice I shuddered, threw myself at her feet, and in the raptures of the liveliest joy pressed her hand to my lips. As for her, I do not know if she had already heard my news, but I saw little surprise in her face, and no expression of sorrow. "Poor boy," she said in a gentle voice, "so here you are back again? I knew you were too young for that journey. I am so relieved that things at least did not turn out as badly as I had feared." Then she had me tell her my story, which did not take too long and which I told very faithfully, omitting, however, this or that detail, but otherwise neither sparing nor excusing myself.

The question of my lodgings was raised. She consulted her chambermaid, and I held my breath throughout their deliberations. But when I heard that I was to sleep in the house, I could barely contain my joy, and watched my little bundle being carried into the room I was to stay in much as Saint-Preux must have watched his chaise being drawn into Madame de Wolmar's coach house.[241] I had the added pleasure of learning that this kindness was not to be transient, and at a moment when they thought my attention was elsewhere, I heard Madame de Warens tell her maid, "Let people say what they will, but as Providence has sent him back to me, I am determined not to abandon him."

So there I was, finally established in her house; but not yet established as I was to be later, from when I was to date the happiest days of my life. But it was a preparation for that time. Although the sensibility of heart that makes us truly enjoy our own selves is the work of nature and perhaps a product of our constitution, it needs certain circumstances to develop. Without these, even a man who is born sensual will feel nothing, and one day will die without having known his true self. That is how I had been more or less up to that time, and perhaps how I would have remained had I not known Madame de Warens, or if I had known her but had not lived long enough at her side to have acquired the sweet habit of the affectionate feeling that she inspired in me. I will venture to say that he who feels only love does not feel what is sweetest in life. I know another feeling, perhaps less impetuous but a thousand times more delightful, that is occasionally joined to love, though often separated from it. This feeling is not simply friendship; it is more voluptuous, more tender. I cannot imagine that it could be felt for someone of the same sex—at least, though I have been a good friend if ever a man has been, I have never experienced this with any of my friends. Though what I am saying might not be clear, it will become so presently. Feelings cannot be properly described except through their effects.

Madame de Warens's house was old, but large enough to have a good spare room that she had turned into her drawing room, and this was the room in which I was put up. It over-

442 · *The Essential Writings of Rousseau*

looked the passageway of which I have spoken, where our first meeting had taken place. Beyond the brook and garden one could see the countryside. This view was not a matter of indifference to the room's young occupant. It was the first time since Bossey that I could see some green outside my windows. Always cut off by walls, I had had nothing before my eyes but roofs and the gray of streets. How new and delightful this was! It greatly increased my disposition to tenderness. I looked upon this charming countryside as yet another of the kindnesses bestowed upon me by my beloved patroness. It was as if she had put it all there on purpose, just for me. I took my place there by her side. I saw her everywhere among the flowers and greenery. Her charms and those of springtime mingled in my eyes. My heart, constricted until that moment, was now released in all that openness, and I breathed my sighs more freely among the orchards.

Madame de Warens's household had none of the magnificence I had seen in Turin, but it was clean and decent and had a restrained patriarchal abundance that bore no trace of opulence. She had few silver dishes, no china, and no game in her kitchen or foreign wines in her cellar; and yet both her kitchen and cellar were well enough stocked to satisfy everyone, and she served excellent coffee in faience cups. Whoever came to see her was invited to dine either at her table or in her kitchen; no workman, messenger, or traveler ever left her house without having been given food or drink. Her household consisted of a chambermaid from Fribourg called Merceret, who was quite pretty, a valet from her own region called Claude Anet, about whom I will have more to say,[242] a cook, and two sedan-chair carriers whom she hired on the rare occasions she went visiting. This was a great burden on a two-thousand-franc pension; nevertheless, her modest income, had it been well managed, could have borne all this in a land where the earth is bountiful and money is scarce. Unfortunately, economy had never been one of her favored qualities, and she went further into debt: money came and went, and everything continued on its course.

The manner in which her household was arranged was precisely that which I would have chosen, and one may imagine that I took advantage of it with pleasure. What pleased me less was having to stay a very long time at table. Madame de Warens could hardly bear the first smell of soup and the main dishes. It almost made her faint, and this revulsion lasted for quite some time. She would gradually recover and make conversation, but would not eat at all. At least half an hour would pass before she took her first bite. I could have dined three times within that period, and had finished my meal well before she had even begun hers. To keep her company I would eat again, and so eat for two without finding myself any the worse for it. I was abandoning myself to the sweet feeling of well-being that I experienced at her side, particularly as this well-being was not clouded by any anxiety about how it was to be sustained. Since I was not yet privy to her affairs, I assumed them to be in a condition in which they could continue as they were forever. Later I was to find the same pleasures in her house, but as I was then better informed about her true situation, and seeing that these pleasures were borrowed against her pension, I could no longer enjoy them with such ease. Foresight has always ruined my enjoyment; seeing into the future has always been of no avail to me, as I have never been able to avoid my destiny.

From the first day we were on terms of the sweetest familiarity, which continued for the rest of her life. *Little One* was my name, *Maman* was hers, and we were always to remain Little One and Maman, even after the years all but erased the difference in age between us. I find that these two names wonderfully convey the essence of our affection, the simplicity of our manner, and above all the close connection of our hearts. She was for me the most tender of mothers, never seeking her own pleasure but always thinking of what was good for me. And if sensuality entered my attachment to her, it was not to change its nature but to render it more exquisite, to intoxicate me with the delight of having a young and pretty mother whom I loved to caress, and I mean caress in the literal sense, as she never thought to deprive me of kisses or the most tender maternal caresses, just as it never occurred to me to take advantage of them. It will be said that we did end up having relations of a different kind; I admit it. But we must wait a little, for I cannot tell everything at once.

That glance at our very first meeting was the only truly passionate moment she ever made me feel, and in fact that moment was the work of surprise. My indiscreet glances never attempted to peek beneath her shawl, even if an ill-concealed plumpness might well have drawn them there. I felt neither rapture nor desire in her presence, just an exquisite calm, delighting in I knew not what. I could have spent my whole life that way, even all eternity, without a moment of boredom. She is the only person with whom I never felt a faltering in our conversation that made the chore of sustaining it a torture. Our tête-à-têtes were not so much discussions as a ceaseless talking that ended only if it was interrupted. Far from needing to force myself to speak, I had much greater need to force myself to keep quiet. As she was always thinking about her many enterprises, she often fell into a reverie. So I would let her dream. I sat there gazing at her silently and was the happiest of men. I had another singular peculiarity: without claiming the favor of a tête-à-tête I sought them out incessantly, and savored them with a passion that turned into fury if importunate people sought her out. As soon as anyone came to see her, whether man or woman, I would leave the room muttering, unable to remain in her presence as a third. I would then pace her ante-chamber, counting the minutes, cursing those eternal visitors a thousand times, unable to imagine that they had such a lot to say to her when I had so much more.

I felt the full strength of my feeling for her only when she was out of my sight. In her presence, I was perfectly contented. But my restiveness during her absence reached a point of being painful. My need to be with her inspired in me bouts of tender-ness that often brought me to tears. I will always remember that on one of the great festive days, while she was at Vespers, I went for a stroll outside town, my heart filled with her image and the ardent desire to spend my entire life at her side. I had enough sense to know that this was not possible at present, and that the happiness I now felt so deeply would be brief. This colored my reveries with melancholy, which, however, had nothing somber about it but was tempered by flattering hopes. The sound of bells, which has always singularly affected me, the singing of the birds, the beauty of the day, the sweetness of the countryside, and the scattered rural dwellings in which I imagined us living together, all made such a lively, tender, sad, and touching impression on me that I saw myself transported as if in ecstasy to that happy time and place where my heart, possessing all the delight it could desire, would savor it in inex-pressible raptures, without even a thought of the voluptuous-ness of the senses. I cannot recall ever having launched myself into the future with more force and illusion than I did then. What has struck me most in remembering this reverie once it came true was that I found things exactly as I had imagined them. If ever a waking dream resembled a prophetic vision, this was certainly the one. The only thing in which I was deceived was its duration, as I had envisioned the days and years, a whole lifetime spent in unchanging tranquility, whereas in reality it lasted only but a moment. Alas! My most enduring happiness was in a dream, its fulfillment followed almost immediately by an awakening.

Were I to launch into the details of all the follies to which my memories of my dear Maman led when I was not with her, I would never finish. How many times did I kiss my bed, for she had slept in it, kiss the curtains and the furniture in my room, for they belonged to her, her pretty hand having touched them; I even prostrated myself on the floor, for she had walked there! At times even in her presence some of the extravagances that only the most violent love can inspire escaped me. One day as we sat at table, she had just taken a bite of food when I called out that I had seen a hair on it. She immediately put it back on her plate, upon which I eagerly seized it and devoured it. In short, there was only a single but essential difference between myself and a most passionate lover, rendering my condition almost incomprehensible.

I had come back from Italy not quite the same as I had gone, but perhaps as no youth my age had ever returned. I had brought back not my chastity but my virginity. I had felt the passage of years. My restive temperament had finally declared itself, and its first involuntary outbreak alarmed me about my health, which proves better than anything else the innocence in which until then I had been living. Soon reassured, I learned that dangerous substitute that tricks nature and saves young men of my temperament from many disorders, but at the cost of their health, vigor, and sometimes their lives. This vice, which shame and timidity find so convenient, is, furthermore, alluring to those with a vivid imagination: being able, so to speak, to dispose as they please of all womanhood and make the beauty that tempts them serve their pleasure without needing to obtain its consent. Seduced by this fatal advantage, I labored to destroy the good constitution that nature had restored to me, and which I had nurtured. If one adds to this disposition the surroundings I was in, living at the side of a beautiful woman, cherishing her image deep in my heart, seeing her continuously throughout the day, at night surrounded by objects that reminded me of her, and sleeping in a bed that I knew she had slept in—then, ah, what temptations! Any reader who pictures them would think me close to death! But quite the opposite. What ought to have been my ruin was precisely what saved me, at least for a time. Intoxicated with the charm of living close to her, ardently desiring to spend all my life with her, I always saw in her, whether she was present or absent, a tender mother, a beloved sister, exquisite friend, and nothing more. I always saw her thus, always the same, and saw nobody but her. Her image, ever present in my heart, left no room for any other. She was for me the only woman in the world, and the extreme sweetness of the feelings she inspired did not leave my senses time to be aroused for others, which protected me from her and all her sex. In short, I was chaste because I loved her. From these effects that I describe so poorly, let those surmise who can the nature of my attraction to her. For myself, all I can say is that if it already appears extraordinary, it will appear even more so in what follows.

I spent my time in the most agreeable manner but was occupying myself with things that pleased me least. There were plans to be drawn up, notes to be copied out, receipts to be recorded, herbs sorted, drugs pounded, and alembics monitored. Amidst all this came crowds of travelers, beggars, and visitors of every kind. We would have to receive at the same time a soldier, an apothecary, a canon, a pretty lady, and a lay brother. I cursed, grumbled, swore, and sent the whole damned lot to the Devil, but she, who took everything with a touch of humor, laughed at my rages till she cried. What made her laugh even harder was to see me yet more enraged at not being able to stop myself from laughing. These little intervals, in which I had the pleasure of grumbling, were delightful, and if during our quarrel still another unwelcome visitor arrived, she knew how to prolong the amusement by cruelly prolonging the visit, casting glances at me for which I would gladly have struck her. She would struggle not to burst out laughing, seeing me constrained by decorum, staring at her like one possessed, while at the bottom of my heart, and even in spite of myself, I found all this most comical.

Though I found all this irksome, it did amuse me since it was part of a way of life I found charming. Nothing that was happening around me, nothing that I was made to do, suited my taste, but everything suited my heart. I believe that I would have come to like the medicinal arts if my disgust had not provided hilarious scenes that never ceased to amuse us. It is perhaps the first time that medicine ever produced such an effect. I claimed to know a medical book by its smell, and the amusing thing is that I was rarely wrong. She made me taste the most disgusting potions, and it was useless to try to run away or defend myself. Despite my terrible grimaces and resistance, despite my clenched teeth, when I saw her smeared, pretty fingers nearing my lips, I could but open my mouth and suck. When her entire modest household was gathered in a room one would have thought, hearing us running around and shrieking with laughter, that some farce was being staged, and not that opiates or elixirs were being concocted.

I did not, however, pass my time entirely with tomfoolery. I had found several books in the room I was occupying: *The Spectator,* Pufendorf, Saint-Évremond, and *The Henriade.* Although I no longer had my former mad passion for reading, I now read in them a little, as I had nothing else to do. I particularly liked *The Spectator* and profited from it.[243] The Abbé de Gouvon had taught me to read less avidly and with more reflection, so I derived more from my reading. I accustomed myself to reflect on language, style, and elegant constructions. I practiced distinguishing pure French from my own provincial speech; for example, the two following lines of *The Henriade* cured me of a spelling mistake typical of Genevans: *"Soit qu'un ancien respect pour le sang de leurs maîtres / Parlât encore pour lui dans le cœur de ces traîtres."*[244] I was struck by the word *parlât,* which taught me that a *t* is necessary in the third person subjunctive, whereas before I had written and spoken the word as *parla,* as in the present indicative.

Sometimes I talked with Maman about what I was reading, and sometimes I read to her. I took great pleasure in this. I practiced the art of reading aloud, and that, too, was useful to me. As I have said, she had a cultivated mind, and at the time it was in full vigor. Several men of letters had striven to win her favor and had fostered her taste for great works. She had, if I may venture to say so, somewhat Protestant tastes. She talked only of Bayle,[245] and thought highly of Saint-Évremond, who had been long forgotten in France. But this did not prevent her from knowing good literature and discussing it with eloquence. She had been raised in the best society, and, having come to Savoy at a young age, had in the elegant company of Savoyan aristocracy shed the mannered style of the Pays de Vaud, where women mistake commonplace truisms for fine wit and speak only in clichés.

Though she had been at court only in passing, her quick

glimpse of it had been enough to familiarize her with it. She always cultivated friends there, and, despite the covert jealousies and the tittle-tattle concerning her conduct and her debts, she never lost her pension. She had experience of society and the skill for reflection that can make use of it. It was her favorite topic of conversation and precisely the kind of instruction I most needed, given all the fanciful notions I had. We read La Bruyère together, and she liked him more than La Rochefoucauld,[246] a sad and dismal book, particularly when one is young and does not like seeing man as he is. When she discussed moral questions, she sometimes wandered a little, but I remained patient, kissing her lips or her hands from time to time, and I did not find her digressions tedious.

This way of life was too sweet to last. I felt it, and the worry of seeing it end was the only thing that clouded my enjoyment. Even at her most playful, Maman studied me, observed me, questioned me, and to secure my fortune thought up a number of schemes that I could have done without. Happily, it was not enough to know my inclinations, tastes, or modest talents; it was in fact necessary to find or create opportunities and take advantage of them, which was not to be done in a day. Even the judgments the poor woman had formed in my favor concerning my merits only delayed putting them into practice, by making her more fastidious in the choice of means. In short, everything went according to my desires owing to the good opinion she had of me, but I was soon enough to be brought back down to earth, and from that moment on, farewell tranquility!

One of her relatives, Monsieur d'Aubonne, came to visit her. He was a man of considerable intelligence, a schemer, and like her a genius at contriving enterprises, but without allowing them to ruin him—a sort of adventurer. He had just proposed to Cardinal de Fleury a most intricate plan for a lottery, which the cardinal had turned down, and which he was now going to propose to the Court of Turin, where it was subsequently adopted and put into practice. He stopped for a while in Annecy and fell in love with the wife of the commissioner, a most amiable woman and very much to my liking, the only person I was happy to see at Maman's. Monsieur d'Aubonne noticed me, Maman spoke to him about me, and he undertook to examine me in order to consider what I might be fit for, and, should he find me worthy, to try to find me a position.

Madame de Warens sent me to him two or three mornings in a row on the pretext of some errand, without forewarning me. He succeeded splendidly in drawing me into conversation, was most congenial, put me at ease as much as possible, chatted with me about this and that and all kinds of nonsense, all with a quite natural air and without appearing to be studying me, as if he were merely in a jovial mood and was interested in a casual chat. I was enchanted. But the result of his examination was that in spite of my appearance and lively physiognomy I was, if not completely inept, at least a boy of little intelligence, with no ideas and small accomplishment—in short, quite limited in every way. The honor of someday becoming a minor village curate was the highest station to which I could aspire. Such was the account of me that he gave Madame de Warens. This was the second or third time I had been judged this way, and it was not to be the last, for Monsieur Masseron's opinion has often been repeated.

The reason for these judgments is too closely intertwined with my character not to need some explanation at this point, for it must, in all conscience, be appreciated that I cannot sincerely subscribe to them. With all possible impartiality, despite whatever Monsieur Masseron, Monsieur d'Aubonne, and many others might have said, I cannot agree with them.

Two almost irreconcilable things are united in me in a manner I am unable to fathom: a most ardent temperament with its lively and impetuous passions, together with ideas that are confused and slow to form, and that present themselves to me only after the fact. One would think that my heart and mind did not belong to the same person. Feeling, quicker than lightning, fills my soul, but instead of illuminating, it burns and dazzles me. I feel everything and see nothing. I am transported but dull. I need to be unruffled in order to think. What is astonishing is that my judgment is nevertheless quite sound, insightful, and even sophisticated, if one is patient. I make excellent impromptu remarks at leisure, but have never done or said anything remarkable on the spur of the moment. I could conduct the most graceful conversation by post, in the way that Spaniards are said to play chess. I once read the story about the Duke of Savoy, who, returning to his estate, looked back in the direction of Paris to shout, "Damn you, Parisian merchant!"[247] I immediately saw myself.

This slowness of thought coupled with vivacity of feeling is not just in conversation, but even when I am alone and at my work. My ideas arrange themselves in my head with remarkable difficulty. They meander dully in circles and ferment until they stir me, fire me up, make my heart beat faster, but amidst all this excitement I can see nothing clearly and am not able to write a single word. I have to wait. Imperceptibly the great agitation subsides, the chaos clears, and each thing returns to its place, but only gradually and after a long and confused interval. Have you ever seen an opera in Italy? During the scene changes in the great theaters there is an unpleasant disorder that lasts for quite a long time. All the sets are in a disagreeable jumble, you see everything dragged this way and that, and you think that it will all come crashing down. And yet little by little everything falls into place, nothing is missing, and one is quite astonished to see a magnificent spectacle follow the great tumult. This process is almost identical to what takes place in my brain when I attempt to write. Had I known first of all to wait, and only then render in all their beauty the things my mind had seen, few authors would have surpassed me.

This is the reason for the extreme difficulty I have in writing. My manuscripts, full of scribbles and blots, with everything mixed up and illegible, attest to the strife they have cost me. There is not one manuscript I have not had to transcribe four or five times before sending it to the press. At my table, pen in hand, a sheet of paper before me, I have never been able to achieve a thing. It is on a walk, among rocks and woods, or at night in my bed during my insomnia that I write in my mind, and one can imagine how slowly, especially as I am a person with no verbal memory, who in all his life has not been able to learn six lines of poetry by heart. There have been passages I have turned over in my head again and again, five or six nights in a row, before they were ready to be put on paper. This has also resulted in my succeeding better with works that require some labor than with those that need to be written with a certain lightness, such as letters, a genre in which I have never been able to catch the tone, and the writing of which I find the utmost torture. Even letters on the most trifling subjects cost me hours of toil; or if I set out to write down immediately what comes to my head, I know neither how to begin nor how to end, the letter turning into a long and confused ramble that is barely intelligible.

Not only is it a struggle for me to express ideas, it is also a struggle to receive them. I have studied people and believe myself to be a good observer; nevertheless, I am unable to see anything in what I am seeing. I can see well only what I remember, and have intelligence only in my memory. Of everything that is said, everything that is done, everything that happens in my presence, I feel nothing, understand nothing. The outward sign is all that strikes me. But afterward everything comes back to me: I remember the place, the time, the tone, the look, the gesture, and the circumstance. Nothing escapes me. It is then, from what has been said or done, that I am able to discover what a person has thought, and I am rarely wrong.

If I am so little master of my mind when alone, one can imagine how I must be in conversation, a situation in which one has to think about a thousand things at once. Just the thought of the many social conventions, of which I am sure to forget at least one, is enough to intimidate me. I cannot even understand how anyone can dare speak in company, for with every word one utters one must weigh all the people present and know their characters and their histories so that one can rest assured that nothing one says might offend anybody. In this regard, those who move in higher circles have a great advantage; knowing better what to be silent about, they can be more certain about what they say. But even they will often blunder. Imagine, then, someone who has just dropped from the clouds—he cannot expect to speak for a minute with impunity. In a tête-à-tête there is another difficulty that I find even worse: the need to speak continuously; when someone says something to you, you must answer, and if nothing is being said, you must revive the conversation. This unbearable constraint alone would have been enough to make me turn my back on society. I find no effort more terrible than the obligation to speak on the spur of the moment and continually. I do not know if this is linked to my mortal aversion for all subjugation, but it is enough for me to be compelled to converse: I will without fail say something foolish.

What is even more fatal is that instead of remaining silent when I have nothing to say, it is then, in order to fulfill my obligation, that I am seized by a compulsion to speak. I will hasten to stammer some pointless words, only too happy if they mean nothing at all. In attempting to overcome or hide my ineptness, I rarely fail to show it. Among a thousand examples I could cite, I shall choose one that is not from my youth, but from a time when, having lived a number of years in society, I ought to have acquired its facility and tone, had such a thing been possible. One evening I was sitting with two great ladies and a gentleman whose name I may divulge—the Duke de Gontaut. Nobody else was in the room, and I was struggling to add a few words—God knows what!—to a conversation among four people, three of whom quite clearly had no need of my contribution. The mistress of the house had had an opiate brought to her, which she took two times a day for her stomach. The other lady, seeing her grimace, said with a smile, "It must be Monsieur Tronchin's opiate." "I do not think so," the first lady replied, in the same tone.

"I imagine it cannot be that much better," witty Monsieur Rousseau added gallantly. Everyone fell silent in astonishment.[248] There was neither a word nor the hint of a smile, and in an instant the subject was changed. Had it been another lady, the blunder might have been a mere pleasantry, but such a comment was a terrible blunder when addressed to a lady who was too agreeable not to have made herself talked about a little, but whom I definitely had no intention of offending. And I believe that the two witnesses, the gentleman and the lady, had great difficulty in restraining their laughter. This is one of those turns of wit that escape me on account of my wish to speak without having anything to say. I am unlikely to forget this incident, as aside from its being quite memorable in itself, I am convinced that it bore consequences that remind me of it only too often.

I believe that this is enough to make it sufficiently clear that though I am not a fool I have often been taken for one, even by people who are good judges of character. What is all the more unfortunate is that my physiognomy promises much, and that the frustrated expectations that ensue render my stupidity even more startling to others. This account, to which I was led by that particular instance, is quite useful in understanding what follows. It contains the key to many extraordinary things I have been seen to do, which have been attributed to a boorish disposition, which I definitely do not have. I would love society as much as the next person if I were not certain that I was showing myself not only to my own disadvantage, but also as being quite different from who I really am. The decision I made to hide myself away and write was precisely the one that suited me. If I had always been in society no one would ever have known my worth, or even suspected it, which is what happened with Madam Dupin, despite her being a woman of intelligence and my having lived in her house for several years. She has told me so herself many times since.[249] There have been some exceptions, which I will mention later.

The limited scope of my talents having been pronounced by Monsieur d'Aubonne, and the position that would be suitable for me designated, all that remained was for me to fulfill my vocation a second time. The problem was that I had not studied anything and that I did not even have enough Latin to be a priest. Madame de Warens thought she would have me study at the seminary for a while. She spoke to the Superior, a Lazarist by the name of Monsieur Gros, a good little man, half-blind in one eye, thin, graying, and the most intelligent and least pedantic Lazarist I have ever known, which, to be honest, does not say very much.[250]

Monsieur Gros sometimes came to see Maman, who received him warmly, made much of him, bantered with him, and sometimes even had him lace her up, a task he undertook willingly. While he was thus employed she flitted about the room, doing this and that, dragging the grumbling Superior behind her by her laces, he following her, protesting, "But Madame, stay still for a minute!" It was a most picturesque scene.

Monsieur Gros eagerly agreed with Maman's plan. He was happy to accept a very modest fee, and undertook to instruct me. All that was now required was the bishop's consent, which he not only granted, but he offered to pay for my board. He also allowed me to remain in lay dress until it could be ascertained what success was to be expected.

What a change! I had no choice but to submit. I went to the seminary as I would to a torture chamber. What a sad home a seminary is, particularly for one who has just left the house of a lovely woman. I took with me a single book that I had begged Maman to lend me, and which was a great comfort. One would not guess what it was—a book of music. Among the talents she had cultivated, she had not neglected music. She had a good voice, sang quite well, and played the clavichord a little. She had had the kindness to give me a few singing lessons, and she had to begin from the beginning, as I barely knew even the music of our Psalms. But nine or ten lessons, given to me by a woman and often interrupted, were scarcely enough to teach me the scales or for me to learn even a quarter of the musical signs. Nevertheless, I had such a passion for this art that I resolved to practice on my own. The book I had taken with me, the cantatas of Clérambault, was not the easiest. One can conceive how determined and obstinate I was when I say that with no knowledge of either key change or the duration of a note, I managed to decipher and sing correctly the first recitative and aria from the cantata *Alphée et Aréthuse*. It is true that this aria scans so precisely that one has only to recite the verses in their measure to catch the measure of the music.

There was a repulsive Lazarist at the seminary who took charge of me and instilled in me a horror of Latin, which he was attempting to teach me. He had oily black hair, a muddy complexion, the voice of a buffalo, the eye of an owl, and boar's bristles for a beard. His smile was sardonic and derisive, and his limbs jerked like those of a puppet on a string. I have forgotten his odious name, but his cloying, frightening face has remained with me, and I cannot recall it without a shudder. I still see myself coming upon him in a corridor, and him sardonically motioning me with his dirty square hat to enter his room, which was more terrifying than a dungeon. Imagine such a tutor for a pupil who had once studied with an abbé of the royal court!

Had I remained at the mercy of this monster for two months, I am certain I would have lost my mind. But the kindly Monsieur Gros, seeing how miserable I was and that I was not touching my food, and that I was growing thin, guessed the reason for my distress, which was not difficult. He rescued me from the clutches of this beast and, in even more marked contrast, placed me with the gentlest of men: Monsieur Gâtier, a young abbé from Faucigny, who was completing his seminary studies, and who, as a mark of consideration for Monsieur Gros, and I believe out of humaneness, too, was prepared to take enough time from his studies in order to direct mine. I have never seen a more touching physiognomy than that of Monsieur Gâtier. He was blond, his beard reddish, and he had the look typical of the people of his region, who tend to conceal a great deal of intelligence beneath a rough exterior. But what was particularly striking about him was his sensitive, affectionate, and loving soul. There was a mixture of gentleness, warmth, and sadness in his large blue eyes, so that one could not look upon him without being drawn to him. Judging by this poor young man's expression, one could believe that he foresaw his destiny, and that he felt himself born to be unhappy.

His character did not belie his physiognomy. Full of patience and kindness, he seemed to be studying with me rather than instructing me. This was more than enough to make me like him, something his predecessor had made easy. Nevertheless, I made very little progress in spite of all my effort and the time he dedicated to me, the goodwill on both our parts, and his good teaching. What is strange is that although my capacity to understand is pronounced, I have never been able to learn anything from a tutor, except from my father and Monsieur Lambercier. The little that I know beyond what they taught me I have learned on my own, as will become clear. My mind, impatient of every sort of yoke, cannot submit itself to the rule of the moment. Even the fear of not learning keeps me from being attentive; afraid that I might exasperate the person speaking to me, I pretend to understand. He continues speaking and I no longer understand anything. My mind needs to march to its own beat—it cannot submit to anyone else's.

The time for ordination came, and Monsieur Gâtier went back to Faucigny as a deacon. He took with him my regrets, affection, and gratitude. I offered prayers for him that were no more granted than those I made for myself: some years later, I heard that while he was a vicar in a parish he had had a child by a young woman, the only woman his tender heart ever loved. A terrible scandal ensued, as the diocese was particularly strict. The rule is that if priests are to get a woman with child she must be married, and for having transgressed this rule of decency Monsieur Gâtier was thrown in prison, disgraced, and expelled.[251] I do not know whether he subsequently managed to regain his position, but the feeling of his misfortune, deeply engraved on my heart, came back to me when I was writing *Émile*, and combining Monsieur Gâtier with Monsieur Gaime, I turned these two worthy priests into the original of my Savoyard vicar. I flatter myself that my imitation did not dishonor my models.

While I was at the seminary, Monsieur d'Aubonne was obliged to leave Annecy. The commissioner decided that he was not pleased at Monsieur d'Aubonne's attentions to his wife, which was a case of his simply assuming the role of the jealous husband, since, despite Madame Corvezi's pleasant disposition, he had a contentious relationship with her. His *Italian predilections*[252] rendered her of no interest to him, and he treated her so brutally that there was talk of separation. Monsieur Corvezi was a vile man, black as a mole and roguish as an owl, who caused so much trouble that he was finally dismissed himself. They say that men from Provence wreak vengeance on their enemies with song—Monsieur d'Aubonne wrought vengeance on his by means of a comedy. He sent his play to Madame de Warens, who showed it to me. I liked it, and it sparked in me the idea of writing one myself to see whether I was indeed as slow-witted as the playwright had affirmed to Madame de Warens. But it was only later at Chambéry that I carried out this project, writing *The Lover of Himself*.[253] So when I wrote in the preface to that work that I had penned it at eighteen, I was lying by a few years.

It was around that time that an event took place that was of little importance in itself, but that had consequences for me, causing a commotion in the world after I had forgotten about it. Every week I had permission to leave the seminary once. Need I say how I made use of it? One Sunday when I was at Maman's, a building next to her house belonging to the Franciscans caught fire. Their ovens were in this building, and it was packed full of dry firewood. In no time at all the whole place was engulfed in flames, and Maman's house was in great danger, covered by fire being driven by the wind. We set about emptying the house in great haste, carrying the furniture out into the garden that was opposite the windows of my old room, across the brook that I have mentioned before. I was so distressed that I threw everything that came to hand out the window, including an enormous stone mortar, which in other circumstances I would have had difficulty lifting. I would have even thrown a large mirror out the window if someone had not restrained me. The good bishop, who had come to see Maman that day, was not standing idly by. He led Maman out into the garden, where he prayed with all who were there, so that when I came out some time later, I found everyone on their knees, and knelt beside them. While the saintly man prayed, the wind changed, so abruptly and at such a crucial moment that the flames that were covering the house and already darting through the windows were blown to the other side of the courtyard and the house remained unharmed. Two years later, after Bishop de Bernex's death, his former Antonin brethren began gathering instances that might serve toward his beatification. At Father Boudet's request I added an attestation of what I had witnessed, and was right in doing so, but wrong in presenting it as a miracle. I had seen the bishop praying, and during his prayer I had seen the wind change, and change most favorably. That was all I could say and swear to. But I ought not to have attested that one of these two things was the cause of the other, something I could not have known. Nevertheless, to the extent that I can recall my convictions, being at the time a sincere Catholic, I did so in good faith. The love of miracles that is so natural to the human heart, my veneration of that virtuous prelate, and the secret pride of having perhaps myself contributed to the miracle, helped seduce me, and it is certain that if this miracle had been the effect of the most ardent prayers, I could claim to have played my part.

More than thirty years later, when I published my *Letters from the Mountain,* Monsieur Fréron[254] somehow or other managed to unearth that certificate and put it to use in his pamphlets. I must admit that it was an opportune discovery, and its discovery at that particular moment struck even me as most amusing.

I have been destined to be rejected by people of every station. Although Monsieur Gâtier rendered as favorable a report as he could, it was evident that my progress did not correspond to the amount of work I had done and did not argue for a continuation of my studies. The bishop and the Superior were also discouraged, and I was sent back to Madame de Warens as one not even fit to be a priest; otherwise not a bad boy, they said, and good-natured enough, which was why, despite so many prejudicial judgments, she did not abandon me.

I brought back in triumph her book of music, of which I had made such good use. The aria from *Alphée et Aréthuse* was almost the only thing I had learned at the seminary. My marked taste for this art inspired in her the idea of making me a musician. The conditions were favorable: at least once a week she had music at her house, and the choirmaster of the cathedral, who directed her little concerts, often came to see her. He was a Parisian by the name of Monsieur le Maître, a good composer, lively and jovial, still young and quite presentable, not very intelligent, but all in all a very good man. Maman introduced me to him. I was drawn to him and he liked me, too. We discussed the fee and came to an agreement. In short, he took me on as a boarder and I spent the winter there, all the more pleasantly as the choir school was only some twenty paces from Maman's house, so that Monsieur le Maître and I could be there in no time at all, and the three of us often dined together.

One can imagine that I much preferred life in the choir school among the musicians and the choirboys filled with song and good cheer, to life in the seminary among the Fathers of Saint Lazarus. Nevertheless that life, despite being freer, was no less regular or strict. I was born to love independence and never to abuse it. For six whole months I did not go out a single time except to visit Maman or to go to church, and was not even tempted to do otherwise. This period was one of those in which I lived in the greatest tranquility and which I recall with the greatest pleasure. Of all the different situations in which I have found myself, some have been marked by such a feeling of well-being that in remembering them I am touched as if I were still there. Not only do I remember the times, places, and people, but also all the surrounding objects, the temperature of the air, its smell and color, and a certain impression of the locality that cannot be felt anywhere else but at that place, and the vivid memory of which carries me there again: everything practiced in the choir school, everything sung in the choir, the rituals, the canons' fine and noble garments, the priests' chasubles, the chanters' miters, the musician's faces, an old lame carpenter who played the contrabass, a little blond abbé who played the violin, the tattered cassock that Monsieur le Maître donned over his lay clothes after removing his sword, and the beautiful, fine surplice with which he covered the cassock before stepping up to the choir. I remember the pride with which, flute in hand, I took my place in the orchestra up in the tribune to play a little solo that Monsieur le Maître had composed especially for me, as well as the fine dinner that awaited us afterward, and our hearty appetites. Vividly retracing this confluence of things has delighted me countless times, in memory as much as and even more than it had in reality. I have always had a tender affection for a certain air from the *Conditor Alme Siderum*[255] that has an iambic rhythm, because one Advent Sunday before daybreak, as I lay in bed, I heard this hymn being sung on the cathedral steps, according to a custom of that church. Mademoiselle Merceret, Maman's chambermaid, knew a little music, and I will never forget a humble motet called *Afferte* that Monsieur le Maître had me sing with her, and which her mistress listened to with such pleasure. In short, everything, including good Perrine, the dear servant girl whom the choirboys drove to distraction, everything in my memories of those times of happiness and innocence often returns to enchant and sadden me.

I had been living in Annecy for almost a year without incurring the least reproach. Everyone was pleased with me. Since leaving Turin I had done nothing foolish, nor did I do anything as long as I was under Maman's eyes. She guided me, and always guided me well. My attachment to her had become my only passion, which proves that it was no mad passion, as my heart governed my reason. It is true that this single feeling, absorbing, one could say, all my faculties, put me in a state in which I was unable to learn anything, even music, despite my efforts. This was not my fault: I was most willing and assiduous. But I was abstracted, a dreamer, given to sighs. What could I do about it? My progress was not being hampered by anything that depended on me. However, all I needed to commit some new folly was something new to appear and inspire me. It arrived. Chance arranged matters, and, as will be seen, my foolish mind seized the opportunity.

One cold evening in the month of February we were all sitting around the fire when there was a knock at the street door.

Perrine took her lantern, went downstairs, opened the door, and brought up a young man who introduced himself with an easy air, making a short and elegant compliment to Monsieur le Maître, presenting himself as a French musician whose straitened circumstances obliged him to travel from village to village offering to play at church services. At the words "French musician" Monsieur le Maître's heart leaped with joy, for he loved his country and his art with a passion. He welcomed the young wanderer and offered him the night's lodging he seemed in great need of, which the young man promptly accepted. I observed the newcomer as he warmed himself and conversed while waiting for dinner to be served. He was of short stature but had broad shoulders; there was something misshapen about him, though he did not have any particular deformity, as if he were somehow a hunchback but with straight shoulders, though I believe he did limp a little. He had on a black jacket that was more worn than old and was coming apart, a shirt with elegant ruffled cuffs that was very fine but very dirty, gaiters into either of which he could have slipped both his legs, and, to protect himself from the snow, a little hat that was good only for holding under his arm. In this comical outfit there was, however, something noble that his comportment did not belie. His physiognomy had a refinement and amiability. He spoke easily and well, but with little modesty. Everything pointed to his being a young rake of good education, who went begging for alms not as a beggar but out of some eccentricity. He told us he was called Venture de Villeneuve, that he had come from Paris and had lost his way, and, somewhat forgetting the role of musician he had assumed, added that he was on his way to Grenoble to see a relative who was in the *parlement* there.

During dinner, the discussion turned to music, and he spoke quite knowledgeably. He knew all the great virtuosos, all the famous works, all the actors and actresses, all the beautiful women, and all the great noblemen. He seemed familiar with everything touched upon, but no sooner had a subject been broached than he threw into the conversation an improper jest that made everyone laugh and forget what we were talking about. It was a Saturday. There was to be music in the cathedral the following day, and Monsieur le Maître proposed that he sing there. "I would be delighted," he replied. He was asked what his voice was. He said high tenor, and changed the subject. Before we all went to the church the following day he was given his part to look over, but did not so much as glance at it. Monsieur le Maître was quite taken aback at this. "You'll see," he whispered into my ear. "I wager he does not know a note of music." "I am afraid you are right," I replied. I followed them anxiously, and my heart was pounding when the music began, for I had already taken a great liking to him.

I was soon very much reassured. He sang his two solos with the utmost precision and taste imaginable, and what is more, in a most beautiful voice. I had never been more pleasantly surprised. After the Mass, Monsieur Venture received endless compliments from the canons and musicians, to whom he replied roguishly but with great elegance. Monsieur le Maître embraced him heartily, as did I. Monsieur Venture could see how glad I was, and seemed pleased.

One would agree, I am sure, that having been infatuated with Monsieur Bâcle, who after all was just an oafish ne'er-do-well, I could easily become infatuated with Monsieur Venture, who was educated, had talent, wit and experience in society, and who might be called a pleasant rake. And that is in fact what happened, something that would have happened to any other young man in my place, the more easily if he had enough discernment to understand merit, and taste to be drawn to it.

Monsieur Venture, without doubt, possessed merit, and the particular merit most rare for his age of not hastening to display his accomplishments. It is true that he boasted of many things he knew nothing about, but of the things he knew, which were numerous, he kept silent, waiting for the occasion to show them; he then seized the occasion without eagerness, which had the greatest effect. Since he changed the subject often without discussing anything at length, one never knew how much of his knowledge he was revealing. Witty, playful, irrepressible, seductive in conversation, always smiling but never laughing, he would say the most vulgar things in the most elegant tone, and get away with it. Women, even the most modest, were amazed at what they were prepared to endure from him. Try as they might to be angry at him, they simply could not be. He was interested only in fallen women, and I believe that he was not successful in love, though he gave infinite pleasure to the society of people who were. It was unlikely that with so many agreeable talents, in a country where these are understood and appreciated, he would be long confined to the status of musician.

If my liking for Monsieur Venture was more reasonable in its cause, it was also less extreme in its effects, despite its being more lively and durable than my liking for Monsieur Bâcle had been. I delighted in seeing Monsieur Venture and listening to him. Everything he did struck me as charming, everything he said appeared to me oracular, but my infatuation did not go so far that I could not bear being separated from him. I had, after all, a good safeguard nearby against such excess. Furthermore, I found that his principles were good for him, but felt that they were of no use to me. I sought another kind of pleasure, of which he had no idea and about which I did not even dare talk to him, certain that he would make fun of me. Nevertheless, I would have liked to link my attachment to him with the one that ruled me. I spoke to Maman about him enthusiastically, and Monsieur le Maître, too, spoke highly in praise of him. She agreed to meet him, but the interview did not go at all well. He thought her affected and she thought him a libertine, and, alarmed at my cultivating such a bad acquaintance, she not only forbade me to bring him to her house again, but painted so vividly the dangers I was courting with this young man that I became somewhat more circumspect in acceding to his influence, and, luckily for my morals and my reason, he and I were soon separated.

Monsieur le Maître, like so many of his profession, was fond of wine. Though he remained sober at table, he insisted on drinking when he worked in his office. His maid knew this well, and the instant he reached for a sheet of paper to begin composing or took up his violoncello, a jug of wine and a glass would appear, and the jug was replenished from time to time. Without ever being completely drunk, the wine always affected him, which was a pity, as he was essentially a good fellow, and so jovial that Maman was always calling him "my little kitten." Unfortunately, he loved his art, worked a lot, and drank a lot. This affected his health, and ultimately his disposition; at times he was sullen and quick to take offense. He was incapable of coarseness or showing disrespect to anyone, never uttering a rude word, not even to a choirboy. But he also insisted on being shown respect, which was only right. The trouble was that, not being particularly intelligent, he could not distinguish other people's nuances in tone and behavior, and he often flew into a rage for no reason.

The former Chapter of Geneva, which so many princes and bishops had considered an honor to join, had in exile lost its past splendor but retained its pride. To be admitted, one still had to be a gentleman or a Doctor of the Sorbonne, and if there is pride that can be pardoned, it is, after personal merit, pride of birth. Moreover, all the priests who have laymen in their employ tend to treat them with considerable hauteur, which was how the canons often treated poor Monsieur le Maître. Particularly the choirmaster, the Abbé de Vidonne, otherwise a gallant man, though too proud of his high birth, did not always show Monsieur le Maître the respect that his talents deserved, nor did the latter take kindly to his disdain. During Holy Week of that year, they had a more intense dispute than usual at the dinner the bishop customarily gave for the canons, and to which le Maître was always invited. The Abbé de Vidonne slighted him in some way and spoke harshly to him, which he could not accept. He decided then and there to leave the following night. Nothing could deter him, even though Madame de Warens, to whom he went to say farewell, spared no effort to appease him. Monsieur le Maître could not resist the pleasure of avenging himself on his oppressors, deserting them during the Easter ceremonies when he was most needed. But there was the problem of taking his music with him, which was no easy matter, as it filled a chest that was too large and heavy to be carried under his arm.

Maman did what I would have done in her place, and would still do. After all her fruitless efforts to keep him, seeing that he was resolved to leave come what may, she decided to help him in every way she could. I dare say it was her duty to do so, for le Maître had devoted himself to her service. He had put his art and, indeed, his person entirely at her disposal, and his devotion had made his desire to oblige her all the more valuable. Accordingly, she was only repaying a friend at a critical moment for what he had done for her in so many little ways during three or four years. But she was the kind of person who had no need to consider what she owed someone in order to help. She sent for me and told me to accompany Monsieur le Maître at least as far as Lyon, and to stay with him for as long as he might need me. She subsequently admitted to me that her wish to separate me from Venture had played a significant part in this arrangement. She consulted Claude Anet, her faithful servant, about how the chest should be transported. He thought that instead of taking a donkey at Annecy, which would inevitably lead to our being discovered, we would have to carry the chest for some distance after dark and then hire a donkey in one of the villages, so that the chest could be conveyed as far as Seyssel, where we would be on French soil and no longer in danger. We followed his advice, departing that same evening at seven, and Maman, on the pretext of covering my expenses, fattened the *poor little kitten*'s purse, which he greatly needed. Claude Anet, the gardener, and I carried the chest as best we could to the nearest village, where a donkey assumed our burden, and we managed to reach Seyssel that same night.

I believe I have already remarked that there are times when I am so little like myself that one might mistake me for another man with an entirely opposite character. What follows is an example. Monsieur Reydelet, the curate of Seyssel, was the canon of Saint-Pierre, and consequently acquainted with Monsieur le Maître, and was one of the men from whom le Maître had most reason to hide himself. My advice, on the contrary, was to present ourselves to him and request lodgings under some pretext, as if we were there with the consent of the Chapter. Le Maître liked the idea, which added a touch of comedy and ridicule to his vengeance. So we brazenly called on Monsieur Reydelet, who received us very well. Le Maître told him that he was on his way to Belley at the request of the bishop to direct the music for the Easter ceremonies, and that he was thinking of passing this way again a few days later. In support of this lie, I threw in dozens more with such ease that Reydelet, finding me a most charming boy, took a liking to me and was exceedingly forthcoming. We were well entertained and well lodged. Monsieur Reydelet heaped us with kindness, and we parted the best of friends, promising to stay longer on our way back. We could hardly wait to be alone to burst out laughing, and I admit I still laugh when I think of it, for one cannot imagine a prank better planned and executed. It would have kept us in the best of spirits for the rest of our journey if Monsieur le Maître, who would not stop drinking and raging, had not been seized two or three times by a fit of the kind to which he was becoming quite prone, and which very much resembled epilepsy. This alarmed and frightened me, and I soon resolved to escape any way I could.

We went to Belley to spend Easter there, as we had told Monsieur Reydelet we would, and were welcomed by the choirmaster and everyone with great pleasure, though we had not been expected. Monsieur le Maître was much respected as a musician, and deservedly so. Belley's choirmaster regarded it as an honor to play his own best works, hoping to obtain the approbation of such a good judge, for le Maître was not only a great connoisseur, but equitable, not in the least jealous, and no flatterer. He was so superior to all the provincial choirmasters, of which they were all aware, that they saw him less as a colleague than as a master.

After spending four or five agreeable days at Belley, we set out again and continued on our way without any mishaps, except of the kind I have already mentioned. Arriving in Lyon, we were put up at Notre-Dame de Pitié. While we waited for the chest to arrive—which, by way of another lie, we were having sent down the Rhône with the help of our good host, Monsieur Reydelet—Monsieur le Maître called on some of his acquaintances, among them Father Caton, a Franciscan of whom I shall speak later, and Abbé Dortan, the Count de Lyon. Both received him well, but were to betray him, as will soon be seen. His luck ended with Monsieur Reydelet.

Two days after our arrival in Lyon, as we were walking through a small street not far from our lodgings, le Maître had one of his seizures. It was so violent that I was gripped by panic. I called out, shouted for help, told the people where he lodged, and begged them to carry him there. Then, as they rushed to the fallen man who lay senseless and foaming at the mouth in the middle of the street, he was abandoned by the one friend on whom he ought to have been able to rely. I seized a moment when I was unobserved, slipped around the corner of the street, and disappeared. I thank God that I have completed this third painful admission. If there were many more of this kind, I would abandon the work I have begun.

Of everything that I have related up to this point, some traces have remained in the places in which I have lived, but what I will tell in the following book is almost entirely unknown. I will speak of the greatest follies of my life, and it is fortunate that they did not turn out worse than they did. My mind, tuned to a foreign instrument, was beyond its scale, though it did return of its own accord and I ceased my follies, or at least thereafter committed follies that were more in keeping with my nature. This period of my youth is the one of which I have the most confused recollection. Almost nothing of sufficient interest moved my heart to enable me to recover a clear memory of this time. It would be difficult, with so much coming and going, so many moves from place to place, not to transpose some dates and locations. I write entirely from memory, without high points or materials that could help me remember. There are events in my life that are as present as if they had just taken place; but there are also gaps and empty spaces that I can fill only with the aid of anecdotes that are as confused as the memories that have remained of them. I might, therefore, at times have made mistakes, and might well make more when it comes to certain trifles, until I again reach the period of which I have clearer information about myself. But in matters truly important to my subject, I am sure that I am precise and faithful, as I always endeavor to be in everything. That is something one can rely on.

No sooner had I left Monsieur le Maître than I made up my mind to return to Annecy. The reason for our departure and the secrecy surrounding it had made me preoccupied with our safety, a preoccupation that consumed me and had kept me for several days from the thought of going back to Annecy. But as soon as this fear for my safety lessened, my abiding feeling took its place; nothing flattered or tempted me, I now had no desire but to return to Maman. The tenderness and depth of my feelings for her banished from my heart all the fantastical schemes and all the follies of ambition. I could see no other happiness than living at her side, and I never took a step without feeling that I was leaving this happiness further behind. So I returned as soon as I could. My return was so swift, and my mind so distraught, that though I remember all my other journeys with such pleasure, I do not have the slightest recollection of this one. I remember nothing about it except leaving Lyon and arriving at Annecy. Let the reader judge if this last period ought to have been expunged from my memory! When I returned, Madame de Warens was no longer there. She had left for Paris.

I never really learned the secret behind this journey. I am certain she would have revealed it to me had I pressed her, but no man has ever been less curious than I about the secrets of his friends. My heart is occupied only with the present, which fills it entirely and exclusively, and besides past pleasures, which from now on will be my only joy, there does not remain even an empty corner in it for what no longer exists. From everything she told me, the only inkling I have is that the revolution at Turin, following the abdication of the King of Sardinia, led her to fear that she might be neglected, and that through the schemes of Monsieur d'Aubonne she sought to secure similar support from the French court. As she often told me, she would have preferred this, because the multitude of great affairs at the French court would have meant that she would have been subjected to less scrutiny. If that is true, it is quite astonishing that she was not given a cooler welcome on her return to Annecy, and that she continued receiving her pension without interruption. Many have believed that she had been entrusted with some secret commission, either by the bishop, who at the time had dealings with the French court and was himself obliged to go there, or by someone even more powerful who was able to ensure that she would be welcomed on her return. If this was the case, then she definitely would have been a fortunate choice as ambassadress; still young and beautiful, she had all the necessary talents to conduct such a negotiation with success.[256]

REVERIES OF THE
SOLITARY WALKER

During the final two years of his life, when Rousseau was taking long botanizing walks in the countryside outside Paris, he would jot down notes for the group of essays that became known as the Reveries of the Solitary Walker. *By the time of his death in 1778 there were ten of them, the final one unfinished. No longer concerned to recount his life story chronologically, as he had done in the* Confessions, *Rousseau enjoyed letting his mind move freely over a variety of topics. We give here the first and fifth essays in the series. The first reflects his fixed conviction, ever since his exile in England a decade earlier, that a vast hidden plot had been mounted against him; by avoiding contact with strangers he chose to be "solitary" in a way that felt positive and empowering. The fifth essay recalls a brief but idyllic period when he and his common-law wife, Thérèse, lived on a small island in a lake near Neuchâtel.*

FIRST PROMENADE

So I am now alone on this earth, no longer having any brother, companion, friend, or society other than my own. The most sociable and loving of human beings has been cast out by unanimous agreement. In the subtle intricacy of their hatred they sought out the torment that would be most cruel to my sensitive soul, violently severing all the ties binding me to them. I would have loved mankind despite its ways; it is only by ceasing to be humane that men have alienated my affection. Now they are strangers, unknown and nothing to me, since that is what they wanted. But I, separated from them and from everything, what am I? This is what remains for me to discover. Unfortunately, this must be preceded by examining my position. It is an idea by way of which I must necessarily pass to get from them to me.

Despite the more than fifteen years that I have been in this strange position,[257] it still seems to me like a dream. I still imagine that indigestion torments me and that I am sleeping restlessly but will wake up completely relieved of my distress, finding myself once again among my friends. Doubtless I have plunged, without realizing it, from wakefulness to sleep, or, rather, from life to death. Dragged I know not how out of an order of things, I have seen myself hurled into an incomprehensible chaos in which I cannot distinguish a single thing; and the more I consider my present situation, the less I can understand where I am.

But how was I to foresee the destiny that awaited me? How could I, even today, conceive my having been delivered to it? Could I ever have supposed, with all my good sense, that one day I, the same man I was and still am, would without question be seen and thought of as a monster, a prisoner, and a murderer, that I would become the horror of the human race and an object of ridicule for the rabble? Could I have imagined that the only greetings I could expect from passersby would be to be spat upon, that an entire generation would take unanimous pleasure in burying me alive? When this strange revolution occurred it took me by surprise, and at first I was shattered. My despair and outrage plunged me into a delirium that took more than ten years to subside, and during that period, stumbling from error to error, from mistake to mistake, from one foolishness to another, my imprudence provided the masters of my destiny with all the many instruments that they put to good use in order to seal my fate.

For a long time I struggled violently and in vain. Without skill or craft, dissimulation or prudence—sincere, open, impatient, angry—the more I struggled the more I managed only to entangle myself further, giving my enemies new weapons of which they were quick to make use. Feeling that all my efforts were in vain, tormenting myself to no avail, I chose the only course of action that remained to me: submitting to my destiny without rebelling against it any longer. I have found in this resignation a recompense for all my misfortunes in the tranquility it affords me, a tranquility that could not coexist with the incessant struggle of a resistance as painful as it was futile.

Something else contributed to this tranquility. Among all the subtle intricacies of my persecutors' hatred, they omitted one that their animosity made them forget, namely, to gradually increase the effects so cleverly that they could ceaselessly sustain and replenish my pain by continually confronting me with some new attack. Had they been crafty enough to leave me a glimmer of hope, they would have had a hold on me; they could have made me their plaything through some false illusion, and then assail me with ever new torments of shattered hope. But they immediately exhausted all their resources; in leaving me nothing, they deprived themselves of all their means. Defamation, debasement, derision, and the opprobrium they heaped on me are no more susceptible to increase than they are to abatement. My persecutors are as incapable of heightening my torments as I am of escaping them. They were in such a hurry to take the measure of my wretchedness to its extreme that all human power, backed by all the cunning of Hell, could not have added anything more to it. Physical pain itself, instead of increasing my anguish, offered a diversion from it.[258] By making me cry out in agony it perhaps spared me from lamenting my fate, and the rending of my body perhaps stopped the rending of my heart.

What more have I to fear from them since everything is done? Unable to worsen my condition, they can no longer inspire terrors in me. Worry and fright are torments from which they have delivered me forever—that is in any case a relief. True torments have little hold on me; I readily accept those I suffer, but not those I fear. My agitated imagination throws them together, turns them over and over, draws them out and amplifies them. Anticipating these torments distresses me a hundred times more than their presence, the threat terrifying me more than the blow. Their arrival robs them of all that was imaginary and reduces them to their actual value. Then I find them much inferior to what I had imagined, and, even immersed in my suffering as I am, I do not fail to feel relieved. In that state, freed from all new fears and released from all the agitation of hope, habit alone can with the passing of time make a situation more bearable that nothing now can worsen. And the more that passing time deadens this feeling, the more my persecutors have no means left to revive it. This is the good that they have done me, depleting as they have in all their abandon every aspect of their animosity. They have deprived themselves of all control over me, and henceforth I can laugh in their faces.

It is not quite two months since utter calm reestablished itself. For a long time I had no longer feared anything, but I still had hope, and that hope, one moment lulled, the next thwarted, was a way by which a thousand diverse passions unceasingly agitated me. An incident that was as sad as it was unforeseen finally erased this weak ray of hope from my heart, making me see that my destiny in this world was unalterably sealed.[259] Since then, I have entirely resigned myself to my fate and have once again found peace.

No sooner had I begun to glimpse the plot in all its breadth than I forever lost the hope of winning back the public during my lifetime; and as this winning back could now never be reciprocal, it would henceforth be of no use to me. In vain would they all return to me—they would no longer find me. With the disdain they have inspired in me, any association with them would be trite and even arduous for me, and I am a hundred times happier in my solitude than I could be living in their midst. They have torn from my heart any pleasure in society, and at my age, that pleasure can no longer sprout anew. It is too late. Whether they do me good or evil, anything regarding them is a matter of indifference to me—whatever my contemporaries may do, they will be as nothing to me.

And yet I still counted on the future, hoping that a better generation, looking more closely both at how the current generation judged me and at how it treated me, will easily unravel the trickery of those behind it and will finally see me as I am. This is the hope that made me write my *Dialogues* and led to my many foolish attempts to see them passed on to posterity.[260] This hope, though remote, kept my spirit in as much turmoil as when I was still seeking a just heart in this world, and this hope, which I might as well have cast to the winds, made me an object of ridicule for the men of today. I said in my *Dialogues* what it was on which I based my hopes. I was mistaken. Luckily I sensed this early enough to find an interlude of utter calm and absolute rest before my final hour. This interlude began during the period of which I am speaking, and I have reason to believe that it will not be interrupted again.

Few days pass without my having new reflections that confirm how wrong I was to count on winning back my public, even in a new era, since in all that concerns me the public is influenced by leaders who keep springing up anew in the groups that despise me. Individuals die, but collective bodies do not. The same passions are perpetuated in them, and their ardent hatred, immortal as the demon that inspires it, never flags. When all my personal enemies are dead, doctors and Oratorians will live on,[261] and even if these two groups were my only persecutors, I can be certain that they will not leave my memory in greater peace after my death than they have left my person during my life. Perhaps with the passing of time the doctors whom I have truly offended might be appeased, but the Oratorians, whom I loved, whom I esteemed, whom I trusted in every way, whom I never offended, those Oratorians, men of the Church and half monks, will never be appeased. My crime is nothing more than their own iniquity, for which their pride will never forgive me, and the public, whose hatred for me the Oratorians will take care to fan and nourish, will be no more appeased than they.

Everything has come to an end for me on earth. Men can no longer do me good or evil. I have nothing left to hope for or fear in this world, and now I am here, in all tranquility at the bottom of the abyss, a poor unfortunate mortal, but impassive like God Himself.

Everything external will henceforth be alien to me. I no longer have in this world companions, fellow men, or brothers. I am on earth as on an alien planet onto which I have fallen from the one where I once lived. If I recognize anything around me, it is only objects that distress and tear my heart, and I cannot cast my eyes on what touches me and surrounds me without finding an instance of the disdain that offends me or the pain that afflicts me. So let us remove from my mind all the distressing things with which I would preoccupy myself both painfully and pointlessly. Alone for the rest of my life, since only in myself can I find consolation, hope, and peace, I must not and do not want to concern myself with anything but myself. It is in this state that I take up the sequel of the sincere and unforgiving scrutiny that I called my *Confessions.* I am devoting my final days to studying myself and preparing in advance the account that soon enough I will have to give of myself. Let us deliver ourselves entirely to the sweetness of conversing with my soul, since it is the only thing that men cannot take away from me. If by reflecting on my inner disposition I succeed in putting it in better order and setting right the harm that might still reside in it, my meditations will not be entirely for naught, and though I might no longer be of any use on this earth, I will not have entirely wasted my final days. The leisure of my daily walks has often been filled with delightful contemplation that I regret having forgotten. I will put down in writing those thoughts that might still come to me, and each time I reread them, their pleasure will return to me. I will forget my misfortunes, my persecutors, and all the opprobrium as I dream of the prize my heart deserved.

These pages will in fact be no more than a sketchy diary of my reveries. They will principally center on myself, because a recluse given to contemplation will necessarily concentrate on himself. Furthermore, all the strange ideas that come to me while I stroll will also find their place in these pages. I will express what I have thought just as it came to me and with as little connection as ideas of the previous day have with those of the day following. But this will result in a new understanding of my nature and disposition through an understanding of my feelings and thoughts that are the daily fodder of my mind in the strange state I am in. These pages can thus be regarded as an appendix to my *Confessions*, but I will not call them that, as I feel I no longer have anything to say that would merit such a title. My heart has been purified under the aegis of adversity, and even with most careful probing I find hardly any vestige of reprehensible inclinations. What will I still have to confess when all earthly affections have been torn from this heart? I have as little reason to praise myself as I do to blame myself—I am henceforth nothing among men, and that is all I can be, as I no longer have true relations or actual society with them. Since I am no longer able to do any good that does not turn bad, no longer able to act without harming another or myself, abstaining has become my only duty, and I fulfill this duty to the extent that I am able to. Yet within this inactivity of body my spirit is still active, still producing feelings and thoughts, and its inner and moral life seems to have grown even more with the passing of all worldly and temporal interests. My body is no longer anything but a burden to me, a hindrance, and I am already extricating myself from it to the extent that I can.

A situation so unique surely merits being examined and described, and it is to this examination that I dedicate my final leisure. To do this successfully, one ought to approach it with order and method; but I am incapable of such labor, which would draw me away from my goal of weighing changes in the state of my soul and how they occur. I will, in a sense, carry out on myself the measurements that natural scientists perform on the air to ascertain its daily state. I will apply a barometer to my soul, and the measurements, effectively implemented and repeated over a long period, may provide me with results that are as sound as theirs. But I will not extend my project that far. I will be content to write down the measurements without seeking to arrange them into a system. I am undertaking the same project as Montaigne, but with a goal that is the complete opposite of his, for he wrote his *Essays* for others, whereas I am writing my reveries for myself alone.[262] If at an advanced age, with my final hour near, I still have the same disposition, as I hope I will, then reading these reveries will remind me of my delight in writing them, and thus in a sense by reviving the past once more doubling my existence. In spite of mankind, I will still be able to delight in society and, decrepit as I shall be, live with myself in another age as if I were living with a friend who is less old.

I wrote my first *Confessions* and my *Dialogues* in a constant state of anxiety to keep them out of the rapacious hands of my persecutors, in the hope of passing them on, if I could, to future generations. With this work the same anxieties no longer plague me, as I know that such worries would be pointless, and as the desire to be better known by my fellow men has been extinguished in my heart, leaving only a profound indifference for the fate of both my truest writings and of the monuments to my innocence, all of which have, perhaps, already been destroyed forever. Let my persecutors try to penetrate what I am doing, let them be worried about these pages, seize them, suppress them, falsify them; henceforth I no longer care. I will not hide these pages, nor will I show them. If they do seize them from me during my lifetime, they will rob me of neither the pleasure I had in writing them, nor of the memory of what they contain, nor of the solitary meditations of which they are the fruit. Their source can only expire with my soul. Had I known from the time of my first calamities not to rebel against my destiny and to follow the course that I am following today, all the efforts of my persecutors, all their terrible machinations, would have had no effect on me, and they would no more have troubled my peace of mind with all their plots than they can henceforth trouble it with any successful schemes against me. They may delight in my disgrace all they will, but they shall not prevent me from enjoying my innocence and ending my days in peace in spite of them.

FIFTH PROMENADE

Of all the places where I have lived (and there have been some charming ones), none has made me so truly happy or left me such tender regrets as the Isle of St. Pierre in the middle of Lake Bienne.[263] Few people, even in Switzerland, know this little island, which in Neuchâtel they call Isle de la Motte. No traveler, as far as I know, has ever mentioned it. And yet it is a most pleasant island, situated like no other for the happiness of a man seeking to withdraw from the world; for though I might be the only man on this earth whose destiny has made this a law, I cannot imagine that I might be the only one who has such a natural inclination, although I have never found the like in any other.

The shores of Lake Bienne are wilder and more romantic than those of Lake Geneva, as its rocks and woodlands lie closer to the water; but they are no less inviting. If there are fewer fields and vineyards, towns and houses, there is more green, more pastures and secluded shady groves, more contrast and surprise in the landscape. As there are no roads wide enough for carriages on these happy shores, the area is less frequented by travelers; but it attracts solitary thinkers who are drawn by the charms of nature, and who gather their thoughts at leisure in a silence where the only noises are the calls of eagles, the intermittent warbling of birds, and the rushing of waters tumbling from the mountains. This beautiful lake, almost circular in shape, encloses in its center two small islands: one, inhabited and cultivated, about half a league around; the other, smaller, uninhabited and wild, is an island destined for destruction, as its soil is constantly being hauled away to repair the damage that waves and storms inflict on the larger one. Thus the substance of the weak is always used for the benefit of the strong.

On the larger island there is only one house, but it is spacious, pleasant, and comfortable, and, like the island, belongs to the Hospital of Berne. A tax collector lives there with his family and servants. He has a large farmyard, a dovecote, and fishponds. Small as the island is, it has such a variety of aspect that it offers every kind of terrain, every kind of cultivation. There are fields, vineyards, woods and groves, and lush meadows shaded by copses and bounded by many kinds of shrubs whose freshness is sustained by the nearby waters. There is a high terrace planted with two rows of trees that runs the length of the island. In the middle of this terrace a pretty pavilion has been built, where people of the neighboring shores gather to dance on Sundays during the feast of the grape harvest.

It was on this island that I sought refuge after the rocks thrown at my house in Môtiers.[264] My stay there was so charming, my life so suitable to my disposition, that I was determined to remain there to the end of my days. My only worry was that I might not be allowed to execute this project, which did not fit with that of dragging me to England,[265] of which I was already feeling the first effects. Such forebodings unsettling me, I would have wanted this refuge to be made my eternal prison, to be confined in it for life without any hope of leaving, to be refused any communication with the world outside so that, unaware of everything that was taking place there, I would forget its existence and it, too, would forget mine.

I was allowed to remain barely two months on this island,[266] but I would have stayed two years, two centuries, and all eternity without a moment's tedium, even without having other company beside the tax collector, his wife, and his servants, all of whom were good and simple folk; but that was precisely what I needed. I consider those two months as the happiest of my life—so happy that it would have lasted all my days without allowing for a single moment the desire for another state to arise in my soul.

What was this happiness, and what was the nature of my delight? By describing the life I led on this island, I will let everyone of worldly society surmise. The first and most important of these delights was the precious *dolce far niente*[267] that I sought to savor in all its sweetness, and during my stay I did nothing other than fulfill the delightful and necessary duties of a man who has devoted himself to idleness.

The hope that I would be asked for nothing more than to be allowed this isolated sojourn to which I had bound myself of my own accord, and from which it would be impossible for me to leave without help and without being noticed, and where I could have no communication or correspondence with the outside world except with the aid of the people around me—this hope, I say, sparked in me the aspiration of ending my days in greater tranquility than I had passed them until then. The idea that I had the time to settle in on the island at leisure led to my not settling in at all. Transported there suddenly alone and just as I was, I subsequently had my housekeeper, my books, and my few belongings brought over, but I had the pleasure of not unpacking anything, leaving my boxes and trunks untouched the way they had arrived, and living in the abode in which I counted on finishing my days as at an inn in which I would stay for only one night. Everything was going so well that seeking to arrange things better would have been to ruin something. One of my greatest delights was to leave my books nicely packed and to have no writing desk. When unfortunate letters forced me to pick up my pen in order to reply, I borrowed the tax collector's writing desk, muttering, and hastened to return it in the vain hope of never needing to borrow it again. Instead of filling my room with dreary papers and heaps of books, I filled it with flowers and grasses, as I was in my first botanical fervor, for which Doctor d'Ivernois[268] had inspired a taste that was soon to become a passion. Seeking to escape all onerous tasks, I needed an amusing activity that appealed to me and that was only as taxing as an idle man could bear. I undertook to compose the *Flora petrinsularis*[269] and to describe all the plants of the island without omitting a single one, and in so much detail that it could occupy the rest of my days. It is said that a German wrote a book about a lemon peel—I intended to write one about each weed of the meadows, each moss of the woods, each lichen that blankets the rocks, in short I did not want to leave a single blade of grass or part of a plant not amply described. As a result of this fine project, every morning after breakfast, which we all ate together, I set out with a magnifying glass in hand and my *Systema Naturae*[270] under my arm to visit an area of the island, which I had divided for this purpose into small squares that I intended to comb through one after the other during each season. Nothing is more unique than the rapture and transport I felt at every observation I made of the structure and organization of the plants and of the part that sexual roles played in fructification, the system of which was entirely new to me at the time. I had not had the slightest idea about the distinction of generic characteristics, and was delighted in verifying them in common species while looking forward to coming upon rarer ones. The forking of the two long stamens of the prunella, the spiraling stamens of the nettle and the lichwort, the exploding pods of the touch-me-nots and boxwood shrubs: a thousand little strategies of fructification that I observed for the first time filled me with joy, and I went about asking if people had seen any prunella shoots much the way La Fontaine would ask if people had read Habakkuk.[271] I would return after two or three hours bearing an ample harvest that would provide enough amusement in my lodgings for rainy afternoons. I would spend the rest of the morning with the tax collector, his wife, and Thérèse, visiting their farmhands at the harvest, and quite often giving them a helping hand. Visitors from Bern who came to see me might find me perched in a tall tree with a sack tied to my waist, which I would fill with fruit and then lower to the ground with a rope. The exercise I had taken in the morning and the good humor that comes with it made the respite at lunch very agreeable; but when lunch took too long and good weather summoned me, I could not wait, and while the others were still at table I slipped away and hurried to a boat, which, when the waters were calm, I would row to the middle of the lake. There, stretching out fully in the boat, my eyes raised to the sky, I let myself slowly drift at the water's will, sometimes for several hours, immersed in a thousand confused and exquisite reveries, which, without having any fixed or constant object, were still a hundred times more preferable than all I had found most sweet and that one calls the pleasures of life. Often alerted by the setting of the sun that the hour of return was approaching, I found myself so far from the island that I was forced to row with all my might to return before nightfall. At other times, instead of setting out into open water, I took pleasure in skirting the verdant shores of the island, the clear waters and cool shade often enticing me to bathe. But one of my most frequent outings was to row from the large island to the small one, to disembark there and spend the afternoon, sometimes going on short hikes through the willows, the alder buckthorns, smartweeds, and shrubs of every kind, sometimes settling down on a sandy hillock covered in grass, thyme, and flowers; even sainfoin and clover that had probably been sown there in the past and were ideal for raising rabbits, which could multiply in peace without having anything to fear and without causing damage. I suggested this to the tax collector; he brought some male and female rabbits from Neuchâtel, and we proceeded in great pomp to the island, his wife, one of his sisters, Thérèse, and I, to establish the rabbits there. They began to populate the island before I left, and they will no doubt have prospered if they managed to survive the rigor of the winters. The founding of this small colony was a celebration. The pilot of the Argonauts could not have been more proud than I,[272] leading the company and the rabbits in triumph from the big island to the small one, and I note with pride that the tax collector's wife, who was exceedingly frightened of water and always felt ill in a boat, set out under my leadership with confidence and showed no fear during our crossing.

When the lake was too rough for boating I spent the afternoons walking around the island, picking wild herbs here and there, at times stopping in the most cheerful and solitary spots to dream at my leisure, at times on the terraces and knolls to run my eye over the ravishing view of the lake and its shores.

The lake was crowned on one side by the nearby mountains and spread out on the other in rich and fertile plains, where the view opened out to the more distant bluish mountains that framed it.

With the approach of evening I would descend from the heights of the island, and liked to sit on the shore by the lake in some hidden refuge. There the sound of waves and the restless waters captured my senses and chased all restlessness from my soul, plunging it into a delightful reverie, nightfall often catching me unawares. The ebb and flow of these waters, their sound continuous but rising suddenly and striking my ears and eyes without respite, supplanted the internal movements of fading reverie, enough to make me feel my existence with pleasure without having to take the trouble of thinking. From time to time a short and dim reflection would emerge about the instability of things in this world, of which the surface of the waters offered an image. But these light impressions were quickly erased in the evenness of the unabating motion that cradled me, and which, without the active help of my soul, held me fast to such an extent that I could not tear myself away without effort when called by the late hour and the agreed-upon signal.

On fine evenings after dinner we would all go for a stroll on the terraces to breathe in the fresh air of the lake. We would sit in the pavilion, laugh, talk, sing old songs that were at least as good as what passes for music these days, and then go to bed contented with our day, hoping that the next would be like it.

Except for unexpected and importune visits, this is how I spent my time on that island during my sojourn. Tell me what might be so alluring to excite in my heart now such intense, tender, and lasting memories, so that after fifteen years it is impossible for me to think of this beloved abode without feeling transported once more by the impulses of desire.

In the vicissitudes of a long life I have noticed that periods of the sweetest delight and most intense pleasure are not those to which memory draws me and touches me most. These short moments of delirium and passion, however intense they may be, are, despite their intensity, only occasional points on the path of life. They are too rare and fleeting to constitute a state of being, and the happiness my heart yearns for is not made up of fleeting moments, but is a simple and permanent state that has no intensity in itself, though its duration increases its charm to the point that I finally find in it supreme happiness.

Everything on earth is in continual flux. Nothing keeps a fixed and constant form, and our affections, which attach themselves to external things, invariably pass and change as they do. Always before or behind us, they recall the past that no longer exists or foretell the future that often is not to be. There is nothing firm to which the heart can attach itself. Therefore we have hardly anything but passing pleasure here below. As for happiness that lasts—I doubt it is known here. In our most intense pleasures there is hardly an instant when our heart can truly say to us: *I wish this moment to last forever.* And how can we call happiness a fleeting state, since it still leaves our heart anxious and empty, and makes us yearn for something in advance or still yearn for something afterward?

But if it is a state in which the spirit finds a base solid enough on which to rest and gather there all its being without needing to recall the past or step into the future; a state in which time is nothing for the spirit, in which the present lasts forever without, nevertheless, marking its duration, and without a trace of succession, without any other feeling of deprivation or delight, pleasure or suffering, desire or fear, except that of our mere existence: such a feeling alone can fill the soul completely. As long as this state lasts, he who finds himself in it can call himself happy, not with an imperfect happiness that is poor and relative, of the kind one finds in the pleasures of life, but a happiness that is sufficient, perfect, and complete, that leaves in the soul no emptiness that it feels it must fill. Such was the state in which I often found myself on the Isle of St. Pierre in my solitary reveries, lying in my boat floating at the water's will, or sitting on the shores of the restless lake, or elsewhere on the banks of a beautiful river or a brook murmuring over pebbles.

What does one enjoy in such a situation? Nothing external to oneself, nothing if not oneself and one's own existence. As long as this state lasts one is sufficient unto oneself, like God. The feeling of existence stripped of all other attachment is in itself a precious feeling of contentment and peace, which would suffice by itself to render this existence dear and sweet to whoever can cast off all the sensual and earthly impressions that here below ceaselessly come to distract us from this feeling and disturb its sweetness. But most men, agitated by continual passions, hardly know this state, and, having tasted it imperfectly for a few moments, have kept only an obscure and confused notion of it that does not let them feel its charm. In the present constitution of things it would not even be good. Avid for these sweet ecstasies, most men become disgusted with their busy lives, which constantly recurring needs prescribe as a duty. But the unfortunate man who has been cut off from society and who can no longer do anything useful and good for others and for himself here below can find in this state compensation for all human felicity, which fortune and men cannot take from him.

It is true that this compensation cannot be felt by every soul or in every situation. The heart must be at peace, and no passions must come to trouble the calm. He who experiences these compensations must be inclined to them; there needs to be support from what surrounds him. Neither absolute rest nor too much agitation is called for, but a uniform and moderate movement that has neither disorder nor gaps. Without movement, life is nothing but lethargy. If the movement is uneven or too strong, he is awakened; reminding us of the surrounding objects destroys the charm of the reverie. It tears us away from within ourselves and places us back under the yoke of fortune and men, bringing back to us the awareness of our misfortunes. Absolute silence brings sadness; it offers an image of death. Then the aid of a happy imagination is necessary, and presents itself naturally to those whom Heaven has favored. What does not come from outside is then created within us. The respite is less, it is true, but also more pleasant, since gentle and sweet ideas do not perturb the depths of the soul but merely skim its surface, so to speak. All one needs is to remember one's self while forgetting all one's misfortunes. This kind of reverie can be enjoyed wherever one can be peaceful and undisturbed, and I have often thought that in the Bastille, or even in a dungeon where not a single object would draw my attention, I could have dreamed happily.

But I must confess that it was far better and more happily realized on a solitary and fertile island, self-contained and separated from the rest of the world by nature, where only happy images offered themselves to me, where nothing reminded me of saddening memories; where the society of the small number of inhabitants was accommodating and convivial without being interesting to the point of occupying me continually; an island where I could, in short, deliver myself all day and without worry or impediment to occupations that were to my taste or to utter idleness. The circumstances were without doubt excellent for a dreamer who knew how to feed on pleasant fantasies, even when surrounded by all that was most unpleasant, and who could sate himself on these fantasies at his leisure by making everything that struck his senses cohere. Emerging from a sweet and lengthy reverie, I would see verdure all around me, flowers, and birds, and let my eyes wander over distant romantic shores that bounded vast stretches of crystalline water; and as I drew these pleasant objects into my fantasies, and by degrees was brought back to myself and my surroundings, I could not determine the point separating fiction from reality. Everything conspired equally to render dear to me the solitary and contemplative life I led during that beautiful sojourn. If only it could be once more! If only I could end my days on that beloved island without ever leaving it, without ever again seeing people from the mainland who would remind me of the many calamities they have taken pleasure in heaping upon me for so many years. I would soon forget these people entirely, though doubtless they would not forget me; but what would I care, as long as they were unable to trouble my peace. Delivered from all earthly passions that the tumult of social life engenders, my spirit would soar above all this and anticipate communing with celestial intelligences, whose number it hopes to augment in a little time.

Men will, I am certain, make sure not to give me back such a sweet refuge where they had no intention of leaving me. But at least they cannot hinder me from being transported there every day on the wings of imagination, to taste there for a few hours the same pleasure as if I were still living there. There the sweetest thing I would do would be to dream at my leisure. In dreaming that I am there, am I not doing the same thing? I am doing even more. I add to the attraction of an abstract and monotonous reverie charming images that enliven it. In my ecstasies their objects often escape my senses, and now, the more profound my reveries, the more vividly they paint the objects for me. I am often more immersed in them, and more pleasantly so, than when I was actually there. What is unfortunate is that the more my imagination fades, the more my reveries fade and recede as well. Alas, it is when one begins to leave one's mortal body that one's visions are most dimmed.

ACKNOWLEDGMENTS

PETER CONSTANTINE is grateful to the Dorothy and Lewis B. Cullman Center for Scholars & Writers. The New York Public Library's substantial collection of French eighteenth-century materials was of great help in the translation of *The Essential Writings of Rousseau*.

TIMELINE

1712 Jean-Jacques Rousseau born in Geneva, June 28, to Suzanne and Isaac Rousseau; his mother dies July 7, and his aunt Suson cares for him thereafter.

1718 Moves with his father, aunt, and older brother to Coutance in the artisans' quarter of Saint-Gervais.

1722 After his father leaves Geneva to avoid arrest, boards with the pastor Lambercier in the village of Bossey.

1725 Apprenticed to the engraver Ducommun.

1726 His father remarries, in the town of Nyon.

1728 Abandons his unfinished apprenticeship and runs away from Geneva at age sixteen; meets Mme de Warens in Annecy; goes to Turin (capital of the Savoy) for conversion to Catholicism, and holds low-level jobs there; is strongly influenced by a wise priest, the abbé Gaime.

1729 Returns to Annecy and moves in with Mme de Warens.

1730 Spends a year of wandering, attempting to be a music teacher in Lausanne and Neuchâtel.

1731 Brief and disappointing stay in Paris; returns to Mme de Warens, who is now living in Chambéry, and begins an eight-month employment as a clerk in the land survey office.

1734 Death (probably by suicide) of Claude Anet, Mme de Warens's steward and lover, who has been obliged to share her with Rousseau.

1735 Begins intermittent residence in a country house, Les Charmettes, outside Chambéry.

1737 At twenty-five, reaches the age of majority in Geneva and recovers part of his modest inheritance; journeys to Montpellier to seek a cure for imagined health problems.

1738 Returns to Chambéry and finds his place taken by another young man, Wintzenried; lives alone at Les Charmettes and reads widely.

1740 Takes a position as tutor to the young sons of M. de Mably in Lyon, where he comes into contact with Enlightenment ideas.

1742 Moves to Paris at the age of thirty, hoping for a career as a musician.

1743 Takes a post as secretary to the French ambassador in Venice, the comte de Montaigu; develops a passion for Italian music, and due to his employer's incompetence, takes on much of the work of the embassy.

1744 Discharged by Montaigu, returns to Paris and develops a close relationship with Diderot, who becomes an intellectual mentor, in a circle that includes d'Alembert and Condillac.

1745 Forms lifelong alliance with Thérèse Levasseur, aged twenty-three (Rousseau is thirty-three); composes an operatic ballet, *The Gallant Muses,* but fails to get it produced.

1746 Birth of the first of five children, all of whom are consigned to a foundling home; takes a secretarial job with Mme Dupin.

1747 Death of Rousseau's father, whom he has not seen for many years.

1749 Writes articles on music for the projected *Encyclopédie* edited by Diderot and d'Alembert; on the road to Vincennes, on the way to visit Diderot, who is imprisoned for subversive writings, conceives the idea of the *Discourse on the Sciences and Arts*.

1750 The *Discourse* wins first prize from the Dijon Academy, is published, and brings Rousseau fame at the age of thirty-eight.

1752 Rousseau's opera *The Village Soothsayer* is performed at court to great acclaim.

1753 Publication of *Letter on French Music*, which becomes the center of a fierce controversy on the respective merits of French and Italian music.

1754 Visits Geneva and reconverts to Protestantism in order to regain citizenship; sees Mme de Warens for the last time.

1755 Publication of a second discourse, *On the Origin of Inequality*, that confirms Rousseau's originality as a thinker.

1756 At the invitation of Mme d'Épinay, moves with Thérèse to a country house, the Hermitage, at La Chevrette near Paris; begins work on a novel, *Julie, or, The New Héloïse*.

1757 Intoxicating but largely platonic affair with Mme d'Houdetot, which ends in recriminations; also breaks with Mme d'Épinay, her lover Grimm, and Diderot.

1758 Moves to Montlouis in the nearby village of Montmorency; *Letter to d'Alembert on the Theater* defends Genevan mores (and earns Voltaire's enmity).

1759 Develops a close friendship with the duke and duchess of Luxembourg, and often stays in the Petit Château on their estate.

1761 Publication and immense success of *Julie*.

1762 Publication of the *Social Contract* and *Émile, or, On Education*, both of which are immediately condemned in Paris and Geneva on religious and political grounds; when an arrest warrant is issued, Rousseau flees France and settles with Thérèse in the village of Môtiers near Neuchâtel in Switzerland; develops a keen interest in botany.

1763 Renounces Genevan citizenship in disgust over political developments there; notoriety as religious freethinker is exacerbated by *Letter to Christophe de Beaumont*.

1764 Rousseau's trenchant critique of Genevan politics, *Letters from the Mountain*, alarms conservatives there and elsewhere; Voltaire's anonymous *Sentiment of the Citizens* reveals the secret of Rousseau's abandoned children.

1765 Protestant ministers organize a campaign against Rousseau, and he is driven from Môtiers when his house is stoned; brief idyllic stay on the Isle of St. Pierre, which he is likewise ordered to leave.

1766 Journeys to England with David Hume and settles with Thérèse at Wootton in Staffordshire; begins work on the *Confessions*; becomes convinced that Hume is plotting against him, and writes a long accusatory letter that Hume makes public.

1767 In a state of panic, returns to France where the arrest warrant of 1762 is still in force; takes an assumed name and lodges in a château in Normandy under the protection of the prince de Conti, whom he had known in Montmorency.

1768 Overwhelmed by paranoia, moves to eastern France and

adopts an assumed name; goes through a form of marriage (not legally valid) with Thérèse, after twenty-three years together.

1769 During a grim winter in the French countryside, brings the *Confessions* close to completion.

1770 Resumes his real name and moves to Paris with the intention of confronting his enemies, who fail, however, to appear; supports himself by copying music, and takes long excursions collecting plants outside Paris.

1771 Attempts to rehabilitate his reputation by giving readings of the *Confessions*, but is ordered by the police to stop.

1772 Begins a new attempt at self-justification, *Dialogues: Rousseau Judge of Jean-Jacques*, and works at it intermittently.

1776 Tries in vain to deposit the manuscript of the *Dialogues* in the cathedral of Notre-Dame, and abandons all hope of rehabilitating his much-maligned reputation; begins an unfinished final work, *Reveries of the Solitary Walker*; is knocked unconscious and incurs lasting damage when a huge dog runs him over in the street.

1778 In failing health, accepts the hospitality of the Marquis de Girardin at his château at Ermenonville outside Paris; dies there of cerebral bleeding on July 2, at the age of sixty-eight, and is buried on the Isle of Poplars in an ornamental lake.

1780 *Dialogues* published.

1782 First half of the *Confessions* published.

1789 Remainder of the *Confessions* published.

1794 Rousseau's remains transferred with great pomp to the Panthéon in Paris.

1801 Thérèse dies, in extreme poverty.

NOTES

INTRODUCTION

1. *Émile* II, in Jean-Jacques Rousseau, *Oeuvres Complètes,* ed. Marcel Raymond et al., 5 vols. (Paris: Gallimard, Bibliothèque de la Pléiade, 1959–95), 4:323.

2. Jean Starobinski, introduction to the *Discours sur l'Origine de l'Inégalité,* in *Oeuvres Complètes* 3:xlix.

3. *Lettre à d'Alembert sur les Spectacles, Oeuvres Complètes* 5:123–24.

4. Blaise Pascal, *Pensées,* no. 455 (Brunschvicg numbering).

5. *Social Contract* I.vi, p. 103 below.

6. *Confessions* IX, *Oeuvres Complètes* 1:417.

7. *Lettre à d'Alembert, Oeuvres Complètes* 5:73.

8. Thérèse Levasseur to Rousseau, June 23, 1762, in *Correspondance Complète de Jean-Jacques Rousseau,* ed. R. A. Leigh, 52 vols. (Geneva: Institut et Musée Voltaire, 1965–71; Oxford: Voltaire Foundation, 1971–98), 11:141.

9. *Dialogues: Rousseau Juge de Jean-Jacques, Oeuvres Complètes* 1:847.

10. Jacques-Henri Bernardin de Saint-Pierre, *La Vie et Ouvrages de Jean-Jacques Rousseau,* ed. Maurice Souriau (Paris: Cornély, 1907), p. 110.

11. *Confessions* VI, *O.C.* 1:225–26.

12. Rapport fait au Comité d'Instruction Publique de la Convention Nationale, 20 Vendémiaire, an III (Oct. 11, 1794), *Correspondance Complète* 48:79.

13. Maria Edgeworth to Mary Sneyd, Jan. 10, 1803 (recounting a conversation with the now elderly Mme d'Houdetot), *Correspondance Complète* 5:280.

14. Alexandre Deleyre to the Marquis de Girardin, Aug. 5, 1778, *Correspondance Complète* 5:291.

DISCOURSE ON INEQUALITY

15. The motto of the temple of Apollo at Delphi was "Know Thyself."

16. In Book X of *The Republic*, Plato uses the analogy of a statue, crusted over after long immersion in the sea, to suggest an original unity of body and soul that has become deformed over time. Rousseau adapts the analogy to suggest the natural goodness of man before the fatal departure from the state of nature into that of civilization.

17. Rousseau is emphasizing that he is not attempting a historical survey, which he thought would tend to make inequality seem inevitable, but a thought experiment seeking to understand the essence of human nature by abstracting it from the myriad ways in which society has altered it.

18. Jean-Jacques Burlamaqui, like Rousseau a Genevan, had recently published *Principles of Natural Right*.

19. This is a crucial move in Rousseau's argument. Previous theorists assumed that human beings have an innate ability to recognize natural law, and that society has been founded upon it; the full question posed by the Academy of Dijon, to which this *Discourse* is a response, was "What is the origin of inequality among men, and is it authorized by natural law?" Rousseau denies the existence of an innate rationality that would have made natural law—including the alleged "naturalness" of inequality—obvious to primitive mankind.

20. In the present context, Rousseau may mean by "the facts" the biblical story of the Creation and Fall; he has no wish to arouse the anger of religious authorities, so he simply bypasses it. However, he may also have in mind the ahistorical thought experiment suggested above.

21. The Lyceum was the public meeting place in Athens where Aristotle and his "peripatetic" school met. Xenocrates, a student of Plato, succeeded his master as head of the Platonic Academy.

22. In *Leviathan* (1651), Thomas Hobbes argued that man in the state of nature would be incorrigibly aggressive, creating a "war of all

against all." Richard Cumberland and Samuel Pufendorf were critics of Hobbes who argued that humans are naturally disposed to
cooperation and peace. The "illustrious philosopher" is Montesquieu, whose *On the Spirit of the Laws* had just come out when Rousseau was writing the *Discourse.*

23. Rousseau added this paragraph after reading Coréal's *Travels in the
West Indies;* it appeared in a posthumous edition in 1782.

24. This provocative statement quickly became notorious, in an era
that placed a high value on reason.

25. Sentence added in 1782; Hippocrates was the great Greek physi-
cian whose name is remembered in the Hippocratic Oath, and Cor-
nelius Celsus was a Roman writer on medicine.

26. The philosophe Condillac was a close friend whom Rousseau had
known since acting as a tutor of Condillac's nephews in Lyon. At
this point in the *Discourse* Rousseau briefly sketches an argument
that he would develop more fully in a never-published *Essay on the
Origin of Languages.*

27. "So much more does ignorance of vice profit the one kind than
knowledge of virtue profit the other." Rousseau is quoting the *Histories* of Justin (third century A.D.), distinguishing between Scythian
ignorance and Greek knowledge.

28. In some contexts Rousseau's word *pitié* is probably closer to the English "compassion" than to our cognate word "pity."

29. The Dutch-English writer Bernard de Mandeville created a scandal with *The Fable of the Bees: Private Vices, Public Benefits* (1723), by
arguing that greed and competitiveness contribute to the collective
good.

30. The "restraint" is instinctive compassion.

31. Rousseau's point is that, like romantic love, these emotions are so-
cially conditioned. As he describes in the *Confessions* from personal
experience, shame—reluctance to expose one's misdeeds to other
people—becomes more powerful than the inward consciousness of
guilt.

32. John Locke, *An Essay Concerning Human Understanding* (1690),
IV.iii.18. Locke's original reads: "Where there is no property there
is no injustice." Rousseau has evidently substituted "injury" for "injustice" because he is imagining an era before legal systems were
invented.

33. Ceres (from whose name the word "cereal" is derived) was the
Roman goddess of agriculture. In Greece, where she was known as
Demeter, the Thesmophoria was celebrated in her honor.

34. This distinction between "being" and "appearing" has been seen as central to Rousseau's thought. In French the two words rhyme: *être* and *paraître*.

35. "Dismayed by the novelty of the evil, he seeks, wretched in his wealth, to flee his riches, and hates what he had once prayed for" (Ovid, *Metamorphoses* XI.127).

36. Lycurgus was a legendary lawgiver who created the militarized society of Sparta.

37. Pliny the Younger served as a magistrate under the first-century Roman emperor Trajan.

38. Herodotus quotes this saying in his *History*, Book VII (with different characters than the ones named by Rousseau). A satrap was a provincial governor in the Persian empire, with its capital at Persepolis; here the Spartan general Brasidas is contrasting the effete luxury of Persia with the collective simplicity of the Spartan way of life.

39. "The most abject slavery they call peace" (Tacitus, *Histories* IV.xvii).

40. Quoted from Jean Barbeyrac's translation of Pufendorf's *The Law of Nature and Nations* (added in the 1782 edition).

41. The *gerontes* were thirty elders who served as magistrates.

42. "If you bid me plunge my sword into my brother's breast, my father's throat, or the entrails of my wife who is with child, I shall do it all, even if my hand be reluctant" (Lucan, *Pharsalia*, Book I). The *Pharsalia* is an epic poem about the Roman civil war, taking its name from the Battle of Pharsalus at which Julius Caesar defeated the forces of the Senate, with which Lucan sympathized.

43. "Where there is nothing to hope for from honesty": quoted from the Roman historian Tacitus.

44. Diogenes the Cynic, who denounced Athenian civilization and lived in voluntary poverty, liked to carry a lighted lamp in daytime while claiming that he was searching in vain for a true man (or, as it is often quoted, an honest man). The Roman statesman Cato the Elder likewise espoused a return to simplicity from modern decadence.

45. Rousseau is actually thinking of the Epicureans, who taught *ataraxia*, a state of tranquility untroubled by anxieties of any kind. The Stoic philosophers, rather differently, counseled *apatheia*, absence of emotion.

SOCIAL CONTRACT

46. By converting to Catholicism, Rousseau had lost his Genevan citizenship, but he thought it important to stress the relevance of Geneva to his political thought.

47. "Let us make just treaty terms" (Virgil, *Aeneid* XI.321–22; Rousseau evidently read it as meaning "In an equitable federation, we will make laws").

48. Although Rousseau uses the term "administration," his real subject is the ideal constitution.

49. Rousseau drastically alters the usual meaning of "the sovereign," which in his day normally meant the monarch, not the people as a whole.

50. The verb translated here and in later occurrences as "give up their liberty" or "offer up their liberty" is *aliéner* in the original, which inspired Thomas Jefferson's famous phrase "unalienable rights." In modern English, however, "alienation" suggests "estranging" or "isolating," which is not at all Rousseau's meaning.

51. The Dutch jurist Hugo Grotius, a pioneer theorist of international law, argued in *Of the Law of War and Peace* (1625) that wars could be legitimate if waged in accordance with natural law. As Rousseau notes, he held that a people may choose to surrender any or all of their rights, and may even sell themselves into slavery.

52. "Learned inquiries into the public right are often no more than the history of past abuses, and those who have taken too much trouble studying them have wasted their efforts" (*Manuscript Treatise on the Interests of France in Relation to Its Neighbors*, by the Marquis d'Argenson). And that is precisely what Grotius did. (Rousseau's note.)

53. Thomas Hobbes, *Leviathan* (1651) II.xviii; Hobbes argued that to escape a "state of nature" in which men would freely kill one another, a strong central authority is necessary, and that even a tyrannical one is preferable to anarchy.

54. Philo Judaeus, a Jewish philosopher in the first century A.D.

55. Aristotle, *Politics* I.ii.

56. See a short treatise by Plutarch entitled *That Beasts Use Reason* (Rousseau's note); the essay appears in Plutarch's *Moralia*.

57. "The powers that be are ordained of God" (Romans 13:1).

58. Homer, *Odyssey* IX.

59. Rousseau had set out his concept of the state of nature in the *Discourse Concerning the Origin of Inequality*. Whereas Hobbes described the state of nature as a perpetual warfare of "all against all," Rous-

seau sees it as a presocial condition of individual freedom and independence.

60. In the thirteenth century, Louis IX—canonized thirty years after
his death as Saint Louis—forbade private warfare between feudal
nobles, in what was known as the Peace (or Truce) of God.

61. The Romans, who better understood and showed more respect for
the right of war than any other nation on earth, carried their scruples in this regard so far that a citizen was not permitted to serve as
a volunteer without engaging himself specifically against the
enemy, in fact an enemy specified by name. When a legion was re-
deployed in which Cato the Younger bore his first arms under Popilius, Cato the Elder wrote to Popilius that if he wanted his son to
continue serving under him, his son would have to swear a new
military oath because, the initial one having been annulled, his son
could no longer bear arms against the enemy. And Cato wrote to his
son, telling him that he should refrain from taking part in a battle
for which he had not sworn a new oath. I know that the siege of
Clusium and other particular events can be cited to counter my
argument, but I am citing laws and practices. The Romans were the
people that least transgressed against their laws, and their laws
were the finest. (Rousseau's note, added after his death to the third
edition of 1782.)

62. I.e., this should be the goal of any legitimate form of social contract,
whether the one Rousseau is proposing or some other.

63. The true meaning of this word has almost entirely disappeared in
modern times. Most people mistake a physical city for a *city*, and a
city-dweller for a citizen. They do not know that houses make a
city, but citizens a *city*. The same mistake once cost the Carthagin-
ians dearly. I have never read anywhere of the title *cives* ever being
given to the subject of any prince, not even by the Macedonians of
ancient times, nor, in our days, the English, though they live in
greater liberty than anyone else. It is only the French who quite
casually assume the name *citizen*, because they have no idea of what
it means, as one can see from their dictionaries; otherwise they
would be guilty of the crime of lèse-majesté in appropriating it.
C*itizen* for the French expresses a virtue, not a right. When Bodin
wanted to speak of our citizens and city-dwellers, he made a big
blunder by mistaking the one for the other. Monsieur d'Alembert
did not err, and, in his article *Geneva*, correctly distinguished the
four orders of men (even five, counting foreigners) in our city, and
of which only two compose the Republic. No other French author

I am aware of has understood the true meaning of the word *citizen*. (Rousseau's note, citing the sixteenth-century French jurist Jean Bodin, and his own friend Jean le Rond d'Alembert, co-editor of the great *Encyclopédie*; in French "citizen" meant someone living in a city, whereas Rousseau understands it to mean free and equal voting members.)

64. I.e., the "sovereign" is composed of all citizens, acting collectively; they may make mistakes, but they cannot cease to be the sovereign.

65. I.e., the state is not an impersonal entity; as the embodiment of the common will, it acts as a collective person with moral responsibilities.

66. This sentence became the most notorious one in the entire book. What Rousseau has in mind is not tyrannical coercion but rather an acknowledgment of the shared commitment that locates freedom in citizen participation rather than resistance. (He also believes that someone unable to conform to the will of the whole should be free to emigrate to someplace else.)

67. Under bad governments, this equality is only apparent and illusory, serving to keep the poor in their misery, and the rich in possession of all they have usurped. In reality, laws are always useful to those with possessions and harmful to those who have nothing. From which it follows that the social state is advantageous to men only insofar as they all have something, but none of them too much. (Rousseau's note.)

68. I.e., just as with the inalienable rights of each individual, the sovereignty of the state cannot be "alienated" or transferred.

69. For a will to be general, it does not always need to be unanimous; but it is necessary for all voices to be counted. Any formal exclusion is a breach of generality. (Rousseau's note, 1782.)

70. In Book II, chapter VI.

71. The jurist Jean Barbeyrac translated Samuel Pufendorf's Latin treatise *Of the Law of Nature and Nations*. In the so-called Glorious Revolution of 1688, James II of England was deposed on the grounds that by seeking to reconvert his nation to Catholicism, he had effectively abdicated the throne. The nearest Protestant in the line of succession was James's daughter Mary, who was married to the Dutch prince William of Orange. It was on this basis that when they ruled England jointly as William and Mary, William could be considered a legitimate king and not a usurper.

72. "Every interest," says the Marquis d'Argenson, "has different principles. The accord between two individual interests is formed by

their opposition to the interests of a third." The Marquis might have added that the accord of all interests is formed by opposition to the interest of each individual. If there were no different interests, the common interest would barely be felt, since it would never encounter an obstacle: everything would run by itself, and politics would cease to be an art. (Rousseau's note, citing d'Argenson's *Considerations of the Past and Present Government of France*.)

73. I.e., small groups of citizens meeting as separate interest groups, rather than participating in the collective whole.

74. "The truth is," says Machiavelli, "that some divisions harm republics, while others benefit it: the divisions that harm it spring from factions and parties, while those that benefit it are divisions that do not rely on factions or parties. As a founder of a republic cannot avoid having enemies in his republic, he must at least avoid that there be factions." *Florentine Histories*, Book VII. (Rousseau's note.)

75. Lycurgus was the legendary founder of Sparta, whose political system Rousseau thought preferable in some ways to the Athenian, where demagogues easily swayed the people. Solon was an early Athenian leader; Numa Pompilius and Servius Tullius were legendary Roman kings.

76. Attentive readers, do not, I pray, be in a hurry to charge me with contradicting myself. The terminology made it unavoidable, considering the poverty of language; but I shall explain later. (Rousseau's note.)

77. Montesquieu claimed that political laws are based upon laws of nature.

78. By this word I do not merely understand an aristocracy or democracy, but generally all government directed by the general will, which is the law. To be legitimate, the government cannot be indistinguishable from the sovereign authority but must be its minister. Consequently, even a monarchy is a republic. This will be made clear in the following book. (Rousseau's note.)

79. A people becomes famous only when its legislation begins to decline. We do not know how many centuries the institutions of Lycurgus ensured the happiness of the Spartans before they were noticed by the rest of Greece. (Rousseau's note.)

80. Charles-Louis de Secondat, Baron de Montesquieu, author of the great *On the Spirit of the Laws* (1748); Rousseau refers here to his *Considerations of the Causes of the Greatness of the Romans and Their Decline* (1734).

81. Those who think of Calvin as only a theologian fail to see the scope

of his genius. The drawing up of our wise edicts, in which he played an important part, does him as much honor as his Institute of the Christian Religion. Whatever change time may bring about in our religion, the memory of this great man will not cease to be honored and blessed as long as our love for our country and our love of liberty are not extinguished. (Rousseau's note; the theologian Jean Calvin, one of the first leaders of the Reformation, drew up a code for Geneva that turned that independent city into a "Calvinist" theocracy.)

82. The *decemviri* ("ten men") were a committee of ten patricians appointed in 451 B.C. to draw up a code of laws for Rome.

83. "In fact," says Machiavelli, "there has never been a legislator of drastic laws who did not turn to God, for otherwise his laws would not have been accepted. A wise legislator can see many good things that are perhaps not evident enough in themselves to persuade others." (*Discourses on Livy*, Book I, chapter xi; Rousseau's note.)

84. Muhammad (the Arabs were considered descendants of Ishmael).

85. William Warburton was an English bishop and political writer.

86. Roman tyrants overthrown by Lucius Junius Brutus.

87. Although the leaders of the French Revolution would venerate Rousseau's memory, passages such as this show how little hope he held for revolutionary reform.

88. Peter the Great, czar of Russia from 1682 to 1725, carried out a massive project of modernization that made his nation a major European power.

89. Satrapies were the provinces of Persia.

90. Denying that gravitation could operate in a vacuum, Descartes and his "Cartesian" successors postulated an invisible medium that pervaded the universe, in which the planets and other bodies were whirled around as if in "vortices" or whirlpools.

91. If there were two neighboring peoples, one of which could not make do without the other, it would be a very difficult situation for the former, and a dangerous one for the latter. In such a case a wise nation would strive to free the other from this dependence. The Republic of Thlascala, surrounded by the Mexican Empire, preferred to make do without salt to buying it from the Mexicans, or even accepting it as a gift. The wise Thlascalans saw the trap concealed beneath such generosity. They preserved their freedom; their small state, enclosed within the great empire, ultimately proved the instrument of that empire's ruin. (Rousseau's note.)

92. Corsica had recently liberated itself from rule by Genoa, becoming

an independent republic in 1755, and after the publication of the *Social Contract* Rousseau was invited to help it draw up a constitution. In 1769, however, seven years after the *Social Contract* was published, Corsica became subject to France, as it is to this day.

93. In Book I, chapter 8.

94. If you wish to give a state stability, you must bring the two extremes as close to each other as possible: Tolerate neither men of great wealth nor beggars. These two conditions, naturally inseparable, are equally fatal to the common good; from the one come the champions of tyranny, and from the other, tyrants. It is always between these two that public liberty is traded, the one purchasing, the other selling it. (Rousseau's note.)

95. "Any branch of foreign commerce," the Marquis d'Argenson says, "brings only an apparent advantage for the kingdom as a whole; it may enrich a few individuals, perhaps even a few towns, but the whole nation will gain nothing by it, and the people will be no better off." (Rousseau's note.)

96. Thus in Venice the College of Senators is given the name "Most Serene Prince," even when the Doge is not present. (Rousseau's note.) The Doge (or duke) was a nobleman elected by his fellows to be their leader.

97. The French word translated here as "relation" is *rapport*; Rousseau plays on the fact that it can mean a mathematical ratio as well as a relationship. His mathematical analogies are notoriously obscure, but the essential point is that each citizen should be treated as a whole number, not a minuscule fraction.

98. "Prince" is confusing in Rousseau's usage, because he uses it (as he does "sovereign") to refer to a collective body, for example the Venetian senate, and not just to a monarch.

99. Montesquieu, *Spirit of the Laws* III.iii.

100. From *Observations on the Government of Poland* by its nominal king, Stanislas Leczinski (1749).

101. It is clear that among the ancients, the word *optimates* does not mean the best but rather the most powerful. (Rousseau's note.)

102. It is extremely important that the method of election of magistrates should be regulated by laws, for if it is left to the will of the princely authority, one cannot avoid falling into hereditary aristocracy, as happened to the republics of Venice and Berne. Venice has long since been a state in dissolution, while Berne maintains itself through the great wisdom of its senate. It is a most honorable, though dangerous, exception. (Rousseau's note.)

103. Aristotle, *Politics* III.vi–vii (but Aristotle in fact defines aristocracy as government by the *aristoi*, "the best," and not by the rich).

104. 1 Samuel 8:10–18, warning the people of the pitfalls in their demand to be ruled by a king.

105. Machiavelli was an honorable man and good citizen; but as he was attached to the House of the Medici he was forced, during his country's era of oppression, to disguise his love of liberty. The very choice of his execrable hero [Cesar Borgia] shows his hidden intention clearly enough; and the contradiction of the principles in his book *The Prince,* and those in his *Discourses on Livy* and *History of Florence,* prove that this profound political thinker has so far been read only by superficial and corrupt readers. The [Pope's] Court of Rome has strictly prohibited his book, and one can see why; it is that court that he portrays most clearly. (Rousseau's note, 1782 edition.)

106. Rousseau inserted this paragraph when the *Social Contract* was in press, intending to pay a compliment to the French first minister, the Duc de Choiseul. But as Rousseau recounted in Book IX of the *Confessions,* Choiseul felt insulted.

107. From Plutarch's *Sayings of Kings.*

108. Tacitus, *Histories* I.16.

109. *The Statesman.* (Rousseau's note.)

110. See Book III, chapter 3.

111. The purported influence of climate on social systems was a central theme in *The Spirit of the Laws.*

112. Jean Chardin, *Travels in Persia* (1711).

113. This does not contradict what I have said before (Book II, chapter IX) about the disadvantages of large states, as there it was a question concerning the authority of the government over its affiliated members, while here it a matter of its strength over its subjects. Its scattered members serve as points of support to act on the people at a distance, but it has a direct point of support to act on its affiliated members themselves. Consequently, on one hand the length of the lever is its weakness, and on the other its strength. (Rousseau's note.)

114. The same principle should be used to judge which centuries deserve to be considered the best in terms of human prosperity. Those in which letters and arts flourished have been too much admired, the hidden object of their culture not having been fathomed and their grim effects not taken into account. *"Idque apud imperitos humanitas vocabatur, cum pars servitutis esset"* [And the inexperienced

called that "humanity" which was part of slavery]. Tacitus, *Agricola*, xxi. Will we never see in the maxims of books the vulgar interest that makes authors speak? No, whatever these authors may say, when, despite a country's renown, its population dwindles, it is not true that all is well, and it is not enough that a poet should have an income of a hundred thousand francs so that his century be the best of centuries. Less attention should be paid to the apparent repose and tranquility of the rulers than to the well-being of entire nations, and above all of the most populous states. A hailstorm can devastate several districts, but it rarely leads to a shortage of food. Uprisings and civil wars alarm rulers greatly, but they are not an actual misfortune for the people, who may even get a respite during disputes about who will tyrannize them. It is from the people's enduring situation that actual prosperity and calamities arise: it is when all is crushed beneath the yoke that decline sets in, and that the rulers destroy the people at leisure, and *"ubi solitudinem faciunt, pacem appellant"* [where they create a desert, they call it peace]. Tacitus, *Agricola*, xxx. When the squabbling of the nobles unsettled the kingdom of France, and the Coadjutor of Paris attended parliament with a dagger in his pocket, the people of France were not prevented from prospering and multiplying in free and honest well-being. In ancient times, Greece flourished in the midst of the most savage wars; blood flowed in torrents, and yet the country was filled with people. "It appears that in the midst of murder, proscription, and civil war," Machiavelli says, "our republic became more powerful because of them: its citizens' valor, their mores and independence, did more to strengthen it than all its dissensions had done to weaken it. A little agitation gives the soul resilience. What makes our species truly prosper is not so much peace as liberty." (Rousseau's note.)

115. We have omitted here a page-long footnote by Rousseau that relates details from Roman history.

116. By "anarchy" Rousseau means not just chaos but also a government that is not legitimate.

117. *"Omnes enim et habentur et dicuntur tyranni, qui potestate utuntur perpetua in ea civitate quoe libertate usa est"* [Cornelius Nepos, *Life of Miltiades:* For all are considered and called tyrants who hold perpetual power in a state used to liberty]. It is true that Aristotle (in *Ethics,* Book VIII, chapter x) distinguishes between a tyrant and a king in that the former governs for his own benefit, and the latter only for the benefit of his subjects. But aside from Greek authors in general having taken the word *tyrant* in a different sense, as appears particu-

larly in Xenophon's *Hiero*, it would follow from Aristotle's distinction that since the beginning of the world not a single king has yet existed. (Rousseau's note.)

118. French society was conventionally divided into three *états* or "estates": the nobles, who governed and fought; the clergy, who prayed; and the Third Estate of commoners. The (rarely convened) Estates General was divided into three separate bodies, in which the small minority of nobles and clergy could outvote the commoners who represented everybody else.

119. Almost in the sense given to this word in the English Parliament. The similarity of their functions would have brought the consuls and the tribunes into conflict, even if all jurisdiction had been suspended. (Rousseau's note.)

120. A *cité* was an incorporated body with distinct rights, and a "citizen" was a city-dweller.

121. Unpaid labor, usually of a specified number of days per year, required of the peasants and other commoners.

122. The *tribunes* were elected officials in ancient Rome; *lictors* were bodyguards of the magistrates. The Gracchi brothers were tribunes in the second century B.C. who promoted popular reforms and were assassinated.

123. Embracing in cold countries the luxury and ease of the Orientals is to embrace their fetters, and we would be submitting to them with far greater inevitability than the Orientals. (Rousseau's note.)

124. This is what I had planned to do in the sequel to this work, where, dealing with foreign relations, I would have taken up the matter of confederations; an entirely new subject, whose principles have yet to be established. (Rousseau's note, referring to his never-completed larger project.)

125. This statement was considered so subversive by authorities in Paris and Geneva that it was specifically cited when the *Social Contract* was proscribed and burned.

126. Book III, chapters XIII–XIV.

127. On the understanding that one is not leaving in order to elude one's duty and to avoid serving one's country at a moment it needs one. Flight in such a case would be criminal and punishable; it would no longer be withdrawal but desertion. (Rousseau's note.)

128. Oliver Cromwell, victorious Puritan general in the English civil wars of the seventeenth century, became a virtual dictator as Lord High Protector; the Duc de Beaufort was a leader in the French civil war known as the Fronde.

129. I.e., free speech is not permitted.

130. Tacitus, *Histories* I.85.

131. This should naturally be understood as applying to a free state, since elsewhere family, belongings, necessity, violence, and lack of a place to live can keep an inhabitant in a country against his will; and then his residence in such a state no longer implies his consent or violation of the contract. (Rousseau's note.)

132. In Genoa, above the entrance to prisons and on the chains of galley slaves, one can read the word *Libertas*. This application of the term is good and just. It is indeed only malefactors of all classes who prevent the citizen from being free. In a country in which all such men would be in the galleys, the most perfect liberty would be enjoyed. (Rousseau's note.)

133. Book III, chapter XVII.

134. *Spirit of the Laws* II.ii.

135. Impoverished members of the Venetian nobility who lived in the San Barnabà district.

136. See Book III, chapter IV.

137. *Polysynodie* (1718), by the Abbé de Saint-Pierre, was an argument in favor of limited monarchy. As a young man, Rousseau was hired to organize and abridge the abbé's posthumous papers, including a plan for universal peace.

138. It was usual in eighteenth-century political writing to deploy extensive analogies from ancient history, and Rousseau, though not classically educated, felt obliged to conform. No attempt will be made here to explain all of his references in this chapter.

139. The name *Rome,* which is said to come from *Romulus,* is Greek, and means "force." The name *Numa* is also Greek, and means "law." What likelihood is there that the first two kings of that city had in advance names that were so appropriate to what they did? (Rousseau's note.)

140. I say "Campus Martius" [the field of Mars] because it was there that the Comitia Centuriata assembled; in the two other Comitia, the people assembled in the Forum or elsewhere; and then the *capite censi* had as much influence and authority as the foremost citizens. (Rousseau's note.)

141. This Centuria, chosen this way by lot, was called *praerogativa* on account of its being the first that was asked to vote, and this is where the word *prerogative* comes from. (Rousseau's note.)

142. *Custodes, diribitores, rogatores suffragiorum.* (Rousseau's note.)

143. Sparta had two kings, but the five elected *ephors* were the most powerful leaders.

144. This nomination was made secretly and by night, as if the Romans were ashamed of placing a man above the law. (Rousseau's note.)

145. In the first century B.C. the patrician Catiline headed a conspiracy to overthrow the Roman republic; Cicero's speeches led to the execution of the other leading conspirators, and Catiline himself died in battle.

146. Cicero could not have been sure of succeeding in this had he proposed that a dictator be nominated, since he did not dare nominate himself, and could not be certain that his co-consul would nominate him. (Rousseau's note.)

147. The Roman censors were responsible for overseeing public morality in general, not just writings.

148. In this chapter I am merely touching on a subject I have treated at greater length in my *Letter to M. d'Alembert.* (Rousseau's note; in that work he defended the traditions of his native Geneva against d'Alembert's arguments in favor of modernization and liberalization.)

149. They were from another island, which the delicacy of our language forbids me to name on this occasion. (Rousseau's note; the island was Chios, which resembles *chier,* "defecate," in French.)

150. *Nonne ea quae possidet Chamos deus tuus, tibi jure debentur?* [Judges 11:24]. This is the text in the Vulgate. Father de Carrières translates: "Do you not believe that you have the right to possess that which belongs to Kemosh, your god?" I do not know the force of the Hebrew text, but I see that in the Vulgate Jephthah positively recognized the right of the god Kemosh, and that the French translator weakened this admission with an "according to you," which is not in the Latin. (Rousseau's note.)

151. It is very clear indeed that the Phocian War, which was called a Holy War, was not a war of religion. Its object was to punish sacrilege, not to subjugate nonbelievers. (Rousseau's note, referring to a war among Greek city-states in the fourth century B.C.)

152. It should be noted that what binds the clergy into a body is not so much formal assemblies, such as those in France, as the communion of Churches. Communion and excommunication are the clergy's social pact, one that will always make the clergy master of peoples and kings. All the priests who are in the same communion are fellow citizens, even if they come from opposite ends of the earth. This invention is a masterpiece of politics. There was nothing like it among pagan priests, which is why they never formed a clerical body. (Rousseau's note.)

153. Note, among other things, in a letter from Grotius to his brother on

April 11, 1643, what that learned man approves of in Hobbes's book *De Cive* and what he condemns. It is true that having a penchant for indulgence, he seems to forgive the author the good for the sake of the bad; but not everyone is so forgiving. (Rousseau's note.)

154. "Let him be sacred," i.e., let him be consigned to the judgment of the gods.

155. Book II, chapter IV.

156. "In a republic," the Marquis d'Argenson says, "each man is perfectly free in whatever does not harm others." Here we have the invariable demarcation. It is impossible to define it more exactly. I have not been able resist the pleasure of occasionally quoting this manuscript, though it is unknown to the public, in order to honor the memory of an illustrious man of integrity who, even in the ministry, retained the heart of a true citizen, with sound and correct views on the governing of his country. (Rousseau's note.)

157. Caesar, in Catiline's defense, tried to establish the dogma of the mortality of the soul: Cato and Cicero, in order to refute it, did not waste time philosophizing, but limited themselves to demonstrating that Caesar was speaking as a bad citizen, and that he was proposing a doctrine that would be pernicious to the state—it was this on which the Roman Senate had to pass judgment, and not on a question of theology. (Rousseau's note.)

158. Marriage, for example, being a civil contract, has civil effects without which society cannot subsist. Let us suppose that the clergy would claim the exclusive right of authorizing this act, a right it must usurp in every intolerant religion. Is it not clear that furthering the authority of the Church in this sense undercuts that of the princely authority, which will no longer have any subjects except for those the clergy chooses to relinquish to it? If the Church is to be master of marrying or not marrying people according to whether they accept or reject a particular doctrine, whether they admit or reject a particular religious formula, whether they have greater or less piety, is it not clear that the Church, by exercising prudence and firmness, will alone dispose of inheritances, public offices, and even of the state itself, which cannot subsist if it is entirely composed of bastards? But there will be appeals on the grounds of abuse, it will be argued, there will be summonses and decrees, worldly possessions will be seized. What a pity! The clergy, however little good sense (I will not say courage) it possesses, will let this come to pass and continue on its course. Unperturbed, it will allow appeals, summonses, decrees, and seizures, and will end up as

master. It is not, I believe, a great sacrifice to give up part of something when one is certain of taking possession of everything. (Rousseau's note.)

159. In 1593 Henri IV ascended to the throne of France by converting from Protestantism to Catholicism; he was reputed to have said *Paris vaut bien une messe* ("Paris is well worth a Mass").

160. These topics were to have been taken up in the projected, but never written, *Political Institutions*, of which the *Social Contract* would have been a part.

ÉMILE

161. "This little boy here," Themistocles once said to his friends, "rules all of Greece, for he rules his mother, his mother rules me, I rule the Athenians, and the Athenians rule the Greeks." What small generals one often finds in the greatest empires, if one descends by degrees from the prince to the first hand that secretly sets things in motion! (Rousseau's note, following Plutarch.)

162. One must understand that just as pain is often a necessity, pleasure is sometimes a need. There is therefore only one desire of the child to which one should never acquiesce, and that is for the child to be obeyed. Consequently, whatever children ask for, it is important to pay special attention to what it is that compels them to ask. Accord them everything that can give them real pleasure, to the extent that you can, but refuse them everything they ask for for whimsical reasons, or in order to assert their authority. (Rousseau's note.)

163. In the empiricist psychology that was widely accepted in Rousseau's time, all "ideas" began as individual sense perceptions. The mind could then combine these, often erroneously, into "complex ideas."

164. John Locke, *Some Thoughts Concerning Education* (1693).

165. One can be certain that the child will regard any will that opposes his own as one's caprice when he cannot see the reason for it; and the child will never see the reason for anything that goes against his whims. (Rousseau's note.)

166. In the margin of his copy of *Émile*, Rousseau wrote a note for possible inclusion in a later edition: a critic of this episode "wasn't able to imagine that this little scene was arranged, and that the conjuror had been instructed in the role he was to play. But how many times, on the other hand, have I declared that I wasn't writing for people who have to be told everything?"

167. Self-regard, or self-love, is *amour propre*, which orthodox religion

considered to be the result of sinful pride, but which Rousseau attributed to the deformation of natural man by society.

168. Rousseau took his personal motto from the poet Juvenal: *Vitam impendere vero* ("Dedicate life to truth").

169. This story is closely based on Rousseau's own experiences in Turin, where he went at the age of sixteen to be converted to Catholicism. Reduced to employment as a humble lackey, he was in danger of becoming a hapless drifter until a kindly priest, the Abbé de Gaime, took an interest in him and encouraged him to believe in himself. The Savoyard Vicar is in large part a portrait of Gaime.

170. "Not unto us, O Lord, not unto us, but unto Thy name give glory, for Thy mercy, and for Thy truth's sake." Psalm 115. (Rousseau's note.)

171. *Sophia*, in Greek, means "wisdom."

172. Rousseau refers to the *Treatise on the Education of Girls* (1681) by François Fénelon, Archbishop of Cambrai and a member of the Académie Française. Sophie is later described as imagining her ideal lover by reading Fénelon's didactic novel *The Adventures of Telemachus*.

173. A child becomes importunate when it is to his advantage, but will never ask for the same thing twice if the first response is unquestionably final. (Rousseau's note.)

174. In Book X of *The Odyssey*, Circe changes the shipmates of Ulysses (or Odysseus) into swine; Ulysses himself was protected by a drug given him by the gods.

JULIE

175. "Too easy woman, do you want to know whether you are loved? Study your lover as he leaves your arms. O love! If I miss the age at which one tastes you, it is not for the hour of gratification; it is for the hour that follows it." (Rousseau's note.)

176. I.e., Saint-Preux's friend Lord Edward Bomston.

177. "Apparently she had not yet discovered the dire secret that was to torment her so, or she did not at that time wish to confide it to her friend." (Rousseau's note.) The secret was that Wolmar, although a man of absolute moral integrity, was an atheist, dismissing religion—in language that anticipates Marx—as "an opium for the soul" (Part VI, Letter 8).

178. "I would have been quite surprised if Julie had read and was quoting La Rochefoucauld under any other circumstances. Never will his unsavory book be savored by good people." (Rousseau's note.) Like his mentor Mme de Warens, Rousseau regarded the *Maximes*

of the seventeenth-century aphorist François, Duc de la Rochefoucauld, as excessively cynical and disillusioned.

179. "These mountains are so high that half an hour after sunset their summits are still lit by the rays of the sun, its red casting a lovely rose color onto the white peaks that can be seen from a great distance." (Rousseau's note.)

180. "And so much faith, and such sweet memories, and such long habit!" (Metastasio, *Demofoonte,* Act III, scene 9).

181. Julie thinks of her loyal friend Claire as her "better part."

182. As an atheist, Wolmar is unable to look forward to the life eternal, since he believes that death is final.

183. Saint-Preux had drawn up an educational plan for Julie's children.

CONFESSIONS

184. "Inside, and under the skin" (Persius, *Satire* III.30).

185. Only a small minority of Genevans were legally "citizens" with the right to vote.

186. Calvin had established his militant version of Protestantism in Geneva in the sixteenth century, and the pastors still oversaw morals with close supervision.

187. Rousseau believed the family story of the simultaneous weddings, but in fact his parents' siblings had married five years earlier, only a week before the bride gave birth to a child. Moreover, his mother's father had died young and in disgrace; the pastor Samuel Bernard who raised her was her uncle, not her father.

188. Heading an Austrian army, Prince Eugène of Savoy defeated the Turks at Belgrade in 1717, but Rousseau's uncle was back in Geneva at the time.

189. "She had accomplishments that were too brilliant for her station in life, her father the minister having taken great pains with her education. She drew and sang, accompanying herself on the lute, was well read, and wrote passable verse. Here is an impromptu poem she composed during the absence of her husband and brother, while taking a walk with her sister-in-law and their two children, in response to someone's comment on that topic:

> *These two gentlemen who are absent*
> *Are dear to us in many ways:*
> *They are our friends and our lovers,*
> *They are our husbands and our brothers,*
> *And the fathers of our children.*" (Rousseau's note.)

190. Though Rousseau does not mention it here, after his mother's death his father left the Bernard home in the affluent cathedral district and moved with his sons to an apartment in the artisans' quarter, Saint-Gervais, in the lower town.

191. An impressive list of histories, biographies, poems, and plays; Plutarch in particular inspired Rousseau with an ideal of dedication to the public good.

192. The first group were ancient heroes; the second were characters in romance novels.

193. Taken prisoner by his enemies, Scaevola held his hand in a fire to show his firmness of spirit.

194. Curiously, Rousseau does not mention his brother's name, which was François.

195. "Suson" was an affectionate nickname for Suzanne (the name of Rousseau's mother as well as of his aunt).

196. Though Geneva had no hereditary aristocracy, Gautier belonged to the patrician class and took offense at the insolence of an ordinary watchmaker. He and Isaac Rousseau had already quarreled on a previous occasion, and rather than standing up nobly for his rights as his son believed, Isaac quietly left Geneva forever to avoid imprisonment. Geneva was nominally an egalitarian democracy, but in fact the Little Council, made up of members of the wealthiest families, controlled its affairs.

197. Bossey is a small village (in French territory today) within sight of Geneva.

198. As Rousseau mentions later, in 1754 he revisited Geneva and Bossey. His cousin Abraham Bernard was the same age as himself.

199. In fact Mlle Lambercier was forty and Jean-Jacques eleven.

200. "Executioner!"

201. The nearby territory of Savoy, where Rousseau would soon live, was governed by the King of Sardinia from its capital in Turin; it was annexed by France in 1860.

202. "Persevering labor conquers all" (Virgil, *Georgics* I.146).

203. The Athenian Aristides was known as "the Just"; Brutus was admired for assassinating the dictatorial emperor Julius Caesar.

204. Actually Rousseau was there for less than a year; although his memory for details was remarkably accurate, he often remembered periods of time as longer than they really were.

205. This grandfather was David Rousseau.

206. "Bridled ass" (alluding to the ass Bernard in the medieval *Roman de Renard*).

207. "Goton" was a nickname for Margeton or Marguerite.

208. Ducommun was only twenty.

209. In one of La Fontaine's fables, Caesar is a self-reliant outdoor dog, whereas Laridon hangs around idly in the kitchen.

210. One of Hercules' twelve labors was stealing golden apples from the garden of the Hesperides.

211. When Rousseau was a secretary and researcher for the wealthy Dupin family, he became close friends with a son named Charles-Louis Dupin de Francueil.

212. The priest Benoît de Pontverre was well known for giving hospitality to young Genevans who might convert to Catholicism, as Rousseau certainly knew when he called on him. Pontverre was not in fact descended from a leader of the sixteenth-century Gentlemen of the Spoon, who wore spoons around their necks in allusion to their vow to eat up the Calvinists who were ruling Geneva.

213. In fact a condition of the pension of Mme de Warens, a very recent convert from Protestantism herself, was that she should actively promote the conversion of others.

214. Annecy, a town of 5,000 in the Savoy (Geneva at that time had 20,000 inhabitants) lay twenty-five miles to the south; it was the headquarters of the Catholic bishop in exile from Geneva.

215. The gilt railing exists today, having been placed there on the two hundredth anniversary of this famous meeting.

216. Mme de Warens did flee an unhappy marriage in this way, but she undoubtedly expected to appeal for protection to the King of Sardinia, who was in the town of Évian across Lake Geneva at the time. Rousseau ascribes her dramatic public conversion to the eloquence of Bishop Bernex, who became her friend and supporter, but others were convinced that she staged the whole thing as a way of securing an income.

217. Seventeenth-century French noblewoman, patron of the arts and associated with a failed rebellion against the monarchy.

218. Saint François de Sales, an eloquent writer, was Bishop of Geneva when the advent of the Reformation forced him to move to Annecy; he and Jeanne-Françoise de Chantal, also canonized as a saint, founded the Order of the Visitation.

219. Rousseau does not mention, and perhaps preferred not to recall, that sending converts on to Turin was a regular part of Mme de Warens's duties.

220. Antoine Houdar de la Motte, a contemporary poet whom Rousseau admired.

221. Since Rousseau had abandoned his apprenticeship, his family had to pay a financial penalty to Ducommun, and they may well have felt that after his misbehavior it was just as well for him to leave. At that time it was quite usual for young journeymen to wander from place to place looking for work.

222. In actuality Rousseau could not stand his stepmother and was deeply hurt by his father's indifference.

223. George Keith, an Earl Marischal of Scotland who went into exile after a failed rebellion to restore the Stuarts to the British throne. In the 1760s, when Rousseau was driven from France and settled near Neuchâtel in Switzerland, Keith was governing that district as an emissary of Frederick the Great of Prussia, and he and Rousseau became close friends.

224. Denis Diderot, co-editor of the great *Encyclopédie* and author of the novel *Jacques the Fatalist,* was for many years Rousseau's closest friend and was influential in his decision to become a writer. Frederick Melchior Grimm, a German living in Paris, was also a friend, though by the time he wrote the *Confessions* Rousseau had quarreled with both of them.

225. Church bells were forbidden in Calvinist Geneva, as connected with Popish ritual, but could be heard from the Catholic countryside beyond the city.

226. A seventeenth-century work by the Protestant pastor Jean Le Sueur, one of the books Rousseau mentioned reading as a boy.

227. In the Piedmontese dialect, "Damned filthy beast!"

228. Homosexuals.

229. According to the hospice records, Rousseau actually departed after only two weeks.

230. The Protestant Henry of Navarre converted to Catholicism in order to ascend to the French throne.

231. The lover of Clytemnestra when her husband, Agamemnon, was away at the Trojan War.

232. Seventeenth-century writer whose letters to her daughter became a literary classic.

233. In fact Rousseau got the same 30 francs that all of the servants did, and there was no obvious reason why the steward Lorenzi should have given him special treatment.

234. In other words, he exposed his rear end.

235. Like Gouvon, Gaime was an abbé, but essentially an ordinary priest rather than someone destined for a distinguished career. An abbé was someone with an ecclesiastical position whose income came from a monastery, but he need not live there or be a monk.

236. In *The Iliad,* the greatest Greek hero and a sneering malcontent, respectively.

237. "Such a one who strikes but does not kill." Rousseau may well have recalled an interpretation of the saying in which it is love that strikes but doesn't kill.

238. The Accademia della Crusca in Florence promoted a purified form of the Italian language, which was spoken in widely differing dialects before the unification of Italy in the nineteenth century. The Abbé de Dangeau wrote treatises on grammar.

239. "Wry-neck."

240. A fountain, invented by the Greek scientist Hero of Alexandria, that used air pressure to make water spurt in a surprising way.

241. In Rousseau's novel *Julie, or the New Héloïse,* Saint-Preux is a young tutor who falls in love with his student Julie, but she is an aristocrat and her family could never allow marriage to a commoner. Though she loves him deeply, Julie commands him to go away, and when he returns years later he finds that she has married an older man, M. de Wolmar, and become a mother. The theme of the novel is that romantic passion can be transformed into something less volatile, as Saint-Preux is accepted as a friend by both Julie and her husband.

242. Rousseau regarded Anet, whose manner was strangely distant, as a good friend, and was astounded much later to realize that he was secretly Mme de Warens's lover. He was the son of her gardener during her marriage and had followed her to Annecy; without doubt he was intensely jealous of Rousseau and may well have committed suicide on that account.

243. *The Spectator* was a widely read collection of periodical essays by Joseph Addison and Richard Steele, combining social commentary with literary criticism and popularized philosophy. Pufendorf was an important political theorist whom Rousseau would later critique in the *Social Contract;* Saint-Évremond was an essayist; *The Henriade* was an epic poem by Voltaire.

244. "Or whether an ancient respect for the blood of their masters still spoke on his behalf in the heart of these traitors."

245. The French Protestant Pierre Bayle wrote a *Historical and Critical Dictionary* that caused scandal by its skepticism.

246. Two extremely worldly authors in the court of Louis XIV; Jean de La Bruyère gave brief descriptions of character types in *Les Caractères,* and the Duc de la Rochefoucauld a disillusioned view of human behavior in his epigrammatic *Maximes.*

247. The actual insult was *à votre gorge,* "by your throat," implying a wish

to strangle someone. When the Duke of Savoy offered a low price for some goods in Paris, the merchant didn't know who he was and made this abusive reply, after which the Duke yelled the same thing at the merchant.

248. These were distinguished nobles, and Rousseau's inept remark could be taken as referring to a treatment for venereal disease, for which the Genevan doctor Théodore Tronchin was well known.

249. After Rousseau became a celebrated writer, his former employer Mme de Dupin, with whom he remained on friendly terms, confessed that she would never have believed it possible.

250. The Lazarists were an order founded by Saint Vincent de Paul to work with the poor.

251. Surviving records do not confirm this story.

252. I.e., he was homosexual.

253. A short (and unsuccessful) play by Rousseau, *Narcissus, or, The Lover of Himself.*

254. *Letters from the Mountain* was a polemical critique of Genevan politics, written when Rousseau was living in the mountains above Neuchâtel, playing on the title of *Letters from the Country* by the Genevan lawyer Jean-Robert Tronchin. Élie-Catherine Fréron was a French critic and opponent of the philosophes.

255. "Creator of the Stars," an Advent hymn.

256. The nature of Mme de Warens's mission in Paris remains mysterious, but the best guess is that she was indeed carrying an important message for the King of Sardinia that he did not wish to commit to writing. Shortly after this event, however, the king abdicated, and for some years Mme de Warens had great difficulty collecting her pension.

REVERIES OF THE SOLITARY WALKER

257. In 1762, at the height of his fame, Rousseau was unexpectedly forced to flee France in order to avoid arrest for his political and religious writings. Since that time he had lived in exile and fear of prosecution.

258. For many years Rousseau had suffered from a painful urinary complaint that doctors were unable to cure.

259. It is not clear what Rousseau had in mind: perhaps his quixotic attempt to interest Parisian passersby in a pamphlet of self-defense, or else the sudden death of a former patron who might have helped to clear his name with the authorities.

260. During the preceding several years Rousseau labored intermit-

tently on a strange work entitled *Dialogues: Rousseau Judge of Jean-Jacques*, attempting to examine his conduct from the viewpoint of an unprejudiced stranger. For a time he hoped that this work, which was not published until after his death, would rehabilitate his image with posterity.

261. Rousseau had publicly criticized contemporary medicine, with a good deal of justification since it often did more harm than good. He apparently believed as well that the order of secular (not monastic) priests known as Oratorians bore him a grudge, but the reason is not known.

262. Rousseau thought that Montaigne's claim to write only for himself was an insincere pose, whereas his own *Reveries* would be destroyed after his death by his enemies and would never find readers.

263. The island, half a mile across, was owned by a hospital in Berne that used it for farming and vineyards. Rousseau and Thérèse lived in the steward's house, which had been a monastery before the Reformation. The Lac de Bienne is also known by its German name as the Bielersee.

264. Rousseau and his companion were driven from this remote mountain village, where they had lived peacefully for nearly three years, when the local Calvinist minister stirred up his parishioners to attack the supposed infidel. Their house was violently stoned during the night, and they fled the next day.

265. The philosopher David Hume, though he had never met Rousseau, heard of his plight and generously offered to help him find a refuge in England. After he got there, however, Rousseau became convinced that Hume was masterminding a secret plot against him, and by the time he wrote the *Reveries* he saw his expulsion from the Isle of St. Pierre as a cunning stage in the plot.

266. In actuality it was only six weeks, after which the Berne government demanded that he leave.

267. "Sweet doing nothing" (Italian). Rousseau often praised "idleness" for making possible the openness to the flow of experience that he goes on to describe in this Promenade.

268. At Môtiers the local doctor, d'Ivernois, inspired a passion for botany that continued to be a favorite avocation of Rousseau's.

269. *Flora of St. Peter's Island*, in playful imitation of standard botanical titles.

270. The standard work on classification of plants by the Swedish naturalist Carl Linnaeus, whom Rousseau greatly admired.

271. Actually it was the Book of Baruch, which is included in the Vul-

gate Bible but relegated to the Apocrypha in the King James Bible. The story was that the poet La Fontaine had little interest in religion, but to stave off boredom during a church service began to read this book, thought it was brilliant, and afterward kept urging other people to read it.

272. In Greek legend, the Argonauts sailed in quest of the Golden Fleece. Rousseau's rabbit colony thrived, and after the publication of the *Reveries* their home was given the name *l'Île des Lapins,* "Rabbit Island."

About the Translator

PETER CONSTANTINE, winner of the PEN Translation Prize and a National Translation Award, has earned wide acclaim for his tranlations of *The Undiscovered Chekhov* and of the complete works of Isaac Babel, as well as for his Modern Library translations, which include Gogol's *Taras Bulba,* Voltaire's *Candide,* Machiavelli's *The Prince,* and Tolstoy's *The Cossacks.*

penguin.co.uk/vintage